WITHDRAWN
WRIGHT STATE UNIVERSITY LIBRARIES

EXHIBITIONISM: DESCRIPTION, ASSESSMENT, AND TREATMENT

Garland Series in Sexual Deviation

EXHIBITIONISM: DESCRIPTION, ASSESSMENT, AND TREATMENT

Daniel J. Cox
and
Reid J. Daitzman

GARLAND STPM PRESS
NEW YORK & LONDON

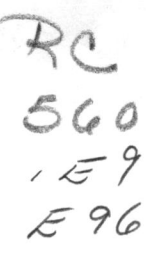

Copyright © 1980 by garland Publishing, Inc.

All rights reserved. No part of this work covered by the copyright hereon may be reproduced or used in any form or by any means—graphic, electronic, or mechanical, including photocopying, recording, taping, or information storage and retrieval systems—without permission of the publisher.

Published by Garland STPM Press
136 Madison Avenue, New York, New York 10016

Library of Congress Cataloging in Publication Data

Main entry under title:

Exhibitionism: description, assessment, and treatment.

 (Garland series in sexual deviation)
 Bibliography: p.
 Includes index.
  1. Exhibitionism. I. Cox, Daniel J. II. Daitzman, Reid J. III. Series. RC560.E9E96 616.8′583 79-14660
ISBN 0-8240-7033-X

15 14 13 12 11 10 9 8 7 6 5 4 3 2 1

Printed in the United States of America

DEDICATION

DJC: *to Debra and my extended family*
RJD: *to Paula and Sarah*

CONTENTS

CONTRIBUTORS ix
PREFACE xi
ACKNOWLEDGMENTS xv

      SECTION ONE   Introduction

1. EXHIBITIONISM: AN OVERVIEW 3
   Daniel J. Cox
2. LEGAL STAND TOWARD EXHIBITIONISM 11
   Steven R. Smith

      SECTION TWO   Psychodynamic treatments

3. GROUP THERAPY 41
   James L. Mathis
4. A PSYCHOANALYTIC VIEW 59
   David W. Allen

SECTION THREE Behavioral Treatment

5. ELECTRICAL AVERSION THERAPY 85
   David R. Evans
6. AVERSIVE BEHAVIOR REHEARSAL:
   A COGNITIVE–BEHAVIORAL PROCEDURE 123
   Ian Wickramasekera
7. MULTIFACETED BEHAVIOR THERAPY 151
   Kelly D. Brownell
8. ASSISTED COVERT SENSITIZATION 187
   Barry M. Maletzky
9. AN EXTENDED CASE REPORT: THE NUTS AND
   BOLTS OF TREATING AN EXHIBITIONIST 253
   Reid J. Daitzman and Daniel J. Cox

SECTION FOUR Concluding Comments

10. VICTIMS OF EXHIBITIONISM 289
    Daniel J. Cox and Barry M. Maletzky
11. THEORETICAL AND THERAPEUTIC INTEGRATION 295
    John M. Rhoads
12. WORKINGS BETWEEN THE LEGAL SYSTEM AND
    THE THERAPIST 311
    Steven R. Smith and Robert G. Meyer
13. FUTURE RESEARCH ISSUES 339
    William D. Murphy, Gene G. Abel, and Judith V. Becker

AUTHOR INDEX 393

SUBJECT INDEX 403

CONTRIBUTORS

Gene G. Abel New York State Psychiatric Institute
New York, New York

David W. Allen San Francisco Psychoanalytic Society and
Institute
San Francisco, California

Judith V. Becker New York State Psychiatric Institute
New York, New York

Kelly D. Brownell University of Pennsylvania
Philadelphia, Pennsylvania

Daniel J. Cox University of Virginia Medical Center
Charlottesville, Virginia

Reid J. Daitzman Connecticut Center for Behavioral and
Psychosomatic Medicine
New Haven, Connecticut

David R. Evans — University of Western Ontario
London, Ontario
Canada

Barry M. Maletzky — University of Oregon Health Science Center
Portland, Oregon

James L. Mathis — East Carolina University School of Medicine
Greenville, North Carolina

Robert G. Meyer — University of Louisville
Louisville, Kentucky

William D. Murphy — University of Tennessee
Memphis, Tennessee

John M. Rhoads — Duke University
Durham, North Carolina

Steven R. Smith — University of Louisville Law School
Louisville, Kentucky

Ian Wickramasekera — University of Illinois School of Medicine
Chicago, Illinois

PREFACE

The idea for this volume evolved over a number of months subsequent to the editors' treatment of a case of exhibitionism that was presented at a regular staff conference meeting of the Adult Psychiatry Clinic, University of Virginia School of Medicine. We both became fascinated at the basic learning foundations of the development of exhibitionistic symptomology and how readily the behavioral literature offered a number of intervention options for the clinician. These options appeared to be empirically based and effective. In discussing the case with our colleagues at the medical school, we soon became aware of the fact that although there were many published accounts of exhibitionism in the behavioral and nonbehavioral literature, treatment still tended to be unsystematic. We also noticed a high relapse rate: many of the exhibitionists referred to our clinic had undergone previous behavioral and nonbehavioral forms of intervention. In addition, as clinicians we invariably were confronted with a myriad of legal and ethical/confidentiality issues give the "aversive" nature of some of the currently available interventions. The legal system was always involved, since most exhibitionists were repeat offenders and therapy was sometimes a part of their "sentencing" and rehabilitative process.

The junior editor subsequently left the University for independent practice and the senior editor assumed the major task of contacting potential contributors for a book on the subject. The idea of a book evolved after we wrote a chapter on exhibitionism for the *Progress in Behavior Modification Series*. As we learned more about this fascinating area, the only alternative turned out to be a comprehensive book on the description, assessment, and treatment of exhibitionism.

We approached the subject from the point of view that exhibitionism, being the most common sexual deviation, could also be considered a "model" deviation. Many of the descriptions, legal issues, assessments, and interventions which have evolved for exhibitionism probably can also be related to the other sexual deviations. In addition, this volume is first in the *Garland Series in Sexual Deviation,* which will include other books on sexual assault, incest, homosexuality, gender identity problems, pedophilia, and fetishism.

A fascinating experience both authors had while preparing this book was to learn of the deficits in our knowledge of the relationship between psychology and the law. We feel that this lack of knowledge is generally the case for many clinical psychologists. For this reason, fully one-sixth of the book involves the legal system's relationship with and input into the treatment of the exhibitionist.

Another area of practical importance is in the variety of techniques and theoretical positions that seem to work more or less effectively. Chapters are presented on individual psychodynamic therapy, group therapy, individual psychoanalytic therapy, electric shock therapy, aversive behavior rehearsal, assisted covert sensitization, multifaceted behavior therapy, and an extended case report illustrating some of the "nut and bolt" problems in applying some of these techniques. There are also chapters describing the characteristics that differentiate exhibitionism from other forms of sexual deviance, and the legal status of the crime of indecent exposure and how therapists, judges, attorneys, and clients should communicate. Another chapter puts forth an integration of the therapeutic models, and the last chapter describes the future clinical and research efforts for assessment, treatment, and follow-up.

Exhibitionism: Description, Assessment, and Treatment is written for clinicians and researchers in psychology, psychiatry, social work, counseling, and other professional groups that have contact with the assessment or treatment of the exhibitionist. In addition, the book is written for law students, attorneys, and judges as a sourcebook on how to communicate with mental health professionals; and as a primer on some of the significant theoretical and practical mental health issues involved with treating the sexual deviate in the context of the legal/social problems of being caught. Finally, the book is a model presentation for the beginning law student or therapist on the multiple problems involved in the assessment and treatment of clients and patients within the context of our contemporary mental health and legal systems. As our culture continues to evolve and to become more concerned with social versus individual rights, confidentiality, consent, and the protection of defendants' rights, we hope that this volume will contribute to the growth of understanding in these areas.

R. D.

ACKNOWLEDGMENTS

The editors would like to express their appreciation to Dean Steve Smith of the University of Louisville Law School and Professor Robert Meyer of the University of Louisville Department of Psychology, who so persuasively and enthusiastically encouraged the integration of law and psychology. They would also like to express appreciation to Professor Lovic Miller of the University of Louisville Departments of Psychology and Psychiatry for his role in modeling an appreciation of a holistic view to man and man's problems. This work was partially supported by the Institutional Biomedical Research Support Grant No. 5S07RR05431-17 National Institutes of Health USPHS-N.T.H.

SECTION ONE
INTRODUCTION

| 1 | Exhibitionism: An Overview | 3 |
| 2 | Legal Stand Toward Exhibitionism | 11 |

1

EXHIBITIONISM: AN OVERVIEW

Daniel J. Cox

HISTORY AND DEFINITION

The term exhibitionism was first introduced into psychopathology by Lasègue in 1877, though Theophrastus described the act as early as 4 B.C. (Stevenson & Jones, 1972). Lasègue (1877) described exhibitionism as a "state intermediate between reason and madness." The most notable feature was a compulsion to exhibit the sexual organs in situations where the apparent desire for, or expectation of, a normal sexual act was absent. Other characteristics noted by Lasègue were that the act usually took place at a distance, no attempts were made to have sexual intercourse, there was often a return to the same place at the same time of day for subsequent acts, and there was no other obviously abnormal behavior. The act itself seemed to be instantaneous, recognized as futile, elicited by situational factors, limited to a single act on any occasion, periodic in its occurrences, and usually without subsequent sexual activity. At the time of the act, the subject appeared to be indifferent to the social or legal consequences.

These observations generally seem as accurate today as they were 100 years ago. However, Mohr et al. (1964) more recently and precisely define exhibitionism as the *expressed impulse to expose the male genitals to an unsuspecting female as a final sexual gratification* (p. 111). This definition excludes exposure which preludes sexual contact, occurs in the context of public urination or intoxication, or results from severe mental disorders such as retardation, temporal lobe epilepsy, or schizophrenia.

From this latter and generally accepted definition, it is evident that the legal category of indecent exposure includes but is not restricted to what is referred to in this book as exhibitionism. Consequently, any extrapolation from legal records must be done with caution.

INCIDENCE

The incidence of exhibitionism is stated to be high by most authors. It is estimated to account for one-third of all sexual offenses in England, Wales, the United States, and Canada (Rooth & Marks, 1973; Smukler & Schiebel, 1975). Gebhard et al. (1965) found exhibitionists to be second only to pedophiles in the number of convictions, and to rank first among sexual deviations in the number of misdemeanors resulting in imprisonment. Though only a small percentage of exposure acts are ever reported to police (17 percent, see Chapter 11), conviction rates are assumed to be high for reports of this sexual deviation because of their flagrant, repeated public behavior toward a victim from whom an overt emotional response is apparently expected and desired.

Though no known available statistics for the United States exist, Bancroft (1976) estimates that exhibitionism is the second most common sexual variation that presents itself at mental health facilities in England. The most common sexual variation reported by Bancroft is homosexuality.

On the basis of victim reports, Gittleson et al. (1978) indicated that approximately one-third of a British female medical student sample had been exposed to, and 44 percent of a nursing sample (mean age = 32.8 years) had reported similar experiences. Cox and McMahon (1978) found that approximately one-third of a United States survey of female college students (mean age = 20) had been exposed to.

However, on the basis of a mail survey to psychiatrists of 40 countries (only 24 of which responded), Rooth (1973a) presents data indicating that the high frequency of exhibitionism may be unique to Western cultures. His data indicates that exhibitionism is virtually unknown to Asian and African psychiatrists. Rooth speculates that the phenomenon is unrelated to industrialization since reportedly it is virtually nonexistent in Japan. Recent data from Taiwan and Hong Kong, in which female college students were sampled (Cox & Sang 1979), suggests that the frequency of occurrences is much higher in the East than Rooth's data suggests.

Incidence of exhibitionism, according to MacDonald (1973), occurs primarily outdoors (71 percent, see Table 1) during the months of May to September (see Table 2); primarily in the middle of the week (see Table 3); and during the hours of 3:00 P.M. to 6.00 P.M. (see Table 4). In conclusion, it appears that exhibitionism occurs during warm days in the middle of the week in public settings.

Table 1. Places of Indecent Exposure

PLACE	NUMBER	PERCENT
Outdoors		
Streets	91	45.5
Alleys	22	11.0
Parking lots	19	9.5
Parks	6	3.0
School playgrounds	4	2.0
Subtotal	142	71.0
Indoors		
Homes	29	14.5
Apartment houses	16	8.0
Laundromats	9	4.5
Offices or Stores	4	2.0
Subtotal	58	29.0
Total	200	100.0

(Adapted from MacDonald, 1973. Courtesy of Charles C Thomas and the author.)

Table 2. Indecent Exposures in Denver by Months

	1968	1969	1970
January	12	17	18
February	17	15	14
March	14	16	22
April	28	31	22
May	28	16	13
June	20	22	22
July	15	22	15
August	24	23	9
September	21	22	22
October	14	11	25
November	20	15	19
December	11	10	14
Total	224	220	215

THE EXHIBITIONIST

At the outset of this section, it is necessary to point out that all research investigating the exhibitionist suffers from the same shortcoming—sample selection bias. All of these studies have worked with arrested exhibitionists. Since this sample bears an unknown relationship to exhibitionists in the natural environment, extrapolation of these findings to all exhibitionists must be done with caution.

Table 3. Days of Indecent Exposures in Denver

Saturday	26
Sunday	16
Monday	33
Tuesday	43
Wednesday	23
Thursday	25
Friday	34
Total	200

Table 4. Times of Indecent Exposures in Denver

Time	Count
12:00–4:59 A.M.	8
5:00–6:59	3
7:00–7:59	7
8:00–8:59	24
9:00–9:59	11
10:00–10:59	8
11:00–11:59	15
12:00–12:59 P.M.	9
1:00–1:59	14
2:00–2:59	9
3:00–3:59	25
4:00–4:59	25
5:00–5:59	13
6:00–6:59	6
7:00–7:59	2
8:00–8:59	6
9:00–9:59	3
10:00–10:59	6
11:00–11:59	5
Unknown	1
Total	200

Gebhard et al. (1965) investigated the early life of convicted exhibitionists as well as other sexual deviates. Between the ages of 14 to 17, exhibitionists reported a poor relationship with their fathers relative to a control, that is, a prison and other sexually deviant groups. Thirty-two percent reported a poor father–son relationship, and 34 percent reported getting along well with their father. Exhibitionists were partial to their mother: 45 percent reported getting along better with their mother than their father, while 20 percent reported a better relationship with the father. Approximately one-half came from broken homes, which is not excessive when compared to prison or other sexually deviant groups. For ages 10 to 11, the future exhibitionist presented a picture of rather poor socialization with peers, in this regard being almost as badly off as Peeping Toms. Only 14 percent had had numerous male and female companions. Although there was no significant medical history during childhood, health of the exhibitionists was inferior to that of prison and control groups. In adult life, masturbation was of unusual importance regardless of other sexual outlets. Unlike control and prison groups in which 85 percent were married, only 65 percent of the exhibitionists had been married by a mean age of 35. At the time of first conviction, only 31 percent were currently married. These marriages were relatively infertile, producing an average of 1.4 children.

Mohr et al.'s (1964) sample indicates that the mean age of first arrest was 24.8 years, while the self-reported mean age of first exposure incident was 19.4 years. However, the mean age of onset reflects a bimodel distribution with peaks in the 11 to 15 and 21 to 25 age ranges. This agrees with Gebhard et al.'s (1965) finding that the mean age of first conviction was 26.5 years. The discrepancy between first incident and first conviction attests to the inconsistency between police records and actual occurrence of exhibitionism.

Most clinical reports describe exhibitionists as moderately schizoid and as having difficulty relating to others. They are seen as somewhat obsessive and passive-dependent, with marked difficulty acknowledging and handling aggressive impulses. Psychometrically, McCreary (1975) reported a mean MMPI Welsh Code of 102 exhibitionists to be 4-58932 671/0: KFL/. A mean Welsh Code of 842 756 139/ KLF/ was reported by Smukler and Schiebel (1975) for 19 court-referred exhibitionists. Rader (1977) reported the mean Welsh Code of 36 exhibitionists referred for pretrial psychodiagnosis to be 4856-23910/ KFL/. Not only did these psychometric findings produce group profiles that fall entirely within normal limits, but Rader reported that his exhibitionists were significantly less deviant than 47 rapists (48' 26739-10/ F-KL/) on 7 of the 13 standard MMPI scales. On the basis of MMPI data, exhibitionists may be described as mildly nonconforming individuals who have a history of mild run-ins with the social norms, but with *no typical psychopathology*.

Cox and Daitzman (1979) conclude that exhibitionists seldom gravitate to more serious sexual offenses, despite the isolated reports of such cases (Cabanis, 1966; Grassberger, 1964) and the suggestion that exhibitionists who preferentially expose to children are likely to develop pedophilic behavior in later life (Mohr et al., 1964). Rooth and Marks (1973) actually present data showing that past exposure to children predicts a better therapeutic outcome. In Gebhard et al.'s (1965) sample, two-thirds of the sexual offenses reported were exhibitionistic. Of the nonexhibitionist sex offenses, one-third were performed with willing females and one-fifth involved force on unwilling females.

It is reported that exhibitionism, along with homosexual pedophilia, has the highest recidivism rate among sexual offenders. Mohr et al. (1964) report that 20 to 25 percent of the exhibitionists coming to court have a record of previous convictions of a sexual offense, while approximately another 20 percent have previous nonsexual offenses. Of the exhibitionists followed up for a mean three-year period of time, Mohr et al. report a 20 percent recidivism rate. However, they report an increasing recidivism rate for those convicted more than once: a reconviction rate of 9 percent for first offenders, a 57 percent rate for those with more than one previous sexual offense, and a 71 percent rate for those with previous sexual and nonsexual offenses. Of Gebhard et al.'s (1965) sample, 13 percent had only one conviction, 33 percent had four to six convictions, and 16 percent were convicted seven or more times. MacDonald (1973) reports a relapse rate of 20 percent after one year and 41 percent after four years. Radzinowiez (1957) reported that exhibitionism accounts for one-third of all sexual recidivists. In their retrospective study, Mohr et al. report that the recidivism rate was uninfluenced by traditional psychotherapeutic efforts. However, this latter report suffers from no control over therapy or patient assignment to therapy versus nontherapy conditions. In reviewing the behavior therapy research, Cox and Daitzman (1979) report no documented relapses after 18 months post-treatment assessment. This suggests that if exhibitionists refrain from exposing for 18 months after behavioral treatment, they are not likely to expose thereafter.

CONCLUSION

On the basis of this review, it is evident that exhibitionism is a very frequent form of sexual deviance. It is experienced by young adult males who have general difficulties in interpersonal relations, but with no typical psychopathology. Although exhibitionists do not generally gravitate to more serious and aggressive sexual offenses, they are prone to relapse over time.

REFERENCES

Bancroft, H. Behavioral treatment of sexual deviations. In H. Leitenberg (Ed.), *Handbook of behavior modification and behavior therapy.* New York: Prentice-Hall, 1976.

Cabanis, D. Medizinisch-Kriminologische Untersuchung uber Exhibitionismus. Unpublished habilitationsschrift, Berlin University, 1966.

Cox, D. J., & Daitzman, R. J. Behavior therapy, research and treatment of male exhibitionists. In M. Hersen, R. Eisler, and P. Miller (Eds.), *Progress in behavior modification* (Vol. 7). New York: Academic Press, 1979.

Cox, D. J., & McMahon, B. Incidence of male exhibitionism in the United States as reported by victimized female college students. *International Journal of Law and Psychiatry*, 1978, *1*, 453–457.

Cox, D. J., & Sang, W. Cross-cultural comparison in the incidence of male exhibitionism. Unpublished manuscript, 1979.

Gebhard, P. H., Gagnon, J. H., Poimerory, W. R., & Christenson, C. Y. *Sexual offenders*. New York: Harper & Row, 1965.

Gittleson, N. L., Eacott, S. T., & Mehta, B. M. Victims of indecent exposure. *British Journal of Psychiatry*, 1978, *132*, 61–66.

Grassberger, R. Der Exhibitionist. *Kriminalistic*, 1964, *18*, 557–562.

MacDonald, J. M. *Indecent exposure*. Springfield, Ill.: Charles C Thomas, 1973.

McCreary, C. P. Personality profiles of persons convicted of indecent exposure. *Journal of Clinical Psychology*, 1975, *31*, 260–262.

Mohr, J. W., Turner, R. E., & Jerry, M. B. *Pedophilia and exhibitionism: A handbook*. Toronto: University of Toronto Press, 1964.

Rader, C. M. MMPI profile types of exposers, rapists and assaulters in a court service population. *Journal of Consulting and Clinical Psychology*, 1977, *45*, 61–69.

Radzinowiez, L. *Sexual offenses: A report of the Cambridge Department of Criminal Science*. London: Macmillan, 1957.

Rooth, G. Exhibitionism outside Europe and America. *Archives of Sexual Behavior*, 1973(a), *2*, 351–363.

Rooth, G. Exhibitionism, sexual violence and paedophilia. *British Journal of Psychiatry*, 1973(b), *122*, 705–710.

Rooth, R. G., & Marks, I. M. Persistent exhibitionism: Short-term response to aversive therapy, self-regulation and relaxation treatment. *Archives of Sexual Behavior*, 1973, *3*, 227–248.

Smukler, A. J., & Schiebel, D. Personality characteristics of exhibitionists. *Disease of the Nervous System*, 1975, *36*, 600–603.

Stevenson, J., & Jones, I. H. Behavior therapy technique of exhibitionism. *Archives of General Psychiatry*, 1972, *27*, 839–841.

2
LEGAL STAND TOWARD EXHIBITIONISM

Steven R. Smith

To a psychotherapist, exhibitionism is the display of one's genitals, for the purpose of obtaining sexual gratification through the exhibition, to an audience that is probably unwilling to view it (MacNamara & Sagarin, 1977). In most jurisdictions there is no law specifically prohibiting exhibitionism as it is defined by the psychotherapist. Undoubtedly, the laws which most closely resemble a prohibition on exhibitionism are the criminal laws on indecent exposure; although instead of being described as laws related to indecent exposure, they may relate to "exposure of sexual organs," "public lewdness," "public indecency," or "lewd and obscene conduct."

The typical law prohibiting indecent exposure covers a good deal more than the activities of exhibitionists. These statutes generally cover the display of genitals which is not done for the purpose of sexual gratification, such as nude sunbathing and sometimes public urination. In addition, in most jurisdictions women can be charged with indecent exposure even though women are not generally thought by therapists to be exhibitionists.

Exhibitionism includes conduct that is almost always included in indecent exposure statutes. That is, the conduct of exhibitionists will almost always result in a violation of the indecent exposure laws. It is conceivable, however, that there are some circumstances in which the nature of the "audience" or conduct of the exhibitionist would not technically be included in an indecent exposure law. Because indecent exposure laws vary so greatly, conduct which is outlawed by one statute may be permitted by another.

The reason for the variation in indecent exposure laws is that these statutes are creatures of state and local law. Virtually every state and some localities have laws concerning indecent exposure. The indecent exposure statutes of one state may vary somewhat from the statutes in neighboring states. There is no general federal indecent exposure law which covers the entire country, although federal criminal law does apply in some federal areas. Further complicating the law relating to indecent exposure is the fact that indecent exposure statutes have been interpreted in different ways by the supreme courts of the various states. It is entirely possible that even if two states have statutes which are similar, the statutes will have been given somewhat different interpretations by the courts of the two states.

The behavior of the exhibitionist may be punished under several statutes other than indecent exposure laws, such as "disturbing the peace" laws. A number of states have sexual psychopath laws which may apply to the exhibitionist. These sexual psychopath laws are a serious matter, and will be considered in a separate section of this chapter.

BASIC CRIMINAL LAW PRINCIPLES

Before indecent exposure statutes and their interpretation by the courts can be fully appreciated, some understanding of basic criminal law principles is necessary.

Conviction of a crime generally requires a showing of actus reus and mens rea; literally, a showing of a bad act and evil mind. The defendant must have actually done something wrong, rather than just having thought about doing something or having intended to do it. He or she must also have had the state of mind (mens rea) prescribed by the law. Typically, this state of mind is described as some level of intent. Thus, to prove a theft offense, it would be insufficient to demonstrate that the defendant walked out of a restaurant with someone else's coat. It would be necessary to demonstrate a mens rea; that is, the defendant intended to deprive another of the use of the coat without just cause.

Actus reus and mens rea must both be demonstrated to convict an individual of indecent exposure. There has been considerable disagreement, discussed later in this chapter, about the kind of act and state of mind required for conviction.

Generally in a criminal proceeding the judge or jury determining guilt must be convinced of the defendant's guilt "beyond a reasonable doubt." In a criminal case the defendant generally has a right to a jury trial but he may waive that right and agree to be tried before a judge without a jury. The state is required to prove each one of the elements (i.e., criteria necessary for conviction) of the crime beyond a reasonable doubt before a conviction is appropriate. "Beyond a reasonable doubt" is considered to be a high standard of proof as compared with the "preponderance of the evidence" or "clear and convincing evidence" standards found in civil law.

Criminal laws must be clear and unambiguous. If, because of the lack of clarity of the criminal law, a person can only venture a guess as to whether his behavior is criminal or not, he cannot reasonably be expected to conform his actions to the requirements of the law. The requirement of certainty in criminal law is clearly established as a requirement of due process contained in the Fourteenth Amendment of the United States Constitution. Criminal statutes which are not reasonably clear may be struck down as unconstitutional as being "void for vagueness."

In addition, a criminal defendant has a variety of constitutional rights, including the right to confront and cross-examine witnesses, the right to have the effective assistance of counsel, the right to avoid self-incrimination, and the right to have reasonable bail set. All of these rights would be applicable to someone charged with indecent exposure. There are two additional constitutional rights that are of particular relevance to an individual charged with indecent exposure; the guarantee of the Eighth Amendment against cruel and unusual punishment, and the First Amendment's right of free speech and association.

THE CRIME OF INDECENT EXPOSURE

The common law and indecent exposure. Even before public indecency was prohibited by statute, the English common law made public sexual exposure a crime. The crime, defined as open and gross lewdness and lascivious behavior, was a misdemeanor (a relatively minor offense) punishable by a fine and imprisonment. The common law was a system of law based primarily upon court decision, rather than on statutes, which developed over a long course of years through judicial decisions. Because of its dependence upon court decisions rather than statutes, the common law is often referred to as judge-made law. The common law which developed in England was transported to the colonies and became the basis of law in the United States.

The common law offense of indecent exposure required "the intentional exposure of the person in a public place and in the presence of others." The purpose of the law was to protect public morals by prohibiting acts which would lower the community's moral standards or otherwise offend the community's sense of decency (Application of Indecent Exposure, 1972). The elements of this offense—or criteria for conviction of indecent exposure—required (1) the person's exposure of genitals or other private, anatomical parts; (2) intentional exposure; (3) exposure in a public place; and (4) exposure in the presence of, or seen by, others. These are the traditional elements of indecent exposure and they have provided the basis for most modern criminal statutes dealing with indecent exposure. The variety of interpretations, given the elements of the crime and modifications which have been made in modern statutes concerning indecent exposure or public lewdness, are considered in some detail in this section.

State statutes. Each state possesses police power which permits it to pass laws for public protection and welfare. This power includes the authority to pass indecent exposure statutes so long as they do not conflict with the Constitution or with valid federal statutes. As might be expected, state laws vary in defining and punishing indecent exposure.

The following are examples of statutes concerning indecent exposure or its equivalent in the United States. They are meant to illustrate, among other things, that the statutes of the state must be carefully examined to determine the elements and nature of indecent exposure in any jurisdiction. It is also important to remember that localities, typically cities and counties, often also have the right to enact laws, generally called ordinances, prohibiting indecent exposure. Special laws relating to federal territories also exist.

Alabama

13-1-111. *Indecent exposure*

It is unlawful for any person to expose or exhibit, or to procure another to expose or exhibit, his sexual organs or private parts in any public place or on the private premises of another, or so near thereto as to be seen from such private premises, in a vulgar and indecent manner.

Any person who violates the provisions of this section may, on conviction, be imprisoned in the county jail or sentenced to hard labor for the county, for not more than 12 months, or fined not more than $500.00, or both.

California

314. *Lewd or obscene conduct; indecent exposure; obscene exhibitions; punishment*

Every person who willfully and lewdly, either:

1. Exposes his person, or the private parts thereof, in any public place, or in any place where there are present other persons to be offended or annoyed thereby; or,
2. Procures, counsels, or assists any person so to expose himself . . . or to make other exhibition of himself to public view, or the view of any number of persons, such as is offensive to decency, or is adapted to excite to vicious or lewd thoughts or acts, is guilty of a misdemeanor.

Upon the second and each subsequent conviction under subdivision 1 of this section, or upon a first conviction under subdivision 1 of this section after a previous conviction under Section 288 of this code, every person so convicted is guilty of a felony, and is punishable by imprisonment in state prison.

Colorado

18-7-301. *Public indecency*

1. Any person who performs any of the following in a public place or where the conduct may reasonably be expected to be viewed by members of the public commits public indecency:
    (a) An act of sexual intercourse; or
    (b) An act of deviate sexual intercourse; or

(c) A lewd exposure of the body done with intent to arouse or to satisfy the sexual desire of any person; or
   (d) A lewd fondling or caress of the body of another person.
2. Public indecency is a class 1 petty offense.

18-7-302. *Indecent exposure.*

1. A person commits the crime of indecent exposure if he intentionally exposes his genitals to the view of any person under circumstances in which such conduct is likely to cause affront or alarm to the other person.
2. Indecent exposure to a child under the age of 14 years is a class 2 misdemeanor; to anyone 14 years of age or older, it is a class 3 misdemeanor.

[Note: A class 1 petty offense carries a fine of not more than $500 and imprisonment of not more than 6 months. A class 2 misdemeanor carries a maximum penalty of a $1,000 fine and 12 months imprisonment. A class 3 misdemeanor carries a maximum penalty of a $750 fine and 6 months imprisonment.]

Florida

800.03 *Exposure of sexual organs*

It shall be unlawful for any person to expose or exhibit his sexual organs in any public place or on the private premises of another, or so near thereto as to be seen from such private premises, in a vulgar or indecent manner, or so to expose or exhibit his person in such place, or to go or be naked in such place. Provided, however, this section shall not be construed to prohibit the exposure of such organs or the person in any place provided or set apart for that purpose. Any person convicted of a violation hereof shall be guilty of a misdemeanor of the first degree, punishable as provided in Section 775.082 or Section 775.083.

[Note: A misdemeanor of the first degree is punishable by a jail term of not more than one year and a fine of not more than $1,000.]

Kentucky

510.150 *Indecent exposure*

1. A person is guilty of indecent exposure when he intentionally exposes his genitals under circumstances in which he knows or should know his conduct is likely to cause affront or alarm.
2. Indecent exposure is a class B misdemeanor.

[Note: A class B misdemeanor may result in imprisonment for not more than 90 days.

An interesting note appears in the commentary accompanying the Kentucky statute. "Exhibitionism is an emotional illness resulting in compulsive behavior. It is questionable whether penal sanctions are effective in controlling this illness. The offense is penalized in this chapter because the resulting social harm is sufficiently serious to warrant penal sanctions."]

New York

245.00 *Public lewdness*

A person is guilty of public lewdness when he intentionally exposes the private or intimate parts of his body in a lewd manner or commits any other lewd act (a) in a public place; or (b) in private premises under circumstances in which he may readily be observed from either a public place or from other private premises, and with intent that he be so observed.

Public lewdness is a class B misdemeanor.

[Note: A class B misdemeanor is punishable by a fine of not more than $500.]

Texas

21.08 *Indecent Exposure*

(a) A person commits an offense if he exposes his anus or any part of his genitals with intent to arouse or gratify the sexual desire of any person, and he is reckless about whether another is present who will be offended or alarmed by his act.

(b) An offense under this secion is a class C misdemeanor.

[Note: A class C misdemeanor carries with it a fine of up to $200.
The Texas statutes demonstrate a fairly common approach to indecent exposure. In addition to the indecent exposure statute printed above, the state also has related statutes concerning public lewdness and disorderly conduct.]

Washington State

9A.88.010 *Public indecency*

1. A person is guilty of public indecency if he makes any open and obscene exposure of his person or the person of another knowing that such conduct is likely to cause reasonable affront or alarm.
2. Public indecency is a misdemeanor unless such person exposes himself to a person under the age of 14 years, in which case indecency is a gross misdemeanor.

[Note: A misdemeanor may involve a jail term of not more than 90 days and a fine of not more than $500. A gross misdemeanor may involve a jail term of not more than one year and a fine of not more than $1,000. As with other criminal statutes, a court may obviously impose a sentence or fine less than the maximum.]

Model Penal Code

Section 213.5. *Indecent Exposure*

A person commits a misdemeanor if, for the purpose of arousing or gratifying sexual desire of himself or of any person other than his spouse, he exposes his genitals under circumstances in which he knows his conduct is likely to cause affront or alarm.

Section 251.1 *Open Lewdness*

A person commits a petty misdemeanor if he does any lewd act which he knows is likely to be observed by others who would be affronted or alarmed.

[The following drafting comments accompanied these sections of the Model Penal Code. "Lewd or indecent behavior is punishable in all jurisdictions. The prohibited conduct amounts to gross flouting of community standards in respect to sexuality or nudity in public. Sometimes legislation against indecency has been construed as applicable to cult nudism. This would not be so under our formulation since we require awareness of likelihood of affronting observers. Nor would our provisions reach debatable brevity of attire on the beaches, since we condemn 'lewdness' rather than the less definite 'indecency'. Control of dress, if desirable, had best be accomplished by regulatory ordinances outside the scope of this code.

"The special case of genital exposure for sexual gratification is punishable more severely than ordinary open lewdness, since the behavior amounts to, or at least is often taken as, threatening sexual aggression. For the same reason this offense is placed in the article of the Code dealing with other types of sexual aggression, whereas open lewdness is included in the article that emcompasses obscenity and prostitution."]

Interpretation of Indecent Exposure Statutes

The terms of indecent exposure statutes vary considerably from state to state and therefore the requirements for conviction of the crime also vary from state to state. There are, however, several elements of the crime which are fairly standard and which have required judicial interpretation. The definitions and elements which have been particularly difficult are (1) the definition of public place; (2) the definition of private parts; (3) the necessity of a witness or witnesses to the exposure; (4) an understanding of the intent of the defendant which is necessary to convict him of the crime and the related issue of the definition of lewd and indecent conduct; and (5) the effect of the consent of the victim to observing the exposure.

Generally one may be convicted of indecent exposure only if the exhibition occurs in public or in a public place. Without this provision, one could theoretically be arrested for disrobing in his own home even though no one on the street could see his activity. A public place is generally construed to be a place where the public has a right to go and to be. It includes publicly owned property and property privately owned but generally available to the public, such as a store or restaurant. Although there has been some debate about the matter, it is now generally accepted that an exposure is made in a public place even if the exposure is a private place but can reasonably be seen by persons in a public place (Fisherow, 1973). Thus, a person who stands in front of a picture window in his own home and exposes himself to school children on a public road is guilty of indecent exposure. Although courts have recognized that the privacy of a residence would normally prevent one from being prosecuted for indecent exposure, they have held that this protection is destroyed when an individual "deliberately disregards protection of his walls and makes use of their (sic) windows instead to make such conduct public."[1] There has been some debate about whether nude swimming beaches and burlesque houses are public places. Although there may be good reasons for not including individuals who are naked in such places within the purview of the indecent exposure statutes (discussed later), it must be admitted that these are public places.

Although some statutes make it clear that a person may be charged with indecent exposure for exposing "any part of his genitals," most statutes lack this specificity. When criminal statutes are so vague that they do not give fair notice of the conduct which is prohibited, they violate the due process clause of the Fourteenth Amendment to the Constitution and are therefore unconstitutional. These laws are said to be "void for vagueness." Indecent exposure laws typically indicate that it is an offense for a person to expose "his person" or "the private parts of his body" or "the intimate part of his body." Such phrases are so vague in that they fail to give a person fair notice of what is prohibited. Such language has, however, generally withstood void for vagueness attacks. In part, the statutes have withstood constitutional vagueness attacks because state courts have made it clear that the statutes are limited to the exposure of the genitals or, in a limited number of cases, the genitals or anus. For the most part it has been recognized that a woman's breasts are not private parts within the meaning of indecent exposure statutes inasmuch as they are not genital organs. Although the exposure of a woman's breasts has not traditionally been included in the crime of indecent exposure because of the use of the word genitals in describing indecent exposure, it is important to note that modern statutes may include a broader description of the anatomical features included under the law. For example, female performers have been charged with "appearing in a public place naked or partly so, with the intent of making a public exhibition of nudity."[2] There is a modern trend toward defining in the indecent exposure statute what body parts are included under the statute. Such a trend is desirable if indecent exposure statutes are to continue to withstand void for vagueness attacks.

It was generally accepted at common law that the crime of indecent exposure require at least two potential observers; one person who actually saw the exposure plus one other person who could have seen the exposure had he or she looked (Fisherow, 1973). It is uniformly recognized that a large number of witnesses to the exposure is not important.

Obviously, there are other definitional problems concerning what constitutes exposure of the genitals. Although this issue has not yet received a great deal of attention from the courts, it has been suggested that "the guilt or innocence of indecent exposure is not a matter of measuring the amount of flesh exposed; one does not caliper the revealed epidermis and certify guilt as increasing by the square inch; the indecency of exposure is always a matter . . . to be gathered from all of the circumstances."[3]

Undoubtedly, the most difficult and confusing aspect of indecent exposure statutes is the level of intent necessary to support a conviction. The mens rea, or intent necessary for conviction under an indecent exposure statute, varies greatly from state to state. This variation is due to the variations in the language of indecent exposure statutes from state to state and to the varying interpretations of the statutes given by state courts.

There are, however, a few areas of general agreement concerning the intent necessary to support a conviction for indecent exposure. There seems to be no disagreement that the defendant must have intentionally, designedly, willfully, or at least recklessly exposed himself to the public. If the exposure to the public is in any way unintentional, accidental, or inadvertent, conviction for indecent exposure is not proper. Thus, the necessary intent cannot be shown if: (1) the exposure is accidental, as when a person is wearing a swimming suit which he does not know to be ripped in such a way as to expose his genitals, or the exposure occurs because of an undetected broken zipper; or (2) an exposure is intentional but the viewing by the public was "unintended," as when the naked image of a person is reflected from his bedroom to the street in a way that he could not have anticipated, or when the curtain surrounding a shower stall is blown aside by a sudden gust of wind. Despite this level of agreement, there is serious disagreement about whether it is sufficient that the exposure to the public be reckless, whether it must be intended (or virtually certain) that members of the public would see the exposure, or whether it is required that the exposure be intended and lewd or otherwise indecent. We will consider this issue further.

It is also generally agreed that certain persons are incapable of forming the intent necessary to support a criminal conviction for indecent exposure. For example, a very young child who takes off his clothes in the street or the mentally incompetent patient who walks naked into a hospital corridor could not be found guilty of the crime. They would be incapable of understanding their actions. The age at which a child might become responsible for indecent exposure varies not only with the general criminal policy of the state, but also with the level of intent required by the state. For example, it would probably require additional mental maturity to intend to act in a lewd way than it would to intentionally expose one's genitals to the public. Most children who would be subject to indecent exposure statutes are still under the authority of juvenile courts. While they might be determined to be delinquent, it is not likely that they would technically be convicted of the crime of indecent exposure. Because of the theoretical emphasis in the juvenile process on seeking assistance rather than punishment for the juvenile, it is likely that any juvenile determined to be a delinquent on the basis of indecent exposure would be sent for some form of psychotherapy or other treatment.

It is generally agreed that while a defendant cannot be convicted of indecent exposure unless the necessary element of intent is alleged and proved, it is not necessary that the defendant admit he intended to expose himself in an indecent fashion. Indeed, a person could be convicted over his protestations that he did not intend indecent exposure. Although the matter of intent deals with the state of mind of the defendant, the law permits the state of the defendant's mind to be inferred from his actions. It is, therefore, possible for the prosecution to present proof of the intent of the defendant based on his actions. For example, it is possible to infer the necessary intent when a defendant was witnessed through a window by several persons as being naked when he tapped on the window to draw attention to himself. In several cases, persons have been found guilty of indecent exposure with the necessary intent inferred when they exposed their genitals while seated in an automobile, so that other people could see them.

It is not unusual for the intent of exposure to be unmistakably clear, as is the case with the typical flasher, or where the defendant was engaged in open sexual conduct in some bushes near a sidewalk during daylight, or where the defendant stood completely naked in the doorway of his house and attracted the attention of passing high school girls by calling out to them. In other cases the intent of the defendant is difficult to determine. A good example is the case where a woman testified that she had seen the defendant standing naked approximately 4 feet behind his first floor windows, which were between 15 and 20 feet from the walk. The defendant said that he often dressed in the living room between the windows because his bedroom was cold, but that he took care not to be seen from the windows.

It is up to the finder of fact, usually the jury, to determine what the intent of the defendant was. This decision is made on instructions from the court (judge). The judge will generally simply state the law of the jurisdiction concerning the intent required and tell the jury in its deliberations to determine whether the defendant violated the statute, including a determination of whether he possessed the necessary intent.

Despite the many areas of agreement concerning the intent necessary to convict a person of indecent exposure, we have noted that there is a major disagreement concerning the issue of what is known as the specific intent required for conviction. Some states seem to require only that the defendant exposed himself in a place where "a reasonable man" knew or should have known that his act would be observed by others (members of the public). Other states have a similar standard but require that the defendant be reckless, as opposed to negligent as the "reasonable man" standard implies, in exposing himself. Still others require that the exposure be "lewd." What is required for conduct to be lewd is uncertain. Courts have defined it as meaning "dissolute," "wanton," "debauched," and "obscene." Lewdness has also been interpreted as meaning "product of immorality that has relation to sexual impurity." These words or definitions are hardly more clear than "lewd." The requirement that the conduct be lewd may be interpreted as being no more than indecent conduct (exposure) which occurs at a time and a place that a reasonable person should have known would be observed by other people (members of the public). The better reasoning is that lewdness requires something more than intentional exposure.

Perhaps the best example of the kind of case in which the definition of lewdness is important are nude sunbathing cases, which are discussed in the next section on consent. If someone goes to a beach and disrobes for the purpose of sunbathing and does nothing more to attract attention to himself, he might be convicted of indecent exposure under a standard requiring only intentional disrobing in public, or when lewd conduct is interpreted as requiring nothing more than disrobing in public. However, he ought not to be convicted if lewd conduct, in addition to mere public nudity, is required. In a notable case, the California courts held that a man who went to a public beach used by relatively few people, disrobed, lay on his back, and fell asleep, but did not at any time engage in any activity which would direct attention to his genitals, did not engage in lewd conduct. The court indicated that to be lewd, the exposure must direct public attention to the genitals for the purpose of sexual arousal, gratification, or affront.[4] As we shall see, some question has been raised concerning the constitutionality of indecent exposure statutes that do not require lewd or obscene conduct in addition to nudity. One state court has noted, "The Supreme Court of the United States has held that the representation of a nude human form in a nonsexual context is not obscene. . . . No matter how ugly or repulsive the representation, we are not to hold nudity, absent a sexual activity, to be obscene."[5]

The mens rea currently required under various state laws for conviction of indecent exposure may, perhaps simplistically, be divided into two major categories: (1) those in which the intent is simply the willful exposure of one's private parts in an area where members of the public are likely to see the exposure; and (2) those in which a specific willful, lewd, or obscene intent which goes beyond mere willful exposure of genitals to others is required. Under the first of these standards, the prosecution must allege and prove that the defendant acted willfully in exposing himself to others, show that it was forseeable that the exposure would be seen by someone, and demonstrate that the act was offensive to those who saw it or to the community's sense of decency. Under the second standard, the prosecution must allege and prove the first standard plus the fact that there was lewd conduct; that is, at least conduct which drew attention to the genitals and perhaps conduct which was in some way related to sexual activity or arousal.

Another issue which has been raised is whether the consent of the "victim" of the exposure is a defense to, or otherwise negates, the criminality of the exposure. This issue particularly arises in cases involving nudist groups or camps, nude sunbathing and nude beaches, and burlesque performances. Few statutes include provisions that clearly indicate whether the consent of those who view the exposure is a defense to the crime. On the other hand, the language in some statutes at least implies that the informed consent of those who view exposure is not a defense to the crime. Even the consent of "witnesses" in a nudist camp is not clear. While some courts have held that nudism is not indecent exposure where those seeing it consent to it and are not offended by it and where the place is screened from view from the general public, other courts have held that the consent of the witnesses does not excuse the act.

The policy behind convicting someone of indecent exposure where those viewing the exposure have agreed to it and where the place is screened from the view of the general public, such as a posted nude sunbathing area, nudist camp, or burlesque performance, is not clear. If there is a public interest in preventing exhibitionism because the nudity may shock citizens, there is certainly no such interest when the "victim" has consented to the nudity. The only rationale would seem to be an interest in protecting public morals by preventing all members of society from seeing naked bodies. Such a position would rest initially on the somewhat tenuous proposition that public morals are harmed when any member of society sees another naked body in a public place, even if he has consented to the viewing.

Much of the confusion and uncertainty regarding indecent exposure statutes appears to arise out of the lack of any clear understanding of the public policy these statutes are meant to promote. Undoubtedly, the statutes are based in part on a perceived desire by the public to avoid having to look at naked bodies in a public place. But this would not explain why a person could be prosecuted for indecent exposure for nudity in places where it was generally understood that nudity would occur. The laws concerning indecent exposure could be improved considerably if the specific policy reasons behind the law were rethought and the laws redrawn more narrowly to meet these goals.

Constitutional Limitations

The constitutionality of most indecent exposure statutes has been upheld. However, a number of constitutional attacks on these statutes have been made which stand some chance of success. Many of the statutes are unclear and may be attacked as being constitutionally void for vagueness. Because of a long history of interpretation of these statutes, however, the judicial gloss (i.e., judicial interpretation) may have sufficiently clarified the meaning of the statute so as to allow it to pass constitutional muster.

The indecent exposure statutes of some states may also be subject to a First Amendment attack on limiting freedom of expression and association. Since nudity can be a form of expression (if not actually speech), it receives some protection under the First Amendment. State v. Nelson[6] suggests the political nature of some conduct covered by indecent exposure statutes. In State v. Nelson, it was held that complete disrobing at a public meeting by college students to protect the exploitation of females in a national men's magazine was a violation of the statute. The Supreme Court has made it clear that movies and even live performances of shows involving nudity are entitled to First Amendment protection. The courts have also held that just because speech or conduct is offensive to some members of the community does not mean that it can be prohibited. In Cohen v. California,[7] for example, the court held that a person could not be prosecuted for wearing a jacket bearing the words "fuck the draft" even though it might be seen by women and children who would be shocked by it.

Even if exposing one's body only amounts to "symbolic speech," it is apparent that there are limits to the extent to which a state may punish nudity as criminal conduct.

Perhaps the appearance of a naked person is more threatening to other citizens and therefore more clearly limited than slogans such as that involved in Cohen v. California. Nevertheless, one might expect courts increasingly to require states to have narrowly drawn and clear statutes if the state is to prohibit indecent exposure. It might be reasonable to expect that courts ultimately will apply the same standard to indecent exposure statutes as they do to printed material to determine whether it is obscene and therefore subject to state control. Indeed, the Supreme Court has recognized that states have greater power to regulate nonverbal, physical conduct than to suppress depictions or descriptions of the same behavior.[8] The Supreme Court currently maintains that a state may prohibit material as obscene if:

1. The "average person, applying contemporary community standards, would find that the work taken as a whole appears to the prurient interest."
2. "The work describes, in a patently offensive way, sexual conduct specifically defined by the applicable state law," such as patently offensive representations of ultimate sex acts, normal or perverted, or patently offensive descriptions of masturbation, excretory functions, and lewd exhibition of the genitals.
3. The "work, taken as a whole, lacks serious literary, artistic, political, or scientific value" (Miller v. California).

Penalties

The penalties for violation of indecent exposure statutes vary greatly from one jurisdiction to another. Generally, indecent exposure is a misdemeanor unless committed under "aggravating" circumstances. Aggravating circumstances include exposure to minors or repeated convictions of indecent exposure. The penalties range from a minor fine to a jail term of up to a year. Under aggravated circumstances, the crime may be defined as a felony, and a significant prison term as well as a stiff fine may be imposed. The California statute, for example, provides that a person is guilty of a felony upon conviction of indecent exposure for a second time. Until the California courts struck down the provision as being cruel and unusual punishment, the second conviction of indecent exposure made an individual subject to a felony prison term of indeterminate length; a person could in effect receive a life sentence for two episodes of indecent exposure.[9] California statutes still provide that upon the second conviction of indecent exposure a person is guilty of a felony and punishable by imprisonment. Conviction of any felony is a serious matter since a felon, until pardoned, loses many civil rights including the right to vote, hold office, and be licensed in certain professions. Because of exhibitionists' high rate of recidivism, any law which provides stiff penalties for repeated indecent exposure convictions is likely to affect them adversely. In addition to the penalties in the indecent exposure statutes, in some jurisdictions a person who is convicted of indecent exposure may be subject to the sexual psychopath laws. If one is determined to be a sexual psychopath, he may be committed either to a state mental hospital or correction facility for an indeterminate period.

It is not at all unusual for the person convicted of indecent exposure to be given the alternative of seeking some form of therapy rather than actually going to prison. A Canadian study indicated that 76 percent who were paroled or given probation were seen by a psychiatric therapist either by court order or through referral by probation officers (Gigeroff, Mohr, & Turner, 1968). The advantages, consequences, and problems associated with referral for psychiatric assistance are examined more fully in Chapter 12.

The penalties that one convicted of indecent exposure incurs extend, of course, considerably beyond those imposed by law. Because indecent exposure conjures up an image of a crazed sex criminal in the mind of the public, the social stigma attached to having been convicted of indecent exposure may result in difficulty in obtaining employment, difficulty in being certified to take licensing examinations in a variety of professions including medicine and law, and extraordinary social stigma. Generally, conviction of indecent exposure will not ultimately prevent someone from taking licensing examinations so long as the conviction is not for a felony and there is no indication that the conviction represents a lack of moral integrity at the time of the application for a license.

Exhibitionists and the Crime of Indecent Exposure

Regardless of the legal issues concerning the extent of coverage of indecent exposure statutes, it is clear that virtually all of the statutes cover the activities of the true exhibitionist. It is also true, of course, that indecent exposure statutes cover a great many other people. The exhibitionist by his very nature will expose his genitals in a public place to unsuspecting strangers and draw attention to his genitals for sexual gratification. Virtually none of the defenses to, or weaknesses of, indecent exposure statutes discussed in this section can be successfully applied to a true exhibitionist. Even clarification of existing laws to rule out indecent exposure convictions when there has been a consenting witness would still leave the exhibitionist subject to criminal punishment, because the true exhibitionist does not expose himself to "consenting" victims. There is little chance that the true exhibitionist could avoid punishment unless the courts were to hold that indecent exposure statutes are so vague as to be completely void (unlikely), or that the First Amendment protects nudity even when conducted for the purpose of shocking other people or for sexual gratification (even more unlikely).

Operation of the Indecent Exposure Laws

In many areas of criminal law, the operation of the law in practice is somewhat different than one might expect by reading the statute, because a fairly small percentage of the criminals are apprehended. However, exhibitionists have a high rate of recidivism and a significant number expose themselves in places (homes and cars) where they are easily identified, so that a large number are apprehended. On the other hand, the evidence concerning indecent exposure often rests heavily on eye-witness testimony. The unreliability of eye-witness testimony has been noted repeatedly. Eye-witness testimony may be particularly subject to question in indecent exposure cases because the exposure is frequently to strangers, the victims are often in a state of shock and surprise, and many victims are children. In addition, the victims of the exhibitionists are likely to be alarmed but unhurt, and reporting and testifying about the exhibition may be troublesome and embarrassing. Many instances of exhibitionism, therefore, go unreported.

The difficulty of establishing evidence is demonstrated by State v. Wilson,[10] in which a 12-year-old girl testified that a man in an automobile exposed himself to her after stopping to ask directions. She did not write down his license number until she arrived at her home ten minutes later, and she told detectives that she could not positively identify the man. After an interview with the defendant, however, she said that he was the man. The court held that the prosecution had not established guilt in view of the girl's inability to describe anything about the man or the interior of the automobile, strong character evidence in the defendant's favor, and some evidence that the man was elsewhere at the time the crime was committed. On the other hand, another court in People v. Palladino[11] held that evidence by three girls under 10 years of age and one girl of 11 years of age that they had seen the defendant opening and closing his auto door until they noticed he was exposing himself was sufficient to sustain a conviction for indecent exposure. The girls had memorized the defendant's license plate number and identified him in court.

Another reality in the application of indecent exposure statutes, or other criminal laws for that matter, is plea bargaining. In most jurisdictions, a very large percent—often in excess of 85 percent—of criminal defendants plead guilty. This plea is often a result of bargaining between the prosecutor and the defense attorney. The aim of this bargaining is to get the defendant to plead guilty to a lesser offense than he was originally charged with. Because of the extreme stigma attached to a person convicted of indecent exposure, defendants often have a strong incentive to plead guilty to a charge such as disorderly conduct or disturbing the peace. These crimes may carry penalties similar to indecent exposure, but they do not carry with them the stigma of being a sex offender. As we have noted, charges against defendants may also be filed away or dismissed, or the defendant given probation, on the condition that he receive psychotherapy.

In some areas, the charge of indecent exposure is still filed against persons for any form of public urination. These charges are not uncommon even in circumstances where it would have been virtually impossible for any member of the public to view the exposure, and therefore where it is doubtful that the standards of the statute have been met.

EXPOSURE TO CHILDREN

A number of states have statutes expressly prohibiting indecent exposure to children or special sections in the general indecent exposure statute which apply to exposure to children. Typically these statutes impose greater penalties for exposure to children than to adults. It is not unusual for exposure to children to be classified as a serious misdemeanor or even a felony. When both penalties for general exposure and more severe penalties for exposure to children exist, the prosecutor will determine the statute with which to charge the person. In some cases it is possible to prosecute the person under both statutes. An exhibitionist could also be charged with a child molestation crime. The theory is that child molestation statutes are meant to protect children under 16 from being subjected not only to physical molestation, but also from emotional molestation such as lewd conduct and indecent exposure.[12] Child molestation statutes may carry very harsh penalties to which an exhibitionist could be subject.

The extent to which a very broad definition of child abuse might include indecent exposure is illustrated by the Federal Child Abuse Prevention and Treatment Act. Passed in January 1974, this act may become an important model for state laws because federal funding for states is tied to the requirements of the act. The federal act defines child abuse and neglect as "the physical or mental injury, sexual abuse, negligent treatment, or maltreatment of a child under the age of 18 by a person who is responsible for the child's welfare under circumstances which indicate that the child's health or welfare is harmed or threatened thereby." The statute includes a mandatory reporting section; that is, persons knowing of child abuse must report the abuse to proper authorities. This federal act does not generally apply directly to exhibitionists since the abuse must be "by a person who is responsible for the child's welfare" and most indecent exposure is to strangers. However, the expansive concept of child abuse as including "mental injury" suggests that actions which are conceived by law-makers as causing emotional injury to a child may become a punishable form of child abuse or molestation.

It is important that the psychotherapeutic disciplines understand the consequence of indecent exposure on a child, so that they can adequately advise legislators and other policy-makers concerning the kinds of mental injury likely to occur to victims.

SEXUAL PSYCHOPATH LAWS

In addition to violating indecent exposure laws and laws prohibiting lewd or indecent conduct, an exhibitionist may be subject to sexual psychopath laws.

Sexual psychopath laws provide for the long-term incarceration of persons determined to be "sexual psychopaths," "sexually dangerous persons," "sex offenders," or "mentally disordered sex offenders." Typically, they are committed to a hospital or psychiatric facility and held there until they are determined by the medical staff of the institution to have been cured. These laws are particularly ominous in that they provide for an incarceration which is indeterminate, that is, which may run from one day to the death of the person declared a sexual psychopath. In addition, there are serious social and economic consequences to being labeled a sexual psychopath.

Sexual psychopath laws now exist in more than half of the states. They were, for the most part, passed during the 1940s and 1950s, often in response to sensational sex crimes. They have been promoted as both providing for humanitarian treatment of the sex offender through civil commitment and providing protection for the public from sex maniacs.

Sexual psychopath laws are lengthy and detailed. Unfortunately, the detail of these statutes seldom clearly defines the persons who are to be considered sexual psychopaths. Following are examples of definitions of sexual psychopaths, or the equivalent, which can be found in this country.

> *California* § *6300.* As used in this article, "mentally disordered sex offender" means any person who by reason of mental defect, disease, or disorder is predisposed to the commission of sexual offenses to such degree that he is dangerous to the health and safety of others. Wherever the term "sexual psychopath" is used in any code, such terms shall be construed to refer to and mean a "mentally disordered sex offender."

Colorado § *16-13-202* defines the sexual offender as a person convicted of a sex offense.

> [Sex offense] means sexual assault, except misdemeanor sexual assault in the third degree . . . sexual assault on a child . . . aggravated incest . . . and an attempt to commit any of the offenses mentioned.

> *Illinois* § *105-1.01.* All persons suffering from a mental disorder, which mental disorder has existed for a period of not less than one year, immediately prior to the filing of the petition herein provided for, coupled with criminal propensities to the commission of sex offenses, and who have demonstrated propensities toward acts of sexual assault or acts of sexual molestation of children, are hereby declared sexually dangerous persons.

> *Minnesota* § *526.09.* The term "psychopathic personality" . . . means the existence of any person of such condition of mental

instability, or impulsiveness of behavior, or lack of customary standards of good judgment, or failure to appreciate the consequences of his act, or any combination of such conditions, as to render such person irresponsible for his conduct with respect to sexual matters and thereby dangerous to other persons.

Ohio § 2947.24. Psychopathic offender [is] any person who is adjudged to have a psychopathic personality, who exhibits criminal tendencies, and who by reason thereof is a menace to the public. Psychopathic personality is evidenced by such traits or characteristics inconsistent with the age of such person, as emotional immaturity and instability, impulsive, irresponsible, reckless, and unruly acts, excessively self-centered activities, deficient power of self-discipline, lack of normal capacity to learn from experience, marked deficiency of moral sense of control.

Washington, D.C. § 22-3503. The term sexual psychopath means a person, not insane, who by course of repeated misconduct on sexual matters has evidenced such lack of power to control his sexual impulses as to be dangerous to other persons because he is likely to attack or otherwise inflict injury, loss, pain, or other evil on the objects of his desire.

Wyoming § 7-13-601. [A person is a sexual psychopath] whenever any person is convicted of or pleads guilty to [any one or more of the following crimes]: sexual assault . . . attempted sexual assault . . . taking immodest, immoral, or indecent liberties with any child under 18 years of age, or knowingly committing any immoral, indecent, or obscene act in the presence of any child under 18 years of age and causing or encouraging any child under 18 years of age to cause or encourage any other child to commit or . . . accosting, knowing, or molesting any child under the age of 18 years, with intent to commit any unlawful act.

While the definition of a sexual psychopath obviously varies greatly from state to state, it generally seems to involve a person who has some mental disorder and is perceived as being dangerous because of the disorder, or who has repeatedly committed certain enumerated sex crimes. Persons charged with indecent exposure ordinarily are not prosecuted under sexual psychopath laws, although in some states they may be subject to these laws.

Sexual psychopath statutes usually provide for a hearing to determine whether a person ought to be committed under the sexual psychopath laws. Psychiatric evidence is taken at the hearing to determine whether the person is suffering from a mental disease. Psychiatrists are often also asked to determine whether the person is dangerous. The defendant may be represented by counsel at these hearings and may cross-examine the medical authorities and present witnesses of his own. If the person is determined to be a sexual psychopath as defined in the statute, he will generally be committed to a hospital or psychiatric facility for an indeterminate time. There may be provisions for periodic review of the patient's condition by the court, but generally the staff at the hospital or psychiatric facility will determine when the person is cured and can safely be released.

Although sexual psychopath laws were meant to be civil rather than criminal in nature, courts have increasingly realized that they have criminal-like consequences; a person may be incarcerated against his will and have a serious stigma in being convicted of a criminal offense. These processes are sometimes referred to as quasi-criminal in nature and therefore it is increasingly recognized that defendants must have many of the procedural rights that a criminal defendant possesses, including the right to an attorney, the right to call and cross-examine witnesses, and the right to be present during the hearing.

Although some states provide that a person may be subjected to the sexual psychopath laws instead of the criminal sex laws, many states provide that the sexual psychopath laws may be applied in addition to the imposition of criminal penalties. Some of these states do at least permit time spent in an institution pursuant to a sexual psychopath commitment to be subtracted from the prison term imposed for the criminal charge. Thus an exhibitionist may not only face a criminal sentence, but also be subject to the sexual psychopath law. Since sexual psychopath incarceration may be for an indeterminate time, an exhibitionist may spend much more time in a hospital or psychiatric facility than he would if he were simply convicted of indecent exposure.

There appears to be little justification for classifying exhibitionists with other more violent and dangerous sex criminals such as rapists. The popular notion that exhibitionism is a step on the road toward rape or child molestation is not supported by the facts. The notion that exhibitionism is an act of a dangerous person is perhaps rooted in the old puritan ethic associating sexual deviance with satanic influences (Henry, 1965). Most exhibitionists are unlikely to follow up the exposure with any violent acts or to move to more dangerous crimes. In fact, in the few cases in which the victim of an exposure expressed any interest, the exhibitionist was sent scurrying away (Stoller, 1977).

Studies considering the relationship between exhibitionism and sexual violence have repeatedly shown that exhibitionists are not dangerous and the few cases of violent criminals who have exposed themselves are incidental, as opposed to true or habitual exposers (Rooth, 1973; Gebhard et al., 1965; Freese, 1972). The complex issues regarding the dangerousness of an exhibitionist and the response of the psychotherapist to this issue are discussed further in Chapter 12.

REPORTING REQUIREMENTS FOR SEX OFFENDERS

There have been repeated suggestions that all sex offenders should be required to report and register with local authorities so that the authorities might better keep track of their activities. These suggestions appear to be based on the assumptions that (1) sex offenders are more dangerous to society than other offenders, and (2) sex offenders are more likely than other criminals to be recidivists and therefore they require surveillance.

California has had a sex offender reporting law for some years. California Penal Code Section 290 requires persons who are guilty of offenses ranging from assault with intent to commit rape and abduction for prostitution to indecent exposure and disorderly conduct to register with local officials and to report each change of address within 10 days. This registration requirement, of course, is in addition to criminal penalties imposed by statute and any incarceration provided by the sexual psychopath law in the state. The purpose of the statute is to ensure that persons convicted of sex crimes are identified to the police for easy surveillance; that is, the legislature has determined that they are likely to commit similar offenses in the future and therefore they warrant close observation. This reporting statute has been harshly criticized as inflicting cruel and unusual punishment (Blair, 1976).

Registration laws may label a person as a sexual criminal and make treatment difficult because the patient will find it more difficult to find acceptance in society.

CONSTITUTIONAL LIMITATIONS

We have noted that there are constitutional limitations on enforcing the laws against indecent exposure. The Fourteenth Amendment to the Constitution of the United States requires that a person be given fair notice of what conduct will result in criminal penalties. The First Amendment may impose limits on the state's control of nudity when it is a form of communication, as in a play.

In addition to these limitations, the Eighth Amendment's prohibition of cruel and unusual punishment may prevent states from imposing exceedingly strict penalties for indecent exposure. If the penalties are irrational in relation to the seriousness of the offense, or if the penalty imposed is shocking or unreasonable, it may violate the cruel and unusual punishment provision of the Constitution. Some modes of therapy which might be applied to the exhibitionist would perhaps be considered cruel and unusual. This issue is considered more fully in Chapter 12.

CONCLUSION

The crime that most clearly covers the activities of the exhibitionist is indecent exposure. Other related crimes, under different names, exist in some jurisdictions. The crime of indecent exposure, however, includes not only the activities of an exhibitionist, but also those of a variety of other persons such as the naked sunbather, the burlesque star, or the person urinating in public.

The crime of indecent exposure is a matter of state law, and state laws vary greatly in terms of the nature of the crime of indecent exposure and in terms of the punishment for the crime. Despite the diversity of state law, there is general agreement that the exposure must be of one's genitals, although in some instances the exposure of a woman's breasts may result in conviction of indecent exposure. The exposure must be more than accidental. It must at least be reckless, and it must be observable from a public place. In some jurisdictions, the exposure must have been lewd, which may mean little more than that it must have been done intentionally or to direct public attention to the genitals for the purposes of sexual arousal, gratification, or affront.

There is disagreement among jurisdictions regarding whether the consent of the victim of the exposure negates the crime. There appears to be no strong public policy for charging a person with indecent exposure if the person or persons to whom the exposure has been made have agreed to observe the exposure.

In addition to the criminal penalties specified in indecent exposure statutes, the exhibitionist may be subject to a social stigma which affects his ability to function in society and to obtain employment. He may also be subject to sexual psychopath laws and registration statutes as a sexual criminal. Sexual psychopath laws may allow an exhibitionist to be civilly committed for an indeterminate time, pending the "curing" of his condition.

There are constitutional limitations on the enforcement of indecent exposure laws. The First Amendment limits the ability of the state to control freedom of expression, including expression which utilizes nudity. The Fourteenth Amendment requires some level of clarity in criminal statutes so that one is on fair notice concerning proscribed conduct. The Eighth and Fourteenth Amendments prohibit cruel and unusual punishment and may limit the severity of punishment for indecent exposure and the kinds of therapy that the state can require an exhibitionist to undergo.

NOTES

1. Byous v. State, 121 Ga. App. 654, 175 S.E. 2d 106 (1970).
2. Robinson v. State, 489 SW 2d 503 (1973).
3. Voelker, dissenting, People v. Hildabridle, 353 Mich. 562, 592, 92 NW 2d 6, 19 (1958).
4. In re Smith, 7 Cal. 3rd 662, 497 P2d 807, 102 Cal. Rptr. 335 (1972).
5. 67 Cal. 2d 791, 797, 433 P.2d 479, 483, 63 Cal. Rptr. 575, 579 (1967).
6. State v. Nelson, 178 NW 2d 434 (Iowa, 1970).
7. Cohen v. California, 403 U.S. 15, 91 S.Ct. 1780, 29 L.Ed. 284 (1971).
8. See note 8, Miller v. California, 413 U.S. 15, 93 S.Ct. 2607, 37 L.Ed. 1119 (1973).
9. In re Lynch, 3 Cal. 3d 410, 503 P2d 921, 105 Cal. Rptr. 217 (1972).
10. State v. Wilson, 244 Minn. 382, 69 NW 2d 905 (1965).
11. People v. Palladino, 237 NY Supp. 2d 266 (1962, Co. Ct.).
12. State v. Trenary, 70 Ariz. 351, 290 P2d 250 (1955).

REFERENCES

Application of indecent exposure statute to nude sunbathing. *Washington University Law Quarterly*, 1972, *1972*, 817.

Blair, J. Sex offender registration for section 647 disorderly conduct conviction is cruel and unusual punishment. *San Diego Law Review*, 1976, *13*, 391.

Fisherow, W. California penal code section 314(1): Nudeness or lewdness. *Hastings Law Journal*, 1973, *24*, 1327.

Freese, A. Group therapy with exhibitionists and voyeurs. *Social Work*, 1972 (March), 44.

Gebhard, P., Gagnon, J., Pomery, W., & Christenson, C. *Sex offenders: An analysis of types.* New York: Harper & Row, 1965.

Gigeroff, A., Mohr, J., & Turner, R. Sex offenders on probation: The exhibitionist. *Federal Probation*, 1968, *32*, 18.

Henry, G. *Society and the sex variant.* New York: Collier Books, 1965.

MacNamara D., & Sagarin, E. *Sex, crime and the law.* New York: The Free Press, 1977.

Rooth, G. Exhibitionism, sexual violence and pedophilia. *British Journal of Psychiatry*, 1973, *122*, 705.

Stoller, R. Sexual deviations. In F. Beach (Ed.), *Human sexuality in four perspectives.* Baltimore: Johns Hopkins Press, 1977.

SECTION TWO
PSYCHODYNAMIC TREATMENTS

3	Group Therapy	41
4	A Psychoanalytic View	59

3

GROUP THERAPY

James L. Mathis

Pratt (1907) met with groups of indigent patients with tuberculosis in 1906 with the goal of teaching them the value of adequate rest, diet, and fresh air. The meetings were no more group therapy sessions than those of Socrates and his students. The erroneous equation of Dr. Pratt's early educational meetings with group therapy led some early researchers to call him the father of this form of treatment. It is not germane to our topic whether or not he deserves this honor, but what is important is that the habit of appending the term "group therapy" to any and all meetings of groups of people with a leader persists undiminished today.

The term "group psychotherapy" was introduced by Moreno in 1932 (1932). Interest in primarily psychoanalytically oriented group work grew slowly throughout the 1930s and early 1940s, but the growth went from steady and controlled to explosive and unrestrained during and after World War II. Much of the impetus for this

---

The background of this chapter is 15 years of work with exhibitionists at four university medical Centers, but the primary base is a specific project begun at the University of Oklahoma Medical Center Department of Psychiatry in 1965. The co-therapist, Mabelle Collins, continued the work after the author moved in 1968.

increased interest came from pure necessity when the number of psychiatric casualties from the military forces exceeded the number of trained personnel available to see them individually. More positive criteria for this form of treatment later evolved from the experiences of critical observers.

Early group work was largely psychoanalytically oriented, but it became evident in time that the classical analytical techniques were not always applicable or that not all patients were responsive to them. A second type of supportive group psychotherapy evolved, even though the dividing line between these two forms was not as precise as the names would imply (Bion, 1961). Modified psychoanalytical techniques were found to be valuable in supportive group psychotherapy. The term "supportive" refers to the therapeutic objective of strengthening or supporting the aspects of the patient's ego that appear to be healthy and more or less acceptable by the patient and his social milieu. This concept becomes very significant in the treatment of exhibitionism.

We will not be concerned with the several splinter groups of recent years such as encounter groups, sensitivity groups, "feely" groups, "nudie" groups, marathon groups, and so on (Yalom & Lieberman, 1971). Many of them have a quasi-religious flavor and appear to rely on conversionlike experiences and charisma of the leader. The more outré the philosophy of the group, the less it is apt to be based on objective data and experience, and the more likely it is to reflect the idiosyncracies of the individual in charge.

It is difficult to obtain valid controlled data on individual psychotherapy and it is almost impossible to do so with group psychotherapy. There is no firm agreement on the criteria for patient selection, the optimal duration of sessions, the frequency of sessions, methods of interaction, or even on who is or is not a group therapist. It is generally accepted that a workable group consists of from eight to ten patients who meet for a minimum of one session weekly for one to one and one-half hours. Most experienced and well trained group therapists agree that it is desirable for the leader to have a comprehensive background in individual psychodynamics and psychotherapy; and many, the author included, think that such training is mandatory (Abse, 1974). The recent tendency to relegate group therapy to the least experienced and trained member of the therapeutic team is to be decried. Good group therapy is harder, not easier, than one-to-one psychotherapy.

We began the project on group psychotherapy of exhibitionists partly out of necessity and also because it appeared to be a logical way to treat the condition. The number of referrals from the police department, courts, and other legal modalities became too large for us to continue individual psychotherapy without a long waiting list; but even without the press of numbers, we had grown unhappy with the apparent low success rate of traditional one-to-one psychotherapy. The patients tended to enter individual treatment willingly and eagerly when under legal pressures or social embarrassment, but the defense of denial rapidly redeveloped and produced a therapeutic stalemate that lasted until the pressures were removed, at which point the therapy was discontinued with no apparent change in the patient's pattern of behavior.

Group psychotherapy, like any other form of psychological intervention, is not apt to be effective or even continued by an individual who is comfortable with himself and his situation. Exhibitionism is an ego-syntonic condition in that it produces very little overt anxiety or any other form of internal discomfort. In fact, the act of exhibiting is a method of relieving anxiety and of producing a sense of well being or even temporary euphoria. Discomfort arises only when the individual is apprehended and for a brief period of time is unable to deny the social unacceptability of his behavior, or when he suffers actual environmental losses (jail, fine, or job loss) as a result of his behavior.

It is this remarkable denial system of the exhibitionist which leads to much of the difficulty in one-to-one psychotherapy. Why should any individual volunteer for treatment when no problem exists? And if forced into therapy by unsympathetic legal authorities or nonunderstanding relatives, why should the reluctant patient subject himself to the discomforts of psychic probing when he already feels well? We observed that our patients in one-to-one psychotherapy came as unwilling "prisoners" and then discontinued as soon as the external pressures were removed.

We founded our group therapy program for exhibitionists at the University of Oklahoma Medical Center on four basic factors:

1. The use of group therapy as an effective method of counteracting the ego-defense mechanism of denial.
2. A treatment goal and symptom common to each patient.
3. Mandatory attendance.
4. Male and female co-therapists.

GROUP THERAPY AND DENIAL

We have introduced the concept that denial is a major stumbling block to successful one-to-one psychotherapy. An individual therapist may confront the exhibitionist with his denial system session after session and the patient appears to agree intellectually, but without changing his true feelings or behavior. The exhibitionist habitually tends to deny feelings and to avoid their expression, much to the frustration of the therapist. We hypothesized that one or two members of a group with some contact with their feelings could act as a stimulus or catalyst to the more constricted patients. It would be difficult for a patient to maintain his denial when faced with counterparts of himself week after week. He would have little choice but to "see himself as others see him," to paraphrase Burns. We planned to include in each group, whenever possible, at least one man who had passed the denial phase either from prolonged therapy of any sort or simply by reason of time. (We had noted that the older exhibitionists tended to "grow up," perhaps as the result of repeated legal difficulties and social embarrassments and partly as a factor of aging.)

A TREATMENT GOAL AND SYMPTOM COMMON TO EACH PATIENT

Each of the men had been apprehended by law officers at least once for exhibitionism, and many of them had had multiple arrests, including one man who has served two prison terms for a total of five years for exhibiting to prepubertal girls. It was felt that the mechanisms of denial, intellectualization, and isolation could be handled best in a setting in which the exhibitionist was faced by other exhibitionists with varying types and degrees of experience with the condition. The opportunity to exhibit verbally before a group of men who were expected to be sympathetic listeners was conceptualized to play a therapeutic role. It was hoped that the group could furnish something lacking in the past histories of most exhibitionists; namely, male support and peer relationships of a healthy nature. An intense siblinglike relationship did in fact develop with time. We had noted that environmental factors which produced anxiety tended to precipitate exhibitionistic episodes in many cases, and it was felt that more acceptable methods of manipulating these factors or of responding to them could be learned from open discussion with fellow sufferers.

For example, one severe exhibitionist, a man who had not gone one week in many years without an episode, shared with the group a method of temporary control that he and his wife had developed. She had made a pair of shorts by cutting the legs from some of his old trousers. He wore these in reverse under his ordinary clothing. The process of having to manipulate the clothing to exhibit himself was so time-consuming that he frequently was able to gain control of the impulse and avoid exhibiting. This type of anecdote also served to bring out the ridiculous aspect of the act to the group members who had to laugh as he recounted the experience.

Like others who had dealt extensively with exhibitionists, we had noted a remarkable similarity in their personalities and lifestyles. We reasoned that a common symptom in people quite similar to each other would facilitate empathy, group cohesion, and social concern.

Our goal was very simple and easy to document: the prevention of further apprehensions by the law. We had learned that the exhibitionist rarely makes a serious effort to evade detection and identification, so we felt confident that arrests would occur with recidivism. We made it plain that this was our only goal and if other personality or life-style changes occurred, they were to be considered fringe benefits.

MANDATORY ATTENDANCE

The mandatory nature of the program stemmed from our experiences with individual psychotherapy for exhibitionists who were not forced to attend for an extended period (Mathis & Collins, 1970a). The usual course was for the patient to cooperate fairly faithfully and to work upon his problems at a superficial level for not more than three months. The external pressure usually had abated by this time, and it was routine for the patient to terminate therapy with the firmly and honestly held conviction that "it will never happen again." Many of these men were rearrested for exhibitionism within six months. We became convinced that the mechanism of denial, bolstered as it was by intellectualization and isolation, was so powerful in these men that most of them were unable to maintain a motivation for treatment to an effective end.

It seemed illogical to expect a man to volunteer for a prolonged treatment program for a condition which he considered to be a thing of the past. One reasonable method of holding the man in treatment long enough to overcome the denial was if the legal authorities gave him the choice of serving whatever sentence he received, which at that time was from one to three years, or having the sentence suspended so long as he attended the therapeutic program for the required length of time. Some first offenders had their cases continued indefinitely contingent upon conscientious participation in the programs, and later we were able to have the official booking delayed upon the same grounds. The advantage in delayed booking over a suspended sentence was the avoidance of a permanent court record and the official label of sexual offender.

We originally felt that a minimum of six months mandatory attendance would suffice, but we quickly learned that this was not enough time for some men and we revised our minimum to one year. It later became the unanimous opinion of the group members themselves that this figure should be raised even higher for some of the more recalcitrant patients. One man with almost daily compulsions to exhibit requested an additional two years suspended sentence when his original one-year term had ended. The judge obliged him.

We were aware of the fact that coercion into treatment is a time-honored "no no" in psychotherapy. We had been taught that psychotherapy patients are supposed to be highly internally motivated or else the treatment will not be effective. Our experience led us to believe that to expect this ideal motivation was to ignore the psychodynamics of the condition in question. We hoped that motivation would follow automatically once the denial mechanism became less operative, and this proved to be true.

Being forced into a treatment situation obviously produced ambivalent feelings in the early phases. The arrest was usually followed by an immediate sense of relief which quickly gave way to fear and anxiety over the possible consequences to job, family, and future. The initial acceptance of treatment was primarily to avoid the legal penalties; so the patients tended to view the therapists as part of the punitive system. On the other hand, they also saw the therapists as potentially able to save them from punishment. They knew that the group leaders were required to give reports of all unexcused absences to the legal officials, and they quickly learned that early in the program this had resulted in one multiple offender going to jail for two years. The initial distrust and resentment toward the group leaders were rather short-lived in the group situation. It was soon replaced by an almost equally unrealistic sense of dependency and trust which we will discuss later.

THE USE OF MALE AND FEMALE CO-THERAPISTS

We hoped to simulate a family constellation that would be the reverse of the pattern most of the patients had known in childhood. The group members knew that the male therapist was the originator of the program. He adopted an obviously leading role without appearing overbearing or domineering. The female therapist remained relatively passive, but never obsequious; understanding and kind, but not seductive or susceptible to seduction. She allowed the patients to practice being masculine without the threat of reprisal or rejection. The background of most exhibitionists suggested that past relationships with females had kept them constantly anxious to prove their masculinity, yet equally afraid of doing so.

The group leaders fell into fairly constant roles with a minimum of preplanning. The male therapist tended to confront the patients with their overt behavior and its direct effect upon their lives, while the female therapist interpreted the more subtle psychological factors and delved more deeply into the psychodynamics. Interpretations of psychodynamic factors rarely were accepted by the patients during the first few months of therapy, since the mechanism of denial allowed them to hear and believe exactly what they wished. Denial systems became more and more difficult to maintain as interpretations began to be made by the group members and to be augmented and explained by the group leaders.

The use of male–female co-therapists was highly valuable, but there is no reason to assume that it is essential for a successful group. Success with a single group therapist has been reported by Witzig (1968). We recognize that our failure in individual psychotherapy does not necessarily mean a condemnation of it. We were and are aware that successful reports exist on many forms of therapy.

TREATMENT MECHANISMS

Each referral was seen within seven days by one of the therapists for a psychiatric evaluation, but every effort was made to see the man on the day of his arrest when his defenses were down. Psychological testing was done rarely and only when there appeared to be a problem in differential diagnosis such as organic brain syndrome, mental retardation, or psychosis. The group leaders then met to discuss the patient and his assignment when he was found to be an acceptable candidate for group therapy. We did not accept patients in whom the exhibiting behavior appeared to be a symptom of some other disorder. For example, one unacceptable referral was a young man who had been arrested twice for disrobing in public. His exhibitionism was part of temporal lobe seizures and had occurred at no other time. Several referrals were found to be schizophrenics whose public exposure was a symptom of the psychosis rather than true exhibitionism. Two referrals were severely retarded men.

The acceptable candidates first were asked to discuss their feelings about and their knowledge of exhibitionism, and then they were given a full explanation of our concepts of exhibitionism and group therapy. This explanation varied somewhat according to the intellectual attributes and the educational background of the man, but in general it was in very simplified terms. Jargon was avoided. The candidate was told that we conceptualized exhibitionism as a compulsive disorder over which the man had little or no control. We emphasized the fact that although we did not see it as criminal behavior, neither did we view it as harmless in that it was a potential disaster for the man and frequently for his family.

The candidate was told that there were three major components in the growth of every human being: the physical, the mental, and the emotional. In effect we said, "The physical and the mental parts of you have grown normally throughout your life, but the emotional aspect has lagged behind for reasons presently unknown to us. Most of the time you are a normal male, but upon certain occasions the emotional part of you reacts as if you were a little boy. The object of group therapy will be to help this fraction of the emotional part of your being to grow to manhood."

A complete sexual history was taken as a routine matter, but sex was not emphasized. We tended to infer, if not actually state, that exhibiting was not a sexual act any more than other neurotic symptoms. It could more accurately be conceptualized as a disavowal of sexuality on the adult level and a plea to be accepted as an irresponsible boy.

We made certain that the man understood our agreement with the legal authorities. We reassured the man that we considered his behavior to be the product of an illness and we disagreed adamantly with those who wished to punish him, but we also assured him that we had no choice but to report him to the authorities if he failed to cooperate in the program. We explained to him that the fate of many men depended entirely upon our fulfilling our end of the agreement, and that we would not hesitate to sacrifice one man for the benefit of many. We pointed out to him that many of the judges and police officials were not in sympathy with our program, and they would like nothing better than to see it fail.

We asked the man if there was anyone with whom he would like us to speak about his condition. He was told that we would be available for personal consultation with his wife, mother, girlfriend, employer, or any other significant person in his life. He was assured that we would speak to no one except the legal authority in charge of his case without his permission and that all records would be confidential. Very few of the men wanted us to have any contact with family members during the initial phases.

We arbitrarily decided that we would limit the size of the group to ten men. We reached this number quickly and then began a second group. Group assignment depended upon which group had an opening, but occasionally we assigned a man on the basis of group composition. For example, we learned in time that we preferred to have all ages and degrees of severity of exhibitionism represented in each group.

The groups met one and one-half hours weekly in the psychiatric outpatient department of the medical center. They were registered, treated, and billed as private patients and charged a fee which ranged from $1.00 to $5.00 per session, according to the ability to pay. Most of our patients were in a low socioeconomic bracket, and many had suffered financial setbacks secondary to the complications of the arrest—frequently loss of employment.

Each man was told that the leaders did not consider themselves to be experts on exhibitionism and would be learning along with the group. Each man was told that how much he did or did not tell about himself was up to him, but honesty and frankness were expected.

The importance of speaking to no one of the specifics of what was heard in the group was stressed and reemphasized many times in the group context.

PHASES OF TREATMENT

The treatment phases (Mathis & Collins, 1970b) will be described in order of their appearance. There were qualitative and quantitative variations which appeared to be related mainly to the severity of the patient's symptomatology, past experiences with the law, and degree of family support. Whereas the phases might be overlapping and ill-defined in a young first offender, they usually were distinct and discretely defined in the older patient with multiple arrests. There were six phases delineated as denial, acceptance, anger, disappointment, upward movement, and separation.

The Phase of Denial

Denial is defined as the ego-defense mechanism in which external reality is rejected because the conscious acceptance of reality is intolerable. We have discussed the exhibitionist's overuse of this mechanism to a destructive degree in much of his living, and especially in relation to his symptomatology. He usually feels shame, guilt, and remorse after the first few exhibiting episodes, but these uncomfortable feelings are soon denied access to consciousness. Each episode, even after multiple arrests, fines, and jail terms, is quickly followed by the conviction that it will never happen again. He enters the treatment as an alternative to the legal consequences, but usually he is convinced that it is an unnecessary expenditure of time and energy since the problem is now under control. Even the abnormality of the act is denied by many men who wish to see it as a particular form of manliness, or as risk-taking behavior proving their courage.

It becomes obvious in the group situation that the mechanism of denial is not only confined to the act of exhibitionism, but it characterizes much more of the exhibitionist's life-style. He shows an unusually low tolerance for any form of anxiety and little awareness of the emotional aspects of everyday living. This frequently produces a constricted view of his position in society and a poverty of human relationships.

The exhibitionist usually remains isolated, denying his need for any relationship to the group, for a period of up to six months. The breakdown of this mechanism is gradual, but we (the therapists and group members) arbitrarily decided that a minimum of six months in forced attendance was advisable before the exhibitionist could be considered able to face his reality situation and to continue treatment on a voluntary basis. The breakdown of this massive denial system was accomplished by constant, repetitious confrontations by group members who had passed through this phase. Even those who had not been able to accept their own denial systems as pathological were able to see them plainly in others, and this was a powerful force in the denial phase. Interpretations and explanations by group leaders had little effect during this period unless they were combined with group observations.

M. was a fourth-grade graduate who had exhibited two or three times weekly for at least 19 years. He had been arrested in many states, repeatedly lost jobs, been evicted from communities, and served short jail terms. He explained his denial to the group after his sixth month in treatment. He said that it was like an automatic electric switch in his brain which was necessary for his survival. He told of countless episodes of acute shame and embarrassment, and of grief and despondency, following arrests early in his life. He said that only this automatic ability to turn off reality had kept him sane and allowed him to face family and friends. This was an oversimplified explanation by an unsophisticated man and it neglected the denial as an etiological factor, but it exemplifies the problem.

The Phase of Acceptance

The exhibitionist begins to relate to the group members and to the therapists with some feeling once he has been able to accept the fact that a part of him is emotionally immature and it is destructive to himself and others. He begins to speak of ongoing circumstances and past events with appropriate emotional overtones rather than as if they had occurred to someone else. He appears surprised to learn that his behavior has a significant effect upon the lives of others close to him. This recognition of emotions comes slowly and with painful difficulty for some. For example, one 40-year-old man, for whom this phase did not come until after almost a year in the group, ran from the room the first time that tears threatened to come to his eyes.

The phase of acceptance is accompanied by a tendency to over-idealize the group and its leaders. There is much discussion in the group about why this treatment was not made available to them previously, and it is implied that similar groups could solve most of the problems of the world. They criticize family members and police officials who did not insist upon proper treatment when they were adolescents—the time when most of them first exhibited. The leaders, who a few months or weeks before may have been seen as in league with punitive authorities, are viewed as saviors who can do no wrong. Older group members who have gone through this phase of semideification of the leaders surely but gently deflate this false image with a great amount of pleasure. The older group members, although they are not aware consciously of what they are doing and why they are doing it, in a truly impressive manner become very adept at judging the correct amount of reality to interpret to the member in this phase.

The Phase of Anger

Most people who have worked extensively with exhibitionists observe that overt anger is the one emotion which frightens the exhibitionist most. We initially made the correct assumption that the exhibitionist does not allow himself to express anger because of his fear of retaliation from authority figures, but we eventually learned that an equally important factor is his fear of being overwhelmed by his infantile rage if he allows any show of anger to come forth. It is as if he equates rage and destruction with true masculinity, but also feels that it is not safe to assume that role. The act of exhibiting is about as far as he wishes to go in expressing his specific hostile feelings toward the female. Each man could give a graphic example from his earlier life of the potential danger of expressing anger in any form. For example, B., a 38-year-old man with severe exhibitionism since adolescence, once had worked as a fireman. He recounted how his peers had teased him unmercifully about his "peter pulling" until one day he grew enraged and laid about the fire station with a chair. The end result was six injured men, including some broken bones. B. never again allowed himself to be angry.

The first overt show of anger after entering the program usually occurred within the group setting in relation to actual situations or objects such as the law, social attitudes, or employment. When it came out against other group members or the leaders, it was accepted or even encouraged and used as grist for the group mill. In most instances, there were significant outbursts against the important female in the patient's life—mother, wife, or girlfriend. These incidents invariably frightened the patient and reinforced his conviction that expressions of anger could lead to overt violence.

One patient hit his wife of 15 years on the chin and knocked her unconscious in the first argument he ever had with her. Another very quiet and passive young man threw all the breakfast dishes out the kitchen window when he became angry at his wife one morning. (He had neglected to open the window.) Episodes such as these invariably brought calls from family members who were understandably upset about the drastic change in a previously meek and mild man's behavior. Sessions with wives were often necessary on a semiemergency basis in order to obtain their cooperation and to give them support and reassurance through this phase.

The phase of anger frequently was our first contact with the significant family members since, in most cases, the man initially was reluctant for us to involve them. Some of the wives began to encourage their husbands to withdraw from therapy or, failing in this, began to threaten divorce proceedings. No wife followed through on the threat of divorce, although one did have an affair and confronted her husband with it. Her confrontation prompted him to exhibit that evening: it was his first episode in the seven months he had been in treatment.

We began a separate group for wives at the beginning of the second year because of their increasing demands on our time, and because the patients had begun spending too much time discussing what their wives had said to us or had been told by us. A senior social worker, well versed in both group therapy and exhibitionism, was assigned to the wives in what became primarily an educative and supportive group of a fairly informal nature. This arrangement was continued throughout the project, with each wife attending an average of six times. The mother of one unmarried patient also attended several times.

We retrospectively concluded that we should have insisted upon the involvement of the significant female from the beginning. We began to do this routinely in the latter phase of the project. These contacts mainly consisted of anticipatory guidance in which we projected what the effects of the program would be upon the men and allowed the women to ask questions and express feelings. This did nothing to prevent the angry outbursts of the men, but the women were prepared for them and better able to tolerate the behavior.

The Phase of Disappointment

Disappointment may be considered a normal successor to over-idealization in the phase of acceptance and to the feelings of fright encountered in the angry period. Each man had tended to hold on to dreams of a utopian future despite repeated gentle warnings from the group. He had survived his initial fear that expressions of anger would overwhelm his controls and lead to disaster, and he often had become proud of what he considered a very masculine attribute. However, it eventually became necessary to face the fact that the urges to exhibit were still present, although considerably attenuated. The man tended to assume that this indicated a lack of progress or even hopelessness even when other group members and leaders assured him that his fears and feelings were a normal reaction. The group leaders brought out the fact that the impulses were now conscious and therefore subject to voluntary control. They reiterated that this change indicated personality growth and improvement. The phase of disappointment was usually very short in duration and it responded readily to group support and leader explanation.

The Phase of Upward Movement

Many workers with exhibitionists have noted how often they tend to be underachievers who rarely reach their true potential in the socioeconomic world. This fact made any upward motion in socioeconomic condition readily observable. The timing of this movement was variable, but it rarely occurred before at least one year of group participation. Its appearance was found to be the single most reliable indicator that the treatment experience was producing results.

The upward movement was approached cautiously and only after considerable discussion and support by the group and its leaders. This phase frequently took several months to solidify; not only because of the man's emotional blocks to it, but also because of the realistic factors of previous failures and the records of arrests for sexual offenses. Upward socioeconomic mobility is extremely difficult for a man with two prison terms and many other arrests for a sexual offense. However, this phase was successfully passed by all of the first 15 patients who were discharged from the treatment program.

One young multiple offender who was working as a laborer returned to college to work toward a career in teaching. One unemployed young man found a full-time job and established his independence from his parents for the first time. Another laborer, a man many years older, began attending night school under vocational rehabilitation and obtained good, permanent employment. Another became self-employed in his own small business, and several other men returned to vocational schools to learn trades. Once the anxieties of his upward movement had been worked through, the patient was thought ready to begin working on discharge plans.

The Phase of Separation

The termination of patients in voluntary psychotherapy for neurotic symptomatology presents problems, mostly psychological, but for the exhibitionist who has a police record, these expected problems are compounded by the knowledge that he may be sent to prison upon the first recurrence of his symptom. This knowledge created considerable anxiety in the members of the group and even more anxiety in the group leaders. The group had come to represent to each man not only his haven of safety, but also his new feeling of self-esteem. There was a tendency to focus all of the separation anxieties on the safety factor, and the group was apt to aid and abet this so that frequently active intervention and interpretation on the part of the therapists were essential. It was necessary to encourage and support repeated verbalizations of the normalcy of feelings of closeness and warmth among the group participants, including the leaders. For most of the men, this experience represented the first close relationship of their lives, and breaking this attachment understandably was approached with reluctance and anxiety.

The group leaders recognized their own anxiety and the tendency to be overprotective toward the man facing termination. They brought this out in the group session and they also discussed it frequently between themselves in order to prevent overreaction and rationalization. They noted that there was a tendency to delay discharge when the slightest doubt existed unless they kept constantly aware of the fact.

Termination was a gradual process discussed for several sessions. A member judged ready for discharge by the group and the leaders was placed on what came to be called consulting status. This meant that he was to return at intervals of two to six weeks, depending upon reality factors, to report to the group on his general situation and adjustment. It was felt that this follow-up would be beneficial to the man himself, and also that it would be encouraging to the newer members of the group to see successful graduates. The member on consulting status was allowed to attend the group meetings at any time that he felt a need for it. He was especially encouraged to do so when faced with any unaccustomed stress or adjustment in his living circumstances or if he felt that his exhibitionistic urges were returning.

Consulting group members agreed to be on call if needed by the leaders. For example, it happened that a group was composed temporarily of only young first offenders. We asked P. to return for a few sessions to give the group an older member who could confront the younger men from the stance of his many years of sick behavior modified by newly gained insights. With considerable histrionic embellishments, he was adept at making it very difficult for a young man to deny the abnormality of his actions. He would choose a particularly resistant youth and say to him, "Oh, God! How sick you make me! How much you make me want to vomit when I see in you all that I was 20 years ago! A snot-nosed kid waving his puny pecker in some girl's face and thinking that he is a man! If only someone had given me this chance when I was your age!" This type of confrontation usually produced results much more rapidly than when given by group leaders or others who could be discounted as talking from the book rather than from experience.

These phases in the process of group psychotherapy for men forced by legal authorities into treatment for exhibitionism are rarely so distinct as descriptions make them appear. Indeed, the group leaders only became aware of them after two years of experience and considerable retrospection and record review. Perhaps they represent a normal progression through any group psychotherapeutic experience involving men with behavior disorders, but their recognition appears to have particular heuristic value for the therapist engaged in group treatment of this type of sexual offender. They give the therapist some degree of objectivity in assessing the patient's progress, and they form a structure for a precise understanding of the patient's actions and verbalizations at a given time. We came to view the successful passage through phase five, upward movement, as an absolute necessity before termination of therapy could be considered. We were constantly aware of the fact that many of our patients might not have another chance if they were rearrested for exhibitionism.

The group leaders began the work with the impression that active participation was necessary for the therapeutic process. This concept had to be questioned in time, as the following case illustrates.

B. was a quiet 18-year-old high school graduate arrested for exhibiting to a group of high school girls. He later admitted to four other episodes at the same schoolyard. He was a supermarket bagboy living at home with his parents and with no apparent social life. Two older siblings were college graduates, married, and apparently doing well. B. averaged not more than five words per session for six months, and these were only monosyllabic answers when he was directly forced into a response. The male leader suggested that the group might wish to ask B. to give up his position since he did not participate and there was a candidate on the waiting list for the group. The group reaction surprised the leader. They adamantly supported B. and they were joined by the female therapist. B. remained in the group and continued to attend faithfully and to listen, but not to participate.

An older group member knew B.'s family. He investigated on his own and reported that B. had made many positive moves which he had not reported. He had moved away from his mother, had his first girlfriend, and enrolled in a local college as a part-time student. Had we depended on B.'s group interaction as an indicator of his progress, we would have been grossly in error.

The formal aspect of this program covered a period of three years and included experience with 45 men seen in two separate groups over that time. Thirteen of the men did not complete the first phase because the legal hold on them was dropped before the mechanism of denial was eliminated. Fifteen of the remaining 32 men were on consulting status by the end of the three-year project, and the remaining 17 were still in therapy at various stages. Two of the 13 who discontinued treatment prematurely were arrested within six months, as compared to no arrests among the 32 who remained in the program. (Two men confessed to one exhibiting episode each during treatment, but neither were apprehended.) The program was continued for several years on an informal basis as a regular part of the outpatient clinic at the University of Oklahoma Medical Center's Department of Psychiatry.

The ethical aspects of a mandatory treatment program have been questioned. This is not the place to argue the philosophical point to a conclusion; but as long as society sees the exhibitionist as a dangerous sexual offender, an attitude which fortunately is not so prevalent as in the past, enforced therapy appears to be the lesser of the evils when compared with enforced punishment. To hold for strictly voluntary treatment is to ignore the basic pathology and psychodynamics of the condition, but therapists with strong feelings against the mandatory aspect obviously will avoid it.

SUMMARY

A successful program of treatment for exhibitionists was based upon the following factors: group psychotherapy as a method of counteracting the mechanism of denial, mandatory attendance, a common symptom and goal, and male–female co-therapists.

The treatment phases observed over a period of three years were denial, acceptance, anger, disappointment, upward movement, and separation. Some form of socioeconomic upward movement was found to be the most accurate predictor of successful treatment.

REFERENCES

Abse, D. W. *Clinical notes on group-analytical psychotherapy.* Charlottesville: University of Virginia Press, 1974.

Bion, W. R. *Experiences in groups.* New York: Basic Books, 1961.

Mathis, J., & Collins, M. Mandatory group therapy for exhibitionists. *American Journal of Psychiatry,* 1970a, *126,* 1162–1167.

Mathis, J., & Collins, M. Progressive phases in the group therapy of exhibitionists. *International Journal of Group Psychotherapy,* 1970b, *20*(2), 167–169.

Moreno, J. L. *Group method and group psychotherapy.* New York: Beacon House, 1932.

Pratt, J. H. The class method of treating consumption in the homes of the poor. *Journal of the American Medical Association,* 1907, *49,* 755.

Witzig, J. S. The group therapy of male exhibitionists. *American Journal of Psychiatry,* 1968, *125,* 179–185.

Yalom, I., & Lieberman, M. A study of encounter group casualties. *Archives of General Psychiatry,* 1971, *25*(I), 16–30.

4

A PSYCHOANALYTIC VIEW

David W. Allen

About fifteen years ago a psychoanalytic patient of mine was arrested for genital exhibitionism while I was on a prolonged vacation. On my return I wrote a report to the court to prevent his being sentenced as a criminal sex offender for this single, isolated act. As a result of my report, one of the probation officers began to refer exhibitionists to me. While the exhibitionists were willing to do some psychotherapeutic work, they were unusually resistant to the uncovering process of long-term psychoanalytic therapy. After a few sessions they would assert that they were "okay now" and wanted to discontinue treatment. I rapidly discovered that these patients did not stay in psychoanalytic treatment, and I discouraged further referrals.

Some years later I published a paper in which I described how neurotic conflicts in looking and showing affect learning capabilities, life styles, and the treatment situation (1967). This paper was not about the *perversions* of exhibitionism and voyeurism, but as a result of it and a subsequent monograph (1974), I again began to get referrals of genital exhibitionists. By that time I had analyzed more than a dozen patients with neurotic problems which included exhibitionistic and voyeuristic conflicts, but I was no more successful than before when I attempted to take several of these compulsive genital exhibitionists into analysis. My attempts at intensive psychoanalytic psychotherapy did not fare much better. Each exhibitionist was under legal pressure to seek treatment. Each seemed to want the minimum psychotherapy acceptable to the court. Each tended to be silent, tense, and unsharing either on the couch or face-to-face.

In my experience, *perverse* exhibitionists—or exhibitionists as we shall call them in this chapter—never voluntarily seek treatment for their exhibiting behavior. They are ashamed of it, disapprove of it, but fear losing it or having taken from them their most satisfying way of reducing tension or having a sexual thrill. Like a child, the exhibitionist may feel that others are cruelly attempting to suppress what is pleasurable to him. If he comes to treatment for his exhibitionism, he is presenting someone else's complaint—society's or the court's—but not his own. If an exhibitionist does seek treatment it is for some other distressing symptom, such as anxiety or depression; and only then, in my opinion, is he accessible to psychoanalysis.

WHY IS IT DIFFICULT TO ANALYZE EXHIBITIONISTS?

Psychoanalysis is essentially a method of research, and the resulting therapeutic gains are the byproduct of that research. The benefit to the patient is not necessarily immediate. In psychoanalysis the patient, who is the subject of the research, works toward a verbal revealing of his uncensored thoughts. The more complete the revealing, the more thorough the research and the more effective the treatment.

Psychoanalysis is carried out on a regular schedule of 45 or 50 minutes a session for four or five times a week for several years. Usually the patient lies on a couch with the analyst behind him. The analyst can see the patient but the patient does not see the analyst. The analyst listens, suspends judgment, and does not intervene except to help the patient explore the inferences of his thoughts and actions. The analyst does not participate in the patient's life outside the psychoanalytic situation. He does not reveal details of his own life but tries to provide a mirror for the patient, reflecting only what the patient has revealed. In recent years, adherence to the strict mirroring technique has been modified by many psychoanalysts but the essential one-sidedness of the revealing remains central to psychoanalytic technique (Lipton, 1977).

From the patient's revealing, an understanding is reached which enables the patient to see and feel how much his reactions have been directed by forces not fully under his conscious control. To the extent that the patient is able to observe himself, the process is beneficial.

Even the ideal psychoanalytic patient who is intelligent, with good ego strength and intellectual integrity and curiosity, will resist certain self-perceptions and self-revelations no matter how skillful the analyst. The working through of these resistances is the main task of the analysis. The analytic situation mobilizes showing–looking anxieties for both patient and analyst. Even though they are co-investigators, the showing is one-sided and, in revealing his most intimate thoughts and feelings, the patient makes himself vulnerable to feelings of guilt and shame. The person who is so fearful of the consequences of his curiosity that he acts to close it off is crippled in using the psychoanalytic method.

As we shall see later, the genital exhibitionist, because of the intensity of his preverbal conflict and his anxiety about separation and rejection, has difficulty in looking and is phobic about mental exhibiting. The exhibitionist is frightened by the analytic situation. He hides, silent and guarded, unable to exhibit verbally, more anxious about mental than genital exhibiting. The essence of the exhibitionist's compulsion is to see a strong reaction in an observer, and the psychoanalytic situation denies him this gratification.

There is a potentially irreconcilable dilemma for the exhibitionist in the analytic situation. For the process to continue, the patient must reveal to the analyst his thoughts and feelings. The exhibitionist may not be able to do so unless the analyst yields to the patient's requirements for an immediate response to the exhibiting, but the process is thwarted if the analyst does so. In *The Fear of Looking*, the implications of looking–showing factors in the psychoanalytic process are examined in detail (Allen, 1974).

In the psychiatric literature, the description of the syndrome of the exhibitionist has been clear since Lasègue (1877) first described him. However, the understanding and explanation of the exhibitionist's behavior have been and continue to be less than adequate. As a result of this inadequacy, treatment and prevention have been problematical. Research must be done to help us understand what underlies the compulsion to exhibit.

As a method of investigation and as a theoretical framework, psychoanalysis adds to our understanding of exhibitionism. But classical psychoanalysis has limited applicability for the treatment of perverse exhibitionism. Recent psychoanalytic understandings in the psychology of the self and narcissism, and understanding the reactivation of internalized object relations in sexual perversions, have been much discussed recently (Kernberg, 1975; Kohut, 1976); but whether these directions of investigation will make possible some effective modifications of the psychoanalytic treatment of exhibitionism remains to be determined.

In the psychoanalytic literature I found only one well-described case of a genital exhibitionist who was in standard psychoanalysis for an extended period of time (Sperling, 1947). Although Stekel (1920), Peck (1924), Guttman (1953), and others have reported clinical cases, a close study of the material reveals their inadequacy as psychoanalytic studies. Karpman's (1926, 1948) extensive reviews do not remedy the deficiency.

Most of our psychoanalytic understanding of exhibitionism comes indirectly through the clinical study of normal and neurotic behavioral styles, by direct observation of exhibitionistic behavior in children, and by inference from the study of exhibitionistic behavior in primates. The basic psychoanalytic theory of exhibitionism has been confirmed by the findings of nonpsychoanalytic investigators (Kinsey, Pomeroy, & Martin, 1948; Mohr, Turner, & Jerry, 1964; Rickles, 1950).

WHAT IS THE TRADITIONAL PSYCHOANALYTIC VIEW OF EXHIBITIONISM?

In Freud and his studies of infantile sexuality, we find the roots of psychoanalytic thinking about exhibitionism. Freud saw exhibitionism as a normal childhood activity (Freud, 1901-1905). He believed that primitive sexual impulses begin in infancy and childhood and are physiological responses of particular organs or organ systems. Normally these sexual impulses are gratified in a discharge with an external object. For example, oral impulses would be gratified in the mouth-to-breast relationship with the mother.

A perversion is a form of preferred adult sexual behavior which deviates from the norm of heterosexual union. It is "an habitual (although not necessarily exclusive) type of behavior" (Moore & Fine, 1967, p. 67). Perversions involve fixations or regressions to fixations in the body-zone stages (oral, anal, phallic) of psychosexual maturation (Freud, 1901-1905). These fixations seem to occur when physiological and emotional needs are mismatched with the mother's nurturant patterns through overgratification or undergratification, or when the gratification is traumatically disrupted or threatened (Winnicott, 1953). One such fixating threat may be castration anxiety reacting on childhood exhibitionism in the phallic-oedipal period and earlier (Greenacre, 1968). In "The Splitting of the Ego in the Process of Defense," Freud (1938) demonstrated how a traumatic experience which was overwhelming to the ego of the child may be mastered in part by denial, splitting off from the ego, and subsequent reproduction in a perversion.

In a case study, Sperling (1947) emphasized exhibitionism as a reaction to frustration. The patient, a professional man of 29, exhibited when he was disappointed, narcissistically hurt, or frustrated. He was brought up in a home where everything connected with sex was taboo. In childhood he was frustrated by seeing three younger siblings replace him at his mother's breast. Sperling suggested that the patient had defended himself against the loss of his mother and her breast by identifying with her and equating his penis with her breast. In his exhibiting, the patient was teasing women by showing them his penis but not giving it to them, as his mother had shown him her breast but gave it to his siblings. There is a suggestion in this case, as in others, that the mother's behavior which aroused hunger, rage, and envy in the patient in childhood was being imitated in his adult exhibitionistic behavior. This acting out was the patient's unconscious attempt to retaliate by arousing hunger and envy in the females to whom he exhibited. Later in the analysis, the patient seemed able to comfort himself with food in place of exhibiting.

Sperling thought that the main impediment to this analysis was the patient's narcissism. To protect his uncertain self-image, the patient denied being afraid and instead felt drawn to danger. He courted the thrill of narrow escapes by exhibiting on the subway. He denied castration and unconscious homosexual submissiveness by exhibiting his penis, symbolically saying, "I have a penis and it is so big that I am not ashamed to show it to everybody" (p. 44). He denied weaning trauma by asserting that he had a breast-equivalent in his penis. By other overcompensations he also showed himself to be better than others, especially his younger brother and possibly his punitive father.

Sperling concluded that in her patient "oral fixation" seemed "the most important determinant for the origin of exhibitionism" (p. 45). Oral fixations underpinning perversions have also been suggested by Freud (1938), Fenichel (1945, pp. 63, 351), and others; and Kernberg (1975) has pointed out the oral determinants in infantile narcissistic character formation.

Socarides (1974) has appropriately emphasized that "sexual perversion serves the repression of a pivotal nuclear complex, the urge to regress to a pre-oedipal fixation in which there is a desire for and dread of merging with the mother in order to reinstate the primitive mother-child unity" (p. 187). He also asserts that this nuclear fear results in a primary identification with the mother and a fundamentally faulty gender identity in all cases of perversion, including those of exhibitionists.

The predisposition to exhibitionism appears to be set when the infant observes his frustrating, controlling, and seductive mother. He is afraid of the mother but is also afraid of losing her, and he begins to identify himself with her in an attempt to resolve these fears of loss and merging. An intense ambivalent alliance with the mother develops which interferes with the child's emancipation from her. It is my impression that there is an unusual degree of ambivalence and anxiety in the exhibitionist's relationship with his father. The father was present and affectionate enough to facilitate the child's heterosexual development. But the child's mental image of his father was of an erratic man who was incapable of adequate nurturing and limit-setting, but whose sometimes violent displays of temper made him threatening. Rickles noted that the mothers of exhibitionists tended to be extremely narcissistic and looked upon their sons as phallic extensions of themselves (Rickles, 1950, pp. 53–58). "Exhibitionists come from faulty family environments with mothers or mother surrogates who were overdominating or overprotective. Fathers were unusually poor role models" (Mohr, Turner, & Jerry, 1964, p. 142). Spitz (1956) found that exhibitionists "have an inordinate need to please or be appreciated by significant figures in their early lives. They have difficulty in relating to the opposite sex and often harbor covert hostility toward women" (p. 388).

The main focusing together of all these factors probably occurs in the latency period. By the time of early adolescence, the problem is fully set and activated. The Kinsey studies indicated that the exhibitionist's sexual propensities were already focusing in preadolescent years (1948, pp. 165–67), and Mohr found that "more offenders were charged at fifteen than at any other time in the teens" (1964, p. 126). Behavior that was observed in the seductive, frustrating mother in infancy and early childhood becomes in the phallic-oedipal and latency periods active voyeurism at first and then, through unresolved identification with the mother, active exhibiting.

In early psychoanalytic writing, the castration aspects of exhibitionism, the narcissism, and the need for reassurance were emphasized. Fenichel (1945) noted that exhibiting "is always connected with an increase in self-esteem, anticipated or actually gained through the fact that the others look at the subject" (p. 72).

It is important to note that a sense of self-esteem derives largely from the attitudes expressed by the significant others as the child attempts to satisfy his biological needs. The way the child experiences other people's attitudes toward him, especially the way the child sees himself being seen, will affect his narcissistic character traits. Freud thought that the fixation on exhibiting served as a primitive reassurance against the castration threat. He believed that in exhibiting, a man insists "upon the integrity of the subject's own (male) genitals and it [the exhibiting] reiterates his infantile satisfaction at the absence of a penis in . . . women" (1901–1905, p. 157). The Kinsey group found that "some exhibitionism is largely an affirmation of masculinity, a cry of 'Look, here is proof I am a man!'" (Gebhard, Gagnon, Pomeroy, & Christenson, 1967, p. 399).

Because of the frailty of his sense of masculinity and his uncertainty about being separate from his mother, the exhibitionist needs to focus attention on his penis, the symbol of his masculinity, and to have the confirmation of a female viewer that what he is showing is not a part of her; that he is in fact separate and distinct from her. His failure to be able to exhibit in other gratifying ways adds to his need to exhibit genitally.

Fenichel (1945) wrote, "The very fact that the girl has no penis and feels this as a hurt to her narcissism makes her displace her exhibitionistic impulses and replace her infantile desire to expose her genitals by a desire to expose all of her body with the exception of the genitals. For this reason the displaced exhibitionism is not adapted to serve as reassurance and cannot develop into a perversion" (p. 346).[1] Exhibitionism in women is regularly of the displaced variety in which body parts are exhibited as part of foreplay, seductiveness, or a reassurance of general lovability. Other factors may contribute to the absence of genital exhibitionism in women. The female child is likely to continue a less restricted physical intimacy of looking and showing with the mother, and the mutual grooming of mother and daughter enhances the natural displaced exhibitionism in the female. The male child, on the other hand, is more likely to experience being relatively suddenly shut off from the mother's bathroom, dressing room, and bedroom. If the intimacy does continue, he may experience it as threatening and it may heighten rather than reduce his castration anxiety.

Very often what triggers the compulsive exhibitionist is not sexual deprivation or the need for sexual contact, but rather a narcissistic or emotional hurt, a rejection by someone significant, or a failure in work-related or male role-related achievement. The exhibitionist is unable to assert himself with other men and when his functioning as a normal adult male is threatened, he asserts himself in a more primitive way. Fenichel (1945) noted that "anything that tends to increase the subject's power or prestige can be used as a reassurance against anxieties. . . . The 'threatening' type of exhibitionist . . . enjoys the powerlessness of the partner because it means 'I do not need to be afraid' . . . thereby making possible the pleasure that would otherwise have been blocked by fear" (p. 354). In exhibiting to females and especially to immature females, the exhibitionist reassures himself of his identity as a male; that he is powerful and able to assert himself. He expresses anger and gets narcissistic reparation and a sexual thrill. In exhibiting, he asserts his dominance in a primitive way not unlike the monkeys in Maclean's (1965) studies.

Maclean demonstrated that exhibiting–looking behavior in monkeys expressed aggression and helped to maintain the social hierarchy. Like bishops kissing the Pope's ring or commoners bowing to the king, Maclean's monkeys submitted to the dominant male. Failure to submit to a quasi-mounting genital gesture to the face brought a vicious biting attack from the dominant monkey. This genital exhibiting passed down the male hierarchy until the least dominant male exhibited only to the least dominant females or to humans outside the observation cages. Though similar to exhibiting done prior to coitus, it was not primarily a sexual act: it was an aggressive social act.

The human male exhibitionist is strikingly like a low-status monkey. He does not exhibit to other males and, as a rule, he does not exhibit to dominant females. His tendency is to exhibit down the hierarchy to immature females. When his self-esteem is injured or his status threatened, he seems to revert to primitive anthropoid exhibiting behavior. He has not achieved sublimation of his exhibitionistic impulses for more adult mental or physical activities and instead regresses to infantile sexual behavior.

Perversions are based not only on fixations and regressions but also on splitting and repression. An idea is split off in the consciousness and repressed. For example, a boy may be concerned that a girl does not have a penis. To relieve his anxiety, he represses that knowledge. As an adult, with the idea still repressed, he looks to find a phallus in women. This is perhaps most clearly seen with the fetishist who fixes on a phallic symbol (fetish) associated with a woman, such as braids or high-heeled shoes, without which he cannot allay his anxiety enough to have sexual pleasure.

Both the fetishist and the exhibitionist have an unusually severe castration complex and need affirmation of uncertain masculine identity. Like the fetishist, the exhibitionist needs to reduce castration anxiety; but to accomplish this he uses the reaction of a viewer to the exhibition of his penis, rather than use of a fetish. While using a fetish usually leads to sexual intercourse, compulsive exhibiting generally leads only to masturbation. In exhibiting, the exhibitionist controls the distance between him and the female. Even in his masturbatory fantasies which are often exhibitionistic (Gebhard et al., 1967, p. 384), he tends to avoid the threatening fusion or engulfment of sexual intercourse. He wishes contact with the female but fears the merging or engulfment that he feared with his mother.

The exhibitionist identifies with his mother to an unusual degree. Sperling (1947) found that her patient unconsciously equated penis and breast. The exhibitionist is unusually sensitive to narcissistic injury and threat of loss, especially loss of masculinity. He needs reassurance and oscillates between the desire for separateness and union. This conflict is probably a residual of the incomplete individuation—separation of infancy that Mahler, Pine, and Bergman (1975) have described. The exhibitionist has not fully completed the task of individuation and separation, and he finds true physical intimacy to be too threatening. Instead he seeks a visual fusion with the female.

Exhibitionism is regularly paired with scopophilia in the psychoanalytic literature (Freud, 1901–1905). Initially the needs to look and show achieve pleasure in the early interaction with the mother (Almansi, unpublished paper 1978) and later in displaying and looking at genitals. The gratification of these partial instincts of scopophilia and exhibitionism can be displaced progressively to other body parts such as the feet or hair, or they can be sublimated into displays such as talking or acting. These displacements can occur either as an elaboration of the original instincts to look or show, or as a reaction against them. If the wish to display or look at genitals or sexual activities causes shame, embarrassment, or guilt, this wish may be denied. As a result, the original warded-off impulse comes through in such ways as blushing, stage fright, stuttering, or even in compulsions to look or show. It is typical to find in the early life of the exhibitionist prohibitions to looking and showing that did not permit the usual curiosity to develop (Allen, 1974). In "Hysterical Dream States," Abraham (1910) described a patient who feared appearing ridiculous in the eyes of others. The patient was extremely sensitive to slight and he fantasied about excelling before others and drawing all eyes upon himself. Abraham concluded that this fantasy was a "sublimation of repressed 'exhibitionistic' wishes" (p. 102).

Every active instinct, such as exhibitionism, is accompanied by its passive counterpart, such as scopophilia (Freud, 1901–1905, pp. 166–67), and therefore it can be concluded that an exhibitionist is also a scopophile or a voyeur. The exhibitionist makes contact not by touch, smell, or direct genital comparison but by a kind of once-removed voyeurism. Although he is interested, he fears looking directly at female genitalia. Instead he *looks at the looking* of the female—at her reaction to the exhibition of himself to her. Kinsey et al. (1953) found that many males, especially exhibitionists, are interested in their own genitalia and those of others (p. 657). The exhibitionist senses approval of his interest in genitals and in his wish to look at and be curious about them because the female looks at him when he exhibits, thus showing that she is curious. There is also some disapproval in the female's reaction that is reminiscent of the disapproval he experienced in looking and showing in childhood and in the threat of discovery, arrest, and punishment.

Stoller (1975), one of the most astute of current psychoanalytic investigators into the phenomenology of perversion, draws our attention to the role of aggression and hostility in the development of a perversion. Early writers like Lasègue (1877) and Krafft-Ebing (1886) noted the general lack of aggressiveness in exhibitionists. Their shy, self-effacing, passive, easily frightened nature is something we still note today. They are aggressive almost exclusively through their genital exhibitions. Hackett (1971) emphasized the inhibitions in the expression of anger in the childhood histories and adult behavior of exhibitionists. Stoller (1975) believes that perversion is "eroticized hatred" and is the interplay between hostility and sexual desire. The perversion is produced by anxiety and the historical events underlying that anxiety (p. 4). Stoller demonstrated that a perversion involves a scripted fantasy, played out in detail, which contains the hidden elements of hostility and revenge and converts a childhood trauma to triumph. The fantasy produces the precise amount of anxiety and excitement that permits sexual discharge. The exhibitionist repeats experiences that recapture the original trauma but differ from the original in some essential reassuring detail. The perversion, then, is a defensive structure raised over the years to permit erotic pleasure.

THE CASE OF P.

P. was not in psychoanalysis or intensive psychoanalytic psychotherapy, but his case may be used to illustrate the psychoanalytic understanding of the perversion or compulsion of exhibitionism as summarized in this chapter.

When he first came to see me, P. was 41 years old. He was a tall, husky man with bright red curly hair, mild mannered, intelligent, not psychotic. He had been convicted more than a dozen times for exhibitionism but had no other criminal record. He was on a five-year parole after serving 43 months for exposing to a nine-year-old girl.

At the time of that offense he managed an office for a firm that sold heavy earth-moving equipment. He had been having increasing marital tensions, was drinking heavily, and exposing himself while drunk with increasing regularity. One day after he had been drinking, he went to see a cocktail waitress with whom he was having an affair. When she rejected him, he drove to a nearby high school to expose, as he usually did, to some adolescent girls. He parked his car near the school and looked through a pornographic magazine which showed naked teenage girls looking in awe at men's penises. When no girls walked by, he moved to sit on the school steps. He was wearing basketball shorts and his genitals were showing. The nine-year-old girl saw him and followed him when he moved. Stimulated by her interest, he had an erection. Two school janitors surprised him as he masturbated in front of her. He ran to his car and fled the state but returned after a short time because he knew that his license number had been taken.

He was sentenced to the state facility for sex offenders for a term of one year to life. There he was a model prisoner and attended group therapy with other exhibitionists. After 43 months he was released on the condition that he abstain from drinking and have psychiatric treatment. He briefly saw a psychiatrist suggested by the court but was reluctant to talk freely because he feared that the doctor might report to the court.

P. thought that the psychiatrist he saw next was primarily interested in dream interpretation. P. worried that he would look bad to the psychiatrist because he would not have much to show; he dreamed little and could remember few dreams. In this reaction, one of the themes of the patient's life was revealed—an anxiety about how he looked in the eyes of others.

The psychiatrist referred P. to me for psychoanalysis. P.'s own wish was to come once every two weeks and I accepted this condition. In keeping with the psychoanalytic approach, I told him that I would not report to the court, to his parole officer, or to a lawyer, except to acknowledge the dates of his appointments. I told him that if he had any further legal difficulty, I would not take part in his defense. My only involvement would be to try to understand him as fully as possible and from that understanding to convey to him what I thought he might find useful. To avoid having records which might be subpoenaed, I kept no notes on this case. When I proposed writing it up for this publication, P. readily agreed to a series of tape-recorded sessions to review his history and treatment with the hope that his case might help others with a similar problem.

In the three-and-a-half years that P. was in therapy, the treatment was never intensive. He missed appointments or arrived at the wrong time. He was released from parole after two years but saw me when he was afraid that his acting out would put him back in prison. He was since arrested twice but was able to stay out of prison for the longest period since his first conviction. His first arrest after being released from parole was for exposing in a parking lot while pretending to urinate. The night before he had had sexual intercourse and was not feeling "horny." He was on his way to see his parents who were visiting, and within three blocks of their hotel he felt compelled to exhibit. "I just blanked out or slipped a gear. I don't know why I did it." He was not convicted. His second arrest was in similar circumstances.

P. was born and raised in Amarillo, Texas. His father was a successful businessman and his mother was active in church and community affairs. In her later years, she volunteered as a docent in an art museum. Both parents came from strongly religious homes and were ardent churchgoers and Bible students. The patient's father was a good athlete, a hard worker, and generally considerate of other people. Sometimes he got drunk and had a violent temper which frightened the patient. The patient felt that his father had been an alcoholic but in his old age regained control of his drinking. P. said that his parents were still physically affectionate with him. They were excessively concerned about what others thought of them. P. remembered that when he was a child his parents concealed their smoking and drinking from their own parents.

P. had a sister three years younger and a brother six years younger. P. believed that he was breast fed but did not remember if his siblings were. He recalled no feeding problems and no difficulties in toilet training. However, there was a suggestion of oral deprivation in infancy. He continued to suck his fingers until he was in the second grade despite his mother's efforts to break him of the habit. Only when she threatened to have his teacher write on the blackboard, "P. sucks his fingers," was he so threatened by humiliation that overnight he stopped his finger sucking. His mother, incidentally, was still a chain smoker.

In the first years of his life, P.'s mother let his curly red hair grow long like a girl's. While she dressed him as a boy, he felt that she treated him like a girl in the way she displayed his hair. There are family movies of his mother holding him firmly and displaying his bright curly hair, and he is spitting at the camera. He felt that she treated him as her little half-girl, half-boy work of art.

In these early years P. had had a slight stammer which recurred when he talked about his exhibiting. Sometimes he had temper tantrums. After his younger brother was born, he began threatening his mother that he would run away from home. When she realized that he was only hiding in the yard, she ignored his threats.

P. remembered that he was often in the bedroom with his mother while she was seductively naked or dressing. About the time his brother was born, he was abruptly excluded from this bedroom intimacy with his mother. He also remembered seeing his father naked a few times in those early years. His parents were not excessively physically modest, although the patient was required to be fully dressed even when his mother was not. The patient insisted that his parents were strict disciplinarians who never discussed sex. He said they never gave him any information about sex and never allowed him to show any interest in sex. It hardly needs to be pointed out that the frankness of our discussions of sexual matters was a direct contrast to this experience. At eight or nine he surmised that his parents had intercourse when he discovered condoms which belonged to his father, but he never actually saw his parents have intercourse.

When he was seven, a year after being excluded from his mother's bedroom, P. "intimidated" his sister into allowing him to examine her genitals and he displayed his penis to her. They repeated this activity but kept it hidden from their parents. About a year later a man exposed himself to P.'s sister and asked her to suck his penis. She immediately reported this incident to her parents. The patient remembered his father's violent rage when he searched for the man with the threat that he would kill him. P. was frightened that his father would do something "horrible" to him if he learned of his own exhibiting to his sister.

By this time the patient had begun fighting at school when he was teased about his hair. Though generally well behaved and concerned about his parents' good opinion of him, he became known as a bully and was rejected by his female classmates. We can surmise that the patient was attempting with his bullying to identify with the aggressor to overcome castration anxieties and to deny fears of femininity or of being an extension of his mother.

When he was nine, a year after his sister's experience with the exhibitionist, he visited his maternal grandparents in Denver. Though they were both strict, P. enjoyed his grandfather but felt that his grandmother was repressive. While there he developed a friendship with a little girl and they played together in a shed in the back of her house. P. induced her to expose her genitals to him. He had just taken off her panties when the girl's outraged mother caught him. He was shocked by the mother's threatening voice and apprehensive that "horrible" things would be done to him. Although his parents spoke of his behavior as "wicked," he was not physically punished. "My image in their eyes was just destroyed," P. said. He remembered fearing that the little girl's father might try to kill him.

At 13 or 14 he was again sent to visit his maternal grandparents and there he had his first arrest for exposing. He drove a few blocks from his grandparents' home, opened the car door, and exposed to some adolescent girls. He was arrested and turned over to his parents, who were told that he should have professional help. He saw a woman psychiatrist three or four times.

Although P. felt that he had been preoccupied since early childhood with exhibitionism and peeping, it was this first and only teenage arrest which fully characterized his adult exhibitionism. Usually he exhibited from a car when he was feeling rejected or frustrated. He preferred to expose to girls of about 13 or 14 and usually when there was a great risk of apprehension.

In high school P. was fairly active socially, a good athlete, and a better than average student. His girlfriends were either from middle-class, religious families like his own, and he was "proud" to be seen with them but not sexually active; or they were lower-class girls with whom he was ashamed to be seen, and with whom by his midteens he regularly had sexual intercourse.

After a year of college, P. joined the Marine Corps in the Korean War. He served for three years, was a squad leader, felt thoroughly manly, and did not engage in exhibitionism. In his final year he was stationed in Hawaii as an athletic instructor. There he met and married his first wife. Together they returned to college but he began to feel trapped in the marriage, and when his wife learned of his affairs with other women, she divorced him.

Shortly after his divorce, he became involved with an attractive, intelligent woman whom he had known since childhood. When she became pregnant he was apprehensive about how their parents would react. His parents were embarrassed. Her parents calmly accepted the situation when he indicated that he wanted to marry her. They did marry and his only child, a daughter, was born. When his daughter was still only a few years old, P.'s second wife began to drink heavily and to gain weight. He began to feel trapped in the marriage and his wife began to show sexual interest in other men. When he learned of her affair with a man who had been his best friend since childhood and with whose sister P. had once been in love, P. went looking for his large, husky, football-playing friend with the intent of smashing his head with a two-by-four. Not finding the man at home, he felt relieved and left. Because he felt so "demoralized" that he had lost everything—home, wife, stature—he decided to leave town. Later he took his daughter to live with him because he felt that his former wife was not taking good care of her. The patient felt financially "ripped off" in the divorce. His wife allegedly used the house payments that he sent to her to support her drinking habit. She died in her thirties of alcoholism.

After the break-up of his second marriage, his compulsive adult exhibiting began. He became involved with a "Scandinavian girl with a nice figure but without brain one." He had met her at a "wild bachelor party" where she danced exhibitionistically and he "swatted her on the butt" when she was in bed with another man. They began to live together but his parents strongly disapproved.

While living with this Scandinavian woman and his daughter, he was arrested about eight times in two states for exhibitionism, and was finally convicted and sent to prison. Though she knew that he was going to prison, the Scandinavian woman married him, and after his release they moved to a small town in North Dakota. P. again began to exhibit. His red hair made him easily identifiable in the town where he lived, so he exhibited only when on business trips in Canada. For a while he saw a psychiatrist but objected to the heavy doses of tranquilizers which were prescribed. P. felt that his wife was not taking good care of his daughter, and this third marriage also ended in divorce.

Over the years P. remained on good terms with his daughter. She finished college and went to work in another part of the country. She knew about his imprisonments but was understanding toward her father and treated his exhibitionism as an aberration over which he lacked control. When she was younger, P. occasionally exhibited to her. He would "accidentally" emerge from the shower, sometimes with an erection, when he knew that she could see him.

Following his most recent release from prison, P. was taken under the wing of his younger brother, a successful businessman, who provided work and a sustaining relationship. The brother had been married once but was now divorced and living with an attractive professional woman.

P.'s sister had been a college beauty queen. She was married and had children. Her husband was promiscuous and at times abusive to her. She had manic-depressive episodes, was given lithium treatment for several years, and had extended psychotherapy. P. felt that she had become emotionally "in touch with herself" and was getting along rather well.

A PSYCHOANALYTIC VIEW 75

Not long after his most recent release from prison, P. became involved with the former wife of a bank guard. He was sexually active with this woman but sometimes also "accidentally" exposed to her teenage daughter. As in previous relationships, he was disturbed by this woman's gaining weight and drinking heavily. He did not feel "proud" of her and thought of her like the lower-class girls in high school. Again he began to feel trapped and pressured to exhibit. In addition, his feelings of guilt and anxiety about exposing to her daughter made him want to get out of the situation.

Later he became attracted to an older, well-educated widow of a high-ranking military officer. She had children, including a daughter in her early twenties. He liked the whole family and felt proud to be seen with this woman. Were it not for the disparity in their ages—she was about a dozen years older than he—he would have liked to marry her. On one occasion after a party they spent the night together, and although she was willing, he found it difficult to have intercourse with her. They often played tennis and went to social events together. P. enjoyed her company but was apprehensive about beginning to feel trapped.

Whenever he began to feel trapped or overwhelmed by a woman, he was likely to act out with exhibitionist behavior. He observed that he was more likely to exhibit when he felt dominated or enveloped in any way. This included being made aware of his dependency on his brother. He was acutely ambivalent over dependency feelings with anyone—his parents, brother, a woman, a doctor. He felt the need to maintain the good opinion of these significant others, and at the same time he was resentful of his dependency on them and wanted to act against them. He wanted to be able to show his work achievements and have them acknowledged as separate from others. This need for individual display often took the form of exhibiting, which continued to preoccupy him with varying intensity. He continued to exhibit about once every 10 days or two weeks. When he had been drinking, he was especially prone to exhibit in a way that risked severe penalty. He said that he had never had sexual intercourse without drinking alcohol first. When a condition of his parole was that he abstain from drinking, he felt that it was like cutting off his sexual pleasure altogether.

Since P. continued to expose and risk further imprisonment, I encouraged him not to try to suppress his sexual exhibiting but to accept the impulses as a part of his makeup and to direct them into more acceptable actions. I suggested that he consider going to massage parlors or nudist beaches. The massage parlors were not of much help to him, but the nudist beaches did offer some relief.

Once he exposed himself on the nudist beach to two young women in an offensive way, and their male companions gave him a severe pummeling. P. was forced to fight his way off the beach. When he next came to my office, he showed me where his face was still bruised from the mauling. Later P. found that exposing to already nude women was not sufficiently exciting because he could not get the shock reaction that he found so essential. Ultimately he found that if he went to a nudist beach which was adjacent to a public beach, he could get the reaction he wanted. Standing naked near the public beach where the people wear swim suits, he usually had an erection and often masturbated. He occasionally shocked teenage girls who were entering the nudist beach. Their voluntary entry onto the nudist beach gave the girls no legal recourse, which kept P. out of serious danger of arrest.

Even with this more socially acceptable style of exhibiting, P. feared that under tension he would revert to his old patterns. He did not believe that he was cured of his exhibitionism, but only that he had gained tenuous control of it. He felt that "it still hangs in the offing like an impending doom." P. had known many exhibitionists in prison, and he stated that he had never known one who was cured by any method of treatment.

SUMMARY

Freud (1901–1905) found, and subsequent investigators confirmed, that in normal psychosexual development some of the elements of infantile sexuality are repressed, and the remainder are fused or integrated at puberty into adult sexuality with genital primacy and established preference for heterosexual love objects. In patients with neurotic conflicts, the repression goes too far and balanced genital integration is not achieved. Because of the instability created, the individual is vulnerable to certain precipitating stresses which may cause the repression to fail, with an accompanying breakthrough of the warded-off infantile sexual impulses. This reaction evokes a compromise in the form of symptoms that symbolize and partially gratify the impulses. In the adult, this insufficiently repressed infantile sexual element may attain primacy as a fixed perversion or remain as an alternative sexual mode under slight regressive stress.

Repression, then, is characteristic of both normal and abnormal psychosexual development. In the neuroses there is too much repression; in the perversions, too little (Brenner, 1957, pp. 198–199). In both, the elements of infantile sexuality are deflected from integration into genital primacy. This lack of integration is partial in the neuroses and more or less total in the perversions, and the resulting symptoms are formed in part at the cost of normal sexuality. "Neuroses are, so to say, the negative of perversions" (Freud, 1901–1905, p. 165).

The exhibitionist suffers from disturbances in his psychosexual development with his earliest object relations. In the oral-tactile period, the infant was thwarted or overwhelmed in showing his nurturing needs and in having them observed and fulfilled. This early misunderstanding in his feelings about himself, his bodily reactions, and his interaction with the external world predisposes the infant to greater stress and conflict in the separation-individuation phase; and it impairs comfortable, appropriate gender-identity beginnings. The child is thereby conditioned to react overstressfully to separation, loss, and experiences of bodily injury, and he has increased need for transitional objects. While he has increased needs for closeness, his fear of engulfment disallows satisfying intimate contact.

In the phallic-oedipal period, the child is especially vulnerable to castration anxieties. When he observes the genital differences between the sexes, or witnesses adult sexual and aggressive behavior, or experiences his own erotic and hostile impulses, he feels threatened. Specific voyeuristic-exhibitionistic experiences, especially with parents or siblings in the phallic-oedipal period, so excite and stress the child that the usual developmental transitions are further retarded. In the latency period, a trauma or series of traumas become the nidus for the reenactment behavior. These traumas write the script for the fantasy that directs the perversion. The resulting behavior is a compromise expression that gratifies sexual and aggressive impulses in voyeuristic-exhibitionistic modes and defends against castration fears, narcissistic hurt, and residual primitive identity and gender confusion. These reenactments have compulsive and hysterical aspects and in adolescence become further fixed and fully ritualized. Narcissistic injury, threat of engulfment, or loss of a love object triggers the acting out. The genital exhibiting has elements of self-reassurance and is primarily restitutive or reparative, but it also expresses fear and anger toward women.

The exhibitionist's personality development has progressed in such a way that he not infrequently shows borderline characteristics. This intermediacy has been noted by many observers since Lasègue's original description.

Some investigators (notably Rickles, 1950) who work within the psychoanalytic frame of reference but do not necessarily use standard psychoanalytic technique (Rickles used psychoanalytic psychotherapy which was sometimes supplemented by pentothal interview) view exhibitionism more as a compulsion neurosis than a perversion (p. 41). The basis for this distinction is that in some patients the overwhelming urge to exhibit is not necessarily accompanied by sexual excitment, erection, masturbation, or ejaculation. Instead, the ritualized showing of the flaccid genitals temporarily reduces tension, just as the performance of rituals in compulsion neuroses or religion temporarily relieves tension. Some exhibitionists may show other obsessive-compulsive character traits, such as excessive attention to cleanliness.

It is a mistake to classify exhibitionism as a compulsion neurosis. It should not even be designated as a deviation that lies intermediate between perversion and neurosis with the properties of both. The compulsion to repeat which is apparent in exhibitionism is present in all perversions. If that repetitiveness alone were considered, all perversions would have to be classified as compulsion neuroses. But unlike the neurotic symptoms produced by excessive repression, exhibitionism and the other perversions reveal the infantile sexual element in its direct, preserved form. In exhibitionism, the fixations are mainly preverbal rather than phallic-oedipal as in the neuroses, and these fixations are acted out rather than expressed in neurotic symptoms and suffering. Exhibitionism should, therefore, properly be considered a true perversion. Moreover, the response to psychoanalytic treatment of exhibitionism is like that of the other perversions rather than like the response to treatment of the neuroses.

When neurotic symptoms are investigated psychoanalytically and the warded-off infantile sexual impulse becomes fully conscious, the tendency is for the sexual impulse to find its place within normative primacy. In addition to enhanced gratification, there is an attendant reduction in the suffering of anxiety and guilt. In exhibitionism, the infantile element is already being gratified. While analyzing the factors that permitted its evolvement into adult life may reduce the suffering of self-blame and even make the perversion less compulsive and to some extent more gratifiable within social bounds, the primacy of the perversion remains.

DIRECTIONS FOR PSYCHOANALYTIC RESEARCH

Over the years, ideas which were developed in psychoanalysis have permeated the arts, literature, and popular thinking. Social attitudes have changed. Child-rearing practices have been modified. These changes, along with others in society, have altered the psychiatric syndromes. For example, the major conversion reactions of hysteria are relatively uncommon in the better educated segments of society today and they seem to have been replaced with more character neuroses of the acting-out types. It may be that these changes in society—and particularly the more open attitudes toward sexual matters—may have already made perverse exhibitionists a dying breed. However, it is this breed that we should study.

In medicine, understanding how a condition comes about does not necessarily mean that the condition is reversible or even that it can be prevented. But without such understanding, the possibilities for effective treatment and prevention are limited. If psychoanalysis is to contribute further to our understanding of exhibitionistic behavior, we need thorough analyses of compulsive exhibitionists. Whether psychoanalytic techniques can be modified in some way to make treatment more suitable for exhibitionists remains to be seen. But even if exhibitionists should prove to be unanalyzable, the psychoanalytic investigative technique might be exploited more fully in researching exhibitionism and other perversions.

Stoller and his co-investigators have been working with patients having gender identity deviations and perversions. They have found that a particularly fruitful way of understanding the genesis of perversions has been to analyze the mothers of children who are developing as deviants while co-workers treat the children. A similar method for the study of exhibitionists might be useful. For example, teenage exhibitionists and their parents might be analyzed. Certainly, knowledge of the family structure of the exhibitionist can add much to our understanding of the perversion.

The psychoanalytic study of children has much to offer in understanding the perversions, including exhibitionism. Research such as that done by Mahler and her colleagues (1975) in the separation-individuation phases of development may help to explain how one perversion develops rather than another. Psychoanalytic theory has often provided impetus for controlled psychological experiments and animal studies, but perhaps not enough attention has yet been given to psychoanalytic application of the insights of such studies.

Finally, some work needs to be undertaken to see whether modifications of psychoanalytic technique may be useful for investigating and treating exhibitionism. Since exhibitionists seem to have some of the attributes of borderline syndromes, it seems likely that theoretical and technical derivatives from work with borderline patients may be made applicable to the study of exhibitionists.

ACKNOWLEDGMENT

JoAnn diLorenzo, San Francisco, was the research and editorial associate for this chapter.

NOTE

1. My editorial associate JoAnn diLorenzo has pointed out that male psychoanalysts often give great weight to the idea of castration anxiety deriving from the phallic-oedipal period as a factor in exhibitionism and perversions. She notes that only Sperling (1947) has emphasized the male exhibitionist's display of his penis in a breastlike reenactment of his formidable and displaying mother's behavior in childhood. DiLorenzo's view is consistent, of course, with Socarides's emphasis (1974), on the perverse patient's primary identification with his mother and the faulty gender identity nidus of the perversion.

    DiLorenzo suggests that the male exhibitionist may in his action be insisting that he has at least one body appurtenance, if not the two of his mother or the possibly imagined none at all of his father. She is suggesting that rather than asserting that he has a penis, his fundamental assertion is that he has a breast. I may add that when the gender-uncertain macho male exhibits his chest, it is often to show the hair on it, his bulging pectoral muscles, or some decorative pendant.

DiLorenzo also points out that females are able to exhibit not only in displaced ways but also in genital ways, as in pornographic magazine photographs and intimate situations, without ever having these actions considered "uncontrollable urges."

REFERENCES

Abraham, K. Hysterical dream states [1910]. In D. Bryan and A. Strachey (Trans.), *Selected papers of Karl Abraham, M.D.* New York: Basic Books, 1966.

Allen, D. W. Exhibitionistic and voyeuristic conflicts in learning and functioning. *Psychoanalytic Quarterly*, 1967, *36*, 546–570.

Allen, D. W. *The fear of looking.* Charlottesville, Va.: University of Virginia Press, 1974.

Almansi, J. Scoptophilia and object loss. Unpublished paper, 1978.

Brenner, C. *An elementary textbook of psychoanalysis.* New York: Doubleday Anchor Books, 1957.

Fenichel, Otto. *The psychoanalytic theory of neurosis.* New York: Norton, 1945.

Freud, S. Three essays on the theory of sexuality (1901–1905). *The Standard edition of the complete psychological works of Sigmund Freud* (Vol. 7). London: Hogarth Press, 1953.

Freud, S. The splitting of the ego in the process of defense (1940 [1938]). *The Standard edition of the complete psychological works of Sigmund Freud* (Vol 23). London: Hogarth Press, 1964.

Gebhard, P. H., Gagnon, J. H., Pomeroy, W. B., & Christenson, C. V. *Sex offenders.* New York: Bantam Books, 1967.

Greenacre, P. Perversions: General considerations regarding their genetic and dynamic background. *The Psychoanalytic Study of the Child*, 1968, *23*, 47–62.

Guttman, O. Exhibitionism: A contribution to sexual psychopathology on twelve cases of exhibitionism. *Journal of Clinical and Experimental Psychopathology*, 1953, *14*, 13–51.

Hackett, T. P. The psychotherapy of exhibitionists in a court clinic setting. *Seminars in Psychiatry*, 1971, *3*, 297–306.

Karpman, B. The psychopathology of exhibitionism. *The Psychoanalytic Review*, 1926, *13*, 64–97.

Karpman, B. The psychopathology of exhibitionism. *Journal of Clinical Psychopathology*, 1948, *9*, 179–225.

Kernberg, O. *Borderline conditions and pathological narcissism.* New York: Jason Aronson, 1975.

Kinsey, A. C., Pomeroy, W. B., & Martin, C. E. *Sexual behavior in the human male.* Philadelphia: W. B. Saunders, 1948.

Kinsey, A. C., Pomeroy, W. B., Martin, C. E., & Gebhard, P. H. *Sexual behavior in the human female.* Philadelphia: W. B. Saunders, 1953.

Kohut, H. *The analysis of the self.* New York: International Universities Press, 1976.

Krafft-Ebing, R. von. *Psychopathia sexualis* [1886]. New York: Pioneer Publications, 1939.

Lasègue, C. Les exhibitionnistes. *L'Union médicale troisième série,* 1877, *23,* 709–714.

Lipton, S. D. The advantages of Freud's technique as shown in his analysis of the Rat Man. *The International Journal of Psychoanalysis,* 1977, *58,* 255–273.

Maclean, P. D. New findings relevant to the evolution of psychosexual functions of the brain. In J. Money (Ed.), *Sex research: New developments.* New York: Holt, Rinehart & Winston, 1965.

Mahler, M. S., Pine, F., & Bergman, A. *The psychological birth of the human infant.* New York: Basic Books, 1975.

Mohr, J. W., Turner, R. E., & Jerry, M. D. *Pedophilia and exhibitionism.* Toronto: University of Toronto Press, 1964.

Moore, B. E., & Fine, B. D. (Eds.). *A glossary of psychoanalytic terms and concepts.* New York: The American Psychoanalytic Association, 1967.

Peck, M. W. Exhibitionism: A report of a case. *The Psychoanalytic Review,* 1924, *11,* 156–165.

Rickles, N. K. *Exhibitionism.* Philadelphia: J. B. Lippincott, 1950.

Socarides, C. W. The demonified mother: A study of voyeurism and sexual sadism. *International Review of Psychoanalysis,* 1974, *1-2,* 187–195.

Sperling, M. The analysis of an exhibitionist. *The International Journal of Psychoanalysis,* 1947, *28,* 32–45.

Spitz, H. H. A clinical investigation of certain characteristics of twenty male exhibitionists. *Dissertation Abstracts,* 1956, *16,* 388.

Stekel, W. A contribution to the psychology of exhibitionism. *Psyche and Eros,* 1920, *1,* 1–16.

Stoller, R. *Perversion: The erotic form of hatred.* New York: Pantheon, 1975.

Winnicott, D. W. Transitional objects and transitional phenomena. *The International Journal of Psychoanalysis,* 1953, *34,* 89–97.

SECTION THREE
BEHAVIORAL TREATMENT

5	Electrical Aversion Therapy	85
6	Aversive Behavior Rehearsal: A Cognitive–Behavioral Procedure	123
7	Multifaceted Behavior Therapy	151
8	Assisted Covert Sensitization	187
9	An Extended Case Report: The Nuts and Bolts of Treating an Exhibitionist	253

5

ELECTRICAL AVERSION THERAPY

David R. Evans

It is important, before embarking upon a discussion of the use of electrical aversion therapy in the treatment of exhibitionism, to place its use in an appropriate therapeutic context. Most authors would agree that electrical aversion therapy constitutes only one mode of therapy in a multimodal therapeutic approach toward sexually aberrant behavior (Bancroft, 1975; Hanson & Adesso, 1972; Marshall, 1974; Marshall & McKnight, 1975; Mathis, 1975; Pinard & Lamontague, 1976; Rehm & Rozensky, 1974). This position led Rimm and Masters (1974) to make the following statement at the beginning of their discussion of aversive control:

AVERSIVE TECHNIQUES, ESPECIALLY PUNISHMENT, ARE RARELY UTILIZED ALONE: THEIR EFFECTIVENESS WILL BE MAXIMIZED AND POTENTIAL PROBLEMS MINIMIZED WHEN THEY ARE USED IN CONJUNCTION WITH OTHER TECHNIQUES DESIGNED TO PROMOTE MORE EFFECTIVE BEHAVIOR PATTERNS (capitals in the original, p. 367).

The caveat that electrical aversion therapy should rarely be the sole method of treatment is perhaps best understood in the context of a comprehensive treatment model.

Bancroft (1975) has suggested a comprehensive treatment approach toward sexual disorders. In his model there are four objectives: "(1) the establishment of a rewarding sexual relationship; (2) the improvement of sexual functioning within a sexual relationship; (3) the control of unwanted sexual behaviour; and (4) adaptation to a deviant sexual role" (pp. 186–187). Perhaps a fifth objective should be added—the development of socially acceptable alternative behaviors. For example, where exhibitionism is performed for excitement rather than for sexual gratification, the client may need assistance to develop alternative, socially acceptable excitements. It should be evident that electrical aversion therapy is just one method of assisting clients to control exhibitionism. Further, if exhibitionism is discovered to occur in response to tension-inducing situations, the therapist may decide to use electrical aversion therapy in conjunction with systematic desensitization (Wolpe, 1973) or stress innoculation (Meichenbaum, 1977). It is important for the therapist to establish the status of each of these five objectives for a particular individual. However, despite the importance of each of these treatment objectives, it is probable that for the majority of exhibitionists there is an habitual component to the behavior (Evans, 1970b). Hence, electrical aversion therapy or some alternative method of suppressing habitual behavior will form a constituent part of most multimodal treatment approaches to exhibitionism.

There has been considerable debate in recent years concerning the so-called ethics of employing aversive techniques (Baer, 1970; Davidson, 1974; Logan & Turnage, 1975; Rachman & Teasdale, 1969; Rosenthal, Rosenthal, & Chang, 1977; Russell, Armstrong, & Patel, 1976; Tanner, 1973a; Wallace, Burger, Neal, van Brero, & Davis, 1976). Often, much of the debate that has occurred in the name of ethics has amounted to nothing more than emotionally laden value statements. As a number of authors have pointed out, many of those who have opposed the use of aversive techniques have done so on the basis of emotional rather than logical, scientific grounds (Baer, 1970; Wallace et al., 1976). If the therapist follows the ethical standards prescribed by the American Psychological Association, then aversion therapy will be used appropriately and ethically (*Ethical Principles,* 1973; *Ethical Standards,* 1977). However, as Schwitzgebel (1978) has noted, the therapist contemplating the use of aversive techniques should also be conversant with the laws and rules in his jurisdiction concerning the use of such procedures. Schwitzgebel outlines laws in North Dakota and Ohio that specify the conditions under which aversive procedures can be employed with certain groups of patients.

The ethical use of electrical aversion therapy demands that the therapist consider a number of issues. The therapist should be competent to use electrical stimulation and be certain that the device which is being employed conforms to the most recent safety standards. Bernstein (1975) and Butterfield (1975a, b) have provided excellent discussions of the safety standards which should be employed when using electric shock. "Test Procedures and Specifications for Evaluating Safety: Apparatus used for Aversive Shock Therapy" (Butterfield, 1975a, pp. 10–25) should be followed with each piece of apparatus employed. At the conclusion of Butterfield's article, he lists aversive shock stimulators which in his opinion meet these standards. Siddall, Vargas, and Adesso (1975) have outlined a circuit for a shock generator which also meets Butterfield's standards.

A second important concern is whether electrical aversion therapy is in fact the most appropriate treatment. All available research should, in the opinion of the user, demonstrate that electrical aversion therapy is an effective and efficient means of ameliorating the patient's specific problem. This latter decision should be made on scientific rather than emotional grounds (Baer, 1970; Davidson, 1974; Wallace et al., 1976). Most authors agree that if aversion therapy is the most effective and efficient method of treating a patient's problem, it would be unethical to refuse such treatment (Baer, 1970; Rachman & Teasdale, 1969; Wallace et al., 1976). Baer (1970) observes that a critical dimension in this decision may be the rapidity with which the unwanted behavior can be brought under control. For example, if electrical aversion therapy leads to control of exhibitionism in three months and another form of therapy leads to the same level of control in two years, the patient may suffer far less net discomfort from electrical aversion therapy than from the alternative mode. Logan and Turnage (1975) argue that the welfare of others should also be considered when deciding on the treatment of choice. Thus they argue that in the case of sexually deviant behavior, the speed with which a treatment leads to the reduction of the maladaptive behavior is of prime importance.

The essence of most legislation concerning aversive techniques, and the consensus of most authors, is that the client should give informed consent before electrical aversion therapy is utilized (Davidson, 1974; Logan & Turnage, 1975; Rachman & Teasdale, 1969; Schwitzgebel, 1978). Martin (1975, pp. 27–31) has outlined the legal aspects of the process of informed consent. The client should have the capacity to give consent, and he should be able to give consent voluntarily. Further, the client must be able to comprehend the informational aspect of informed consent. The information conveyed to the client should be noncoercive and include the following:

1. A full description of the procedure to be employed
2. The relative effectiveness of the method compared to other methods
3. Parameters relating to the probable duration of the therapy
4. A statement of the associated risks
5. Indication that the client can withdraw from therapy at any time.

Assuming that these guidelines are followed and met, the therapist using electrical aversion therapy is likely to be acting in an ethically and legally appropriate manner. Obviously, an important aspect of the decision to employ electrical aversion therapy with exhibitionists is its rationale and effectiveness. The section which follows addresses the theoretical rationale behind electrical aversion therapy with exhibitionists, and the subsequent section outlines supportive research.

THEORETICAL RATIONALE

In simplistic terms, electrical aversion therapy involves the pairing of some representation of an individual's deviant behavior with electric shock over a number of trials with the object of eliminating the occurrence of deviant behavior. Inherent in this definition, however, are a number of issues: the mode of representing the deviant behavior, parameters associated with the occurrence of electric shock, models of associating the representation of the deviant behavior and electric shock, the presence or absence of aversion relief, and the duration and spacing of trials (Evans, 1968a; Bancroft, 1974). The theoretical rationale underlying electrical aversion therapy will be discussed in relation to each of these issues.

Representation of the Deviant Behavior

It is rarely possible to pair shock directly with the deviant behavior in the natural setting, and such activity in treating exhibitionism may leave the therapist open to subsequent charges of being an accessory (Evans, 1970a). Hence, it is necessary to represent the deviant behavior in the therapeutic situation. The deviant behavior can be actually performed, represented in pictorial form, imagined, or represented by some combination of these methods. A number of authors have arranged for the client to exhibit in the therapeutic environment (Fookes, 1969; Jones & Frei, 1977; Reitz & Keil, 1971; Rooth & Marks, 1974; Serber, 1970; Wikramasekera, 1972, 1976). Of these authors, only Fookes and Rooth and Marks have associated actual exhibiting with electrical aversion. A second possibility is to photograph the subject while he actually exhibits in a simulated situation, and then to employ the resultant pictures in conjunction with electrical aversion. Forgione (1976) has described a method of obtaining such pictures in the treatment of child molesters by using mannequins. To date, we are unaware of any attempt to employ this method with exhibitionists. The final and most frequent method of representing exhibitionistic activity is to have the individual imagine acting out (Evans, 1970a; Kushner & Sandler, 1966; Mathis, 1975; Miller & Haney, 1976; Wijesinghe, 1977). The individual may be asked simply to imagine the activity (Kushner & Sandler, 1966), to imagine acting out in response to pictures of females (Miller & Haney, 1976; Wijesinghe, 1977), or to imagine exposing while reading or hearing descriptions of the activity (Evans, 1970a, b; Mathis, 1975). There is a paucity of controlled studies indicating the relative efficacy of these methods.

Another important issue related to the method of representing the deviant behavior centers around the topography of the deviant behavior. Frankel (1975) has argued that behaviors should be analyzed not as isolated incidents (the act of exhibiting), but as behavioral chains. A number of authors have analyzed deviant behavior as a sequence of behaviors (Claeson & Malm, 1973; Copemann, 1977; Evans, 1970a, 1971; Lubetkin & Fishman, 1974; O'Brien, Raynes, & Patch, 1972; Steffy, Meichenbaum, & Best, 1970). Most deviant behaviors can be conceptualized in terms of four phases:

1. A cognitive phase involving the urge to act out and the decision to act out

2. A preparatory phase during which the individual enacts behaviors preparatory to acting out
3. An action phase during which the individual acts out
4. A post-action phase during which the individual savours the positive consequences of the act.

There is surprisingly little literature investigating the effect of aversive consequences on chains of behavior. Most authors rely on the work of Wolfe (1936) to predict the effects of various strategies on chains of behavior. It appears that if aversion to the deviant act is provoked, the behavior will quickly reinstate itself once aversion therapy is concluded. In contrast, if aversion to the cognitive precursors of the act is provoked, then the chain is less likely to become reinstated. To date, no comparative studies have been carried out to evaluate the importance of viewing and treating deviant behavior as a chain. Some authors choose to associate shock with behaviors occurring in the action phase; others have associated shock solely with the cognitive phase. Other authors have tended to associate shock with aspects representative of each phase of the behavioral chain. In the absence of any empirical evidence, perhaps the latter strategy is most appropriate.

Electric Shock Parameters

The majority of therapists employing electrical aversion therapy with exhibitionists have administered shock to the fingers or forearm of a single limb (Evans, 1970a; Fookes, 1969; Rooth & Marks, 1974; Wijesinghe, 1977). Typically, the client is able to set his own level of shock at the level which approaches his toleration threshold (Callahan & Leitenberg, 1973; Evans, 1970a; Kushner & Sandler, 1966; Mathis, 1975). Only Miller and Haney (1976) have employed mild electric shock. The literature appears to be bereft of studies examining the effect of shock intensity in electrical aversion therapy with exhibitionists. However, Tanner (1973b) has demonstrated that sexual reorientation of homosexuals is enhanced by higher shock intensities.

Another important parameter may be whether the occurrence of shock is certain or uncertain. O'Neil (1975) concluded that the efficacy of electrical aversion therapy was increased by using unpredictable rather than predictable shock onset. In contrast, Klemp and Rodin (1976) found that level of predictability did not differentially affect the impact of shock; rather, it was the degree of uncertainty associated with the shock which was important. Most therapists employing electrical aversion therapy with exhibitionists have endeavored to increase the level of uncertainty associated with shock onset by randomizing the occurrence of shock trials, randomly changing the delay related to shock onset, and using variable ratio scheduling (Callahan & Leitenberg, 1973; Evans, 1970a; Miller & Haney, 1976; Wijesinghe, 1977).

One final variable pertinent to shock is the question of whether it should be administered by the therapist or by the client. Conway (1977) manipulated this dimension and was unable to reject the null hypothesis associated with this variable. It must be assumed then that therapist- and client-administered shocks lead to similar levels of therapeutic effect. The majority of therapists reporting electrical aversion therapy with exhibitionists have employed therapist-administered shock. However, Rooth and Marks (1974) did supplement this procedure with client-administered shock trials. In some jurisdictions, legal requirements may suggest the use of a client-administered shock paradigm.

Theoretical Models

There are a number of theoretical models that underlie the association of some representation of the deviant behavior with electric shock and the subsequent behavior of the individual in response to his deviant behavior. Bancroft (1974, 1975), Church (1963), Davidson (1974), Forgione (1976), Lovibond (1970), and Rachman and Teasdale (1969) have provided extensive discussions of these models. All too often therapists using electrical aversion therapy have done so without an appropriate consideration of which model they were using. Often the results of electrical aversion therapy are difficult to assess either because the therapist has used a mixed model or because the therapist has failed to provide sufficient information to define the model being used. The four models upon which electrical aversion therapy may be based are a classical conditioning model, an escape-learning model, an avoidance-learning model, and a punishment model.

The classical conditioning model has been discussed by Bancroft (1974, 1975), Davidson (1974), and Rachman and Teasdale (1969). Under this model, some aspect of the deviant behavior is associated with an aversive stimulus over numerous trials. It is postulated that the subject will develop a conditioned aversion to the deviant behavior and hence avoid it. The most prominent theory concerning this model is Mowrer's (1960) two-stage theory. Under this theory, the representations of the deviant behavior associated with the aversive stimulus are conditioned to produce anxiety, which in turn leads to avoidance of the deviant behavior. A number of authors have argued that Mowrer's two-stage theory does not adequately account for the results of aversion therapy using the classical conditioning model (Evans, 1975; Hallam & Rachman, 1972b; Rachman, 1976). Hallam and Rachman (1972a) found that patients reported indifference rather than anxiety toward the deviant behavior following aversion therapy. They proposed a state theory to account for this finding, suggesting that classical conditioning results in suppression of the deviant behavior. Evans (1975) has argued that during aversion therapy which utilizes a classical conditioning model, a general expectancy for guilt is developed in relation to the deviant behavior. Once this general expectancy for guilt has developed, the patient will refrain from the deviant behavior.

The escape-learning model has been reviewed by Church (1963), Forgione (1976), and Lovibond (1970). In escape learning, some representation of the deviant behavior is paired with an aversive stimulus and the client can perform an instrumental response which terminates the aversive stimulus. For example, Forgione paired pictures of the client enacting his deviant behavior with shock. The client could escape shock by saying "no more," or "take it away." Once the verbal response was emitted, shock was terminated and the client was able to view (escape to) a shock-free slide of a nude, mature female. During escape learning the client learns to emit the escape response more rapidly as trials progress. Implicit in this model is the notion that when the client is exposed to the representation of the deviant behavior outside of the therapeutic situation, he will quickly escape from it and perform an alternative behavior. Generally, escape-learning trials have rarely been used exclusively in electrical aversion therapy. More commonly, they are used prior to avoidance-learning trials.

Bancroft (1974, 1975), Church (1963), Davidson (1974), Lovibond (1970), and Rachman and Teasdale (1969) have all presented extensive discussions of the avoidance-learning model. In this model, some representation of the deviant behavior acts as a signal for shock, and the patient can avoid shock by performing a behavior which removes him from the possibility of shock. Ultimately, by refusing to interact with the representation of the deviant behavior, the patient avoids shock. Hence the patient is trained to avoid the deviant behavior actively. Most authors using this model include escape trials or mandatory shock trials either in conjunction with avoidance trials or as precursors to avoidance trials (Forgione, 1976; MacCulloch, Britles, & Feldman, 1971; Sambrooks, MacCulloch, & Waddington, 1978). This latter strategy is probably based upon the assumption that the individual must experience some aversion trials in order to be aware of the rationale for engaging in the avoidance behavior.

The final model often employed is the punishment or response-contingent aversive stimulation model (Lovibond, 1970). This model has been discussed in detail by Bancroft (1975), Church (1963), Davidson (1974), Lovibond (1970), and Rachman and Teasdale (1969). Under this model, it is assumed that the subject will reduce his frequency of deviant behavior after being systematically presented with an aversive or punishing stimulus contingent upon some representation of the deviant behavior. In practical terms, this procedure is similar to a classical conditioning model. However, the theoretical rationale behind the procedure follows operant rather than respondent theory. Lovibond (1970) has raised the question of whether the punishment leads to suppression of the deviant behavior or a change in the patient's motivation to enact the deviant behavior. Technically, the punishment model is not a very compelling model to account for the successful use of aversive therapy. Under operant theory, the therapeutic setting would quickly become a discriminant stimulus for punishment, while all other locales would become discriminant stimuli for nonpunishment. Thus, unless the therapeutic punishment procedure in some way led the patient to develop a self-punishment strategy, it would be most ineffective.

Of the four models discussed, the classical conditioning model and some combination of the escape-avoidance models are most frequently employed in electrical aversion therapy. It is most important that the therapist understand the model upon which his mode of therapy is based, because the model should influence decisions concerning shock and trial parameters. There is little if any empirical evidence available to assist the therapist in selecting which model he should follow. It is now rare for aversion trials alone to be employed. Most therapists add an aversion relief component.

Aversion Relief

Most frequently the pairing of some representation of the deviant behavior with shock, escape from shock, or avoidance of shock is followed by some representation of nondeviant behavior. Essentially, this procedure is discrimination training in which deviant behavior is aversive—to be escaped from or avoided—and nondeviant behavior is relaxing, pleasurable, and desirable to engage in. Feldman and MacCulloch (1964) employed an aversion relief component in conjunction with their anticipatory avoidance method and Thorpe, Schmidt, Brown, and Castell (1964) noted the importance of including an aversion relief component. Despite the lack of empirical evidence supporting the importance of this component, theoretical assumptions support its inclusion in electrical aversion therapy.

Trial Parameters

As Bancroft (1974) observed, there has been no systematic study to determine the optimal spacing or duration of trials in electrical aversion therapy. Most therapists employ a spaced sequence of trials (Evans, 1970a; Fookes, 1969; Miller & Haney, 1976). However, Wijesinghe (1977) has also been successful with massed trials distributed over a single day. Frequently, the number of repetitions included in each session is the number which will conveniently fit into an hour. Invariably, the initial block of trials is concluded when some criterion of nondeviant behavior is reached. Once the initial block of trials is completed, booster trials often are included to offset the possible extinction of the learned response. In a study investigating the necessity for booster sessions, Tanner (1975) failed to find evidence to support the need for booster sessions. In contrast, Maletzky (1977) found that some individuals required booster sessions and others did not. In the absence of more definitive evidence, it seems important to continue to include booster sessions in electrical aversion therapy.

SUPPORTIVE RESEARCH

There have been a number of behavioral approaches to exhibitionism: electrical aversion therapy (Fookes, 1969; Mathis, 1975; Wijesinghe, 1977); shame aversion therapy (Jones & Frei, 1977; Reitz & Keil, 1971; Serber, 1970); aversive behavioral rehearsal (Wickramasekera, 1972, 1976); covert sensitization (Hayes, Brownell, & Barlow, 1978; Hughes, 1977; Maletzky, 1974); and systematic desensitization (Bond & Hutchinson, 1960; Serber & Wolpe, 1972; Wickramasekera, 1968). These approaches are noted in order to offset any belief on the part of the reader that this chapter presents a myopic view in favor of electrical aversion therapy. However, a perusal of the literature should suggest that it is impossible to draw any conclusions concerning the relative merits of each of these methods. With the exception of a study by Callahan and Leitenberg (1973) comparing electrical aversion therapy and covert sensitization over two cases, there have not been any controlled studies comparing these various methods. Aversive behavioral rehearsal and assisted covert sensitization are discussed in subsequent chapters of this book. The comparative data presented in these chapters may permit the reader to draw hypotheses concerning the relative merits of these methods; but in the absence of comparative studies, no definitive answer can be reached.

The available studies employing electrical aversion therapy in the treatment of exhibitionism are summarized in Table 1. Of the nine studies reviewed, five are case studies, two are small single-group studies, and two are within-subject comparative studies. The majority of subjects in these studies were under legal sanction at the time of treatment, and several authors used electrical aversion therapy in conjunction with other treatments. Thus, both of these confounding factors make it virtually impossible to draw conclusions concerning the specific effects of electrical aversion therapy. If one excludes the comparative studies and those having brief follow-up periods, 11 (92 percent) of the 12 subjects followed for one year were symptom-free at that time. Of subjects followed for 18 months or more, results were equally promising.

The information in Table 1 suggests that each of the theoretical models outlined in the previous section were used by authors to direct their use of electrical aversion therapy. There appears to have been little consistency in the use of an aversion relief component,

Table 1. Summary of Electrical Aversion Therapy Studies

AUTHOR	NUMBER TREATED	MODEL	AVERSION RELIEF	REPRESENTATION OF DEVIANT BEHAVIOR	NUMBER OF TRIALS	BOOSTER SESSIONS	FOLLOW-UP LENGTH	FOLLOW-UP NOT EXHIBITING	LIMITATIONS
Kushner & Sandler (1966)	1	Punishment	No	Imagination of aspects of exhibiting	12	No	1 yr.	1(100%)	Case study
Evans (1967, 1970a)	7	Mixed	Yes	Imagination of aspects of exhibiting	12	Yes	6 mo.	5(71%)	Small N; no control; brief follow-up
Fookes (1969)	7	Classical conditioning[a]	No	Imagined exposing while exposing	18	Yes	3 yr.	6(86%)	Small N; no control
MacCulloch, Williams, & Britles (1971)	1	Mixed	Yes	Pictures of older women	18	No	5 mo.	1(100%)[a]	Case study; brief follow-up
Callahan & Leitenberg (1973)	2	Classical conditioning[a]	No	Imagine exhibiting to pictures	18 8	No No	1½ yr. 4 mo.	1(100%)[a] 0(0%)[a]	Case studies; treatment confounding
Rooth & Marks (1974)	12	Classical conditioning[a]	Yes	Imagined exposing while exposing	8	No	1 yr.	4(33%)[a]	No control; treatment confounding
Mathis (1975)	1	Escape	No	Exposing	3	No	2 yr.	1(100%)	Case study; treatment confounding
Miller Haney (1976)	1	Classical conditioning[a]	Yes	Imagine exposing to pictures	22	No	1½ yr.	1(100%)	Case study; treatment confounding
Wijesinghe (1977)	2	Classical conditioning	Yes	Pictures of pubescent girls	6	No	5 yr. 1½ yr.	1(100%) 1(100%)	Case studies

[a] Not directly stated in article, and thus inferred from author's report.

despite its logical appeal. Principally, patients were asked to imagine exhibiting, to exhibit, or do both in conjunction with electrical aversion. Most authors were consistent in allowing them to set the shock at the highest level they could tolerate. The average number of treatment trials was 12 and only two authors reported using booster sessions. Thus there was little concordance across studies in the selection of parameters which are considered to be important in electrical aversion therapy.

The two comparative studies bear further discussion. Callahan and Leitenberg (1973) compared covert sensitization and electrical aversion therapy in a within-subject design. Each subject was first given a base-line period (A). The first client was given four periods of covert sensitization (B) and three of electrical aversion (C), making the design A-B-C-B-C-B-C-B. Each period consisted of six trials. The second client was given two periods of covert sensitization and one of electrical aversion, making the design A-B-C-B. Each period consisted of eight trials. It should be noted that both clients received more trials of covert sensitization than electrical aversion. Based upon the results for these two clients, Callahan and Leitenberg found covert sensitization and electrical aversion equally effective.

The second study by Rooth and Marks (1974) involved 12 clients who received three different treatments: electrical aversion, a self-regulation program, and relaxation. The first 6 clients were given these treatments according to a balanced latin-square design, that is, clients were assigned on a random basis such that one client received each possible order of treatment. The second group of 6 clients were given enhanced versions of the treatments, also according to a balanced latin-square design. Over a number of measures, Rooth and Marks (1974) concluded that electrical aversion was most effective and self-regulation the next most effective. Relaxation was ineffective. These results must be interpreted with extreme caution, given the small number of clients in each cell of the design and the fact that the treatments were modified half-way through the study. The follow-up results reported by Rooth and Marks were discrepant from those reported for other group studies using electrical aversion therapy (Evans, 1967, 1970a; Fookes, 1969) or for studies using other forms of treatment (Mohr, Turner, & Jerry, 1964). It is possible that clients in the Rooth and Marks study developed a negative set toward the treatment experience due to the intermittent effects of the various treatments. If this hypothesis is correct, then researchers need to consider carefully the implications of employing within-subject designs. Alternatively, Rooth and Marks may have obtained more honest reporting from their clients than was true for other authors.

The available research suggests, then, that electrical aversion therapy is an effective means of reducing exhibitionism. However, there is neither evidence to suggest that it is better than no treatment, nor any substantial evidence to suggest how it compares with other modes of treatment.

In order to provide a more comprehensive description of electrical aversion therapy, the next section focuses upon the specific treatment procedures employed by this author with a group of 25 exhibitionists.

SPECIFIC TREATMENT PROCEDURES

The specific treatment procedures were patterned after the method of Feldman and MacCulloch (1964, 1965, 1971) in which deviant, normal, and neutral pictorial stimuli were used in the treatment of various deviant behaviors. Treatment procedures are discussed under the headings of apparatus, stimuli, procedure, and general results.

Apparatus

The apparatus consisted of a Kodak "Carousel" 35 mm automatic slide projector with a foot pedal, remote advance-switch. The projector was modified so that it was an eighty-position rotary switch. Each pole of this switch was connected in series with a single-pole, single-slide switch. This arrangement allowed the therapist to select, by engaging the appropriate slide switches, the slide positions that were to be associated with shock. Once a predetermined slide position occurred, a timer was initiated and after a preselected delay the client was put in circuit with an A.C. shock stimulator. Shock was administered by means of 10 mm silver–silver electrodes attached to the client's ring and index fingers. No electrode paste was employed.

Treatment was conducted in two connecting rooms with a communicating door, a one-way mirror, and a rear projection screen. One room contained the apparatus which was set up so that the stimuli were projected on the rear projection screen. On the other side of the partition, the client was seated in a reclining chair facing the screen. The foot pedal was placed so that he could conveniently advance the slides when he wished.

Stimuli

Stimuli consisted of exhibitionistic, heterosexual, and neutral image-provoking phrases. Each phrase was typed in block capitals on white paper, and 35 mm negative slides were made of each phrase. Hence, when the phrases were projected on the screen, they were in white lettering on a black background. This procedure was followed both because of ease of production and because the phrases stood out better when projected this way. Initially a specific set of phrases was generated for each client. After several clients had been seen, it rapidly became apparent that a general set of stimuli could be used for most if not all clients.

Two assumptions predicated the development of the "Frequency of Deviant Activity—Exhibitionism Inventory" for use in treatment (see Appendix 1, p. 119). First, phrases had to give the client sufficient information to generate an image, but also allow him to impose his own experience upon the image. Second, phrases had to encompass the four phases involved in the behavior: the cognitive phase, the preparatory phase, the action phase, and the post-action phase. Phrases relating to masturbatory fantasy were also included (Evans, 1968b, 1970b). Based upon these assumptions and experiences with early clients, the 40 phrases in the inventory were developed. Slides were prepared of these 40 phrases for use with exhibitionists.

A set of 100 slides of phrases depicting neutral activities were also prepared. Clients, staff, and friends participated in the generation of these neutral phrases. Neutral phrases were employed to provoke images of everyday activities that were unrelated to either deviant or heterosexual activities. Examples of neutral phrases are shown in Table 2.

Finally, two sets of 40 phrases depicting normal heterosexual behavior were generated, the first for married men and the second for single men (see Appendices 2 and 3). Again, patients and staff (male and female) contributed to the development of these phrases. It

Table 2. The Slide Sequence and Content for the Clients' Third Trial

	SLIDE		
Number	Shock delay	Type	CONTENT
1		N	Raking leaves
2		N	Watching curling on television
3	6"	D	Feeling the urge to expose
4		H	Relaxing with your wife and watching television
5		N	Watching a grand prix car race
6	3"	D	Feeling a thrill as you plan to expose
7		H	Caressing your wife's breasts
8		N	Enjoying a drink of ginger ale
9	5"	D	Having a strong urge to expose
10		H	Having sexual intercourse with your wife
11	3"	D	Seeing an attractive young woman and exposing
12		H	Discussing your problems with your wife
13		N	Picking up a newspaper
14	6"	D	Having a strong sensation of pleasure as you expose
15		H	Playing cards with your wife
16	6"	D	Seeing an attractive woman and thinking of exposing
17		H	Kissing your wife passionately
18		N	Doing some repairs to your car
19		N	Having a drink of milk
20	6"	D	Having a strong feeling that you must expose
21		H	Thinking about how much you love your wife
22	3"	D	Having a feeling of suspense as you expose
23		H	Watching your wife undress
24		N	Watching a parade pass by
25	4"	D	Sitting in your car and exposing
26		H	Becoming aroused by a new dress your wife has on
27		N	Mowing a lawn
28	4"	D	Feeling excited after you have exposed
29		H	Discussing future plans with your wife
30	4"	D	Feeling sexually excited as you think of exposing

was assumed that the range of behavior covered by the phrases should include both interpersonal and sexual activities. Slides of both sets of phrases were prepared.

Procedure

During the first session, clients were interviewed and a full history was taken. The general model of interviewing followed that outlined in Evans, Hearn, Uhlemann, and Ivey (in press). At the conclusion of the initial interview, when indicated clients were asked to complete a brief battery of psychological tests (Evans, Covvey, Glicksman, Csapo, & Heseltine, 1976). The Exhibitionism Inventory and either the Married Male Inventory or the Single Male Inventory were also administered at this time. Based upon the history and the results of psychological testing, a multimodal treatment package was developed for the patient. The remaining discussion in this section focuses on one module of the multimodal package—electrical aversion therapy. However, it must be stressed that this procedure is rarely used alone and in some cases is not indicated at all. It is most frequently employed when a strong habitual component is seen to underlie the exhibitionistic behavior.

When electrical aversion therapy was selected, the client was seen for weekly sessions until neither exhibitionistic acts nor urges to exhibit had been reported for four consecutive weeks. Urges usually diminished to zero shortly after exhibitionistic acts disappeared. Booster sessions were given because there is some slight evidence that they are important in maintaining suppression of deviant behavior (Kushner, 1965; Maletzky, 1977; Tanner, 1975). Three bimonthly and three monthly booster sessions were arranged for clients. Follow-up interviews were held at 6 and 12 months following the conclusion of weekly trials.

At each treatment session, the client was shown 60 image-producing phrases. Twenty of the phrases related to exhibitionism (deviant slides), 20 slides related to neutral activities (neutral slides), and the remaining 20 slides related to normal heterosexual activities (heterosexual slides). On the basis of the client's responses on the Exhibitionism Inventory, phrases depicting the 20 least occurring activities were selected for inclusion in session one. Over the remaining sessions, the proportion of phrases depicting more frequently occurring exhibitionistic activities was gradually increased such that during the eighth, ninth, tenth, and subsequent sessions only phrases depicting the most frequently occurring exhibitionistic activities were employed. This strategy of moving from least to most frequently occurring deviant activities has been advocated by Feldman (1966). The assumption is that conditioned aversion becomes more potent as trials progress, and hence using such a sequence ensures conditioned aversion to the most frequently occurring activities. The 20 neutral slides were selected at random for each trial from among a pool of 100 slides. Using the clients' responses on the Married Male or Single Male Inventories, phrases containing the most frequently occurring heterosexual activities were selected for use in session one. Over the remaining sessions, the proportion of phrases depicting less frequently occurring heterosexual activities was gradually increased. During the eighth, ninth, tenth, and subsequent sessions the 10 heterosexual slides depicting most frequently occurring activities and the 10 slides depicting least frequently occurring activities were used. This sequencing of heterosexual slides was based on the assumption that hierarchical desensitization would occur.

In each treatment session, the ordering of deviant, neutral, and heterosexual slides was essentially random except for the following rules: each deviant slide was followed by a normal slide; and no more than two deviant–normal slide sequences could occur consecutively. Table 2 shows the slide sequence for a typical electrical aversion session. In order to facilitate slide program preparation, a set of 20 sequences were developed from which one was selected at random each session. Neutral slides were included to make the occurrence of deviant slides less predictable. As can be observed in Table 2, the delay between the onset of a deviant slide and shock was varied at random between three and six seconds in one-second intervals. The delay was changed manually by the therapist prior to each deviant slide. Shock concluded when the client pressed the foot pedal to advance to the next slide.

At the beginning of each treatment session, the client set his own shock level to what was just intolerable. He was given the following instructions:

> You are going to see a series of slides. I want you to read each and then imagine that activity as vividly as you can. Try and put yourself right in the situation. You may go on to the next slide whenever you wish by pressing the foot pedal. Now press the foot pedal and the first slide will appear.

The therapist then absented himself to the apparatus room to monitor the treatment process. At the conclusion of each session, the client was briefly interviewed concerning his reactions to the session. Finally he was given a checklist upon which to record his acts and urges during the time until the next session.

General Results

Twenty-five clients to whom electrical aversion therapy was offered were systematically followed. The results to be reported cannot be attributed to electrical aversion therapy alone. Two important confounding factors prevent this conclusion. First, 22 clients were on probation orders, the terms of which provided differing degrees of motivation. Second, only rarely was electrical aversion therapy the sole method of treatment. However, it can be concluded that the results do reflect the impact of electrical aversion in conjunction with other aspects of a multimodal treatment approach and court-inspired motivation.

The average age of the total sample was 28 years (18–41 years) and the average educational level was grade 10 (grade 8 to college degree). Nineteen (76 percent) were married and 6 (24 percent) were single, 13 (52 percent) reported heterosexual fantasies during masturbation and 12 (48 percent) reported exhibitionistic fantasies during masturbation. The average reported frequency of exhibiting in the six months prior to court involvement was eight times per month. Of the 25 clients, 4 (16 percent) did not enter electrical aversion therapy. In one case, a physiological cause for exhibiting was discovered and with appropriate treatment the behavior disappeared. Two other clients were seen for an initial interview and decided against treatment, not because of the nature of the treatment, but because they denied having a problem with exhibitionism. Only one client opted out of treatment because he was unprepared to begin electrical aversion therapy.

Hence, 21 (84 percent) of the initial sample participated in electrical aversion therapy and were interviewed at six months and one year following the conclusion of their initial block of weekly trials. For this sample the average number of weeks from commencement of treatment to indication of no reported acts was 4.8 weeks, and to indication of no reported urges was 9.6 weeks. Thus the average number of weekly trials was 13.6. Six months following the conclusion of their weekly trials, 19 (90 percent) reported that they were symptom-free. One year following the conclusion of weekly trials, 17 (81 percent) reported that they had not exhibited during that time. These results compare favorably with those reported by Mohr, Turner, and Jerry (1964) for a sample of Forensic Clinic patients in Toronto. Treatment for their clients consisted of combinations of individual and group therapy. Compared to the present sample, the Forensic Clinic clients were seen on a weekly basis over lengthy periods of time. Thus the cost effectiveness for the present sample was superior to the Forensic Clinic sample.

In order to illustrate the use of these methods with an individual client, a case study follows.

CASE STUDY

History

N. was a 32-year-old male who reported that he had begun exposing at the age of 18. He had been found guilty of indecent exposure by the court and was placed on probation for one year. As a condition of probation, he was referred for treatment. Five years previously he had been found guilty of indecent exposure and at that time was placed on probation for one year without any treatment requirement. During his initial interview he indicated that he had not received previous treatment for his exhibitionistic behavior.

He remarked that his parents were both alive and well, and were presently living together. He was the oldest of four children, having a younger brother and two younger sisters. His upbringing was normal and he considered his home situation to be very good. To his knowledge, no other members of his family had any problem with exhibiting. He stated that he had attended school until the age of 16 and had completed grade 9. For approximately six years he had worked in a factory in a semi-skilled position. Then at the age of 22 he became a fireman, the occupation he held at the time of referral. He was married at the age of 24 and had a 7-year-old son. He reported that he and his wife had intercourse approximately eight times per month and that his fantasies during intercourse were heterosexual in nature. He indicated a good relationship with his wife, with no difficulties with their mutual sexual activities. He masturbated once or twice each month, and his masturbatory fantasies involved exposing to women.

He estimated that during the six months prior to his arrest he had exhibited an average of once or twice a month. Since his arrest he claimed that he had not exhibited. His preferred locale for exhibiting was from a wooded area in a local public park. While exhibiting he remained fully clothed and exposed his genitals to oncoming females. Once observed, he quickly removed himself from the scene. Shortly after and in private, he masturbated to the fantasy of his most recent activity. He preferred to exhibit to attractive females between the ages of 18 and 40 and sought no specific response on their part. He was unable to recall any specific details of the first occasion that he exhibited and intimated that it occurred quite spontaneously. He tended to exhibit when he was bored and wanted excitement, rather than in response to tension.

Assessment

At the conclusion of the initial interview, N. was asked to complete the Raven Progressive Matrices, the WAIS-Clarke Vocabulary Test, the MMPI, the Frequency of Deviant Activity—Exhibitionism Inventory, and the Frequency of Normal Activity—Married Male Inventory. Scores on both the Raven and the WAIS-Clarke Vocabulary Test indicated that N. was of average intelligence. His MMPI scores were all within normal limits, suggesting an individual of essentially normal personality. As a result of the foregoing history and the normal test data, it was concluded that his exhibitionism was essentially a habitual behavior and electrical aversion therapy alone was indicated. The information obtained in the Exhibitionism Inventory and the Married Male Inventory was employed to select image-provoking phrases for the electrical aversion procedure described previously.

Treatment

At the commencement of the first electrical aversive conditioning session, the nature of the procedure was described to N., his questions and concerns were discussed, and he was given the option to refuse the treatment. The remainder of the first session was similar to all other sessions. The electrodes were attached to his fingers, the shock stimulator was turned on, and the shock level was gradually increased. N. was instructed to depress the foot pedal when he could no longer tolerate the shock. This shock level was used for the duration of the session. Thus he could select the shock level he wished, with the implicit assumption that he would voluntarily administer an aversive reinforcement. N. was then told that he would see a series of slides of phrases on the screen, and he was asked to imagine as vividly as possible the situation suggested. The program of slides used during his third session is shown in Table 2. He was instructed to progress to the next phrase by pressing the foot pedal. The slide program was initiated and ran automatically until its conclusion. N.'s reactions to the session were then discussed in full. Finally, he was given a small 10 × 50 mm card containing a day-by-hour (7:00 A.M.–11:00 P.M.) matrix on which he was to enter exhibitionistic acts and urges to exhibit.

N. was given weekly treatment sessions until he reported no urges to expose for four weeks in a row. He was then given bimonthly treatments for six weeks and monthly treatments for three months. In order to monitor his continued progress, he was seen for a follow-up interview at 6 and 12 months after the initial block of 10 weekly treatments.

N.'s frequency of urges to exhibit over treatment are shown in Figure 1. He reported no exhibitionistic acts during the 62 weeks of contact we had with him. Informal contact two years following the initial block of treatments indicated that N. had not exhibited during that period, and urges to exhibit were infrequent and brief in nature. Perusal of court records for his local area indicated that N. had not appeared in court on a charge of indecent exposure in the two-year period. During treatment sessions he had employed an escape strategy; that is, during deviant slides he awaited the onset of shock before moving to the next slide.

ISSUES IN FUTURE RESEARCH

The focus in this chapter has been on studies of electrical aversion therapy with exhibitionism, to the relative exclusion of studies examining the effects of electrical aversion therapy with other disorders. A number of process, outcome, comparative, and factorial studies have examined aspects of electrical aversion therapy with other sexually deviant behaviors such as smoking, alcohol, and drug

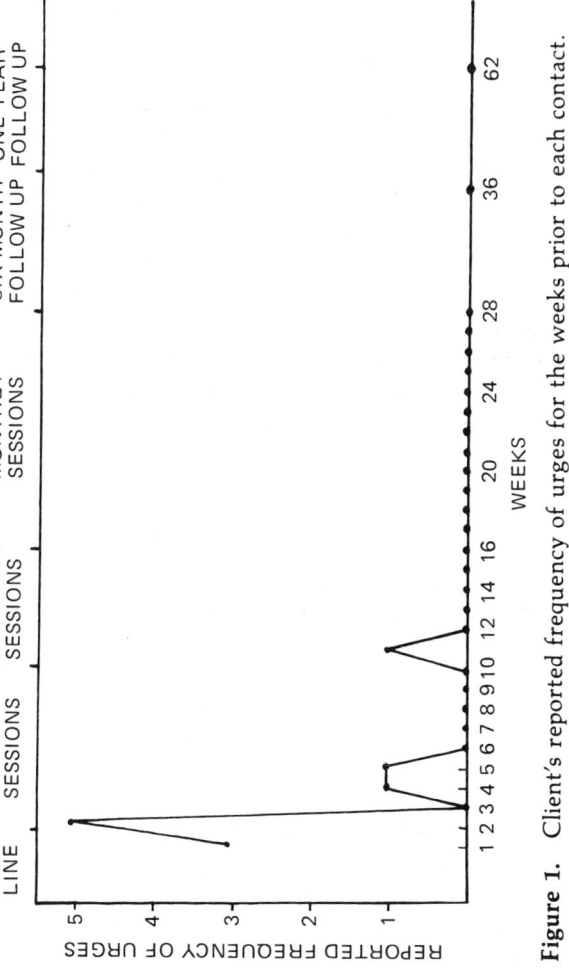

Figure 1. Client's reported frequency of urges for the weeks prior to each contact.

abuse (Davidson, 1974; Hinrichsen & Katahn, 1975; Russell, Armstrong, & Patel, 1976). The findings of these studies purposefully have been omitted from the discussion because of the assumption that the topography of the deviant behavior interacts with the effects of electrical aversion therapy. No doubt, studies with other behaviors can suggest useful hypotheses for examination. However, it would be risky to assume that findings with other behaviors necessarily apply to exhibitionism.

Three types of study are urgently required before therapists can make more research based, ethical decisions concerning the continued use of electrical aversion therapy with exhibitionists. First, there is a need for process studies to identify the dimensions or parameters (such as the representation of the deviant behavior, the inclusion of aversion relief, and the use of booster sessions) that are most effective in enhancing the effects of electrical aversion therapy with exhibitionists. Second, it is important, once the most potent version of electrical aversion therapy has been determined, to compare it with appropriate no-treatment and nonspecific treatment control conditions. Finally, it is crucial that electrical aversion therapy be compared with other aversive and also nonaversive treatments for exhibitionism. Until these studies are carried out, therapists must continue to base their decision to use electrical aversion therapy on the best available clinical data.

In the introduction to this chapter, the caution was made that electrical aversion therapy is rarely used alone. The case studies by Mathis (1975) and Miller and Haney (1976) provide excellent examples of the use of electrical aversion therapy in conjunction with other modes of treatment. Both studies included interpersonal skills training, and Mathis included the additional component of sexual skills training. In such a multimodal treatment, the need at some point arises to discover what components are required for each type of client. Another important concern is to identify the appropriate ordering of components in the treatment of exhibitionism. In their review of the treatment of homosexuality, Hinrichsen and Katahn (1975) outlined patient, intervention, environmental, and change dimensions of importance both in the application and research of the multimodal approach to treatment with exhibitionists. Many of the parameters in their review should be considered when addressing the question of which components, and what order of components, are most appropriate for a given exhibitionist.

Before concluding this chapter, it is important to theorize or at least to speculate about future developments which might enhance electrical aversion therapy. Evidence is rapidly mounting to suggest that none of the conditioning models of aversion therapy account for the effects of this therapeutic approach. Davidson (1974), in concluding his review of aversion therapy studies and alcohol abuse, defines the classical conditioning, avoidance, punishment, and two-stage models underlying aversion therapy. He comments, "Given the research reviewed here, it is not at all clear that any, or all, of the preceding theoretical explanations of the process operating can be invoked as an adequate explanation" (p. 578). Hinrichsen and Katahn (1975), following their review of aversive conditioning studies with homosexuals, conclude, ". . . the available data do not clearly support hypothesized conditioning processes as underlying the successful use of aversive conditioning procedures with homosexuals . . ." (p. 86). Bancroft (1975) comments, ". . . in spite of the fact that aversion therapy has been used for nearly 20 years, there is really no convincing evidence that when it works it does so by means of the conditioned aversion which justified its use on theoretical grounds" (p. 183). In an impressive study of aversion therapy parameters and smoking, Russell et al. (1976) conclude, "There is no certain evidence in the literature and no evidence from this study that traditional conditioning processes play any part in the clinical response to electrical aversion therapy" (p. 122). These comments are representative of a growing trend among therapists and researchers to question and indeed to abandon the conditioning models that underlie aversion therapy. Indeed, some authors (Evans, 1975; Hallam & Rachman, 1972b) have suggested alternative models.

Most authors who have questioned the conditioning rationale of aversion therapy have suggested the possible importance of cognitive factors (Bancroft, 1974; Berecz, 1976; Glover & McCue, 1977; Rosenthal, Rosenthal, & Chang, 1977; Russell, Armstrong & Patel, 1976; Tinling, 1972). Gagné (1970) has proposed a taxonomy of learning which transcends the learning–cognition split in learning theory. Gagné has organized learning into eight types, three of which are pertinent to this discussion: type 1, signal learning (classical conditioning); type 2, stimulus–response learning; and type 7, rule learning. The classical conditioning model of aversion therapy is signal learning and the escape, avoidance, and punishment models are forms of stimulus–response learning. A major concern with these two types of learning is that they require repeated trials in order to offset the extinction of the conditioned response. Under rule learning, in contrast, once the rule or set of rules pertinent to the desired behavior are learned, they are extremely resistant to extinction. For example, once we have learned the set of rules pertinent to driving a car, we are able to enact that behavior even though we may not have driven for some time. A second advantage to rule learning is that once a set of rules pertinent to a class of behavior has been learned, the individual is able to apply the rules to all members of the class. Thus, with regard to the rules associated with driving, we are able to apply those rules to a variety of cars so that most people can rent and drive even a truck when the need arises. The advantages to a rule-learning model of aversion therapy would be that the rules learned would maintain over time and also generalize to all members of the class of behavior called exhibiting.

There are three tangential pieces of evidence which suggest that when aversion therapy is effective it may be as a result of rule learning. The first finding is that even when the parameters associated with the conditioning models are not present, some clients learn to control their behavior. A number of authors have observed that therapeutic interventions based upon conditioning models and therapeutic interventions not based on conditioning models (noncontingent shock, therapist support) tend to be equally effective (McConaghy & Barr, 1973; Russell, Armstrong, & Patel, 1976). A possible interpretation of these findings is that both the true aversion conditions and the control conditions are conducive to rule learning. Further, it is common in aversion therapy to observe that some clients do very well and others do abysmally (Hallam & Rachman, 1972). Such within-treatment differences could be explained by the fact that despite the lack of therapeutic instructions to do so, the clients doing well formulate and learn their own rules as a result of the procedure. This hypothesis could easily be evaluated by asking clients subsequent to conventional aversion therapy to explicate what rules they may have learned.

The second finding which supports the rule-learning model pertains to recent studies of the need for booster sessions. Conditioning models of aversion therapy would predict the need for booster sessions in order to offset extinction of the newly learned behavior. In contrast, a rule-learning model would suggest that booster sessions are not necessary. Of the studies reported in Table

1, only two employed booster sessions and yet all seem to have been equally effective in producing control of exhibitionism. Recently Tanner (1975) failed to find evidence to support the need for booster sessions with homosexual clients who had undergone aversion therapy. Maletzky (1977) similarly found that only some clients required booster sessions following aversion therapy. The present argument would suggest that the clients requiring booster sessions had not yet learned the appropriate rules necessary to control their behavior.

The third line of supportive evidence comes from studies that approximated a rule-learning model of aversion therapy. These studies utilized the escape-conditioning paradigm; but instead of asking the subject to emit an instrumental motor response in order to avoid shock (Bond & Evans, 1967; Mathis, 1975), he was asked to emit a verbal or cognitive response (Abel, Levis, & Clancy, 1970; Lubetkin & Fishman, 1974; Steffy, Meichenbaum, & Best, 1970). Abel et al. exposed patients to 10 trials for each session in which descriptions of their deviant activities were paired with contingent shock. In the final 7 trials, patients were able to stop the description and avoid shock by verbalizing and fantasizing alternative, nondeviant sexual behavior. Interpretation of this procedure as rule learning suggests that clients were learning the following rule: when I think about my deviant behavior, I must quickly think about alternative nondeviant sexual behavior. The trials would act to have the client rehearse the rule and the shock would facilitate the speed with which the new fantasy was emitted. In a similar paradigm with a chronic heroin user, Lubetkin and Fishman (1974) had the client say "stop" and then verbalize a socially adaptive nondrug situation.

Steffy et al. (1970) employed a similar strategy with smokers. Four groups were compared in their study: the first group had to describe the smoking chain, refuse a cigarette, and verbally disavow their enjoyment of cigarettes to avoid shock; the second group had to imagine the smoking chain and then refuse the cigarette or vigorously extinguish it; the third group imagined smoking without actually smoking a cigarette; and the final group discussed insight control. At the conclusion of treatment the refusal groups both reduced their smoking more than the imagination and insight control groups. However, at six months follow-up the group that had imagined smoking and then refused or extinguished a cigarette smoked at 30 percent of baseline, while all other groups had virtually returned to their baseline level. Steffy et al. indicated that overt verbalizations were awkward and embarrassing for patients. No doubt the covert verbalizations allowed the patients to evolve a personal rule and then practice it without embarrassment. Further, the overt verbalizations were experimenter-derived, and the covert verbalizations were client-derived. The authors indicated that patients might have done better if they had verbalized a commitment to change and a statement of their rationale for changing instead of describing the smoking chain.

Given the preceding evidence, it seems that the application of a rule-learning model to electrical aversion therapy is a plausible proposition. Gagné (1970) defines a rule as *"an inferred capability that enables the individual to respond to a class of stimulus situations with a class of performances"* (italics in original, p. 191). He cautions that while an individual may be able to verbalize a rule, this does not mean that he can perform the capability. Thus, rule-governed performance and not verbalization is the measure of rule learning. Gagné outlines the conditions that are requisite for rule learning to occur. No doubt these conditions can be established in the context of electrical aversion therapy in order to establish rules which would offset deviant behavior. The rules could be either patient-derived or based upon rules used by nondeviant individuals to avoid the deviant behavior of concern. Strickler, Bigelow, Lawrence, and Liebson (1976) have presented rules for moderate drinking which may be prototypical of such rules for other problems. Although the application of a rule-learning model to electrical aversion therapy is speculative at this point, it certainly deserves as much attention as other models.

REFERENCES

Abel, G. G., Levis, D. J., & Clancy, J. Aversion therapy applied to taped sequences of deviant behavior in exhibitionism and other sexual deviations: A preliminary report. *Journal of Behavior Therapy and Experimental Psychiatry*, 1970, 1, 59–66.

Baer, D. M. A case for the selective reinforcement of punishment. In C. Neuringer and J. L. Michael (Eds.), *Behavior modification in clinical psychology*. New York: Appleton-Century-Crofts, 1970, 243–249.

Bancroft, J. *Deviant sexual behaviour modification and assessment*. Oxford: Clarendon, 1974.

Bancroft, J. The behavioural approach to sexual disorders. In H. Milne & S. J. Hardy (Eds.), *Psychosexual problems*. Baltimore: University Park Press, 1975, 180–194.

Berecz, J. Treatment of smoking with cognitive conditioning therapy: A self-administered aversion technique. *Behavior Therapy*, 1976, 7, 641–648.

Bernstein, T. Electrical safety in aversive conditioning of humans. *Behavioral Engineering*, 1975, 2, 31–34.

Bond, I. K., & Evans, D. R. Avoidance therapy: Its use in two cases of underwear fetishism. *Canadian Medical Association Journal*, 1967, 96, 1160–1162.

Bond, I. K., & Hutchinson, H. C. Application of reciprocal inhibition therapy to exhibitionism. *Canadian Medical Association Journal*, 1960, 83, 23–25.

Butterfield, W. H. Electric shock-hazards in aversive shock conditioning of humans. *Behavioral Engineering*, 1975a, 3, 1–28.

Butterfield, W. H. Electric shock-safety factors when used for the aversive conditioning of humans. *Behavior Therapy*, 1975b, 6, 98–110.

Callahan, E. J., & Leitenberg, H. Aversion therapy for sexual deviation: Contingent shock and covert sensitization. *Journal of Abnormal Psychology*, 1973, 81, 60–73.

Church, R. M. The varied effects of punishment on behavior. *Psychological Review*, 1963, 70, 369–402.

Claeson, L., & Malm, U. Electro-aversion therapy of chronic alcoholism. *Behaviour Research and Therapy*, 1973, 11, 663–665.

Conway, J. B. Behavioral self-control of smoking through aversive conditioning and self-management. *Journal of Consulting and Clinical Psychology*, 1977, 45, 348–357.

Copemann, C. D. Treatment of polydrug abuse and addiction by covert sensitization: Some contraindication. *International Journal of the Addictions*, 1977, 12, 17–23.

Davidson, W. S. Studies of aversive conditioning for alcoholics: A critical review of theory and research methodology. *Psychological Bulletin*, 1974, 81, 571–581.

Ethical principles in the conduct of research with human participants. Washington, D.C.: American Psychological Association, 1973.

Ethical standards of psychologists. Washington, D.C.: American Psychological Association, 1977.

Evans, D. R. An exploratory study into the treatment of exhibitionism by means of emotive imagery and aversive conditioning. *Canadian Psychologist*, 1967, 8, 162.

Evans, D. R. Conditioned stimuli, unconditioned stimuli, and numbers of trials in the conditioning of aversion to alcohol drinking. *O.P.A. Quarterly,* 1968a, *21,* 47–51.

Evans, D. R. Masturbatory fantasy and sexual deviation. *Behaviour Research and Therapy,* 1968b, *6,* 17–19.

Evans, D. R. Exhibitionism. In C. G. Costello (Ed.), *Symptoms of psychopathology.* New York: Wiley, 1970a, 560–573.

Evans, D. R. Subjective variables and treatment effects in aversion therapy. *Behaviour Research and Therapy,* 1970b, *8,* 147–152.

Evans, D. R. Modifying deviant sexual behaviour in adolescents. In L. A. Hamerlynck & F. W. Clark (Eds.), *Behavior modification for exceptional children and youth.* Calgary: University of Calgary, 1971, 89–96.

Evans, D. R. Theoretical problems of aversion therapy: An extension. *Psychotherapy: Theory, Research and Practice,* 1975, *12,* 396–399.

Evans, D. R., Covvey, H. D., Gliksman, L., Csapo, K., & Heseltine, G. F. D. The automated psychological evaluation system (APES). *Behavior Research Methods and Instrumentation,* 1976, *8,* 108–111.

Evans, D. R., Hearn, M. T., Uhlemann, M. R., & Ivey, A. E. *Essential Interviewing: A programmed approach to effective communication.* Monteray, Ca.: Brooks/Cole, in press.

Feldman, M. P. Aversion therapy for sexual deviations: A critical review. *Psychological Bulletin,* 1966, *65,* 65–79.

Feldman, M. P., & MacCulloch, M. J. A systematic approach to the treatment of homosexuality by conditioned aversion: Preliminary report. *American Journal of Psychiatry,* 1964, *121,* 167–171.

Feldman, M. P., & MacCulloch, M. J. The application of anticipatory avoidance learning to the treatment of homosexuality-1. Theory, technique and preliminary results. *Behaviour Research and Therapy,* 1965, *2,* 165–183.

Feldman, M. P., & MacCulloch, M. J. *Homosexual behavior: Therapy and assessment.* Oxford: Pergamon Press, 1971.

Fookes, B. H. Some experiences in the use of aversion therapy in male homosexuality, exhibitionism and fetishism-transvestism. *British Journal of Psychiatry,* 1969, *115,* 339–341.

Forgione, A. G. The use of mannequins in the behavioral assessment of child molesters: Two case reports. *Behavior Therapy,* 1976, *7,* 678–685.

Frankel, A. J. Beyond the simple functional analysis—The chain: A conceptual framework for assessment with a case study example. *Behavior Therapy,* 1975, *6,* 254–260.

Gagné, R. M. *The conditions of learning* (2nd ed.). New York: Holt, Rinehart & Winston, 1970.

Glover, J. H., & McCue, P. A. Electrical aversion therapy with alcoholics: A comparative follow-up study. *British Journal of Psychiatry,* 1977, *130,* 279–286.

Hallam, R. S., & Rachman, S. Some effects of aversion therapy on patients with sexual disorders. *Behaviour Research and Therapy,* 1972a, *10,* 171–180.

Hallam, R. S., & Rachman, S. Theoretical problems of aversion therapy. *Behaviour Research and Therapy,* 1972b, *10,* 341–353.

Hanson, R. W., & Adesso, V. J. A multiple behavioral approach to male homosexual behavior: A case study. *Journal of Behavior Therapy and Experimental Psychiatry,* 1972, *3,* 323–325.

Hayes, S. C., Brownell, K. D., & Barlow, D. A. The use of self-administered covert sensitization in the treatment of exhibitionism and sadism. *Behavior Therapy,* 1978, *9,* 283–289.

Hinrichsen, J. J., & Katahn, M. Recent trends and new developments in the treatment of homosexuality. *Psychotherapy: Theory, Research and Practice,* 1975, *12,* 83–92.

Hughes, R. C. Covert sensitization treatment of exhibitionism. *Journal of Behavior Therapy and Experimental Psychiatry,* 1977, *8,* 177–179.

Jones, I. H., & Frei, D. Provoked anxiety as a treatment of exhibitionism. *British Journal of Psychiatry,* 1977, *131,* 295–300.

Klemp, G. O., & Rodin, J. Effects of uncertainty, delay, and focus of attention on reactions to an aversive situation. *Journal of Experimental Social Psychology,* 1976, *12,* 416–421.

Kushner, M. The reduction of a long-standing fetish by means of aversive conditioning. In L. P. Ullman & L. Krasner (Eds.), *Case studies in behavior modification.* New York: Holt, Rinehart and Winston, 1965, 239–242.

Kushner, M., & Sandler, J. Aversion therapy and the concept of punishment. *Behaviour Research and Therapy,* 1966, *4,* 179–186.

Logan, D. L., & Turnage, J. R. Ethical considerations in the use of faradic aversion therapy. *Behavioral Engineering,* 1975, *3,* 29–34.

Lovibond, S. H. Aversive control of behavior. *Behavior Therapy,* 1970, *1,* 80–91.

Lubetkin, B. S., & Fishman, S. T. Electrical aversion therapy with a chronic heroin user. *Journal of Behavior Therapy and Experimental Psychiatry,* 1974, *5,* 193–195.

MacCulloch, M. J., Britles, C. J., & Feldman, M. P. Anticipatory avoidance learning for the treatment of homosexuality: Recent developments and an automatic aversion therapy system. *Behavior Therapy,* 1971, *2,* 151–169.

MacCulloch, M. J., Williams, C., & Britles, C. J. The successful application of aversion therapy to an adolescent exhibitionist. *Journal of Behavior Therapy and Experimental Psychiatry,* 1971, *2,* 61–66.

Maletzky, B. M. "Assisted" covert sensitization in the treatment of exhibitionism. *Journal of Consulting and Clinical Psychology*, 1974, *42*, 34–40.

Maletzky, B. M. "Booster" sessions in aversion therapy: The permanency of treatment. *Behavior Therapy*, 1977, *8*, 460–463.

Marshall, W. L. A combined treatment approach to the reduction of multiple fetish-related behaviors. *Journal of Consulting and Clinical Psychology*, 1974, *42*, 613–616.

Marshall, W. L., & McKnight, R. D. An integrated treatment program for sexual offenders. *Canadian Psychiatric Association Journal*, 1975, *20*, 133–138.

Martin, R. *Legal challenges to behavior modification.* Champaign, Ill.: Research Press, 1975.

Mathis, H. I. Instating sexual adequacy in a disabled exhibitionist. *Psychotherapy: Theory, Research and Practice*, 1975, *12*, 97–100.

McConaghy, N., & Barr, R. F. Classical, avoidance, and backward conditioning treatments of homosexuality. *British Journal of Psychiatry*, 1973, *122*, 151–162.

Meichenbaum, D. *Cognitive behavior-modification: An integrative approach.* New York: Plenum, 1977, 143–182.

Miller, H. L., & Haney, J. R. Behavior and traditional therapy applied to pedophiliac exhibitionism: A case study. *Psychological Reports*, 1976, *39*, 1119–1124.

Mohr, J. W., Turner, R. E., & Jerry, M. B. *Pedophilia and exhibitionism.* Toronto, University of Toronto Press, 1964.

Mowrer, O. H. *Learning theory and behavior.* New York: Wiley, 1960.

O'Brien, J. S., Raynes, A. E., & Patch, V. D. Treatment of heroin addiction with aversion therapy, relaxation training and systematic desensitization. *Behaviour Research and Therapy*, 1972, *10*, 77–80.

O'Neil, P. M. Effects of predictability of shock onset in faradic aversion therapy: Illustration in the treatment of onychophagia. Unpublished doctoral dissertation, University of Georgia, 1975.

Pinard, G., & Lamontagne, Y. Electrical aversion, aversion relief and sexual retraining in treatment of fetishism with masochism. *Journal of Behavior Therapy and Experimental Psychiatry*, 1976, *7*, 71–74.

Rachman, S. The passing of the two-stage theory of fear and avoidance: Fresh possibilities. *Behaviour Research and Therapy*, 1976, *14*, 125–131.

Rachman, S., & Teasdale, J. *Aversion therapy and behaviour disorders: An analysis.* London: Routledge & Kegan Paul, 1969.

Rehm, L. P., & Rozensky, R. H. Multiple behavior therapy techniques with a homosexual client: A case study. *Journal of Behavior Therapy and Experimental Psychiatry*, 1974, *5*, 53–57.

Reitz, W. E., & Keil, W. E. Behavioral treatment of an exhibitionist. *Journal of Behavior Therapy and Experimental Psychiatry,* 1971, *2,* 67–69.

Rimm, D. C., & Masters, J. C. *Behavior Therapy Techniques and Empirical Findings.* New York: Academic Press, 1974.

Rooth, F. G., & Marks, I. M. Persistent exhibitionism: Short-term response to aversion, self-regulation, and relaxation treatments. *Archives of Sexual Behavior,* 1974, *3,* 227–248.

Rosenthal, T. L., Rosenthal, R. H., & Chang, A. F. Vicarious, direct, and imaginal aversion in habit control: Outcomes, heart rates, and subjective perceptions. *Cognitive Therapy and Research,* 1977, *1,* 143–159.

Russell, M. A. H., Armstrong, E., & Patel, U. A. Temporal contiguity in electric aversion therapy for cigarette smoking. *Behaviour Research and Therapy,* 1976, *14,* 103–123.

Sambrooks, J. E., MacCulloch, M. J., & Waddington, J. L. Incubation of sexual attitude change between sessions of instrumental aversion therapy. *Behavior Therapy,* 1978, *9,* 477–485.

Schwitzgebel, R. K. Suggestions for the use of psychological devices in accord with legal and ethical standards. *Professional Psychology,* 1978, *9,* 478–488.

Serber, M. Shame aversion therapy. *Journal of Behavior Therapy and Experimental Psychiatry,* 1970, *1,* 213–215.

Serber, M., & Wolpe, J. Behavior therapy techniques. In H. L. P. Resnick & M. E. Wolfgang (Eds.), *Sexual Behaviors: Social, Clinical, and Legal Aspects.* Boston: Little Brown, 1972, 239–254.

Siddall, J. W., Vargas, J. M., & Adesso, V. J. Standards of safety for electrical apparatus used in aversion therapy. *Behavior Therapy,* 1975, *6,* 274–275.

Steffy, R. A., Meichenbaum, D., & Best, J. A. Aversive and cognitive factors in the modification of smoking behaviour. *Behaviour Research and Therapy,* 1970, *8,* 115–125.

Strickler, D., Bigelow, G., Lawrence, C., & Liebson, I. Moderate drinking as an alternative to alcohol abuse: A non-aversive procedure. *Behaviour Research and Therapy,* 1976, *14,* 279–288.

Tanner, B. A. Aversive shock issues: Physical danger, emotional harm, effectiveness and "dehumanization." *Journal of Behavior Therapy and Experimental Psychiatry,* 1973a, *4,* 113–115.

Tanner, B. A. Shock intensity and fear of shock in the modification of homosexual behavior in males by avoidance learning. *Behaviour Research and Therapy,* 1973b, *11,* 213–218.

Tanner, B. A. Avoidance training with and without booster sessions to modify homosexual behavior in males. *Behavior Therapy,* 1975, *6,* 649–653.

Thorpe, J. G., Schmidt, E., Brown, P., & Castell, D. Aversion relief therapy: A new method for general application. *Behaviour Research and Therapy,* 1964, *2,* 71–82.

Tinling, D. C. Cognitive and behavioral aspects of aversive therapy. In R. D. Rubin, H. Fensterheim, J. D. Henderson, & L. P. Ullman (Eds.), *Advances in behavior therapy.* New York: Academic Press, 1972, 73–80.

Wallace, J., Burger, D., Neal, H. C., van Brero, M., & Davis, D. E. Aversive conditioning use in public facilities for the mentally retarded. *Mental Retardation,* 1976, *14,* 17–19.

Wickramasekera, I. The application of learning theory to the treatment of a case of sexual exhibitionism. *Psychotherapy: Theory, Research and Practice,* 1968, *5,* 108–112.

Wickramasekera, I. A technique for controlling a certain type of sexual exhibitionism. *Psychotherapy: Theory, Research and Practice,* 1972, *9,* 207–210.

Wickramasekera, I. Aversive behavior rehearsal for sexual exhibitionism. *Behavior Therapy,* 1976, *7,* 167–176.

Wijesinghe, B. Massed aversion treatment of sexual deviance. *Journal of Behavior Therapy and Experimental Psychiatry,* 1977, *8,* 135–137.

Wolfe, J. B. Effectiveness of token-rewards for chimpanzees. *Comparative Psychology Monographs,* 1936, *12* (60).

Wolpe, J. *The practice of behavior therapy.* New York: Pergamon, 1973.

APPENDIX 1.
FREQUENCY OF DEVIANT ACTIVITY INVENTORY: EXHIBITIONISM

Check the appropriate box on the answer sheet to indicate how often you find yourself engaging in the following activities.

1. Suddenly having a strong desire to expose.
2. Becoming excited as you think about exposing.
3. Deciding to expose.
4. Wanting to expose.
5. Looking for a place to expose.
6. Having a strong urge to expose.
7. Driving along and deciding to expose.
8. Having a strong feeling that you must expose.
9. Seeing an attractive woman and thinking of exposing.
10. Seeing an attractive young girl and having an urge to expose.
11. Feeling sexually excited as you think of exposing.
12. Feeling the urge to expose.
13. Feeling a thrill as you plan to expose.
14. Preparing to expose.
15. Getting ready to expose.
16. Going to a special place to expose.
17. Getting excited as you expose.
18. Feeling satisfaction as you expose.
19. Having a strong sensation of pleasure as you expose.
20. Feeling relieved as you expose.
21. Becoming worked up as you expose.
22. Seeing an attractive young woman and exposing.
23. Seeing a desirable young girl and exposing.
24. Sitting in your car and exposing.
25. In your favorite place and exposing.
26. Having a feeling of suspense as you expose.
27. Feeling sexually excited as you expose.
28. Feeling tense as you expose.
29. Feeling happy as you expose.
30. Wanting to have sexual intercourse as you expose.
31. Feeling very happy after you expose.
32. Being quite calm after you have exposed.
33. Feeling excited after you have exposed.
34. Being pleased after you have exposed.
35. Having a feeling of relaxation after you have exposed.
36. While you masturbate, thinking about exposing.
37. Having a sudden impulse to expose.
38. Looking for someone in order to expose.
39. At work, thinking about exposing.
40. At home, thinking about exposing.

© David R. Evans, 1967. Reproduced here by permission of the author.

APPENDIX 2.
FREQUENCY OF NORMAL ACTIVITY: MARRIED MALE

Check the appropriate box on the answer sheet to indicate how often you find yourself engaging in the following activities.

1. Hugging your wife in the kitchen.
2. Relaxing with your wife and watching television.
3. Making up after an argument with your wife.
4. Caressing your wife's breasts.
5. Feeling the thrill of orgasm with your wife.
6. Feeling content and affectionate after orgasm with your wife.
7. Having sexual intercourse with your wife.
8. Discussing your problems with your wife.
9. Playing cards with your wife.
10. Kissing your wife passionately.
11. Thinking about how much you love your wife.
12. Watching your wife undress.
13. Kissing your wife as you leave for work.
14. Planning a party with your wife.
15. Becoming aroused by a new dress your wife has on.
16. In bed with your wife.
17. Discussing future plans with your wife.
18. Telling your wife how much you enjoy being with her.
19. Talking intimately to your wife as you both undress.
20. Having sex with your wife.
21. Taking a shower with your wife.
22. Talking affectionately to your wife.
23. Going out for the evening with your wife.
24. Telling your wife about problems at work.
25. Kissing your wife affectionately.
26. Imagining your wife doing a strip tease.
27. Choosing perfume for your wife.
28. Going to a party with your wife.
29. Thinking about making love to your wife.
30. Looking forward to seeing your wife after work.
31. Relaxing with your wife.
32. Celebrating your wedding anniversary with your wife.
33. Lying on a beach with your wife.
34. Going to a movie with your wife.
35. Seeing a sexy scene in a movie and thinking about your wife.
36. Feeling your wife respond warmly to your caresses.
37. Seeing your wife in a sexy nightgown.
38. Dancing with your wife.
39. Talking about old times with your wife.
40. Planning a holiday with your wife.

© David R. Evans, 1967. Reproduced here by permission of the author.

APPENDIX 3.
FREQUENCY OF NORMAL ACTIVITY: SINGLE MALE

Check the appropriate box on the answer sheet to indicate how often you find yourself engaging in the following activities.

1. Hugging a female friend.
2. Relaxing with a female friend and watching television.
3. Making up after an argument with a close female friend.
4. Relaxing with a female friend and caressing her breasts.
5. Feeling the thrill of orgasm with a close female companion.
6. Feeling content and affectionate after sexual intercourse with a female friend.
7. Having sexual intercourse with a female friend.
8. Discussing your problems with a female friend.
9. Meeting an attractive female and asking her for a date.
10. Kissing a female friend passionately.
11. Getting excited as you dance with a young woman.
12. Having dinner with an attractive woman you have recently met.
13. Kissing an attractive woman as you say good night to her.
14. Planning a party with a female friend.
15. Becoming aroused by a new dress your female friend has on.
16. In bed with a female friend.
17. Discussing future plans with a female companion.
18. Telling a female how much you enjoy being with her.
19. Talking intimately to a female as you undress together.
20. Having sex with a female companion.
21. Taking a shower with a close female friend.
22. Talking affectionately to a female.
23. Going out for the evening with a female companion.
24. Telling a female friend about problems at work.
25. Kissing a female affectionately.
26. Making love to a female you are attracted to.
27. Buying a present for a female friend.
28. Going to a party with a female.
29. Becoming excited as you get ready to go out with a female.
30. Looking forward to seeing a female friend after work.
31. Undressing with a female companion.
32. Thinking about having sex with a close female friend.
33. Lying on a beach with a female.
34. Going to a movie with a female companion.
35. Relaxing with a female after sex.
36. Feeling an attractive woman respond warmly to your caresses.
37. Having a strong sensation of pleasure as you have sex with a female friend.
38. Dancing with a female.
39. Thinking about having sexual intercourse with a female as you masturbate.
40. Planning a trip with a female friend.

© David R. Evans, 1967. Reproduced here by permission of the author.

APPENDIX 4.
FREQUENCY OF ACTIVITY ANSWER SHEET

	Very Often	Quite Often	Occasionally	Never
1.				
2.				
3.				
4.				
5.				
6.				
7.				
8.				
9.				
10.				
11.				
12.				
13.				
14.				
15.				
16.				
17.				
18.				
19.				
20.				
21.				
22.				
23.				
24.				
25.				
26.				
27.				
28.				
29.				
30.				
31.				
32.				
33.				
34.				
35.				
36.				
37.				
38.				
39.				
40.				

© David R. Evans, 1967. Reproduced here by permission of the author.

6

AVERSIVE BEHAVIOR REHEARSAL:
A Cognitive–Behavioral Procedure

Ian Wickramasekera

The Aversive Behavior Rehearsal (ABR) technique (Wickramasekera, 1972, 1976a) is a procedure for the management of a specific subset of chronic sexual exhibitionists (repeated offenders as defined by police records). The in vivo ABR (I-V-ABR) therapist makes an appointment for a patient to come into the clinic and expose himself at a specific time and place to people who know of him. With the vicarious Aversive Behavior Rehearsal (V-ABR) technique, a therapist arrages for a chronic exhibitionist to observe via video tape the I-V-ABR treatment of a fellow exhibitionist. Twenty-three chronic exhibitionists have been treated within one to four treatment sessions with these methods, and only one relapse has been detected to date in follow-ups ranging up to nine years.

In the past fifteen years, I have experimented with a variety of techniques looking for a reliable and brief method of symptomatic control of sexual exhibitionism. I have tried many interventions including dynamically oriented psychotherapy, rational-emotive therapy, Gestalt therapy, hypnotherapy, systematic desensitization, operant shaping of assertive heterosexual behavior (Wickramasekera, 1968), and aversive conditioning (shock).

In the summer of 1966, I was working with a 19-year-old, chronic male exhibitionist. After repeated pairings of exhibitionistic fantasy with electric shock, the patient reported an inability to form subjective images of the deviant fantasy. I doubted the accuracy of his verbal report, and urged him to imagine that he was being observed by an unseen female while he actually did expose himself. When I insisted on this in vivo behavioral rehearsal of his deviant act, the patient became quite anxious. After considerable pressure, he started to rehearse the deviant behavior in my presence. I planned to apply shock first to the terminal components (unzipping, genital exposure, and masturbation) of the deviant sequence. But as he approximated the terminal components, he began to tremble, burst out crying, and reported lightheadedness, tachycardia, weakness, and nausea. It became apparent that the use of electric shock was redundant in this case. The patient also stated that he saw clearly for the first time how foolish and dumb his behavior looked. I realized that with this type of patient the degree of involvement and arousal generated by this procedure exceeded anything I had observed during psychotherapy or aversive conditioning. Because his response to the procedure was rapid, positive, and appeared durable, I continued to experiment with the technique. To date at least three other clinical investigators (Jones & Frei, 1977; Reitz & Keil, 1971; Serber, 1970; Stevenson & Jones, 1972) also have reported independently stumbling onto a very similar procedure with similar results. Several years later I decided to call this cognitive behavioral procedure Aversive Behavior Rehearsal.

RATIONALE

In Vivo ABR (I-V-ABR) Procedure

The I-V-ABR procedure prescribes and elicits the patient's symptom (exhibitionism) under conditions that overlap substantially with the naturally occuring event but with certain critical alterations:

1. The exposure is deliberately planned by therapist and patient several weeks in advance and scheduled for a specific time and place.

2. The exposure is enacted under conditions of reduced anonymity.
3. During its enactment, the behavior is subjected by the patient and therapist to cognitive-verbal exploration of associated affect, bodily sensations, and fantasy.

The goal is to elicit and demythologize any autistic fantasies that may cognitively mediate the exhibitionistic behavior in its natural habitat. Conditions are arranged to increase the probability that the patient will take a pedestrian, critical, and analytical view of what he is doing during the act of exposure. It is, in a sense, a form of discrimination training for response-produced stimuli (fantasies). It has been hypothesized (Wickramasekera, 1972) that, at least for the subtest of exhibitionists discussed in this chapter, the enactment of sexual exhibitionism occurs under internal conditions of increased fantasy involvement (Sarbin & Coe, 1972) and reduced critical judgment (Hilgard, 1965). These patients show reduced critical judgment when they use public places, compulsively return to the same place with their car license plates clearly visible, and in numerous other ways temporarily ignore situational dangers. It appears that a cognitive shift from fantasy involvement to a critical pedestrian view may alter the future probability of exhibitionistic behavior occurring under the internal conditions (moods of self-pity, boredom, anger, failure) and external conditions (warm weather, parks, girls in short skirts) that previously set the stage for exposure. In some respects this intervention is equivalent to reducing the probability of "hypnotic" behavior under specific internal and external conditions which may operate as discriminative stimuli for hypnotic behavior as it has been conceptualized by some writers (Sarbin & Coe, 1972).

Vicarious ABR (V-ABR) Procedure

A recent variant of the ABR procedure is called Vicarious Aversive Behavior Rehearsal (V-ABR). It is based on instructing and situationally arranging for an exhibitionistic patient to observe a video tape of a real exhibitionist being processed in vivo through the ABR procedure. The symptomatic consequences of V-ABR appear to be similar to the I-V-ABR procedure, but our sample is still small ($N = 4$) and our follow-ups are too inadequate (two to three years) to provide more than a tentative impression of a promising variant of ABR. The V-ABR procedure is probably indicated for the same type of patients who benefit from the in vivo ABR procedure, but who cannot be processed through the entire I-V-ABR for one or more of the following reasons:

1. The patient is deficient in the motivation necessary to go through the in vivo ABR.
2. There are medical contraindications which require that the patient be exempt from the severe stress of the I-V-ABR procedure (e.g., positive history of cardiovascular or CNS complications, angina pectoris, cardiac decompensation, hypertension, or epilepsy.
3. A patient may have weak reality contact or marginal adjustment, or be prepsychotic or acutely disturbed. The V-ABR is offered only to patients who have carefully considered and refused the in vivo ABR procedure or to those who, in the clinical judgment of the therapist or his medical consultant, are likely to be hurt by the in vivo ABR.

Indications for I-V-ABR

Only the following subset of exhibitionists should be considered candidates for this procedure:

1. Chronic sexual exhibitionists. Repeated offenders as defined by police records or those who report a high frequency (several times a day to several times a week) of compulsive urges to expose.
2. Patients who are introverted or neurotic as defined by the Eysenck Personality Inventory (1968), or who have high trait anxiety on the MMPI.
3. Patients who are moralistic, inhibited, and "good" citizens in 90 percent of their public lives.
4. Patients who have failed to respond to conventional procedures such as psychotherapy and aversive conditioning.
5. A "voluntary" patient who wants to try the ABR after he has been offered conventional procedures (Wickramasekera, 1971).

Contraindications for I-V-ABR

1. Prepsychotic or psychotic diagnosis.
2. Any medical condition which is incompatible with severe phasic stress, e.g., cardiovascular or CNS disease or trauma.
3. Sociopathic personality disorder (DSM II3017).

4. Large and ineffective doses of psychotherapy can develop an impenetrable cognitive defense in professional situations against engagement and absorption (Tellegen & Atkinson, 1974) in the deviant fantasy belief system that mediates sexual exposure. The patient must have access to the deviant fantasy in the clinical situation for positive clinical outcome.

Therapy for first or second offenders should first utilize conventional procedures like hypnosis, assertive training, psychotherapy, or a combination of systematic desensitization and operant shaping (Wickramasekera, 1968).

PROCEDURE

Component I (see Flow Chart 1) has diagnostic utility and also appears to potentiate certain active ingredients in the behavior influence process. These ingredients include the patient's self-disclosure, self-exploration, and commitment; structuring of the patient's positive expectations; and giving the patient responsibility for making the technique work. These variables have been empirically demonstrated to be effective in both the psychotherapy and the social psychological research literature (Strupp & Bergin, 1972; Goldstein, Heller, & Sechrest, 1966).

The patient is immediately told in the clinical interview that he suffers from a *chronic addictive* condition with which he cannot be helped unless he is completely honest (no falsification or omission of information) and willing to accept great discomfort and pain. He is told that his problem cannot be cured but if he is willing to be completely honest and accept great pain, he can learn to effectively control his condition. The previous times he has broken promises to himself are cited as evidence of the bankruptcy of his prior efforts.

Component IA eventually elicits and shapes the patient's self-exploratory and self-monitoring behaviors from very specific topics (e.g., first events of exposure, age, and so on) to a very general form of self-monitoring and self-exploration (identification of triggering events). At this more general level, the patient is attempting to relate the onset of his symptom to internal (e.g., conflict, failure, self-pity, boredom, etc.) and environmental events (the warm weather, specific location, length of women's skirts, types of female clothing, etc.).

FLOW CHART 1. ABR PROCEDURE

I. Diagnosis and assessment
    A. Collect the following facts and formulate relationships in the clinical interview.
        1. First event (age, circumstances)
        2. Frequency (in remote and recent past, and in present)
        3. Locations (car, parking lot, library, and so on)
        4. Time of day or night
        5. Duration of episode
        6. Age and sex of victims (special features)
        7. Masturbation, ejaculation, associated rituals, and fantasies
        8. Triggering events (e.g., conflict, failure, weather, female clothing, daydreams, and fantasies)
    B.
        1. Present treatment plan and alternatives with prognosis
        2. Present intervention as research, not routine treatment
        3. State side effects. Give the patient an article on ABR to read
        4. State restriction on intercourse for three weeks following procedures I and II
    C. Psychological and psychophysiological tests
        1. MMPI
        2. Eysenck Personality Inventory
        3. Taylor Manifest Anxiety Scale
        4. Spiegel Eye-Roll Test of Hypnotizability
        5. SHSS Form A
        6. Hypnosis Attitude Scale
        7. Conjugate Lateral Eye Movements (Bakan, 1969; Gur & Gur, 1974)
        8. Absorption scale
        9. Respiration ⎤
       10. Skin conductance ⎥ ← Psychophysiological baseline and response to standardized stimuli
       11. Skin temperature ⎥
       12. Heart rate ⎦
    D. Medical tests and physical examination—any contraindications?

> **FLOW CHART 1** (continued).
>
>   E. Discuss treatment plan with patient's significant others and lawyers. Have patient read and sign consent for treatment and video tape forms
> II. Intervention
>   A. Procedure I: 40 minutes of intensive self-disclosure, intensive self-exploration, and confrontation, of which approximately 20 minutes is actual physical exposure
>   B. Procedure II: 40 minutes of intensive self-disclosure, self-exploration, and confrontation, of which approximately 20 minutes is actual physical exposure
> III. Evaluation Follow-up
>   A. Follow-up three weeks later with observation of video tapes (neutral and aversive) with psychophysiological monitoring
>   B. Follow-ups at intervals of 2, 6, 9, and 12 months; then once each year

These antecedents appear to overlap between subjects to some extent, but they are also highly idiosyncratic. The identification of these internal and external antecedents or triggering events is quite important in terms of helping the patient develop an "early warning" system for his post-therapy prophylactic use.

Component IB essentially involves selling the patient on the ABR technique, but doing so in a cautious and ethical manner. To create positive expectations, for example, the patient is instructed to find and read a favorable review of this intervention (*Human Behavior*, April 1973) written in nontechnical terms. Previously observed side effects are described (repeated nightmares, acute anxiety or depression, secondary impotence) and the requirement of abstinence from sexual intercourse for three weeks after treatment is presented.

Component IC is mainly intended to enable an eventually more precise and objective specification of the type of patient for whom this procedure is indicated or contraindicated. It has been hypothesized (Wickramasekera, 1972) that trait anxiety, hypnotizability, the degree of socialization, and autonomic lability are implicated in the probability of certain sexual deviations. In addition, the combination of extensive psychological, psychophysiological, and medical tests may create the therapeutic expectation in the patient that "grave and healing events" are about to occur. The psychophysiological tests currently involve a 15 to 20-minute adaptation period; a 10-minute base-line period; instructions to the subject to solve simple mental arithmetic problems and to read aloud the titles of the books in the bookcase across the room; instructions to visualize, with eyes closed, a pleasant and relaxing scene (e.g., soaking in the bathtub or sipping a martini while relaxing by a fire); and instructions to visualize, with eyes closed, the last time he was arrested for indecent exposure. On-line data reduction procedures generate mean, standard deviation and range of all psychophysiological measures.

Component IE is the culmination of a series of progressively, tightly interlocking, tacit behavioral commitments to change. It requires the patient to make a full disclosure of his deviation and its frequency and chronicity to significant others (parents, wife) and to his lawyer. It also challenges him to persuade them of his wisdom in undergoing the ABR procedure, which in the process of doing he appears to strengthen his own commitment. One patient was lost at this point because his lawyer labeled the ABR procedure "insane" (which it probably is in some respects), and told the patient that if he cooperated with the video taping, he could expect to appear nude on the "Today Show" or "Huntley and Brinkley News." This component closes with the patient signing a release which allows the therapist to video tape his naked body for the "advancement of science," and releasing the therapist of all responsibility for possible negative consequences of the ABR procedure. The patient acknowledges on the release that the negative side effects have been carefully explained to him. Component I may take as many as four to six sessions to complete (each session 50 minutes), depending on the individual patient's initial level of defensiveness and commitment.

In summary, the preliminary orientation and screening procedures carefully structure the patient's expectations in a positive direction. They increase his commitment to public (self-disclosed) living and to socially appropriate risk taking and assertiveness in order to eliminate his exhibitionistic behavior. It is conceivable that these interventions alone could be sufficient to produce symptomatic control. This is an empirical question which could be answered simply by putting patients processed to this point on a waiting list and comparing their relapse rate with patients who additionally receive the complete in vivo ABR processing.

Component II involves approximately two 40-minute sessions of full self-disclosure, self-exploration, and self-confrontation in the presence of five female and two male mental health professionals (social workers, senior medical students, psychiatric nurses, and psychology interns) in a large room with a one-way mirror and video taping of the entire proceedings. It is sometimes hinted at this point that there may be other authorized observers (e.g., referring probation officer or arresting law officer) on the other side of the mirror. A psychiatric nurse is included in the team in case of a medical emergency, and also a large, sturdy male video-tape operator in case the patient becomes combative (which has not happened to date). The therapist opens the session in a kind, but grave manner and becomes progressively more obnoxious and confronting as the session progresses. He begins by putting a series of rapid questions to the patient (Please state your name, age, address, marital status, occupation, children's names and ages, religion, specific deviant sexual acts, associated rituals and locations, objects of exposure, and so on).

The patient is instructed in the following number system to cue specific acts of exposure and masturbation. The use of numbers appears more effective in securing compliance under stress than verbal requests. The patient is told, "When I say *one,* you will unzip your pants; when I say *two,* you will get a firm grip on your penis (use patient's own word for penis, e.g., cock); when I say *three,* you will start to masturbate ("jack-off," etc.)."

During and between exposures, the patient is pointedly questioned by all the team members individually and requested to attend to different parts of his body or their legs, breasts, crotches, hips, and the like. For example, he might be asked to respond to all or some of the following questions and instructions: What is your mood when you expose yourself? What triggers the mood? What do you see now as you look at yourself in the mirror? Describe what you think we see as we look at you right now. What do you think we are feeling (thinking, etc.) as we look at you now? How do your hands feel? How does your head (legs, penis, stomach) feel? Give your penis a voice, let it talk to us. Tell us about the man you are in your public life. Tell us about your private life. What are your masturbatory fantasies? And so on.

During component II, the patient is asked to disrobe and robe several times as he is encouraged to explore the relationship between his current feelings and his moods prior to and during exposure, and their relationship to antecedents, consequences, and immediate situational factors. He is frequently relieved to be asked to "zip up," or pull up his pants, but this relief is short-lived because soon afterwards he is asked to disrobe again. At the close of the session, the patient is frequently in tears, trembling, weak, and nauseous.

The therapist dismisses the team and changes abruptly into a warm, kind, supportive figure who wipes the patient's eyes and fetches him a drink of water. The therapist sincerely and freely expresses his admiration for the courage and strength the patient demonstrated during the previous "hell," and leaves him in doubt for a few days as to whether another procedure will be required.

The primary contraindications for another procedure are massive sympathetic arousal (check pulse) during the first procedure, insightful verbalizations with active patient participation, and any evidence of bizarre behavior during or after the procedure (very rare event). The primary indication for a second procedure is marginal arousal and "unauthorized" psychological escape behavior while physically present (disassociation). If a second procedure is scheduled, we begin by asking specific details about his cognitive, affective, and motor reactions during and after the first procedure—particularly his immediate and delayed reactions. The session continues with some variation on the previous material, loose ends from the previous session, or any new material. To disrupt any persisting disassociation, team members approach him physically and ask him to describe physical details of other team members, such as their clothing or bodies.

It is first particularly important during the procedure to elicit any idiosyncratic fantasies (e.g. girls being impressed with the girth of his penis) which may mediate the exhibitionism; and second, to subject this material to a critical analytic pedestrian type of verbal processing (left brain). It is also important, after the second step, to encourage the patient to practice and develop any alternative set of more acceptable assertive responses when tempted to expose himself. These may include whistling at an attractive female, or verbalizing aloud what was most attractive about the woman and what he would like to do with the female if not constrained by his own inhibitions and social restraints. He may also be encouraged to verbalize lewd remarks.

RESULTS

The in vivo ABR procedure has been offered to 28 patients. Five have refused or have not completed the I-V-ABR or V-ABR. Twenty-three patients have been treated with the ABR procedure to date, 19 with the in vivo ABR and 4 with the vicarious ABR. Only one patient treated with the ABR procedure has reported exposing himself. We have not detected any other relapses to date. All patients report having between one to four thoughts of exposure at least once in three months, but the thoughts are brief and easily terminated. Approximately one-half of the patients report mild to severe anxiety when thoughts of exposure occur to them. The rest of the patients report a "neutral" feeling if they have thoughts of exposure. All patients report that the frequency of exposure fantasies has been reduced dramatically since treatment, and the quality and duration of the fantasies—if they occur at all—"feel" vastly different from the pretreatment fantasies. The patients also report that they are more appropriately assertive with females.

The follow-ups for the in vivo procedure range from 22 months to almost nine years. The follow-ups for the vicarious ABR are too brief to attach much significance to them at this time. The follow-ups are based on four kinds of data:

1. Patients provide direct verbal reports during the periodic individual interviews. The systematic follow-up interviews appear to be reactive measures, because many patients report that their anxiety level increases prior to their follow-up appointment, and the previous ABR procedure is reactivated in memory. It appears that these regular follow-up sessions strengthen the ABR procedure and should be regarded as part of it. Since these are patients' subjective verbal reports, they are open to all the limitations associated with such sources of information.

2. Private interviews with significant others (wife, employers, parents), or telephone calls to them, are used at the time of the patient's follow-up interview to check on the patient's verbal report.
3. Search of police records on indecent exposure in the three surrounding counties are used to verify the patient's verbal report. This procedure is recent and is still incompletely established. The law enforcement system appears responsive and supportive of this project, but their own records and those at a state-wide level are incomplete. Very few acts of exposure are followed by arrest.
4. Recently we have begun to add a fourth psychophysiological evaluation component to our follow-up system.

To determine the psychophysiological consequences of being processed through the ABR procedure and being reminded of it, the following instructional and situational arrangements are made: (see Flow Chart 2.) The patient is told to return to the therapist's office for "a test" approximately three weeks after the last in vivo ABR procedure. In the therapist's office, the patient is connected to a physiograph (which is screened from the patient) while he sits quietly on a comfortable recliner. In front of the subject, approximately eight feet away, are two video-tape monitors. The monitor above is programmed to show a portion of the video tape (aversive tape) of the patient's treatment. The monitor below is programmed to show a neutral or control tape consisting of a portion of the patient's initial diagnostic interview. After connection to the physiograph, the patient is given 20 minutes to adapt and "relax" in the situation. At the end of the adaptation period, the control tape is activated remotely by the therapist and allowed to run for four minutes. After the control tape is turned off, the aversive tape is activated remotely and allowed to run also for four minutes. The subject has previously been instructed to observe both tapes carefully, but he is not informed about the content of the video tapes or the order in which they will be shown. After four minutes of exposure to the aversive tape, it is switched off and the subject is simply instructed to relax for 10 minutes before he is disconnected from the physiograph, which has been monitoring and recording his heart rate (BPM), respiration, skin conductance, and skin temperature during the adaption, observation, and relaxation periods.

> **FLOW CHART 2. VIDEO-PHYSIOGRAPH ASSESSMENT PROCEDURE**
>
> 1. Adaptation and base-line (20 minutes)
> 2. Control TV tape (4 minutes)
> 3. Aversive TV tape (4 minutes)
> 4. Return to baseline (10 minutes)

The purpose of the control tape is to determine the psychophysiological consequences of the patient becoming oriented to and observing a video tape of himself while connected to a physiograph. Simple inspection of the physiograph record during the patient's exposure to control and aversive tape sequences indicates clear and significant differences in heart rate, skin conductance, and respiration. Statistical analyses have not been done: they do not seem necessary for the seven records of this type we have collected to date with this evaluation procedure.

Figures 1–4 show psychophysiological changes occurring in an adult male during two base-line periods and while observing control and aversive tapes. The aversive video tape was of the patient rehearsing sexual exposure and masturbation in the presence of three females and two males. The upper trace is of heart rate (BPM), the middle trace is of galvanic skin response (GSR), and the bottom trace is of respiration. Paper speed is 6 inches per minute. This patient's record was selected because he demonstrated physiological changes in all three response systems (BPM, GSR, respiration). Not all subjects tested to date demonstrate clear changes in all three response systems. As indicated by Lacey (1959), individual patients appear to show response profiles. The patient is shown the results of this evaluation procedure. Showing him the results increases the credibility of the treatment effects. The routine psychophysiological testing (BPM, GSR, respiration) of the patient during the periodic follow-up interview is presented to the patient "to detect how much of the previous conditioning persists." Some patients perceive this new procedure as a lie detector test, which may have a modest deterrent effect on deviant behavior. During the follow-ups, the patient is instructed after a psychophysiological base-line period to expose

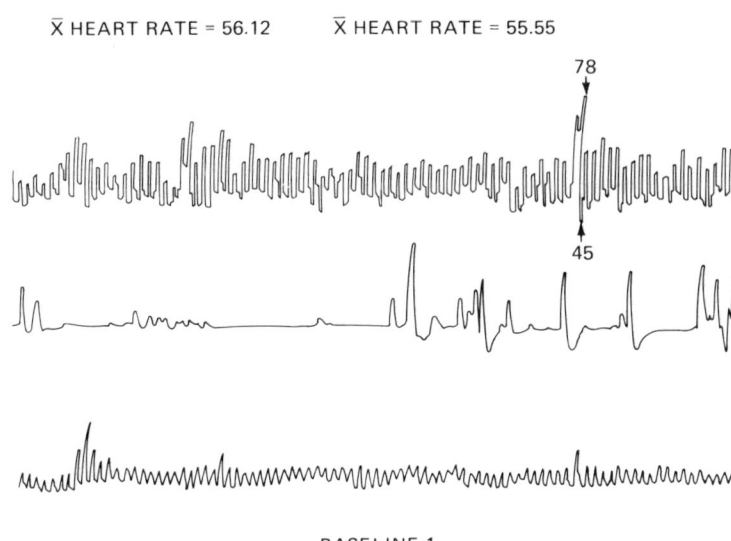

Figure 1. Psychophysiological changes in an adult male during base-line period 1 of the video-physiograph assessment procedure.

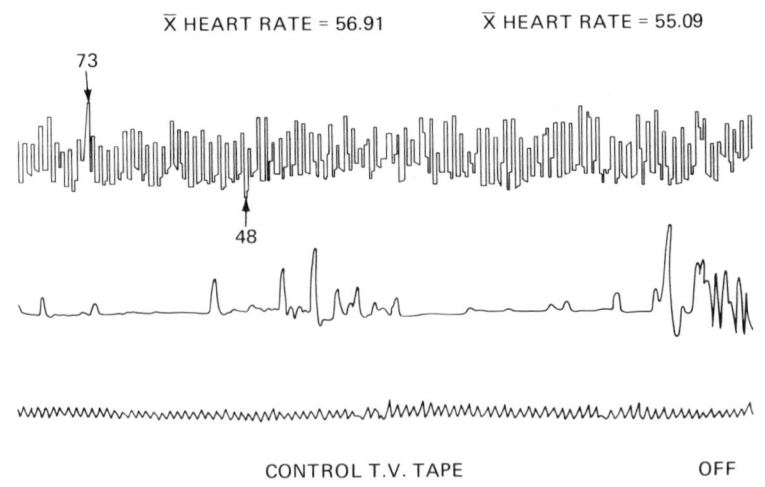

Figure 2. Psychophysiological changes in an adult male while watching himself in a "control" video tape.

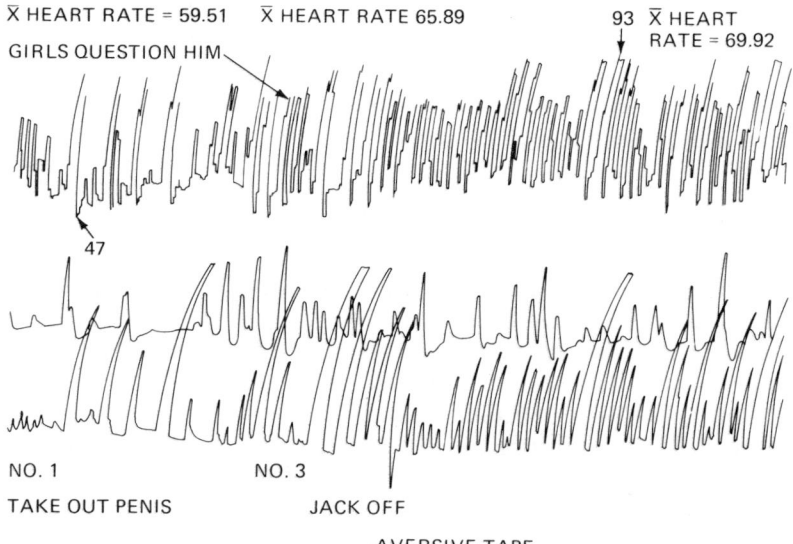

Figure 3. Psychophysiological changes in an adult male while watching an aversive-stimulus video tape.

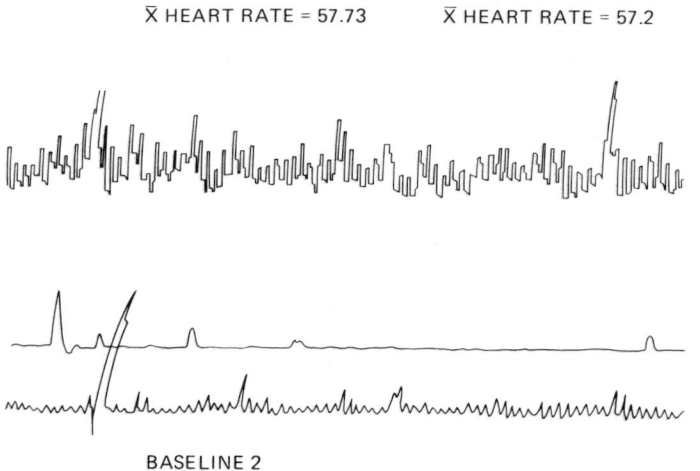

Figure 4. Psychophysiological changes in an adult male during base-line period 2.

himself in fantasy and then is casually asked, while still connected to the instrument, the number of times he has exposed himself since the last follow-up. Table 1 indicates the characteristics and treatment outcome of the 23 exhibitionists who have participated in the ABR treatment program to date.

COMPLICATIONS AND CLINICAL ISSUES

The in vivo ABR does appear to have some side effects which are observed between the two in vivo ABR procedures or immediately after the treatment. These side effects include moderate to mild anxiety, tension, and depression of one to four weeks duration. One or more of these symptoms have been reported by all in vivo ABR patients. These symptoms seem to disappear in all cases after five weeks. Repeated nightmares, in which the ABR procedure or a variant of it is rehearsed in sleep, have been reported by 5 patients. Secondary impotence of brief duration (two to four weeks) has been reported by 3 patients. Temporary loss of interest in sex has been reported by approximately 13 in vivo ABR patients. All symptoms appear to have cleared up two months after treatment.

The secondary impotence has particularly concerned us. In an attempt to reduce the future probability of it, we have introduced a prohibition against all sexual intercourse by patients for three weeks after the first in vivo ABR procedure. The mechanism of erection is primarily parasympathetic, and hence a temporary state of massive sympathetic arousal (post-treatment anxiety and tension) is probably antagonistic to effective sexual functioning in the male patient. Residual anxiety has usually subsided by the third week after treatment.

About one-half of the patients disassociate (become psychologically absent although physically present, or "go someplace else in their head") during either ABR procedure to avoid the impact of the aversive reality that has been carefully arranged for them. They do not attend or they become "numb" to the full concrete impact of the aversive reality. This probably natural response to stress has to be rapidly terminated in this context. The "unauthorized form of escape behavior" (Azrin & Holz, 1966) has been terminated by insisting forcefully that the patient describe the present physical reality (color

Table 1. Characteristics of Male Sexual Exhibitionists and Outcome of their Treatment

SUBJECT	DURATION (IN YEARS) SINCE FIRST EXPOSURE	AGE	FREQUENCY OF EXHIBITIONS PER MONTH	METHOD	NUMBER OF TREATMENT SESSIONS	FOLLOW-UP Years	FOLLOW-UP Months	OUTCOME
1	14	32	2-4	I-V-ABR	3	7	3	N-R
2	16	29	1-2	I-V-ABR	3	6	3	N-R
3	40	49	1-2	I-V-ABR	3	6	9	N-R
4	6	20	3-4	I-V-ABR	4	6	6	N-R
5	18	37	1-4	I-V-ABR	4	8	9	N-R
6	4	26	1-3	I-V-ABR	3	6	11	N-R
7	7	32	1-20	I-V-ABR	2	5	3	N-R
8	12	30	1-3	I-V-ABR	2	5	5	N-R
9	5	22	1	I-V-ABR	2	5	3	N-R
10	25	50	1-7	I-V-ABR	2	5	2	N-R
11	11	29	1-2	I-V-ABR	2	4	3	N-R
12	4	22	1-4	I-V-ABR	2	3	4	N-R
13	20	42	1-14	I-V-ABR	2	2	6	N-R
14	7	23	1-2	I-V-ABR	2	2	9	N-R
15	9	28	1-9	V-ABR	1	2	11	N-R
16	13	29	1-3	V-ABR	1	2	8	N-R
17	10	26	1-2	V-ABR	1	2	6	N-R
18	12	36	2-4	V-ABR	1	2	4	N-R
19	8	24	1-12	I-V-ABR	1	2	3	N-R
20	10	29	1-12	I-V-ABR	1	2	3	N-R
21	18	29	1-4	I-V-ABR	2		22	R
22	35	51	2-8	I-V-ABR	1		20	N-R
23	16	36	1-16	I-V-ABR	1		20	N-R

I-V-ABR: in vivo aversive behavior rehearsal. V-ABR: vicarious aversive behavior rehearsal.
R: Relapsed. N-R: Relapse not detected.

of female's eyes, hair, shape of their breasts, legs, or clothes), his own physical reactions, his current autistic fantasies, and his speculations about the thoughts and feelings behind the females' faces. The therapist can usually subjectively estimate the intensity of the aversion generated by the severity of his own exhaustion or tension after the procedure. The procedure is really quite harrowing to all concerned. It appears that if the ABR technique is continued over several sessions, the patient becomes desensitized to the technique. Hence, treatment should cease with a brief "resensitization" (Wickramasekera, 1970).

Many exhibitionists are quiet, nonassertive, moralistic individuals who take few risks in their public lives but become very daring figures during their "private" exhibitionistic episodes and fantasies. Their public image may be one of respectability, caution, reliability, and industry; whereas in their private feelings they are desperately bored, resentful, and self-pitying, and their fantasies are defiant and dangerously exciting.

During the ABR procedures, the patient frequently develops insight into this inconsistency between his public and private lives, and he is strongly encouraged to act in more adaptive risk-taking and assertive ways in his public life—e.g., asking for a raise or promotion; speaking back to his wife, boss, or a peer; changing jobs; or trying a love affair. It appears likely that the inhibition of aggressive, sexual novelty, and excitement needs episodically increases the probability of their maladaptive expression in indecent exposure. The patients appear to become more appropriately assertive after the ABR.

DISCUSSION OF RESEARCH IMPLICATIONS

Instructionally and situationally the ABR procedure arranges for the elicitation of strong aversive internal consequences. Typically, patients report or manifest one or more of the following before, during, or immediately after the procedure: trembling, nausea, light-headedness, palpitations, weakness, cramps, butterflies in the stomach, headaches, tightness in the chest. "Voluntary" participation (Wickramasekera, 1971) ensures that the patient actively generates the aversive consequences in himself. The aversion is installed inside the subject and outside of his control, so that the aversive contingency cannot be easily dismantled by the patient as, for example, with a portable and remotely controlled shock generator. It has been speculated (Wickramasekera, 1972) that the procedure may involve interoceptive conditioning, and this speculation appears to be reinforced by some theoretical and empirical data (Miller & Murray, 1952; Miller, 1959; Miller, 1964). Miller has suggested (personal communication, 1973) that if aversion is attached to internal cues, the gradient of generalization will be flatter. This hypothesis may explain the apparently reliable transfer of the suppression of exhibitionism from the clinical situation to the patient's natural habitat. But it is doubtful that aversive arousal alone is an essential and sufficient condition for the control of exhibitionism in this subset of patients.

First, it is necessary to recognize that the technique is clearly over-determined because it appears to incorporate several ingredients which previously have been shown to be or claimed to be effective ingredients in the psychotherapy, social psychological, and learning literatures.

It is possible to offer several explanations of why the ABR controls the frequency of exposure. These explanations should have implications for empirical research manipulations. For example, the reduction of exhibitionism may be attributed to extinction or nonreinforcement of the private fantasies and exhibitionistic role behaviors in the clinical exposure situation (females do not react with shock or fear). Punishment (Azrin & Holz, 1966) of the exhibitionistic fantasies and role behavior by the connection of aversive visceral consequences to internal cues, or insight and self-disclosure (Mowrer, 1964) may explain the positive outcomes. Cognitive dissonance theory predicts maximum attitudinal changes under conditions of "voluntary" participation, minimal reward, and maximum effort. All three ingredients are incorporated into the ABR procedure. Powerful structuring of demand characteristics (Orne, 1970) may be said to explain the positive outcome. Credibility or face validity is an important property of a therapeutic procedure to a patient, and five exhibitionists have spontaneously told me that they had anticipated a technique like the ABR and wondered if it would help them.

At an even lower level of abstraction, it may be said that the treatment simply arranges for a series of events that identify highly motivated exhibitionists who would respond to any form of treatment. Hence the results are due to some nonspecific effect. Alternately, it may be said that the screening events are arranged to make the patient increasingly vulnerable to interpersonal influence, and once such an orientation is established, the specific treatment technique is irrelevant. The treatment procedure involves several components, some of which may be effective and the others "superstitions." The technique is highly researchable and may be dismantled along several empirical dimensions such as verbal instructions, situational arrangements, and frequency and duration of treatments. For example, men could be substituted for women or verbal instructions and patient self-exploration could be increased, reduced, or eliminated. The diagnostic screening could be eliminated, or the diagnostic screening retained and the treatment procedures eliminated. Another alternative would be to retain the diagnostic screening and replace the "exposure" procedure with an equally unpleasant aversive (shock) conditioning procedure. At a strictly empirical level, the independent variables need to be manipulated and symptomatic outcome monitored over several years.

Currently we are attempting to look rather grossly at the motivational hypothesis by attempting to narrow the patient's choice from three alternatives, i.e., psychotherapy, threat of legal action, or ABR; to two alternatives, i.e., threat of legal action or ABR; and, finally, to secure involuntary legal commitment of exhibitionists to the ABR procedure. To achieve the last purpose, to expand our follow-up net, and to secure more base-line data on this deviation, we are conducting exploratory negotiations both at local and state-wide levels (while protecting patient confidentiality) with law enforcement agencies and the courts.

We are also attempting to identify the cognitive, behavioral, and psychophysiological characteristics that predict maximum response to this treatment procedure. The extensive diagnostic screening was initially intended to improve prediction of positive outcomes with this procedure, but the small relapse rate to date has frustrated this purpose. It is likely that, as our sample increases, we will detect more relapses which will enable us to look more closely at our techniques. Clinical impressions confirm the view that hypnotizability, the degree of socialization, religiosity, introversion, autonomic responsivity, and manifest anxiety are salient predictors of positive outcome with this procedure. Nearly all the exhibitionistic subjects we have screened to date and treated either with V-ABR or in vivo ABR have had most of these subject characteristics.

MODIFICATIONS OF THE ABR

There are currently two creative modifications of the ABR which seek to extend the technique to other symptoms. Boudewyns has described an interesting and promising adaptation of the ABR for use with obscene telephone callers. Forgione (1974) has described a creative adaptation of the ABR for use with pedophilia. These procedures are described in sufficient detail for clinical implementation, but we do not have experience with them. In fact, the treatment failure about to be described may have been avoided if certain modifications in the ABR technique had been made.

Case Study of a Treatment Failure

T. was a 29-year-old, right-handed married male referred by the court from a very large and distant city. He had been arrested for this offense at least four times since the age of 16. He reported feeling moralistic, guilty, and depressed after each incident. He stated that he had observed his father practice indecent exposure several times, and his mother was the first female to whom he had deliberately exposed himself when he was around age 9. His sexual relationship with his wife was very poor and, in spite of seeing over 10 psychotherapists and marriage counselors, neither his sexual-social relationship with his wife nor his control over his sexual exhibitionism had improved. T. had seldom seen any therapist longer than 15 sessions. He reported exposing himself exclusively to teenage females, ages 13 to 16, and to a very specific type of female: "gum chewing, slutty girls in blue jeans". This patient had greater pre-ABR intellectual insight into the etiology, precipitating factors, and the dynamics of his sexual problem than any patient who had previously received the ABR. In fact, his most recent therapist had been one of the most illustrious medical psychoanalysts in the United States. T. did not appear to know of the analyst's national reputation. He spontaneously stated that he had developed more understanding of himself and his symptoms through this therapist (15 sessions) than from any previous treatment. After his most recent arrest and referral to me, his base-line rate of exposure was quite variable (one to six times a week) and was enacted exclusively in public libraries, parks, and parking lots. The frequency of his exhibitionistic fantasies was more stable, 7 to 10 times per day, and was associated with masturbation and ejaculation about 5 percent of the time. The patient was a very bright, rational-verbal, handsome, and superficially outgoing person. He was always very attractively dressed, but in a manner more appropriate to an older adolescent. Careful evaluation of his conjugate lateral eye movements (Bakan, 1971; Gur & Gur, 1974) indicated over a 90 percent tendency to engage the left hemisphere in response to standard reflective questions.

Procedure

T. was processed through the in vivo ABR technique with no deviations or omissions from the procedure previously described. For obvious ethical and legal reasons, we were unable to use teenage adolescent females and were restricted to three attractive females in their late twenties. The patient was administered two ABR sessions of approximately 60 minutes each, followed three weeks later by the video-physiograph evaluation procedure.

Results

T.'s reactions to the procedure were atypical in at least four objective respects. His behavioral response to the instruction to expose himself was rapid, (10 to 20 seconds) and there was no need for the therapist to use threats or verbal pressure to secure compliance. He showed no overt (blushing, trembling, sweating) or covert (pulse rate 80 to 92) indications of strong sympathetic activation. He demonstrated no observable (e.g., defocused eye movements) indications of dissociation (Hilgard, 1976). His rate of verbal responding did not appear to decrease or increase during the ABR procedure. (See Figures 5–8.)

During the video-physiograph evaluation procedure three weeks after the ABR, T.'s heart rate, respiration, and GSR responses were not significantly different on stimulation by control and experimental video tapes. This atypical finding suggests that the aversive tape was not physiologically stressful to the patient.

During the ABR procedure, T. verbalized many insights he had previously shared with the therapist during the screening period. The patient and a female co-therapist stated that they believed the treatment was effective, but the senior therapist had many reservations, mainly because the patient had manifested no observable signs of alteration in physiological arousal. During the ABR procedure, the therapist urged the patient to terminate future masturbation to deviant fantasy in his natural habitat. Three weeks later, during the video-physiograph evaluation, the patient remained optimistic that the treatment was effective; but the physiological data did not fit our previous observations with successful patients. Based on this data, the therapist made a prediction to his co-therapists that the patient would relapse. T. also reported none of the typical side effects (e.g., nightmares, transient depression, or lack of sex drive) of the ABR. One month after the video-physiograph evaluation, the senior therapist received a long-distance telephone call from T. He stated that he had exposed himself three times on the same day in a parking lot and several times afterwards. He was again depressed, guilty, moralistic, and remorseful.

Current Theoretical Position

Based on the previous clinical observation, it appears that there is at least one strong contraindication for the use of the present ABR procedure. If the patient has had prior exposure to large and frequent doses of ineffective psychotherapy, he probably has developed an impenetrable cognitive defense, in professional situations, against absorption in the deviant fantasy-belief system (Wickramasekera 1972, 1976a) that mediates sexual exposure. It appears that this patient used his motor and verbal-subjective response systems to insulate his visceral response system from the typically intrusive and invasive properties of the ABR. Based on the previous observations, it seems even clearer that cognitive-verbal manipulations which do not elicit and alter the belief system which is regnant during deviant enactment are ineffective in inducing long-term behavioral changes in the case of behaviors enacted in "altered states of consciousness" (Wickramasekera 1972; 1976a, b; 1977). Originally it was hypothesized (Wickramasekera, 1972) that exposure in this subset of patients occurs in an altered state of consciousness, characterized by reduced critical judgment and at least partial amnesia as to motivation, in a quasi-automatic fashion. The critical-analytic cognitive component of the ABR cannot impact the relevant belief-fantasy system of the patient unless there is some approximation to the altered physiological and cortical activation pattern that apparently prevails during enactment in the patient's natural habitat. The belief systems that mediate exposure probably are only partially encoded *verbally* and may be stored in the minor (Galin, 1974) or hypnotic hemisphere (Bakan, 1969; Gur & Gur, 1974; Graham & Pernicano, 1976), to be

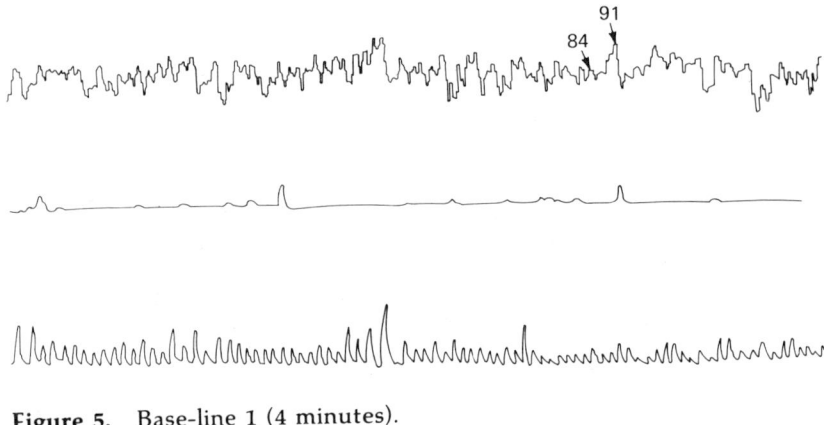

Figure 5. Base-line 1 (4 minutes).

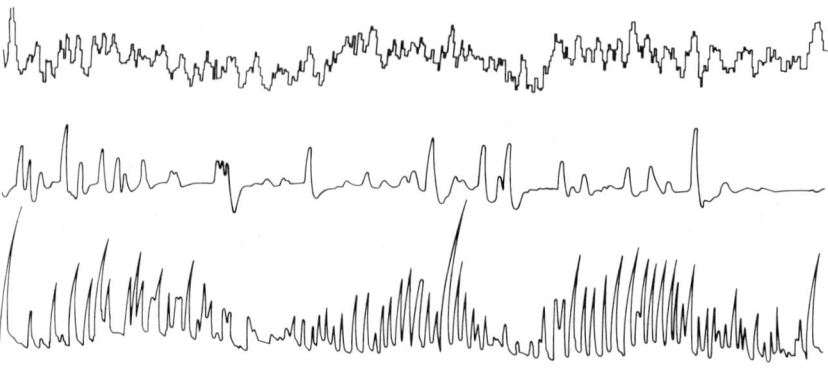

Figure 6. Control TV tape (4 minutes).

elicited only on appropriate *visual* stimulation. This specific type of sexual visual stimulation may be associated with increased probability of enhanced engagement of the right hemisphere (Cohen, Rosen, & Goldstein, 1976) and with potentiation of, and absorption (Tellegen & Atkinson, 1974) in, the deviant fantasy belief system that mediates exposure.

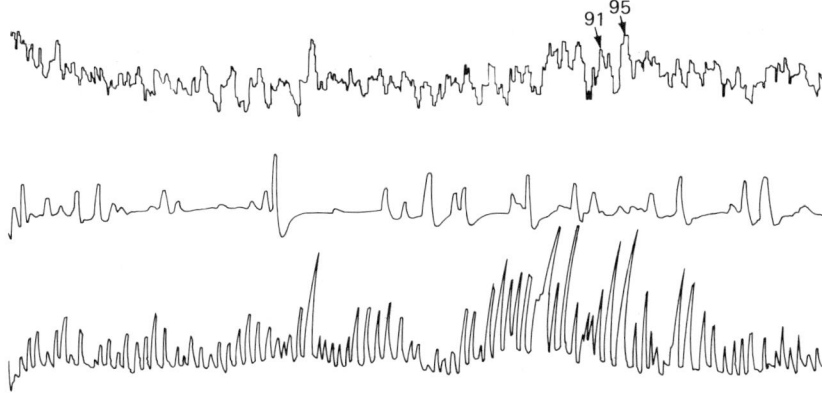

Figure 7. Aversive TV tape (4 minutes).

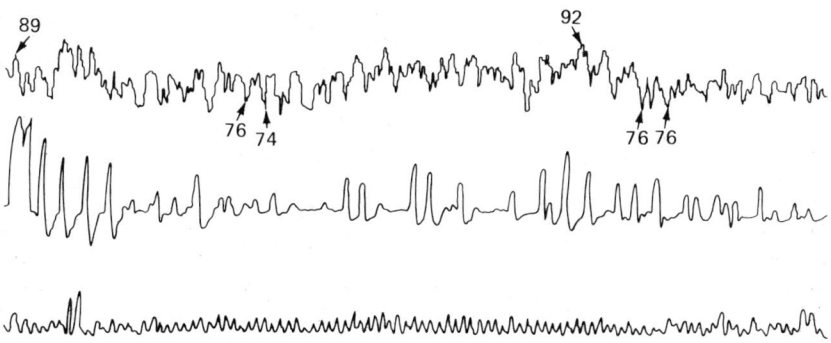

Figure 8. Base-line 2 (4 minutes).

CONCLUSION

It appears that sexual exhibitionism in this subset of patients (Wickramasekera, 1972) is a state-specific learning phenomena that remains impervious to critical-analytic cognitive interventions which are nonintrusive of that specific learning state. It is assumed that this intervention failed because we were unable to approximate the appropriate conditions of visual (adolescent girls) and visceral stimulation sufficiently. It seems that an alteration in arousal and concomitant critical analytic attenuation of the relevant deviant belief-fantasy systems are the essential and sufficient conditions to reduce the probability of sexual exhibitionism in this subset of chronic patients.

REFERENCES

Azrin, N. H., & Holz, W. C. Punishment. In W. K. Honig (Ed.), *Operant behavior, areas of research and application.* New York: Appleton-Century-Crofts, 1966.

Bakan, P. Hypnotizability, laterality of eye movements and functional brain asymmetry. *Perceptual and Motor Skills,* 1969, *28,* 927–932.

Cohen, H. D., Rosen, R. C., & Goldstein, L. Electroencephalographic laterality changes during human sexual orgasm. *Archives of Sexual Behavior,* 1976, *5,* 189–199.

Galin, D. Implications for psychiatry of left and right-cerebral specialization. *Archives of General Psychiatry,* 1974, *31,* 572–583.

Graham, K. R., & Pernicano, K. Laterality, hypnosis, and the autokinetic effect. Paper presented at the meeting of the American Psychological Association, Washington, D.C., 1976.

Gur, R. C., & Gur R. E. Handedness, sex and eyedness as moderating variables in the relation between hypnotic susceptibility and functional brain asymmetry. *Journal of Abnormal Psychology,* 1974, *83*(6), 635–643.

Hilgard, E. R. Neodissociation theory of multiple cognitive control systems. In G. Schwartz & D. Shapiro (Eds.), *Consciousness and self-regulation.* New York: Plenum, 1976.

Hilgard, E. R. *Hypnotic susceptibility.* New York: Harcourt, Brace & World, 1965.

Jones, I. V., & Frei, D. Provoked anxiety as a treatment of exhibitionism. *British Journal of Psychiatry,* 1977, *131,* 295–300.

Lacey, J. E. Psychophysiological approaches to the evaluation of psychotherapeutic process and outcome. In E. A. Rubenstein & M. B. Parloff (Eds.), *Research in psychotherapy.* Washington, D.C.: American Psychological Association, 1959.

Miller, N. E., & Murray, E. J. Displacement and conflict: Learnable drive as a basis for the steeper gradient of avoidance than of conflict. *Journal of Experimental Psychology,* 1952, *43,* 227–231.

Miller, N. E. Liberalization of basic S–R concepts: Extension to conflict behavior, motivation and social learning. In S. Koch (Ed.), *Psychology: A study of a science* (Study 1, 2). New York: McGraw-Hill, 1959.

Miller, N. E. Some implications of modern behavior therapy for personality change and psychotherapy. In D. Byrne & P. Worchel (Eds.), *Personality change.* New York: Wiley, 1964.

Mowrer, O. H. *The new group therapy.* Princeton, N.J.: Van Nostrand, 1964.

Orne, M. T. Hypnosis, motivation and the ecological validity of the psychological experiment. In W. J. Arnold & M. M. Page (Eds.), *Nebraska symposium on motivation.* Lincoln: University of Nebraska Press, 1970, 187–265.

Reitz, W. E., & Keil, W. E. Behavioral treatment of an exhibitionist. *Journal of Behavior Therapy and Experimental Psychiatry*, 1971, *2*, 67–69.

Sarbin, T. R., & Coe, W. C. *Hypnosis: A social psychological analysis of influence communication.* New York: Holt, Rinehart & Winston, 1972.

Serber, M. Shame aversion therapy. *Behavior Therapy and Experimental Psychiatry*, 1970, *1*, 213–215.

Stevenson, J., & Jones, I. H. Behavior therapy techniques for exhibitionism. *Archives of General Psychiatry*, 1972, *27*, 239–241.

Tellegen, A., & Atkinson, G. Openness to absorbing and self-altering experiences ("absorption"), a trait related to hypnotic susceptibility. *Journal of Abnormal Psychology*, 1974, *83*, 268–277.

Wickramasekera, I. The application of learning theory to the treatment of a case of sexual exhibitionism. *Psychotherapy: Theory, Research and Practice*, 1968, *5*, 108–112.

Wickramasekera, I. Desensitization, resensitization and desensitization again. *Journal of Behavior Therapy and Experimental Psychiatry*, 1970, *1*, 257–262.

Wickramasekera, I. The effect of "hypnosis" and task motivational instruction in attempting to influence the voluntary self-deprivation of money. *Journal of Personality and Social Psychology*, 1971, *19*, 311–314.

Wickramasekera, I. A technique for controlling a certain type of sexual exhibitionism. *Psychotherapy: Theory, Research and Practice*, 1972, *9*, 207–210.

Wickramasekera, I. Effects of EMG feedback on hypnotic susceptibility. *Journal of Abnormal Psychology*, 1973, *82*, 74–77.

Wickramasekera, I. Aversive behavior rehearsal for sexual exhibitionism. *Behavior Therapy*, 1976(a), *7*, 167–176.

Wickramasekera, I. *Biofeedback, behavior therapy and hypnosis: Potentiating the verbal control of behavior for clinicians.* Chicago: Nelson-Hall, 1976(b).

Wickramasekera, I. On attempts to modify hypnotic susceptibility: Some psychophysiological procedures and promising directions. *Annals of the New York Academy of Sciences*, 1977, *296*, 143–153.

7

MULTIFACETED BEHAVIOR THERAPY

Kelly D. Brownell

While reading a magazine recently, I saw a picture of a man (with his back to the viewer) in a trenchcoat, apparently exposing his genitals. The word "flash" appeared in bold letters below the picture. This scene was printed on T-shirts which were available for $5.00 and promoted the magazine in which the picture appeared. The magazine? Pornography perhaps, catering to the most prurient interests of the reader? The advertisement appeared in the respected *Philadelphia* magazine.

Exhibitionism has become an acceptable, if not fashionable, topic of conversation. The word "flasher" is in vogue and is commonly used to describe the exhibitionist. Cartoons depicting exhibitionists in the various stages of their distinctive acts appear frequently in popular magazines. At costume parties, at least one guest is likely to be clad in an exhibitionist's garb. One can even purchase a "flasher doll" whose raincoat can be pulled back to reveal an anatomically accurate male complete with pubic hair and a penis.

When exhibitionists are apprehended by police and are accountable to the criminal justice system, however, their behavior is not greeted with the same amusement. In the United States, exhibitionists may be charged with "tending to debauch the morals or manners of the people," and in England an offender may be sentenced as an "incorrigible rogue."

Exhibitionism is one of the most puzzling forms of sexual behavior encountered in the mental health and legal professions. Few professionals can understand why a person would want to expose the genitals to an unsuspecting victim, particularly when the behavior may not be accompanied by overt sexual arousal. This lack of understanding has contributed to the mystery that clouds most discussions of this topic. Furthermore, there has been little agreement among professionals about the cause and treatment of this disorder.

Exhibitionism was first recorded in 4 B.C. in a report on Theophrastus. In 1877 the French physician Lasègue characterized the exhibitionist as a respectable person who feels compelled to expose his genitals repeatedly to the same person in the same location. There is relief of sexual tension after the act, even though shame and remorse also occur. The exhibitionist makes no attempt at intercourse with his victim, and in fact makes no effort even to touch his victim. With the exception of Lasègue's claim that the exhibitionist favors the same victim for repeated acts, this definition is appropriate today.

Krafft-Ebing (1900) included cases of exhibitionism in his work on sexual psychopathy. Havelock Ellis (1927) claimed that sexual pleasure was gained from the emotion of the victim, be it pleasure, confusion, or horror. As MacDonald (1973) has pointed out, these authors were censured by the medical profession for their forthright discussion of this act. In subsequent years, professional discussion of exhibitionism became more appropriate, but the exhibitionist act maintained its disturbing quality for society.

Human behavior is perhaps best viewed from a social learning framework. Social learning theory (Bandura, 1969; 1977a) conceptualizes behavior as developing within a social context in which the environment and the person interact to create normal as well as abnormal behavior. Abnormal behavior is developed, maintained, and modified in the same fashion as normal behavior. The term "abnormal" does not reflect intrinsic differences in social behavior; rather, it indicates arbitrary decisions by society about whether a behavior is appropriate for a given person, at a given place, and at a given time (O'Leary & Wilson, 1975; Ullmann & Krasner, 1975). The fact that some sexual behaviors occur with greater frequency than others indicates that a majority of people are exposed to similar learning processes (Simon & Gagnon, 1970; Wilson & Davison, 1974). This formulation was promoted by Kinsey during his research on sexual behavior:

> Learning and conditioning in connection with human sexual behavior involves the same sorts of processes as learning and conditioning in other types of behavior. . . . The sexual capacities which an individual inherits at birth appear to be nothing more than the necessary anatomy and the physiological capacity to respond to a sufficient physical or psychologic stimulus. . . . As a result of its experience, an animal acquires certain patterns of behavior which lead it to react positively to certain sorts of stimuli, and negatively to other sorts of stimuli. . . . The type of person who first introduces an individual to particular types of social-sexual activities may have a great deal to do with his or her interest in continuing such activity, and his or her dissatisfaction with other types of activity (Kinsey, Pomeroy, Martin, & Gebhard, 1953, pp. 644–646).

From a behavioral perspective, exhibitionism consists of a constellation of sexual and nonsexual behaviors, each of which has been learned from the individual's interaction with his internal and external environment. Particular behaviors are reinforced by sexual arousal culminating in orgasm, or by the influence of the behavior on the environment (reaction of the victim or others).

The role of fantasy is crucial in the development of sexual behavior. There is general agreement that the fantasies during masturbation are powerfully reinforced and therefore tend to mimic actual behavior. But how a particular person chooses masturbatory fantasies is not clear. McGuire, Carlisle, and Young (1965) agree with Kinsey that early sexual experiences provide fantasy material for masturbation that subsequently influences sexual practices. Inherent in this view is the idea that any object or act can be linked fortuitously to sexual pleasure if the two are associated during times of maximum pleasure. A more parsimonious view, however, is that specific fantasies and behaviors are associated with sexual arousal for reasons that can be determined and defined. For example, why do some adolescent males choose to masturbate while clutching women's panties, while others imagine having intercourse with very young girls, and others imagine exposing themselves in a public place?

The exhibitionist fantasy is particularly difficult to explain as accidentally linked to sexual arousal. Few exhibitionists report early incidents in which exhibitionistic behavior just happened to occur and then was reinforced. Stoller (1975) maintains that specific events during childhood which influence sexual identity are instrumental in the subsequent development of sexual fantasy material. I agree with Stoller's view, yet would not evoke the psychodynamic constructs as an explanation for this phenomenon. Stoller, for example, claims that unresolved oedipal conflicts and castration anxiety make a child fear for his masculinity. To prevent this anxiety in later life, a sexual scenario is acted out as restitution for earlier pain. The same outcome can be viewed in behavioral terms. During the early years, a child learns how the males and females act in his immediate environment and, more importantly, he learns how the males and females interact with him. Specific persons are important models for the child's view of himself as a sexual being.

This chapter presents conceptual and technological information on a multifaceted behavioral approach to the treatment of exhibitionism. The social learning theory of the development of sexual behavior is used as a foundation for a comprehensive model for the description and modification of sexual behavior. Research on the treatment of exhibitionism will be discussed and the treatment literature assessed. A detailed case study of a multifaceted behavioral approach also is presented to display the formulation of a treatment program. Finally, problems typically encountered in dealing with exhibitionists are addressed.

A COMPREHENSIVE MODEL OF SEXUAL BEHAVIOR

Professionals have typically viewed a person displaying abnormal sexual behavior as having little more than deviant arousal to inappropriate behaviors or objects. The treatment implications of this view have been obvious and far-ranging. A treatment program is defined as successful by the absence of arousal in response to deviant behavior. The legal system is predicated on the notion that incarceration will be sufficiently punishing to decrease an individual's propensity for deviant behavior. Psychodynamic psychotherapy and early behavioral therapies also have concentrated on deviant behavior to the exclusion of other possible influences.

Barlow (1974) has proposed that sexual deviation consists of excesses and deficits in a number of areas. Problems in areas other than deviant arousal may be the most important targets for the therapist, and decreasing deviant arousal may play little part in the overall therapeutic picture (Brownell & Barlow, in press).

The tendency for therapists to attempt to eliminate deviant arousal has strong historical underpinnings. The Freudian view of heterosexual behavior as the natural outcome of healthy psychosexual functioning led to the theory that heterosexual behavior would take the place of deviant behavior if the inappropriate behavior could somehow be blocked. Gagnon and Simon (1973) point to this untested assumption, which is typified by Bond and Evans's (1967, p. 1162) claim that, "It is possible that if they can abstain from their deviant behavior for a sufficient period of time, normal outlets for the control of sexual arousal will develop." This hydraulic model of sexual functioning has two corollaries: heterosexual responsiveness will increase if deviant arousal is decreased, and deviant arousal will automatically diminish if heterosexual behavior can be increased. Little experimental evidence exists to support this view (Barlow, 1973; Brownell & Barlow, in press). In fact, recent evidence from controlled research has shown that deviant arousal and heterosexual arousal are not interdependent (Brownell, Hayes, & Barlow, 1977).

Sexual behavior can be conceptualized as consisting of four independent components (Barlow, 1974): deviant sexual arousal, appropriate sexual arousal, heterosocial skills, and gender role deviation. There may be excesses and deficits in any or all of these areas. A description of each area and the experimental evidence for treatment efficacy in each category follow.

Deviant Sexual Arousal

For exhibitionists, deviant arousal is sexual excitement in response to some aspect of exposing their genitals to an inappropriate person. Traditionally, aversion therapy has been used to reduce deviant arousal. Various aversion therapy procedures which have been used include peripheral electric shock (Feldman & MacCulloch, 1971), chemical aversion (McConaghy, 1969), covert sensitization (Brownell et al., 1977; Cautela, 1967), shame aversion (Serber, 1972; Wickramasekera, 1972), and olfactory aversion (Maletzky, 1973). Of these, electrical aversion and covert sensitization have been the most widely utilized (Barlow, 1973; Marks, 1976), although there is an impressive body of evidence supporting the use of covert sensitization assisted by olfactory aversion (see Chapter 8, this volume).

Electrical Aversion Therapy

In this form of therapy, painful electric shocks are paired with stimuli meant to elicit deviant arousal. It has been used in avoidance, escape, classical fear conditioning, and backward conditioning paradigms (Barlow, 1972). Stimuli have included verbal descriptions, written material, imagined situations, slides, audio tapes, and video tapes. Feldman and MacCulloch (1971) have reported the most impressive results using electrical aversion. Homosexual subjects were assigned to groups receiving electric shock in an anticipatory avoidance paradigm, shock in a classical conditioning paradigm, or traditional psychotherapy. At a one-year follow-up, 60 percent of the aversive conditioning subjects and only 20 percent of the subjects receiving traditional psychotherapy reported significant improvement. Feldman and MacCulloch (1965) achieved similar findings in an earlier study. Even though these studies suffered from the lack of objective measurement of sexual arousal, the improvement rate is impressive in light of reports from studies using traditional treatments, in which 10 to 30 percent of homosexuals showed reduced deviant arousal in the course of treatment (Bieber, Bieber, Dain, Dince, et al., 1963; Curran & Parr, 1957; Woodward, 1958).

Subsequent studies, using more objective measures of sexual arousal and a stricter definition of sexual-orientation change, have shown lower cure rates than Feldman and MacCulloch (1965; 1971). In these later studies, from 25 to 35 percent of subjects improved significantly (Birk, Huddleston, Miller, & Cohler, 1971; McConaghy, 1969; McConaghy & Barr, 1973).

Many of the early studies on sexual deviation used homosexual subjects who reportedly desired to change their sexual orientation. Some of the subjects, however, were referred from courts where shortened sentences were contingent on completion of a treatment program. More recently, as homosexual behavior has become more accepted by society, there have been fewer attempts to modify homosexual arousal and more attempts at helping a person—regardless of his or her sexual orientation—adopt the life-style that is most suitable for that individual (Wilson & Davison, 1974). Davison (1977) has gone so far as to suggest that merely treating a homosexual patient defines the homosexual behavior as abnormal. Homosexual behavior by definition is not pathological, and many homosexuals requesting change in sexual orientation are reacting to pressure from their environment. A homosexual life-style may therefore be appropriate for some persons. Even though the view of homosexual behavior has changed, early studies on the process of changing sexual arousal patterns in homosexual subjects are still informative.

Covert Sensitization

Cautela (1967) first used covert sensitization, in which aversive scenes are paired imaginally with deviant sexual stimuli, to reduce homosexual arousal. In two studies by Barlow and his colleagues, five homosexuals and one pedophile were successfully treated using covert sensitization: single-subject experimental methodology in these studies demonstrated that the aversion procedure was responsible for decreases in deviant arousal (Barlow, Agras, Leitenberg, Callahan, & Moore, 1972; Barlow, Leitenberg, & Agras, 1969). The specificity of covert sensitization has also been demonstrated in a series of studies on subjects with more than one pattern of deviant sexual behavior (Brownell & Barlow, 1976; Brownell et al., 1977; Hayes, Brownell, & Barlow, 1978). In these studies, a multiple baseline design was used to evaluate the successive application of covert sensitization to different sources of deviant arousal (for example, exhibitionism and sadism). Arousal to each deviation declined only when the scenes were paired with the stimuli specific to that deviation.

The only study to compare covert sensitization to electrical aversion was done by Callahan and Leitenberg (1973). In a within-subjects experimental design, two exhibitionists, one transvestite, two homosexuals, and one homosexual pedophile were given both treatments with the order of presentation counterbalanced across subjects. The treatments were equally effective on a physiological measure of sexual arousal, and covert sensitization was more effective for subjective measures of arousal.

Covert sensitization has been more consistently effective than electric shock in reducing deviant arousal, judging from series of case studies and from well controlled single-subject reports. However, there have been no large-scale trials with covert sensitization as there have been with electric shock (Feldman & MacCulloch, 1971). The relative efficacy of the two procedures has been tested only by Callahan and Leitenberg (1973), with the results favoring covert sensitization. There are several reasons that support the use of covert sensitization rather than electrical aversion. Covert sensitization does not require equipment and does not pose any physiological risk to the patient. The prevailing social climate discourages the use of aversive procedures in general, and electric shock in particular. Covert sensitization can be viewed as a self-control procedure (Brownell & Barlow, in press) which can be self-administered (Hayes et al., 1978).

Appropriate Sexual Arousal

The second component of sexual functioning is arousal in response to sexual stimuli considered appropriate by the patient. In most cases, patients consider heterosexual arousal to be appropriate for their life-style. Occasionally, however, they will consider themselves homosexual and wish to enhance their arousal to members of the same sex. If a thorough assessment shows that a person is indeed homosexual, and homosexual behavior is considered most pleasurable for that person, one of the goals of treatment can be to enhance homosexual arousal. In some states, this may place the therapist in legal jeopardy, particularly if homosexual interactions are prescribed as part of treatment. Caution is in order when dealing with this issue.

Early writings by both behavioral and psychoanalytic theorists proposed that the primary component in the development of deviant sexual behavior was fear of heterosexuality (Rado, 1949; Wolpe, 1973). In exhibitionism, for example, the deviant behavior was said to be a substitute for the heterosexual behavior that was blocked by disabling fear. Therefore, treatment consisted solely of reducing this fear. Recent evidence indicates that deviant and heterosexual behavior are independent of one another (Brownell et al., 1977), and the absence of heterosexual arousal is perhaps best attributed to the lack of early learning experiences that result in heterosexual behavior.

A variety of techniques are designed to increase heterosexual arousal. The three most thoroughly studied techniques—systematic desensitization, aversion relief, and orgasmic reconditioning—are discussed briefly here. For a more thorough discussion, see Barlow (1973).

Systematic Desensitization

Systematic desensitization (see Goldfried & Davison, 1976, for a description) has been used to treat sexual deviation because of findings from several studies that many homosexuals display strong negative emotional reactions toward heterosexual practices (Bieber et al., 1963; Ramsay & Van Velzen, 1968). The theory is that if these persons can be desensitized to their fear of heterosexual behavior, deviant behavior will be replaced by the preexisting heterosexuality. Fookes (1968) showed increases in heterosexual behavior in 7 exhibitionists, 5 transvestites, and 15 homosexuals by pairing heterosexual slides with relaxing music subsequent to electrical aversion. Obler (1973) found that systematic desensitization combined with assertion training was more effective than psychoanalytic group therapy for "severe sexual disorders."

Bancroft (1970) has made the only comparison of systematic desensitization and electrical aversion in his treatment of 30 homosexuals. Both treatments equally increased heterosexual arousal. Other case studies have shown desensitization to increase heterosexual responsiveness among exhibitionists (Wickramasekera, 1968) and homosexuals (Huff, 1970; Kraft, 1969; LoPiccolo, 1971).

Systematic desensitization has been effective in fear reduction for a number of clinical problems (O'Leary & Wilson, 1975). For patients with a fear of heterosexual interaction, desensitization may be valuable. There is no reason to suspect, however, that heterosexual arousal will increase if heterosexual anxiety is alleviated. The source of heterosexual anxiety is also important. If a conditioned fear is present, desensitization may be appropriate; however, many people may avoid interactions with the opposite sex because of a skills deficit (Curran, 1977). In these cases, direct training may be necessary.

Aversion Relief

Aversion relief involves pairing the termination of an aversive stimulus with an appropriate sexual stimulus. The presentation of a deviant sexual stimulus is followed by an electric shock, the termination of which is paired with a heterosexual stimulus. In one such study, electric shocks were paired with words describing deviant behavior that were projected on a screen (Thorpe, Schmidt, Brown, & Castell, 1964). The shocks were terminated when a heterosexual word, such as intercourse, appeared. According to self-report measures, heterosexual responsiveness increased somewhat; but, as with other case studies that have found aversion relief to be effective, the lack of objective measurement makes the results difficult to interpret (Gaupp, Stern, & Ratliff, 1971; Larson, 1970). These results are further complicated by the finding that heterosexual responsiveness sometimes increases when no direct attempt is made to increase it (Bancroft, 1970; Barlow et al., 1969; Gelder & Marks, 1969). In addition, several studies have found aversion relief to be ineffective in increasing heterosexual arousal (Abel, Levis, & Clancy, 1970; McConaghy, 1969; Solyom & Miller, 1965). There is no objective evidence that aversion relief increases heterosexual responsiveness (Barlow, 1973).

Orgasmic Reconditioning

Perhaps the most promising method of increasing heterosexual responsiveness is orgasmic reconditioning. It is based on the behavioral principles of fading, shaping, and reinforcement and is a direct method of facilitating arousal. This technique involves masturbation to deviant imagery, with a heterosexual image substituted just prior to orgasm. The heterosexual image is systematically substituted at an earlier stage of the masturbatory process until it becomes the sole content of the masturbatory imagery. Case studies have shown orgasmic reconditioning to be effective in increasing heterosexual responsiveness in patients seeking treatment for homosexuality (Annon, 1971; LoPiccolo, Stewart, & Watkins, 1972; Marquis, 1970), sadomasochism (Davison, 1968; Marquis, 1970; Mees, 1966), voyeurism (Jackson, 1969), pedophilia (Annon, 1971), vaginismus (Wilson, 1973), and several other deviations (Brownell et al., 1977; Marshall, 1973).

There has been only one attempt to evaluate orgasmic reconditioning in a controlled investigation. Conrad and Wincze (1976) used this procedure to increase heterosexual arousal in four male homosexuals. All subjects reported increases in heterosexual arousal, but behavioral and physiological measures did not show any change. A recent study by Kantorowitz (1978) evaluated orgasmic reconditioning for normal male volunteers. Once again the measures yielded results, but this time contrary to the findings of Conrad and Wincze (1976). In the Kantorowitz study, physiological measures showed change in preferences for specific heterosexual slides, whereas self-report measures revealed no changes.

The discrepancies among measures and studies argue for a thorough assessment of sexual functioning, including physiological, behavioral, and self-report measures. There is also evidence that *when* the appropriate stimuli are presented during the course of arousal may be a critical determinant of whether orgasmic reconditioning is successful in increasing arousal to those stimuli (Kantorowitz, 1978). It can be concluded, however, that the results from orgasmic reconditioning studies are generally favorable. Further investigation of this promising procedure may help to elucidate its active components.

Heterosocial Skills

The third component of sexual functioning is heterosocial skills. In any social situation, including interacting with the opposite sex, a variety of behaviors are necessary for successful performance. In asking for a date, for example, a person must judge the other's interest, make "small talk," determine the appropriate time to ask, be pleasant yet forthright, sound interested, and so forth. If any of these component behaviors are missing, heterosexual interactions could be very punishing. At each stage of a relationship, different skills are required. A deficit in any of these areas could make a person incapable of forming a heterosexual relationship even if high levels of heterosexual arousal are present. This is perhaps the most overlooked area in the treatment of sexual deviation. There are several reports of studies in which subjects have successfully increased heterosexual arousal, but have been unable to act on this new-found arousal due to deficits in social skills (Annon, 1971; Barlow & Agras, 1973; Herman, Barlow, & Agras, 1974).

Heterosocial anxiety occurs with great frequency (Martinson & Zerface, 1970). Because this anxiety may have reactive as well as conditioning components, careful assessment of each patient is necessary (Curran & Gilbert, 1975; Kanfer & Phillips, 1970). Systematic desensitization has been most frequently used for conditioned anxiety. In order to relieve reactive anxiety, a variety of techniques have been used including assertion training, behavioral rehearsal, and social skills training. Several studies have used skills training as one component of a treatment program for sexual deviation (Blitch & Haynes, 1972; Cautela & Wisocki, 1969; Edwards, 1972; Hanson & Adesso, 1972; Ovesey, Gaylin, & Hendin, 1963; Stevenson & Wolpe, 1960). Although the results from these reports have been encouraging, the effect of social skills training on sexual deviation has not been determined and a comprehensive treatment program designed specifically for this disorder has not been tested. However, a technology for teaching social skills to other populations has been developed, and may apply to patients with sexual deviation.

In a direct attempt to improve heterosocial skills in dating anxiety, Curran and Gilbert (1975) trained subjects in listening skills, techniques to deal with periods of silence, giving and receiving compliments, nonverbal methods of communication, and so forth. The treatment program involved homework assignments, social reinforcement, video-taped feedback, behavioral rehearsal, and assertion training. Detailed measurement showed that subjects receiving this training were more successful at improving heterosocial skills than control subjects. These results are consistent with results from studies in which subjects were taught assertion skills (McFall & Marston, 1970; McFall & Twentyman, 1973), and they indicate that heterosocial skills can indeed be learned.

Several investigators have developed comprehensive treatment regimens for social skills training and have found this treatment approach to be useful in psychiatric settings (Finch & Wallace, 1977; Goldsmith & McFall, 1975; Hersen & Bellack, 1976). In addition, there have been several well-controlled attempts to develop a technology for the assessment of social skills (Bellack, Hersen, & Turner, 1978; Curran, 1978). There are two excellent reviews of information on social skills training by Curran (1977) and Hersen and Eisler (1976).

Gender Role Deviation

The fourth component of sexual functioning—gender role, or gender identity—refers to behaviors, thoughts, and feelings about one's maleness or femaleness. In gender role deviation, opposite-sex role behaviors are present and there is a preference for the opposite sex role. Transsexualism, the most pronounced form of sex role deviation, is characterized by a person consistently feeling, acting, and believing as if he or she were of the opposite sex (Green & Money, 1969). Distinguishing characteristics of transsexuals are requests for sex reassignment surgery, persistent cross-dressing, and statements like, "I am a woman trapped in a man's body."

Patients with sexual deviation (for example, exhibitionism) as the major problem often will complain of some gender role deviation. Typically a patient will claim he has always wanted to be a woman or is convinced that life would be better if he were female, and therefore he requests sex-change surgery. There is a tendency among the misinformed to diagnose these persons as transsexuals or to dismiss their problems as unimportant. Either path has consequences for treatment. The ramifications of professionally labeling someone "transsexual" are enormous, as will be mentioned later. Dismissing gender role difficulties can lead to problems if a treatment program fails to deal with each aspect of sexual functioning. Gender role disturbance is present in some exhibitionists. Since most of the research on gender role deviation has been done on transsexuals, a brief review of this literature is pertinent.

Stoller (1969) has rejected the dichotomous view of gender identity as either male or female, and indicated that gender identity in most people lies on a continuum between completely male and completely female. One study of homosexual, transsexual, and heterosexual subjects found evidence for Stoller's position (Freund, Nagler, Langevin, Zajac, & Steiner, 1974). It is also important to note that gender role consists of many components including motor behavior, verbal behavior, and cognitions, and each lies on a male–female continuum for a given patient.

Most attempts to remedy gender role difficulties have been with transsexuals (Green, 1974; Stoller, 1969). The first studies approached the discrepancy between psychological and biological sex by aiming treatment at gender identity. For the most part, psychoanalytic and behavioral methods have not been successful (Gelder & Marks, 1969; Pauly, 1965), and the serious emotional hazards of attempting to change gender identity have been clearly documented (Money & Ehrhardt, 1973; Stoller, 1968). Therefore, the discrepancy was thought best solved by altering a person's biological sex to be consistent with his gender identity. The results from sex reassignment surgery have been much more favorable than the results from the other treatments cited, but sex change is a serious and irreversible procedure and needs to be undertaken with great caution (Green, 1974; Money & Ehrhardt, 1973; Stoller, 1968; 1969). Studies have shown how firmly entrenched gender identity problems can be; yet there are some reports of successful gender role change.

The first successful change of gender identity with behavioral methods was reported by Barlow, Reynolds, and Agras (1973). In this case study with a 17-year-old transsexual male, a massive, multifaceted treatment program was effective in modifying arousal patterns, motor behaviors, and social skills. In a more recent paper, Barlow, Abel, and Blanchard (in press) treated two additional transsexual subjects with behavioral techniques and found similarly encouraging findings even with long-term follow-up. There have also been successful attempts to alter gender role deviation in children (Green, Newman, & Stoller, 1972; Rekers & Lovaas, 1974; Rekers, Lovaas, & Low, 1974).

Gender role deviation needs to be thoroughly assessed in each patient requesting treatment for sexual deviation. In the few cases in which a patient is truly transsexual, referral should be made to a reputable clinic, preferably one where transsexuals are treated routinely. In cases where gender role behaviors can be modified, the behavioral approach has provided the best group of procedures (Barlow et al., in press; Barlow et al., 1973).

Implications for Treatment

In the treatment of exhibitionism, each of the four areas of sexual functioning must be evaluated for excesses and deficits. This is particularly important because many patients report only the most obvious difficulty (Bancroft, 1974). Failure to recognize a problem in any of these areas could lead to incomplete treatment programs which could be harmful. Increasing heterosexual arousal would be of little use, for example, if the requisite social skills were not present for the person to implement the arousal. Decreasing deviant arousal without insuring the presence of alternative sexual behaviors may be tantamount to leaving a person "sexless." The importance of thorough assessment before, during, and after a treatment program cannot be overemphasized.

One method of illustrating the multifaceted behavioral approach to the treatment of exhibitionism is by the use of case material. The following case study was reported in a series of treatment cases by Brownell et al. (1977); but is presented in greater detail here to demonstrate a comprehensive behavioral treatment program. The program included the assessment of each of the four areas of sexual functioning and subsequent treatment. Throughout the program, ongoing assessment was used to determine the effectiveness of the treatment procedures and to evaluate whether any new problems had risen.

CASE STUDY

The patient was a 22-year-old male college student seeking treatment after arrest for public indecency. He was attending college and working at a warehouse to finance his education. He was living with his wife-to-be, although his arrest was the source of great distress to his partner and she was contemplating terminating the relationship. The patient was arrested for exposing himself and masturbating in the presence of a college-age woman while in his car in a parking lot. It was his first arrest, even though he reported exposing himself many times previously. At the time of treatment, charges for the exposure incident had been dropped and the subject was under no legal contingencies to complete a treatment program. The patient also complained of being plagued by sadomasochistic fantasies and reported that his fiancé was rejecting his requests to engage in these practices during their sexual encounters.

Sexual History

The patient had a 10-year history of exhibitionist behavior and thoughts. The first incident occurred at age 12 when he was standing naked in front of the picture window of his home. He had an erection but "didn't know what to do with it." He claimed that he "tucked it between his legs" and walked around the room. He noticed his reflection in a mirror and said it looked like he "had a cunt." As he walked around, he became aroused and ejaculated. Subsequently he aroused himself in this fashion many times. This behavior lasted for approximately two years, during which time seeing the reflection of himself with his penis tucked between his legs was critical to his arousal.

At age 14, the patient reported masturbating in the window when he heard girls' voices. He became intensely aroused and ejaculated even without seeing the girls. Thereafter, he waited for females to be walking by on the street and would masturbate while partially exposed at the window. He reported that no one saw him during these incidents. The presence of females on the street replaced the reflection in the mirror as the necessary component of arousal.

For the next several years, he claimed that "just seeing girls from the window wasn't good enough." He began to venture out of the house to masturbate in their presence. When a girl walked by, he would hide behind a stone wall, a tree, or bushes and disrobe and masturbate. He began getting closer to the females and claimed to be "very brash about it." He reported that there were only a few incidents at this time in which the girls actually saw him. In one such incident, the girl walked toward him. He was startled and ran away. The patient also reported that one time two girls saw him masturbating and throughout the remainder of the summer they walked by his house frequently to see him "jerk off." On another occasion, he claimed that he ran into the street behind two girls who were walking by and began to masturbate while only a few feet away. He stated, however, that they had no reaction.

During the summer, the patient masturbated while exposed "thousands of times," because girls passed his home on their way to a beach. In the winter he would "pull his hair out" and increase the frequency of masturbation to offset the lack of passers-by. He masturbated on the average of 5 times per day, but would masturbate as many as 10 times per day if he had been unable to masturbate the previous day. In later years, the frequency of masturbation increased to a maximum of 12 times per day. He reported that his orgasms from masturbation were very rapid and intense. He masturbated with his penis between his legs until the age of 20, at which time he learned to manipulate himself with his hands.

The patient reported needing to get closer and closer to females in order to become aroused. He stated that "it was a game with me" and he had to "see how close I could get to the chicks without them noticing me." At this point he began to expose himself so that the females would see him. He enjoyed the reactions he got. Prior to his arrest, the patient had been exposing himself frequently in a parking lot near his university. He would sit in his car and then get out, expose himself, and masturbate when he saw an attractive female. If the females were with a male, or if a male was nearby, the patient would become intensely angry at the male and fantasize killing him. Sexual arousal did not occur in these cases.

The patient's arrest occurred in the parking lot. As an attractive female drove by, he left his car, pulled down his pants, and masturbated as she drove by. He returned to his car and masturbated, hoping that she would return. She did return—with the state police. He was then arrested.

The patient reported feeling physiologically different during exposure incidents than during other times of sexual arousal. While exposing himself, he had difficulty breathing, felt weak all over, experienced palpitations, and had shaky hands. His orgasms during these incidents, however, were very quick and intense.

Further assessment revealed an 8-year history of sadomasochistic fantasies and a 3-year history of actual sadomasochistic behavior. The patient first recalled having sadomasochistic fantasies during masturbation, when he would become extremely aroused at fantasizing a female "walking on my balls." The degree of pain he imagined increased over time until he fantasized a female stepping on his testicles, kicking him in the crotch, and finally castrating him. At one point, he reported fantasizing a female biting off his penis and cutting out his abdominal organs with knives. For the three years prior to his arrest, the patient had requested that his girlfriend squeeze his testicles very hard as he approached orgasm. He feared that she would cease to comply with his demands for this behavior and might wish to terminate the relationship because he was "weird." He also wished to eliminate the deviant fantasies because he thought they were pathological, and he wished to fantasize more traditional sexual practices.

The patient's heterosexual experiences had been conventional, although he started at a late age. He had never had social or sexual contact with females until he met his wife-to-be when he was a sophomore in college. At the point of his arrest, they had been together for nearly three years and had been sleeping together for most of that time. The sexual relationship between the patient and his girlfriend proceeded from kissing to petting to intercourse. In the early stages of the relationship, intercourse occurred an average of five times per week. This had declined to one to three times per week at the time of his arrest. The patient had not revealed his sadomasochistic fantasies to his girlfriend, nor had she been informed of his history of exhibitionism until his arrest. She was reportedly distressed by his arrest, but did not alter her plans to marry him.

Assessment

A detailed assessment of each component of the patient's social and sexual functioning was undertaken to determine which intervention strategies should be used.

Deviant Arousal

The patient's exhibitionistic arousal was assessed with two self-report measures. Physiological measurement of sexual arousal was of the utmost importance, and would ordinarily have been taken routinely; however, during the treatment of this patient, problems with laboratory equipment prevented this. Since there is evidence that physiological and self-report measures are correlated (Brownell et al., 1977), the self-report measures reported here were assumed to reflect arousal patterns adequately.

The Card Sort measure (Barlow et al., 1969) was used to assess deviant and heterosexual arousal. Scenes depicting heterosexual and deviant sexual situations were prepared and typed on individual index cards. An example of an exhibitionistic scene was

> I am looking out my apartment window and see a good-looking girl coming my way. I pull down my pants and begin to jerk off. As she comes closer, I get more excited. She looks up and sees me. She has a frightened look on her face.

Five separate scenes were prepared for each category of deviant arousal and heterosexual arousal. The patient was instructed to secure a vivid image of the scene and to rate the degree of his sexual arousal from 0 to 4 (0 = no arousal, 1 = little arousal, 2 = fair amount of arousal, 3 = much arousal, 4 = very much arousal). The Card Sort was administered twice daily during a base-line and treatment phase, weekly during the initial stages of follow-up, and monthly thereafter.

The patient was also instructed to complete a self-monitoring form for urges and fantasies. He carried a notebook in which there were spaces for deviant and heterosexual urges. An urge was defined as a thought, image, or fantasy of a given sexual behavior regardless of whether it occurred in the presence of an arousing object. The number of urges daily was used as a measure of deviant and appropriate thoughts.

Since the patient had sadomasochistic thoughts and behaviors, this source of deviant arousal was measured with both the Card Sort and the record of urges. A sadomasochistic scene from the Card Sort was

> I am walking through the woods and see a nice woman. She makes me kneel down in front of her, then she kicks my balls. When I fall down she starts to step on my balls and then starts to bite my prick. She bites so hard that she bites it off.

The two self-report measures revealed that the subject had high levels of arousal for both exhibitionistic and sadomasochistic behaviors. The Card Sort showed approximately 80 percent maximum arousal for exhibitionistic scenes and 85 percent arousal for sadomasochistic scenes. The patient averaged nine exhibitionistic urges and eight sadomasochistic urges each day. The measures showed stable levels of arousal and urges during a base-line period. This high level of arousal indicated that both types of deviant arousal were important to measure and modify.

Heterosexual Arousal

The patient's heterosexual arousal was assessed with the same self-report measures as for deviant arousal. A typical heterosexual scene from the Card Sort was

> Sharon and I are on the couch kissing. I begin to feel her tits and she puts her hand on my hard prick. She then lays back and we fuck like crazy.

Notice that the Card Sort scenes were in the patient's own words to closely approximate the internal monologue used by the patient to narrate sexual scenes. Base-line measures for the Card Sort revealed approximately 100 percent maximum arousal. The patient averaged eight heterosexual urges each day. The patient reported feeling satisfied with his heterosexual behavior, and the measures substantiated his reported high levels of arousal. Ongoing measurement of heterosexual behavior during treatment was necessary, but direct modification of heterosexual arousal was not deemed necessary at this point.

Heterosocial Skills

The patient reported being capable of performing socially and sexually with his main source of heterosexual contact—his girlfriend. His sexual performances had been adequate (no evidence of premature ejaculation or impotence) both by his report and by his girlfriend's report. To evaluate the patient's performance in social situations, three role-played scenes were video taped in which the patient interacted with a female confederate in a dating-type situation. The tapes were then scored. The patient had no difficulty in these situations, and the tapes revealed adequate performance. Direct training in heterosocial skills did not appear necessary.

The patient complained of having difficulty interacting with other males. He spoke of feelings of inferiority, suspicions that other males were making light of his shortcomings, intense anger reactions, and aggressive behaviors. Assessment revealed that self-defeating cognitions were responsible for the feelings (Ellis & Harper, 1961; Lazarus & Fay, 1975). Because of these problems, the patient was having difficulty interacting with his fellow employees at work and with his fellow students and professors at school. Direct intervention aimed at improving the patient's cognitive style was necessary.

Gender Role Deviation

There was no history of cross-sex behaviors or thoughts in the patient. He scored appropriately on a scale for measuring male and female motor behaviors while sitting, standing, and walking (Barlow et al., 1977). The patient also was administered the Freund Transsexualism Scale (Freund et al., 1974) and displayed a masculine gender identity. It appeared, therefore, that he did not have difficulties in this area.

Treatment Program

The assessment of this patient's sexual and social behaviors led to three treatment goals: a decrease in exhibitionistic arousal and behavior; a decrease in sadomasochistic arousal and behavior; and improved cognitive behavior. In addition, heterosexual behavior and arousal were to be measured during treatment to make certain that they remained at high levels. This assessment of the different areas of sexual and social functioning characterizes the multifaceted behavioral approach to the treatment of sexual deviation. The treatment program necessarily consists of a number of procedures aimed at remedying excesses and deficits in particular problem areas.

Behavior therapy involves the explicit description of treatment goals and procedures. Treatment therefore is individually oriented, and therapy is viewed as an experiment of $N = 1$ (O'Leary & Wilson, 1975). Single-subject experimental methodology (Hersen & Barlow, 1976) is especially well suited to treatment cases of this type, and it allows rigorous evaluation of treatment procedures. In the present case, a multiple base-line across behaviors (arousal patterns) was used to evaluate the effectiveness of specific interventions and to determine the interrelationship between two different patterns of deviant arousal, and between deviant arousal and heterosexual arousal. With this design, intervention techniques were applied sequentially to each behavior (arousal pattern), while base-line measures were continued on the remaining behaviors.

Since exhibitionism was the patient's presenting complaint and his lack of control over this behavior had led to his arrest, decreasing this arousal was the most immediate concern. The order of treatment modalities was (1) decreasing exhibitionistic arousal, (2) decreasing sadomasochistic arousal, and (3) cognitive intervention.

Covert Sensitization for Exhibitionism

As mentioned previously in this chapter, the two techniques for reducing deviant arousal that have received the most attention have been electrical aversion and covert sensitization. In the only study to compare the two techniques, covert sensitization was more encouraging for self-report measures and the two procedures were equally effective for physiological measures (Callahan & Leitenberg, 1973). Since covert sensitization is also more likely to be viewed favorably by the public and it can be used within a self-control framework, it was chosen as the treatment for reducing deviant arousal in this case.

Covert sensitization was first applied to the exhibitionistic arousal patterns while base-line measures continued for sadomasochistic and heterosexual arousal. For the procedure, the five Card Sort scenes were presented in random order, with an aversive image following each presentation. Each scene was presented for approximately three minutes, with a 60-second intertrial interval. The patient constructed three aversive images to be used in the procedure. The images were aversive specifically to him and fell into two categories: realistic consequences of the deviant behavior (for example, arrest, humiliation, imprisonment, loss of love); or less realistic but aversive scenes (vomiting, burning) typical of most covert sensitization studies (Cautela, 1967). Prior to each session, the patient visualized each of the aversive scenes and selected the most aversive. This scene was then used for the session.

During treatment, the patient initially was seen twice weekly, and then weekly thereafter. He was instructed to self-administer the covert sensitization at least twice daily between sessions and was given a recording sheet to note each occurrence of a self-administered trial. During the initial sessions, the therapist administered the procedure. Later the patient administered the procedure in the presence of the therapist so that feedback could be given for use in the sessions to be done at home. An example of a therapist-administered trial follows. The patient was instructed to relax, close his eyes, and attempt to secure a vivid image of the scene being presented.

> *You are driving by the college and you get an urge to go to the parking lot. You drive by the lot and begin thinking of how arousing it is to expose yourself. You pull into the parking lot and stop. You get excited just thinking about it and start to play with yourself through your pants. Then you see a beautiful girl driving her car into the lot. You look around and nobody else is there. As she gets closer, you get harder and harder. You step out of your car as she drives by. As she turns to drive back, you pull down your pants and start to jerk off. It feels wonderful. She sees you now and looks very frightened.*
>
> *And then you hear another car! It is the state police! You feel scared and want to run but you can't move. The police car screeches to a halt in front of you. They jump out and throw you up against the car. They start to laugh at you and tell you that you will go to jail. As they are putting you in the police car, Sharon drives up and sees what you have done. She begins crying and gets hysterical. She says it is all over and that she will never see you again. You know you will lose her, your job, your school—everything. You feel empty, like there is nothing left.*

With this patient, it was apparent that the scenes were actually being imagined, and that the aversive scenes were effective. During the aversive scenes, the patient clutched the arms of his chair, tensed his facial muscles, and occasionally cried. He reported that the scenes were very powerful. It is interesting that he reported the realistic scenes to be more aversive than scenes such as vomiting. Designing a behavioral program of this nature requires a great deal of clinical skill, and the procedures cannot be administered in a mechanical or whimsical fashion. For a more detailed description of how to implement covert sensitization, see Brownell and Barlow (in press).

During covert sensitization for exhibitionism, arousal and urges decreased dramatically (See Figure 1). On the Card Sort measure, arousal for exhibitionistic scenes dropped to approximately 20 percent of maximum after three sessions of covert sensitization, and declined to zero after nine sessions. The frequency of urges declined steadily until they reached zero after 14 sessions of covert sensitization. During this period, the patient reported being "turned off" to exhibitionism because of the aversive images that followed any thoughts or urges he had.

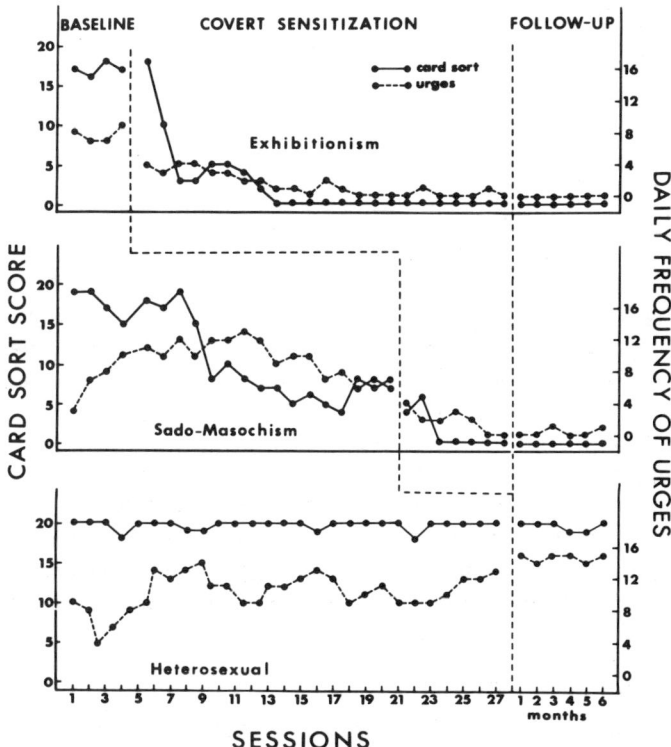

Figure 1. Card Sort ratings of sexual arousal in response to deviant and heterosexual stimuli and daily frequency of sexual urges. Card Sort ratings were averaged to yield a session score, and the number of urges represents a daily average. (From Brownell et al., 1977. Copyright 1977 by the American Psychological Association. Reprinted by permission.)

During covert sensitization for exhibitionism, sadomasochistic urges increased somewhat, and the Card Sort measure of sadomasochistic arousal declined to approximately 50 percent of maximum. Since the multiple base-line design was used, the effect of the intervention on an arousal pattern to which it had not been applied (sadomasochism) could be tested. Even though arousal in this category decreased, it remained at approximately 50 percent of maximum, thus indicating the need for direct intervention. Heterosexual arousal stayed at the maximum level and the frequency of urges increased to approximately 13 per day.

Covert Sensitization for Sadomasochism

At this point, covert sensitization was applied to sadomasochistic arousal patterns. Covert sensitization continued for the exhibitionism scenes and was also applied to the Card Sort scenes for sadomasochism. Figure 1 indicates that arousal to sadomasochistic scenes fell to zero after three sessions of covert sensitization, and the frequency of urges fell to zero after five sessions. At the same time, exhibitionistic arousal remained low and heterosexual arousal remained high.

It was evident that covert sensitization did not reduce deviant arousal completely until it was specifically applied to a given set of arousal patterns. In addition, heterosexual behavior did not change as a function of changes in deviant arousal. These findings are consistent with the other cases reported by Brownell et al. (1977), and they suggest that various patterns of sexual arousal exist independently and require individual assessment and intervention.

After the treatment program, the patient was seen for monthly meetings during a six-month follow-up phase. Reductions in exhibitionism and sadomasochism arousal were maintained, as were high levels of heterosexual arousal.

Cognitive Restructuring

During the final stages of the treatment program, cognitive restructuring was used to improve the patient's view of himself and to teach him to react more adaptively to his interactions with others. The patient was given a recording sheet to monitor his self-deprecating statements and the antecedent events. He was then given self-help books by Lazarus and Fay (1975) and Ellis and Harper (1961). He was taught to analyze the situations in which his self-statements were negative and to combat them with more realistic statements. The frequency of inappropriate self-statements decreased and the patient reported being more comfortable in social situations.

Approximately one year after the final follow-up session, the patient mailed a letter to the therapist saying that he was very happy with his life because he was no longer plagued by urges to engage in deviant behavior. He claimed that the cognitive restructuring was most useful because it had changed his way of viewing his own behavior, and he was no longer prone to prolonged bouts of insecurity.

The assessment of all components of a patient's behavior patterns is a very important issue, and a great deal of excellent research has been done on the assessment of sexual behavior. (See Chapter 13 of this book for a comprehensive view of the methods of assessment.) Specific treatment techniques are chosen not because of a diagnostic label applied to the patient, but according to the patient's specific functioning in discrete areas of sexual behavior. The assumption is not made, for example, that the exhibitionist has inadequate heterosexual arousal or, for that matter, has adequate arousal. Only after assessment of his arousal is a treatment plan devised.

CLINICAL ISSUES

Treating patients in a clinical setting is seldom as easy as it appears from reading case studies. Problems invariably arise and, unfortunately, little is written about how to deal with these problems. In the treatment of exhibitionism, the therapist is likely to encounter idiosyncratic problems. A brief outline of these problems, adapted from Brownell and Barlow (in press), is presented next. More information can be found in the original material.

Desire to Change

One sees vastly different degrees of motivation for change in treatment programs for exhibitionists. Even patients with the same degree of motivation may have different reasons for their motivation. Some patients are forced into treatment by the legal system and have little desire to change a pattern of behavior that is pleasurable to them. These patients may attempt to simulate improvement to produce a favorable disposition from the courts. Others may have been so severely punished for their behavior, or may feel so genuinely guilty, that they desire an end to the urges that plague them.

It is generally assumed that motivation to change is a significant factor in therapy. This, of course, is true of behavior therapy as well as of other therapies. Contrary to public opinion, conditioning and behavior change are not automatic processes that occur without the awareness and willingness of a patient (Bandura, 1974). Many behavioral programs fail when the goals of the patient and the goals of the therapist are discrepant. In these cases, counter-control can develop and little may be accomplished (Davison, 1973). Therefore, lack of motivation may indicate that a patient will profit very little from treatment.

This problem is particularly important in cases where intense legal or social pressures are influencing a patient. Courts often require psychotherapy for exhibitionists. It is not difficult for patients to discover that the therapist's report may determine the severity with which the court will punish their behavior. Significant others may also apply pressure for treatment, especially upon discovering the deviant behavior. In these cases, many patients enter treatment as a display of motivation to the relevant public. Some therapists refuse to treat exhibitionists until the legal sanctions are removed and they are convinced that the patient has a genuine desire to change. This is not easy to determine, however. It is worthwhile to devote time to this issue when first assessing a new patient.

Morality of Deviant Behavior

Many patients do not share society's view of their behavior as deviant. Most are aware that they face legal and social sanctions for their behavior, but do not feel they have committed a moral offense against their victims. Exhibitionists sometimes construct elaborate cognitive systems in which they not only view their behavior as harmless, but feel they are actually aiding the victim in sexual growth. One patient treated by the author was asked what effect his exposure incidents had on the victims. His response was, "The human body is beautiful, and our society is wrong in covering it up. There are many cultures where the body is freely displayed. We wouldn't have sexual hang-ups if we weren't so afraid of the body. The people who see me are not so likely to have hang-ups. They really like it, they just act afraid because they are surprised."

Patients do not part with these beliefs easily. It is important, however, to change these cognitions at some point during treatment. Direct confrontation can be useful in some cases, but repeated attacks on the false beliefs are usually necessary before change can occur. Some patients develop additional motivation to alter their deviant behavior if they know that exhibitionism can be damaging to the victims.

False Suppression of Arousal

In many patients, a false sense of security accompanies entry into a treatment program. Even before treatment begins, a patient may argue that the deviant arousal is under control and there is no chance that it will reoccur. Patients may actually believe this: such punishing legal and social events may have transpired as a result of arrest that they are certain they would never be foolish enough to repeat the act. The strength of these aversive events fades with time, however, and there is a high probability that the behavior will return. Life-long patterns of sexual arousal are not likely to be "scared out" of someone. It is important to confront the patient with this information and to avoid using the patient's self-report as an indication of clinical improvement.

Self-Control Approach

There is evidence from the literature on behavioral treatment that self-controlled behavior change strategies are more effective in promoting change than interventions imposed by an external agent (Bandura, 1977b; Brownell, Colletti, Ersner-Hershfield, Hershfield, & Wilson, 1976). I typically present treatment procedures within a self-efficacy framework (Bandura, 1977b). This approach can also be useful in dealing with sexual deviation. For covert sensitization, the patient is taught to self-administer the procedure in the presence of the therapist, and then told to practice it at home. In some cases, a tape-recorded session can be used at home for this purpose. Each patient is also taught to use the covert process as a coping strategy. If a deviant urge presents itself, the patient is to summon one of the aversive images used for covert sensitization. This strategy shows the patient that the procedure can be useful even if deviant urges continue to exist. Controlled research has to be done to see whether self-administered covert sensitization is as effective when the same procedure is administered totally by the therapist, yet one report argues for self-administration (Hayes et al., 1978).

FUTURE DIRECTIONS FOR RESEARCH

The treatment of sexual deviation must be undertaken with consideration of a number of components of sexual functioning. The multifaceted approach has brought a number of new behavior patterns within the realm of behavioral quantification and modification. For example, there is extensive literature on the treatment of social skills deficits (Curran, 1977; Hersen & Eisler, 1976), yet few researchers have used these principles for the treatment of sexual deviation. In cases where heterosexual arousal may be present, a lack of social skills could make the person incapable of developing a heterosexual relationship. This is but one example of the complexity of sexual and social behavior. Research has only begun to discover effective treatment for problems in these different areas. Some of the issues that merit further investigation follow.

1. Methods of motivating patients who are not interested in changing deviant behavior would be very useful. This may be particularly relevant for practitioners in prison settings. The first logical step in this direction would be the assessment of motivation to change. Little work has been done in this area.
2. Alternative methods for the reduction of deviant sexual arousal are necessary. Covert sensitization appears to be effective in many cases (Brownell et al., 1977) but there are patients for whom imagery procedures are ineffective. Aversive procedures have been the most thoroughly studied, but other approaches may also be useful.
3. Cognitive interventions hold new promise for a comprehensive treatment program for the exhibitionist. Inappropriate cognitions frequently impede treatment, and the successful restructuring of a person's cognitive system may become an important step in the treatment plan.
4. A more detailed understanding of the interaction between physiological and emotional arousal would also be of great importance. It is not known, for example, whether physiological arousal serves as a cue for sexual thoughts, or whether physiological arousal follows cognitive events. The measurement of cognitive arousal will be a critical ingredient in this type of research. Some very promising work has been done by Wincze, Hoon, and Hoon (1977) using a continuous measure of subjective arousal.
5. The specific components of social skills and gender role

behaviors must be elucidated before specific treatment strategies can be developed. This would include work on verbal, motor, and cognitive behaviors.
6. A fascinating area of research is the study of sexual fantasies and their relationship to sexual behavior. Stoller (1975) suggests that the sexual fantasy reveals the psychological trauma that is responsible for the deviant behavior. Fantasies are also quite useful in formulating a behavioral treatment program because they show the idiosyncratic factors that arouse a patient. Part of the assessment program for sexual deviation consists of having the patient write a detailed account of his most arousing masturbatory fantasies. It is possible that fantasy material could be used to predict treatment outcome or to determine the treatment procedures to use for a specific patient.

SUMMARY

The treatment of sexual deviation is a difficult and complex process. Sexual behavior consists of at least four components: deviant arousal, heterosexual arousal, heterosocial skills, and gender role behaviors. Each area must be assessed to formulate a complete picture of the patient's difficulties. Each of the four areas may influence the other areas; yet the components may exist independently. Deficits and excesses in each area can be critical determinants of a patient's progress in treatment and thus cannot be ignored. This is contrary to the tendency to concentrate only on deviant sexual arousal.

Sexual behavior does not occur in a social vacuum (Brownell & Barlow, in press). Many environmental, interpersonal, and cognitive factors operate on a person with sexual problems. Deviant behavior may be overtly or covertly reinforced by family members or friends. Evaluation of this factor by interviewing significant others may be helpful. Consideration of the legal contingencies may also help to get a clear picture of the variables affecting a patient's behavior.

One of the foremost characteristics of the behavioral approach is the emphasis on evaluation of all treatment interventions (O'Leary & Wilson, 1975). This emphasis has eliminated the need for uncontrolled case studies for the dissemination of information on treatment techniques. Single-subject experimental methodology has increased the researcher's ability to test therapeutic techniques (Hersen & Barlow, 1976). The case study presented in this chapter is an example of an attempt to evaluate treatment techniques rigorously within the limits imposed by the clinical realities of a treatment program. Conceptualizing clinical practice as a series of experiments using one subject allows for a scientific approach to therapy.

REFERENCES

Abel, G., Levis, D., & Clancy, J. Aversion therapy applied to taped sequences of deviant behavior in exhibitionism and other sexual deviations: A preliminary report. *Journal of Behavior Therapy and Experimental Psychiatry,* 1970, *1,* 59–60.

Annon, J. S. The extension of learning principles to the analysis and treatment of sexual problems. *Dissertation Abstracts International,* 1971, *32*(6-B), 3627.

Bancroft, J. A comparative study of aversion and desensitization in the treatment of homosexuality. In L. E. Burns & J. L. Worsley (Eds.), *Behavior therapy in the 1970s.* Wright: Bristol, England, 1970.

Bancroft, J. *Deviant sexual behaviour: Modification and assessment.* Oxford: Clarendon Press, 1974.

Bandura, A. *Principles of behavior modification.* New York: Holt, Rinehart & Winston, 1969.

Bandura, A. *Social learning theory.* Englewood Cliffs, N. J.: Prentice-Hall, 1977(a).

Bandura, A. Self-efficacy: Toward a unifying theory of behavioral change. *Psychological Review,* 1977(b), *84,* 191–215.

Barlow, D. H. Aversive procedures. In W. S. Agras (Ed.), *Behavior modification: Principles and clinical applications.* Boston: Little Brown, 1972.

Barlow, D. H. Increasing heterosexual responsiveness in the treatment of sexual deviation. *Behavior Therapy,* 1973, *4,* 655–671.

Barlow, D. H. The treatment of sexual deviation: Towards a comprehensive behavioral approach. In K. S. Calhoun, H. E. Adams, & K. M. Mitchell (Eds.), *Innovative treatment methods in psychopathology.* New York: Wiley, 1974.

Barlow, D. H., Abel, G. G., & Blanchard, E. B. Gender identity change in transsexuals: Follow-up and replication. *Archives of General Psychiatry,* in press.

Barlow, D. H., & Agras, W. S. Fading to increase heterosexual responsiveness in homosexuals. *Journal of Applied Behavior Analysis,* 1973, *6,* 355–366.

Barlow, D. H., Agras, W. S., Leitenberg, H., Callahan, E. J., & Moore, R. C. The contribution of therapeutic instruction to covert sensitization. *Behaviour Research and Therapy,* 1972, *10,* 411–415.

Barlow, D. H., Leitenberg, H., & Agras, W. S. The experimental control of sexual deviation through manipulation of the noxious scene in covert sensitization. *Journal of Abnormal Psychology,* 1969, *74,* 596–601.

Barlow, D. H., Reynolds, E. S., & Agras, W. S. Gender identity change in a transsexual. *Archives of General Psychiatry,* 1973, *28,* 569–576.

Bellack, A. S., Hersen, M., & Turner, S. M. Role-play tests for assessing social skills: Are they valid? *Behavior Therapy,* 1978, *9,* 448–461.

Bieber, B., Bieber, I., Dain, H. J., Dince, P. R., Drellich, M. G., Grand, H. G., Grundlach, R. H., Kremer, M. W., Wilbur, C. B., & Bieber, T. D. *Homosexuality.* New York: Basic Books, 1963.

Birk, L., Huddleston, W., Miller, E., & Cohler, B. Avoidance conditioning for homosexuality. *Archives of General Psychiatry,* 1971, *25,* 314–323.

Blitch, J. W., & Haynes, S. N. Multiple behavioral techniques in a case of female homosexuality. *Journal of Behavior Therapy and Experimental Psychiatry,* 1972, *3,* 319–322.

Bond, I. K., & Evans, D. R. Avoidance therapy: Its use in two cases of underwear fetishism. *Canadian Medical Association Journal,* 1967, *96,* 1160–1162.

Brownell, K. D., & Barlow, D. H. Measurement and treatment of two sexual deviations in one person. *Journal of Behavior Therapy and Experimental Psychiatry,* 1976, *7,* 349–354.

Brownell, K. D., & Barlow, D. H. The behavioral treatment of sexual deviation. In A. Goldstein & E. Foa (Eds.), *The handbook of behavioral interventions.* New York: Wiley, in press.

Brownell, K. D., Colletti, G., Ersner-Hershfield, R., Hershfield, S. M., & Wilson, G. T. Self-control in school children: Stringency and leniency in self-determined and externally imposed performance standards. *Behavior Therapy,* 1977, *8,* 442–455.

Brownell, K. D., Hayes, S. C., & Barlow, D. H. Appropriate and deviant patterns of sexual arousal: The behavioral treatment of multiple sexual deviations. *Journal of Consulting and Clinical Psychology,* 1977, *45,* 1144–1155.

Callahan, E. A., & Leitenberg, H. Aversion therapy for sexual deviation: Contingent shock and covert sensitization. *Journal of Abnormal Psychology,* 1973, *81,* 60–73.

Cautela, J. R. Covert sensitization. *Psychological Reports,* 1967, *20,* 459–468.

Cautela, J. R., & Wisocki, P. A. The use of male and female therapists in the treatment of homosexual behavior. In R. Rubin and C. Franks (Eds.), *Advances in behavior therapy, 1968.* New York: Academic Press, 1969.

Conrad, S. R., & Wincze, J. P. Orgasmic reconditioning: A controlled study of its effects upon the sexual arousal and behavior of adult male homosexuals. *Behavior Therapy,* 1976, 7, 155–166.

Curran, D., & Parr, D. Homosexuality: An analysis of 100 male cases seen in private practice. *British Medical Journal,* 1957, 1, 797–801.

Curran, J. P. Skills training as an approach to the treatment of heterosexual-social anxiety. *Psychological Bulletin,* 1977, 84, 140–157.

Curran, J. P. Comments on Bellack, Hersen, and Turner's paper on the validity of role-play test. *Behavior Therapy,* 1978, 9, 462–468.

Curran, J. P., & Gilbert, F. S. A test of the relative effectiveness of a systematic desensitization program and interpersonal skills training program with date-anxious subjects. *Behavior Therapy,* 1975, 6, 510–521.

Davison, G. C. Elimination of a sadistic fantasy by a client-controlled counter-conditioning technique: A case study. *Journal of Abnormal Psychology,* 1968, 73, 84–90.

Davison, G. C. Counter-control in behavior modification. In L. A. Hamerlynck, L. C. Handy, & E. J. Mash (Eds.), *Behavior change methodology, concepts, and practice.* Champaign, Ill.: Research Press, 1973.

Davison, G. C. Homosexuality: The ethical challenge. *Journal of Consulting and Clinical Psychology,* 1977, 44, 157–162.

Edwards, N. B. Case conference: Assertive training in a case of homosexual pedophilia. *Journal of Behavior Therapy and Experimental Psychiatry,* 1972, 3, 55–63.

Ellis, A., & Harper, R. A. *A guide to rational living.* Hollywood, Ca.: Wilshire, 1961.

Ellis, H. *Studies in the psychology of sex.* Philadelphia: Davis, 1927.

Feldman, M. P., & MacCulloch, M. J. The application of anticipatory avoidance learning to the treatment of homosexuality: Theory, technique, and preliminary results. *Behaviour Research and Therapy,* 1965, 2, 165–183.

Feldman, M. P., & MacCulloch, M. J. *Homosexual behavior: Therapy and assessment.* Oxford: Pergamon Press, 1971.

Finch, B. E., & Wallace, C. J. Successful interpersonal skills training with schizophrenic inpatients. *Journal of Consulting and Clinical Psychology,* 1977, 45, 885–890.

Fookes, B. H. Some experiences in the use of aversion therapy in male homosexuality, exhibitionism, and fetishism-transvestism. *British Journal of Psychiatry,* 1968, 115, 339–341.

Freund, K., Nagler, E., Langevin, R., Zajac, A., & Stiner, B. Measuring feminine gender identity in homosexual males. *Archives of Sexual Behavior,* 1974, *3,* 249–261.

Gaupp, L. A., Stern, R. M., & Ratliff, R. G. The use of aversion-relief procedures in the treatment of a case of voyeurism. *Behavior Therapy,* 1971, *2,* 585–588.

Gelder, M. G., & Marks, I. M. Aversion treatment in transvestism and transsexualism. In R. Green & J. Money (Eds.), *Transsexualism and sex reassignment.* Baltimore: Johns Hopkins Press, 1969, pp. 383–417.

Goldfried, M. R., & Davison, G. C. *Clinical behavior therapy.* New York: Holt, Rinehart & Winston, 1976.

Goldsmith, J. B., & McFall, R. M. Development and evaluation of an interpersonal skill-training program for psychiatric inpatients. *Journal of Abnormal Psychology,* 1975, *84,* 51–58.

Green, R. *Sexual identity conflict in children and adults.* New York: Basic Books, 1974.

Green, R., & Money, J. *Transsexualism and sex reassignment.* Baltimore: Johns Hopkins Press, 1969.

Green, R., Newman, L. E., & Stoller, R. J. Treatment of boyhood transsexualism. *Archives of General Psychiatry,* 1972, *26,* 213–217.

Hanson, R. W., & Adesso, V. J. A multiple behavioral approach to male homosexual behavior: A case study. *Journal of Behavior Therapy and Experimental Psychiatry,* 1972, *3,* 323–325.

Hayes, S. C., Brownell, K. D., & Barlow, D. H. The use of self-administered covert sensitization in the treatment of exhibitionism and sadism. *Behavior Therapy,* 1978, *9,* 283–289.

Herman, S. H., Barlow, D. H., & Agras, W. S. An experimental analysis of classical conditioning as a method of increasing heterosexual arousal in homosexuals. *Behavior Therapy,* 1974, *5,* 33–47.

Hersen, M., & Barlow, D. H. *Single case experimental design: Strategies for studying behavior change.* New York: Pergamon, 1976.

Hersen, M., & Bellack, A. S. Social skills training for chronic psychotic patients: Rationale, research, findings, and future directions. *Comprehensive Psychiatry,* 1976, *17,* 559–580.

Hersen, M., & Eisler, R. M. Social skills training. In W. E. Craighead, A. E. Kazdin, & M. J. Mahoney (Eds.), *Behavior modification: Principles, issues, and applications.* Boston: Houghton Mifflin, 1976.

Huff, F. The desensitization of a homosexual. *Behaviour Research and Therapy,* 1970, *8,* 99–102.

Jackson, B. A case of voyeurism treated by counter-conditioning. *Behaviour Research and Therapy,* 1969, *7,* 133–134,

Kanfer, F. H., & Phillips, J. S. *Learning foundations of behavior therapy.* New York: Wiley, 1970.

Kantorowitz, D. A. An experimental investigation of preorgasmic reconditioning and postorgasmic deconditioning. *Journal of Applied Behavior Analysis,* 1978, *11,* 23–34.

Kinsey, A. C., Pomeroy, W. B., Martin, C. E., & Gebhard, P. *Sexual behavior in the human female.* Philadelphia: Saunders, 1953.

Krafft-Ebing, R. *Psychopathia sexualis.* Chicago: Keener, 1900.

Kraft, T. Treatment for sexual perversions. *Behaviour Research and Therapy,* 1969, *7,* 215.

Larson, D. An adaptation of the Feldman and MacCulloch approach to treatment of homosexuality by the application of anticipatory avoidance learning. *Behaviour Research and Therapy,* 1970, *8,* 209–210.

Lasègue, C. Les exhibitionnistes. *L'Union medicale,* 1877, *23,* 703.

Lazarus, A., & Fay, A. *I can if I want to.* New York: Morrow, 1975.

LoPiccolo, J. Case study: Systematic desensitization of homosexuality. *Behavior Therapy,* 1971, *2,* 394–399.

LoPiccolo, J., Stewart, R., & Watkins, B. Treatment of erectile failure and ejaculatory incompetence of homosexual etiology. *Journal of Behavior Therapy and Experimental Psychiatry,* 1972, *3,* 233–236.

Maletzky, B. M. "Assisted" covert sensitization: A preliminary report. *Behavior Therapy,* 1973, *6,* 117–119.

Marks, I. Management of sexual disorders. In H. Leitenberg (Ed.), *Handbook of behavior modification.* New York: Appleton-Century-Crofts, 1976.

Marquis, J. N. Orgasmic reconditioning: Changing sexual object choice through controlling masturbation fantasies. *Journal of Behavior Therapy and Experimental Psychiatry,* 1970, *1,* 263–271.

Marshall, W. C. The modification of sexual fantasies: A combined treatment approach to the reduction of deviant sexual behavior. *Behaviour Research and Therapy,* 1973, *11,* 557–564.

Martinson, W. D., & Zerface, J. P. Comparison of individual counseling in a social program with nondaters. *Journal of Counseling Psychology,* 1970, *17,* 36–40.

McConaghy, N. Subjective and penile plethysmograph responses following aversion relief and apomorphine aversion therapy for homosexual impulses. *British Journal of Psychiatry,* 1969, *115,* 723–730.

McConaghy, N., & Barr, R. F. Classical, avoidance, and backward conditioning treatments of homosexuality. *British Journal of Psychiatry,* 1973, *122,* 151–162.

McDonald, J. M. *Indecent exposure.* Springfield, Ill.: Charles C Thomas, 1973.

McFall, R., & Marston, A. An experimental investigation of behavior rehearsal in assertive training. *Journal of Abnormal Psychology,* 1970, *76,* 295–303.

McFall, R. M., & Twentyman, C. T. Four experiments on the relative contributions of rehearsal, modeling, and coaching to assertion training. *Journal of Abnormal Psychology,* 1973, *81,* 199–218.

McGuire, R., Carlisle, J., & Young, B. Sexual deviations as conditioned behavior: A hypothesis. *Behaviour Research and Therapy,* 1965, *2,* 185–190.

Mees, H. L. Sadistic fantasies modified by aversion conditioning and substitution: A case study. *Behaviour Research and Therapy,* 1966, *4,* 317–320.

Money, J., & Erhardt, A. N. *Man and woman, boy and girl.* Baltimore: Johns Hopkins Press, 1973.

Obler, M. Systematic desensitization in sexual disorders. *Journal of Behavior Therapy and Experimental Psychiatry,* 1973, *4,* 93–101.

O'Leary, K. D., & Wilson, G. T. *Behavior therapy: Application and outcome.* Englewood Cliffs, N. J.: Prentice-Hall, 1975.

Ovesey, L., Gaylin, W., & Hendin, H. Psychotherapy of male homosexuality. *Archives of General Psychiatry,* 1963, *9,* 19–31.

Pauly, I. Male psychosexual inversion: Transsexualism: A review of 100 cases. *Archives of General Psychiatry,* 1965, *13,* 172–181.

Rado, S. An adaptational view of sexual behavior. In P. Hoch & J. Zubin (Eds.), *Psychosexual development in health and disease.* New York: Grune & Stratton, 1949.

Ramsey, R. W., & Van Velzen, V. Behavior therapy for sexual perversions. *Behaviour Research and Therapy,* 1968, *6,* 17–19.

Reckers, G. A., & Lovaas, O. I. Behavioral treatment of deviant sex-role behaviors in a male child. *Journal of Applied Behavior Analysis,* 1974, *7,* 173–190.

Rekers, G. A., Lovaas, O. I., & Low, B. The behavioral treatment of a transsexual preadolescent boy. *Journal of Abnormal Child Psychology,* 1974, *2,* 99–116.

Serber, M. Teaching the nonverbal components of assertive training. *Journal of Behavior Therapy and Experimental Psychiatry,* 1972, *3,* 179–183.

Simon, W., & Gagnon, J. Psychosexual development. In J. H. Gagnon & W. Simon (Eds.), *The sexual scene.* New York: Transaction, 1970, pp. 3–27.

Solyom, L., & Miller, S. A differential conditioning procedure as the initial phase of behavior therapy of homosexuality. *Behaviour Research and Therapy,* 1965, *3,* 147–160.

Stoller, R. J. *Sex and gender.* New York: Science House, 1968.

Stoller, R. J. Parental influences in male transsexualism. In R. G. Green & J.

Money (Eds.), *Transsexualism and sex reassignment*. Baltimore: Johns Hopkins Press, 1969, pp. 153–171.

Stoller, R. J. *Perversion: The erotic form of hatred*. New York: Pantheon, 1975.

Thorpe, J. G., Schmidt, E., Brown, P. T., & Castell, D. Aversion-relief therapy: A new method for general application. *Behaviour Research and Therapy*, 1964, 2, 71–82.

Ullmann, L. P., & Krasner, L. *A psychological approach to abnormal behavior* (2nd ed.). Englewood Cliffs, N. J.: Prentice-Hall, 1975.

Wickramasekera, I. The application of learning theory to the treatment of a case of sexual exhibitionism. *Psychotherapy: Theory, Research and Practice*, 1968, 5, 108–112.

Wickramasekera, I. A technique for controlling a certain type of sexual exhibitionism. *Psychotherapy: Theory, Research and Practice*, 1972, 9, 207–210.

Wilson, G. T. Innovations in the modification of phobic disorders in two clinical cases. *Behavior Therapy*, 1973, 4, 426–430.

Wilson, G. T., & Davison, G. C. Behavior therapy and homosexuality: A critical perspective. *Behavior Therapy*, 1974, 5, 16–28.

Wincze, J. P., Hoon, P., & Hoon, E. Sexual arousal in women: A comparison of cognitive and physiological responses by continuous measurement. *Archives of Sexual Behavior*, 1977, 6, 232–240.

Wolpe, J. *The practice of behavior therapy*. New York: Pergamon, 1973.

Woodward, M. The diagnosis and treatment of homosexual offenders. *British Journal of Delinquency*, 1958, 9, 44–59.

8
ASSISTED COVERT SENSITIZATION

Barry M. Maletzky

Covert sensitization, a term coined by Cautela (1966), is a procedure which pairs, in the patient's imagination, scenes of an unwanted behavior with scenes aversive to him, in an attempt to diminish the probability of that behavior occurring again. It is covert in that only images are used, and it is sensitizing in that the scenes are paired with unpleasant images. The procedure theoretically offers several advantages over the use of an actual aversive stimulus such as electric shock. It is less noxious, more readily acceptable by patients, and requires no special apparatus.

For example, an exhibitionist, in a state of relaxation, would be asked to imagine a typical scene of himself exposing; at a point where sexual pleasure was building, the therapist would suddenly shift to aversive images, usually making these a natural consequence of the exposing behavior. More specifically, the therapist might say:

> *Imagine now you are hiding in the bushes of the park. Several young girls go by on their way to the swings. You can clearly see their faces, their hair, what they are wearing, their young bodies. You start to unzip your pants and pull your penis out. It is getting hard as you rub it back and forth. The girls can see you now. They're staring right at it, shocked as you pump it back and forth; but suddenly, as you are showing it to them, there is a terrible odor: you've stepped in some brown, slimy, dog crap; it's smeared onto*

your shoe and some has gotten onto your socks and pants. The odor is nauseating. You're going soft. The whole thing is making your stomach turn, making you sick. You zip yourself up and clean yourself off as quickly as you can. As you turn away, you feel more relaxed. You can breathe again now that you are away from there. You feel glad you got away.

Clearly, there are three components to such a scene: mounting sexual pleasure, aversive imagery, and relief upon escape. A fourth, not so clear aspect to such a scene is the cognitive suggestive element inherent in the last sentence of the example just given: it is better not to expose and you feel better for not doing it.

There are a number of reports in the behavioral literature attesting to the efficacy of covert sensitization in the treatment of a host of maladaptive approach behaviors (Ashem & Donner, 1968; Davison, 1968; Fookes, 1960; Liechtenstein & Keutzer, 1969), though not all accounts are complimentary (Diament & Wilson, 1975; Emmelkamp & Walta, 1978; Foreyt & Hagen, 1973; Janda & Rimm, 1972). The typical procedure is first to train the patient in progressive muscular relaxation to enhance concentration and visualization of scenes (Wolpe, 1969), and then to present scenes previously gleaned from the patient, always pairing images of the maladaptive behavior with unpleasant consequences. Aside from nauseating images, scenes of pain (penis stuck in zipper of fly, then bleeding), embarrassment (girl laughing at exposed penis), and danger (police arrive, catching exhibitionist with his pants down), or those producing damage (girl runs away, slips, hits head, bleeds) can be used, limited only by the therapist's ingenuity.

Our early attempts to put what appeared to be an innovative behavioral procedure to work were moderately successful. We constructed scenes of fetishists getting strangled in their garter belts and homosexuals sucking on penises with festering sores, yet in perhaps 50 percent of these cases we achieved less than we had hoped. The patients told us what was wrong. As one homosexual patient complained, "The bad part isn't bad enough." If aversive images were too weak, could they be bolstered with actual aversive stimuli? Since many of the scenes we were using were nauseating ones, we decided to experiment with foul odors.

Aversive Olfactory Stimuli

There is something about a foul odor that antagonizes the appetite for sex as well as for food. The neurophysiology has yet to be grasped, although to mammals the survival value of avoiding putrefying substances is clear. Moreover, evidence is mounting that the use of malodorous substances is a powerful way to decondition some maladaptive sexual approach behaviors (Colson, 1972; Franks, Fried, & Ashem, 1966; Fensterheim, 1974; Foreyt & Kennedy, 1971; Kennedy & Foreyt, 1968; Maletzky, 1973, 1974; Maletzky & George, 1973; Morgenstern, 1974).

Reports of aversive olfactory conditioning began to appear in the early 1960s, although mainly the foul odor employed was more chemical than nauseating. Thus Colson (1972) experimented with ammonia as did Wolpe (1969), who also used asafetida; Kennedy and Foreyt (1968) assaulted the nasal mucosae of their patients with butyric acid, the stench of rancid butter; and stale cigarette smoke was the favorite of Franks, Fried, and Ashem (1966) and Morgenstern (1974) in their studies with nicotine addicts.

These reports encouraged our experimentation with foul-smelling substances, but at first our efforts met with technical defeats: The repeated use of ammonia caused mucosal damage to the nasal passageways; hydrogen sulfide was unstable and, to the dismay of fellow workers, permanently permeated every object in the treatment room; and some deviants actually enjoyed the smell of rotting eggs.

Our consultations with laboratory personnel and our own noses soon produced what appeared to be a suitably horrid substance; valeric acid, an evil older sister of butyric acid, is the 12-carbon straight-chain organic acid that imparts its essence to rotting cheese. Patients compared its olfactory qualities to a combination of rancid butter and smelly gym socks.[1] This liquid, available from chemical supply houses, fueled our early work with troublesome consumatory responses such as alcoholism and addiction to tobacco, as well as the sexual deviations of homosexuality and exhibitionism (Maletzky, 1973, 1974a, b; Maletzky & George, 1973). After working with valeric acid for several years, however, we had some cause to worry about its potency to decondition strongly held sexual habits. Some patients complained that the odor and the suggestions used with it were not strong enough, and some even began to enjoy the stench.

Serendipity nurtures science: a rotting piece of meat in the midst of a garbage strike drew not only the flies but also our attention. What better to elicit feelings of revulsion? This chance occurrence spurred several laboratory experiments to supply the most noxious odor we could produce. At present we prepare the following concoction: a human placenta, newly delivered and readily available in all hospital laboratories, is cut into 2 to 4 cm cubes, placed with some of its liquid into glass bottles with screw-top covers, and innoculated with a bacterial culture of *E. Coli, P. Mirabilis,* or *P. Aeruginosa.* The culture is allowed to incubate at an elevated temperature for 48 hours. The resultant preparation, with its associated foul odor, can be presented to the patient in a number of ways, including merely holding the bottle under his nose, presenting it in a squeeze-bottle snifter apparatus, or more elaborately presenting it in a sleek, custom-designed olfactory stimulator similar to that recently described by Weitzel, Horan, and Addis (1977).

Assisted Covert Sensitization

Bolstering the aversive scenes in covert sensitization with an actual noxious stimulus was cheating in a manner of speaking, for of course the procedure was hardly covert anymore. Nonetheless, we called it "assisted" covert sensitization (ACS), a misnomer to blanch the complexion of even the most liberally minded behaviorist.[2] The procedure is actually nothing more than aversive conditioning with stench substituted for shock, though it must be remembered that imagery is still the medium employed to present the positive sexual stimulus rather than pictures, slides, or other tangible stimuli.

Several nonexhibitionist examples may help to visualize the use of ACS in clinical practice and to demonstrate its applicability to a range of maladaptive sexual approach behaviors.

> *A homosexual pedophile was assisted in constructing several scenes of his typical child-molesting behavior sequence. After relaxation training, a relaxed state was induced and the patient asked to imagine the following scene. "Imagine you are babysitting for a handsome young boy; you are putting him to bed; there is no one else there but you and him. As you tuck him in you can see his blond hair and blue eyes looking at you. You begin to stroke his hair and his face. He is letting you caress him! You slide into bed next to him and start to take off his pajamas. You can see his naked chest and feel his body next to yours; you're really getting hard as you put your mouth onto his. He is really enjoying it! You begin to go down on him, to suck his hard little cock. Suddenly (foul odor introduced), there's a foul putrid odor in the room; it's coming from his penis—there's a sore on the end of it with pus and blood oozing out. It's making you sick to your stomach; some of the pus has gotten into your mouth and is dripping down your throat. Your supper catches in your throat; you try to gag it down but you can't. Chunks of vomit come into your mouth, ballooning out your cheeks. The vomit gushes out and dribbles down your chin onto his naked body. The stench is driving you wild. You quickly run into the bathroom and clean yourself off (odor removed), then go outside into*

the fresh night air. As you get away from the boy you begin to feel better; that horrible odor is gone; you can breathe the fresh, clean air, and your stomach relaxes. You can breathe deeply now that you are away from sex with the boy and you can relax."

A peeping Tom related several scenes typical of his voyeuristic behavior. Under relaxation he was asked to imagine the following scene. "You're behind the Vista Apartments looking for a lighted window. Suddenly you see the lights go on behind a patio door. You hide in the bushes. You can see a young woman starting to undress! She is taking off her blouse, then her bra; you can see her bending over to pull down her slacks. Just as she starts to pull down her panties you inch closer for a better look but suddenly (odor introduced), you trip and slam up against the glass of the door. You crash through, cutting yourself badly. Everyone has heard. All the neighbors come running out. You are getting sick to your stomach and that foul odor is there like rotting human flesh making you want to puke. Quickly (odor removed) you dash away to your car and as you get away from there you begin to feel better. As you drive, fresh air comes in from the open car window and you can relax, glad you're not looking in that window again."

Aversive imagery and concomitant foul odors do not always need to flow naturally with the scene. Images of a young boy's pubic hair crawling with maggots might naturally be associated with a foul odor; but scenes of pain, embarrassment, or apprehension by police can also be associated with the odor to enhance their aversiveness, even though a foul stench would not necessarily follow. A recent report indicates, however, that if negative imagery flows naturally from a scene, some benefits accrue (Little & Curran, 1978). Nonetheless, in our experience extensive and naturalistic aversive imagery need not be employed, as the following scene demonstrates.

A male transvestite was asked, under relaxation, to imagine the following scene. "Imagine you are beginning to pull a beautiful slip on over your naked body. You can feel its satiny, smooth surface glide over your legs and press tightly against your penis. You are beginning to get hard just feeling it on you when (odor introduced) that horrible smell comes back. The odor of rotting flesh makes your stomach turn. Just having the slip and touching it makes you sick to your stomach. You begin to puke and chunks of vomit dribble down onto the slip. It is disgusting to be there like that with the slip on, so sick to your stomach. You quickly pull the slip off (odor removed) and wash yourself off. Now you can breathe again. That horrible odor is gone and you can relax, feeling glad you finally got that slip off."

There are several factors involved in such scenes, as previously mentioned—including aversive conditioning, elements of suggestion, and cognitive reappraisal. Rather than an examination of the contributing strength of each of the individual parts, however, what follows is a description of the development of a treatment *package* for exhibitionism, and the demonstration of its clinical efficacy.

EXPERIMENTATION

We have had the opportunity to examine and treat in excess of 150 exhibitionists over a period of nine years. The majority of these subjects were included in several research studies (Maletzky, 1973, 1974a, b; Maletzky & George, 1973) but others are newly reported here. Subjects included in Experiments 1–5 and 7 were treated with either ACS or other behavioral techniques to be described, and without the addition of adjunctive techniques to constitute the treatment package. No subject was used in more than one study except in Experiments 7 and 8, in which retrospective data were scrutinized. In the synthesis which follows the description of these experiments, the results of these studies are drawn together and some rationale for the use of this treatment package in exhibitionism is provided.

Experiment 1

Purpose

Based upon early clinical successes with a variety of maladaptive sexual approach behaviors (Maletzky, 1973), we designed a prospective clinical study intending to apply the technique of ACS to the next 10 exhibitionist patients referred. The question was asked: Is ACS a useful treatment option in exhibitionism?

Methods

Comments in this section for Experiment 1 are more detailed than in the methods sections of the remaining experiments, so as to provide information applicable to the entire research project.

Subjects. Table 1 lists characteristics of the 10 subjects, all drawn from a small army base. Six patients came willingly for treatment, requesting help because of dissatisfaction with a life plagued by duplicity, social approbation, and the dread of apprehension. Four were referred by legal authorities who had provided them the choice of incarceration or probation with psychiatric care. These cases

Table 1. Demographic Characteristics, Frequency, and Duration of Exhibitionist Behavior

				EXHIBITIONISM	
SUBJECT	AGE	MARITAL STATUS	EDUCATIONAL LEVEL	Frequency (in months)	Duration (in years)
1	27	Married	College degree	4	5
2	45	Married	10th grade	2	16
3	33	Married	12th grade	9	13
4	21	Single	10th grade	1	1
5	24	Married	College degree	2	5
6	37	Married	Two years of college	4	3
7	29	Married	College degree	10	1
8	52	Divorced	9th grade	11	31
9	34	Married	College degree	3	12
10	30	Married	College degree	4	8

afforded us the opportunity of assessing treatment under pressure. The subjects were mostly married men who described fair to excellent sexual adjustment with their wives, thus confirming earlier reports that exhibitionism is not simply a response to otherwise poor heterosexual adjustment (Maletzky, 1973). As with the majority of the men we have treated for exhibitionism (we have not treated a female for exhibitionism), and in agreement with other and more recent reports (Henderson & Batchelor, 1969), they generally had steady records of employment and were outgoing, active in civic affairs, and free of criminal activity outside of exhibitionism. Only a few (approximately 4 percent) had serious difficulties with drugs or alcohol.

To generalize across all our studies, our population could not be distinguished by any single trait of which we were aware; rather, these men were notable particularly for their heterogeneity. Just one feature seemed outstanding in their backgrounds—a seemingly high incidence of early and repeated sexual play with girls in which presentation and inspection of genital areas assumed paramount importance. Whether this indicates an early conditioning factor at a particularly sensitive sexual age or whether it would be true of any sample of men is conjectural, but probably worthy of further investigation. Fully 72 percent of our subjects mentioned such sexual play between the ages of five and nine, and 57 percent used fantasies of being naked among females during masturbation and intercourse.

Many of our patients were referred by attorneys who knew our interests. Over 52 percent were involved in some probationary program and thus receiving treatment under less than voluntary conditions. Efficacy of treatment in this group across the research project did not differ significantly from that of voluntary patients.

Treatment procedures. During an initial interview the therapist gathered historical data and emphasized that exhibitionism was a learned behavior which, with diligence, could be unlearned. In subsequent sessions each subject was taught relaxation exercises to enhance visualization of scenes. Concurrently, the subjects and the therapist constructed a 7 to 10-item hierarchy of scenes collected from accounts of exposing behavior and fantasies. A typical hierarchy with the scenes curtailed for ease of presentation is reproduced in Table 2, along with a scale of sexual pleasure from 0 (no pleasure) to 100 (maximum pleasure). A few extra scenes (see scene 7A in Table 2) were constructed to reward the subject for rejecting the urge to expose. The scenes were arranged so that the early ones were less pleasurable than ones presented later on.

A list of noxious images derived from the subject's account of what most revolted him also was prepared. Such images usually included scenes of vomiting; contact with feces, urine or insects; vile stenches; scenes of apprehension by authorities; scenes of ridicule; or scenes of producing physical injury. All sessions were conducted in a dimly lit room with the subject reclining on a lounger, the therapist seated near his side. Throughout the entire research series, approximately 50 percent of the treatment sessions were conducted by mental health technicians and the remaining 50 percent were conducted by mental health professionals, including the author. Approximately 35 percent of treatments were performed by the Department of Neurology and Psychiatry at Lyster Army Hospital, Ft. Rucker, Alabama; 20 percent at the University of Oregon Health Sciences Center; and 45 percent within the author's private psychiatric practice.

After ensuring that the subject could obtain adequate levels of relaxation and imagine scenes clearly (an idiosyncratic pleasant scene such as a vacation spot, walking on a beach, or sleeping in a meadow was usually combined with relaxation as an induction technique), the therapist proceeded with the sexual scenes. At a point where sexual pleasure was building, the therapist introduced suggestions of noxious

Table 2. Hierarchy of Scenes Presented to Subject 3, Placed in Order of Sexual Pleasure to the Subject

SCENE	CONTENT	SEXUAL PLEASURE RATING[a]
1	Seeing young girls walking home from school, sitting in car across street masturbating, being discovered, getting sick to stomach.	10
2	Standing behind tree in park, masturbating while watching young girls go by, being apprehended by policeman.	30
3	Inviting young girl behind tree in park, exposing self, girl pointing and laughing at him, inviting friends to see, getting sick to stomach.	45
4	Driving past high school, stopping and exposing self to group of girls, fearing apprehension, getting sick to stomach, having diarrhea.	60
5	Driving through shopping center at night, approaching pretty girl in car, unzipping self, getting penis caught in zipper, with much pain, bleeding.	75
6	Driving to laundry during daytime, seeing young blonde on street alone, trying to expose self, but bad smell coming in from factory producing nausea, vomiting.	85
7	Driving to laundry at night, approaching pretty blonde to expose self, getting sick to stomach, vomiting on self, girl getting his license number.	100
7a	Same as scene 7, but odor and sick feelings quickly removed as subject resists temptation to expose self and drives on.	—

[a] The pleasure associated with imagining the first, or sexual part, of the scene.

elements and held an uncapped bottle of valeric acid under the subject's nose. As the scene progressed, the subject in his imagination escaped from the exposing situation. The odor was removed (it left only a slight background odor, to which one accommodated) and suggestions of relaxation with deep, rhythmic breathing were reintroduced.

To demonstrate, a typical scene is presented.

You are driving down Collins Avenue going to the laundry. You can feel yourself in the car, hands on the wheel, looking out the windows. It's dusk and it has been raining. You can see the wet street and puddles. Just as you make that right turn onto Andrews Drive by the ice cream parlor, you see this great-looking girl walking on your right. You slow down to get a better look. She is blond, about 16, and really stacked. You can see her breasts under her tight blouse and her skirt is so short you can see her legs all the way up! You start to get excited just by looking and turn the car around to follow her. Now she is on your left and you slowly pull up to her as you start to play with yourself and your penis starts to get harder and stiffer. You can't help but think about touching and fondling her and you ache just to be naked with her, to see her be surprised and happy at how big and hard your penis is (odor introduced), but as you stop the car and start to take it out that bad smell and that sickening feeling in the pit of your stomach comes back. You really get turned off as your stomach turns over and over and pieces of your supper catch in your throat. You try to gag them back down but you can't. Big chunks of vomit gush out of your mouth, dribble down your chin, and drip all over you. The smell is making you even sicker. The blond can see you now all soft and vomiting over yourself and she is starting to get your license number! People are starting to come out of the ice cream place to see and you've got to get out of there (odor removed). You quickly clean yourself off and drive away, rolling down the windows to get some fresh air. As you get out of there you start to feel much better. That bad smell is gone and you can breathe deeply again. A fresh clean breeze comes in from the windows and you feel more comfortable and relaxed; your stomach starts to settle down and you begin to fully relax again. You're glad you're out of there, breathing freely and able to relax.

Each scene is presented once per session for 5 sessions. Three to five scenes were thus presented for each 50-minute, twice-monthly session, and the hierarchy was completed in 9 to 11 sessions.

During sessions, scenes were tape-recorded. Each patient listened at home to recordings two to three times weekly and self-administered whiffs of valeric acid from his own vial at appropriate intervals. Such self-treatment, already described for covert sensitization, was first rehearsed in the office as it involved not only a measure of discipline but a good deal of coordination.

Toward the end of treatment, each patient was instructed to carry his vial of valeric acid and sniff it in purposely sought situations which had previously elicited exposing behavior. At 3, 6, and 12-month intervals, all patients underwent booster sessions (Maletzky, 1977) in which the last four scenes of their hierarchy were presented along with the valeric acid. Table 3 presents a paradigm of treatment with average durations for each phase.

Assessment. This early experiment represented a broad-based attempt to answer the question of whether ACS was a helpful technique deserving further study. Hence data collection was not up to the current standard of double-blind, expectancy-controlled behavioral research. We simply wanted to know whether the treatment paradigm presented in Table 3 would decrease exposing behavior.

Several of the remaining studies to be described were also unashamedly clinical. They were designed to answer the question of what works with the least time and expense employed and the most permanent remission achieved. Although Experiments 3 and 5 employed penile plethysmograph recordings, we were most concerned not with how much blood rushed to the penises of our patients, but whether they continued to expose or not. Further discussion of the validity of the plethysmograph is discussed in Experiments 3 and 4.

Three types of data were collected in the first experiment:

Frequency records. Each patient maintained the following frequency records.

1. Covert exhibitionist behavior such as urges; for example, wishing to expose oneself in a situation allowing it; fantasies, or extensive daydreaming about exposing oneself; and dreams of exhibitionism.
2. Overt exhibitionist behavior; that is, exhibitionist acts or masturbation to exhibitionist fantasies.

It is widely assumed that subjects' reports are biased and unworthy of serious scientific consideration. In study 3, however (pp. 210–215), plethysmograph records verified subjects' reports with an accuracy of 89 percent. Moreover, contrary to expectation, data from all eight studies showed that patients referred under direct court pressure recorded no more or less exposing behavior throughout the treatment than those self-referred. In addition, police records correlated highly with self-reports: in 54 episodes of police-recorded exposing incidents for 31 men, 47 incidents were reported to the therapist by the patient before the legal record was obtained.

Legal records. Appropriate authorities were contacted regularly to learn whether any patient had been apprehended for, or suspected of, exposing himself.

Table 3. Paradigm of Treatment Schedule for All Subjects

TREATMENT PHASE	DESCRIPTION	AVERAGE DURATION AND FREQUENCY
1. History taking	(self-explanatory)	½ of first hour
2. Education	Explanation of exhibitionism as a learned response, not a manifestation of deviant personality	¼ of first hour
3. Treatment explanation	Description of treatment technique	¼ of first hour
4a. Relaxation training with therapist	Listening to instructions given by therapist in office	½ of two succeeding sessions
4b. Relaxation training without therapist	Listening to taped instructions at home, or in office without therapist present	15 minutes nightly for 2 weeks
5. Scene collection	Collection and revision of exhibitionist and noxious scenes	½ of two succeeding sessions
6a. Sensitization sessions with therapist	Scene visualizations under relaxation, with valeric acid administered by therapist	30 minutes, twice weekly, for an average of 12.4 weeks
6b. Sensitization sessions without therapist	Scene visualizations under relaxation, by tape, self-administering valeric acid	30 minutes, twice weekly, for an average of 10.2 weeks
7. Sensitization sessions in vivo	Smelling valeric acid in situations previously associated with exhibitionism	Several minutes, twice weekly, during the last 5 weeks of active treatment
8a. Booster sessions with therapist	Same as 6a	30 minutes, given at 3-, 6-, and 12-month intervals following active treatment

Table 3 (Continued).

TREATMENT PHASE	DESCRIPTION	AVERAGE DURATION AND FREQUENCY
8b. Booster sessions without therapist	Same as 6b	Whenever subject felt it to be necessary. Average of 5.2 such sessions, at times other than treatment phase 8a, over a one-year period

The temptation test. For futher validation, a test was devised to tempt the subject to expose himself (Maletzky & George, 1973). A comely actress, unknown to the subject, purposely placed herself in situations that previously had a high probability of eliciting exposing behavior. The situations, clothing, and demeanor were tailored to the individual subject (none in this first study exposed only to children). The test was given at the end of treatment and again one year later. Two examples, one a success and one a failure, are offered.

> *A. was in the habit of driving by a high school on his way home from work. He previously had frequently exposed himself from his car to female students. Our actress, dressed to similate a student, waited for A.'s car to approach; then, making certain no one else was near, she walked toward his car seductively on several occasions. A. drove his car past her on all occasions and never exposed himself.*
>
> *B. had frequently exposed himself to neighbors or passers-by while seated on his screened-in porch. Our actress passed his porch several times, and on one of these occasions B. called her over ostensibly to ask the time. While engaging her in conversation, he was noted to be stimulating his penis, and then he finally exposed himself to her. She walked off briskly without responding.*

Ethical objections can certainly be raised about such a test. However, all patients were informed that "experimental and unusual procedures" would be employed, and each agreed to participate. More to the point, striving for objectivity was essential to justify this treatment's continued application. Moreover, it is unlikely that two widely spaced, unrewarded temptations would have affected these patients permanently or adversely.

Results

Frequency records. Figure 1 depicts in graphic form the mean frequencies of exposing behaviors throughout treatment and follow-up. Frequencies for the month prior to and just after treatment and at 12-month follow-up are presented in Table 4, which also depicts individual data. Mean covert exhibitionist behavior decreased from 16.5 exposures per month for 10 patients (range = 6–29) before treatment to 0.6 per month (0–2) just afterward, and remained at 0.7 per month (0–4) one year later. Mean overt behaviors decreased from 5.0 per month (1–11) to 0.1 per month (0–1) just after treatment, and remained at zero throughout the 12-month follow-up.

Legal status. No patient was apprehended for, or suspected of, exposing himself during treatment and the 12-month follow-up.

The temptation test. All subjects but one passed both their tests. One man failed his test after treatment and, because he admitted to

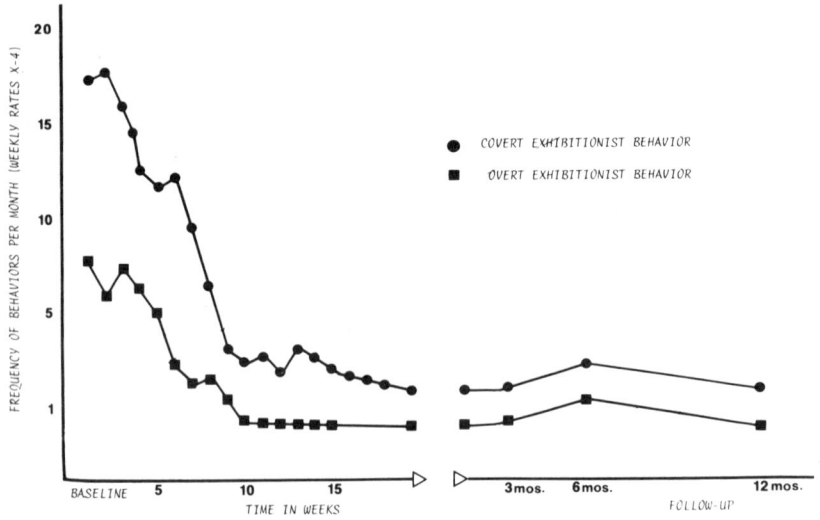

Figure 1. Mean frequencies of covert and overt exhibitionist behaviors during treatment and follow-up.

Table 4. Frequencies of Covert and Overt Exhibitionist Behaviors for the Months before and after Treatment and at 12-Month Follow-up (Analysis of Variance by Subjects)

	COVERT			OVERT		
SUBJECT	Pre-treatment	Post-treatment	12 months	Pre-treatment	Post-treatment	12 months
1	24	1	0	4	0	0
2	6	0	0	2	0	0
3	17	0	1	9	0	0
4	10	0	0	1	0	0
5	9	2	2	2	0	0
6	15	1	0	4	0	0
7	29	0	0	10	0	0
8	27	2	4	11	1	0
9	17	0	0	3	0	0
10	11	0	0	4	0	0
M	16.5*	0.6*	0.7*	5.0*	0.1*	0*

*$p < .001$

lingering exhibitionist urges and fantasies, was treated for 10 additional sessions. Urges and fantasies remained at 12-month follow-up, though much reduced in strength and frequency; moreover, he passed the final temptation test and was considered an ultimate treatment success.

Anecdotal reports collected from wives, girlfriends, and supervisors indicated that most men improved their heterosexual adjustment and job performance during treatment and follow-up (cf. Experiment 3). No evidence of symptom substitution could be found. In addition, most men claimed more self-confidence and pride once they were free of urges to expose themselves.

Discussion

Despite the fact that our early efforts in treating sexual dysfunctions with covert sensitization did not meet with unqualified success, we persisted in developing a stronger form of treatment because the alternatives contained certain flaws.

Issues of convenience. The group and individual psychotherapies used to treat exhibitionism require considerable time and expense (Freund, 1960; Rickels, 1950; Smith, 1968) and are questionably effective (Ewalt & Farnsworth, 1963). Hackett (1971), for example, could treat only 45 of 214 patients with traditional individual therapy, and at a high cost in time. Mathis and Collins (1970, 1971) reported that 15 of their 21 patients were still in group therapy after three years. In addition, 13 of these patients failed to continue treatment. While our groups are not strictly comparable, length of active treatment in Experiment 1 averaged just 12.4 weeks, and booster sessions consumed only a modicum of time. Not one of our subjects abandoned therapy, not even those treated as a condition of probation. Electric shock, the usual behavioral alternative in the treatment of exhibitionism, is not amenable to home practice, especially if used with slides. In contrast, with ACS the tape recorder can be used at home for 50 to 80 percent of scene presentations, freeing the therapist for other tasks.

Issues of acceptability. A number of patients throughout the experiments refused to participate if electricity were used. This position, based upon misinformation, seemed at times unshakeable and has been previously noted (Fookes, 1960; Rachman & Teasdale, 1969).

Issues of cost. Equipment to produce shock, present slides, and coordinate both in individual and group psychotherapy is costly. The cost of ACS is minimal and the valeric acid or placental cultures last interminably. One 500 mg bottle of valeric acid sufficed to conduct all the treatments in Experiment 1. Three placental cultures (distributed in many vials) handled all other treatments in the remainder of these experiments.

The results obtained with exhibitionists in Experiment 1 suggested the effectiveness of ACS in this disorder. As we set about the tasks of devising controls and more objective assessment procedures, we were still impressed that 10 exhibitionists, 4 of whom had been court referred, were significantly helped by this simple and direct technique. Not only were overt exposing behaviors eliminated, but urges, fantasies, and even dreams of exposing were eliminated as well.

Experiment 2A

The success of the assisted covert sensitization technique probably resulted from the use of an aversive stimulus to bolster the covert aspect, especially one that not only assaulted the olfactory senses but also added a certain decaying quality evocative of the scenes usually used in the strictly covert technique. Yet several of our patients, both within Experiment 1 and treated immediately thereafter, complained that even the valeric acid was "too mild." As stated before, some patients began to show no aversion to the odor or to even enjoy it. Our unpleasant but obvious task was to search for even fouler odors. This search resulted in the discovery of the placental cultures previously described.

Purpose

Discovery of the bacterial placental cultures prompted an urge to pit one foul odor against the other to determine which was strongest, in all meanings of the word.

Methods

Subjects. Ten subjects, each serving as his own control, were employed in an A-B/B-A randomly assigned procedure. These patients were not appreciably different from the population described in Experiment 1 except that an even greater number (7) were court referred. Four were civilians and 6 were military personnel. (Experiment 7 presents group demographic data whereas the other experiments do not.)

Treatment procedures. As they were referred, each patient was assigned covert sensitization assisted with valeric acid (condition A) or placental culture (condition B) for five treatment sessions, and told to use the given odor in home practice. At the end of these five sessions, the odors were reversed; the patients beginning with valeric acid switched to placental culture, and vice versa for the succeeding five sessions, in order to control for sequential effects. Otherwise, treatment procedures were exactly as outlined in Experiment 1.

Assessment. It is difficult to determine over a short period of time which treatment is more effective when trying to decondition a low-frequency overt behavior such as exhibitionism. An attempt can be made by comparing both overt and covert behaviors using, as a datum, the percentage of change in several measures from base-line to end of treatment within each treatment condition. In this way, percentage changes could be computed for each odor either at the start of treatment or after the change-over from one odor to the other.

Frequency data for covert and overt exhibitionist behaviors were collected in the same way as Experiment 1. Although the data were recorded exactly as in Experiment 1, the results were analyzed somewhat differently. Beginning with a base-line of frequencies collected for one month before actual treatment began, data were computed as a percentage change from this base-line. After the A-B or B-A switch, data were again computed as a percentage change, employing the base-line from a two-week period between the switch. The purpose was to learn how much change each odor was eliciting, rather than the actual frequencies involved.

Results

Frequency records. Figure 2 presents overt frequency data under both treatment conditions, and demonstrates a faster rate of conditioning and a greater strength of odor with placental culture than with valeric acid. It can be seen that the placental culture emerges as a slight but significant favorite in this contrast of odors. A presentation of percentage frequency data in Table 5 shows that the mean decrease in overt behaviors with the acid was 72 percent while with the culture this figure reached 89 percent, a significant difference ($p < .05$). It is also of interest to note that, as is usual in this work, covert changes lag behind overt changes and yet often, but not always, catch up by the time of follow-up. Thus some patients continue to entertain weak urges or fantasies of exhibitionism, but without acting on them.

Legal status. No differences emerged on this parameter. Two patients were reported for exposing incidents while using valeric acid, and two other patients using placental culture were reported. Three of these four incidents were reported in the first half of the treatment period.

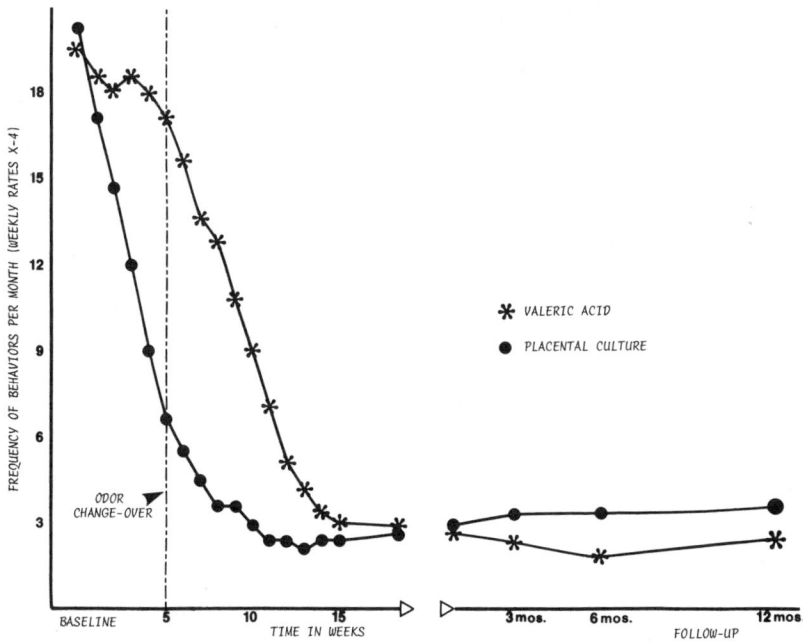

Figure 2. Mean frequencies of overt exhibitionist behaviors with valeric acid and placental culture.

Discussion

Though not an exhaustive test, these results gave us every reason to use placental culture as the preferred stimulus. It was free, easily obtained and handled, and lasted interminably. Moreover, it had the added quality of appearing nauseating—a chunk of slimy brown tissue within its own foul liquor. No small attribute was the patients' knowledge of the tissue's origins.

However, the A-B/B-A switch-over design of Experiment 2A, coupled with the small number of subjects, confounded the variables of experimenter bias for one smell over another. In addition, the variable of increased skill of therapists and patients alike in the technique of treatment, and the aforementioned cognitive properties of the culture, necessitated a more elegant technique in deciding which odor to choose.

Table 5. Percentage Frequency Change in Covert and Overt Exhibitionist Behaviors with Valeric Acid and Placental Culture

TIME OF ASSESS- MENT	VALERIC ACID		PLACENTAL CULTURE	
	Covert	Overt	Covert	Overt
Baseline	0	0	0	0
5 weeks	12.7	24.2	18.9	33.0
10 weeks	29.8	52.7	49.5	65.4
15 weeks	69.6	71.1	73.9	88.5
3 months	69.1	67.9	82.5	87.6
6 months	75.2	79.2	85.1	89.5
12 months	78.0[a]	72.8[a]	90.7[a]	89.3[a]

[a]Differences significant at the .05 level.

Experiment 2B

When one proposes to compare the efficacy of two treatments, one of which is thought to be superior to the other, the most ethical approach is to insure that the patients receiving the suspected lesser treatment are exposed to it over a minimum amount of time, and then to switch them to the more effective treatment when the issue is settled. This is all the more urgent in the treatment of a criminal behavior such as exhibitionism.

Purpose

The purpose of Experiment 2B was to firmly but quickly answer the question of which odor was more effective in eliminating exhibitionist urges and behaviors.

Methods

Subjects. Because of the statistical methods to be described, we did not know how many patients would eventually be treated. As they were referred, they were alternately assigned to either acid or culture. At the end of the study, a total of 30 subjects, or 15 subject pairs, had been established. Fortunately, demographic analysis at the end of the study showed no significant differences between groups in matters such as age, race, or social classification.

Treatment procedures. ACS was administered exactly as outlined in Experiment 1 and presented in Table 3; the only treatment variable was the use of the two odors.

Assessment. To determine efficacy as rapidly as possible, with the fewest number of subjects required to assess a significant difference, the ingenious statistical device of restricted procedures in sequential analysis as introduced by Bross (1952) and modified by Armitage (1960) was utilized. Well known for its usefulness in medication trials (Maletzky & Klotter, 1974a, b), it has apparently not been previously employed in behavior research.

Each subject within a pair was assigned ACS with valeric acid or placental culture. Thus a preference within each pair for acid or culture would emerge over time. By preselecting an arbitrary criterion—in this case a 75 percent reduction in overt and covert exhibitionist behaviors—the researcher determined when the trial was over and assessed a "winner," either acid or culture. Moreover, the experiment could be performed in several arenas, since the criteria could be selected among a number of measures. In this experiment, for example, studies were run to measure percentage change in reported covert and overt behavior frequencies and subjects' assessment of aversiveness of scenes plus odors after each treatment session on a scale of zero (neutral) to 100 (the most disgusting imaginable).

Results

Data are presented in a series of three graphs (Figures 3–5) in which covert behaviors, overt behaviors, and subjects' assessments of aversion are analyzed separately. For each graph, the top and bottom lines represent the .01 level of probability that any preference was due entirely to chance. The variable line depicts a preference either for acid if it descends, or culture if it ascends, for a particular variable and subject pair. As an example, Figure 3 demonstrates preferences on the variable of covert exhibitionist behaviors. The graph ascends for 2 subject pairs, indicating that the culture produced a stronger decrease in urges, fantasies, and dreams of exhibitionist behavior than the acid. But the graph descends for the third subject pair, since acid produced a greater decrease in exhibitionist behaviors than the culture. The ascending graph reaches the top line after 15

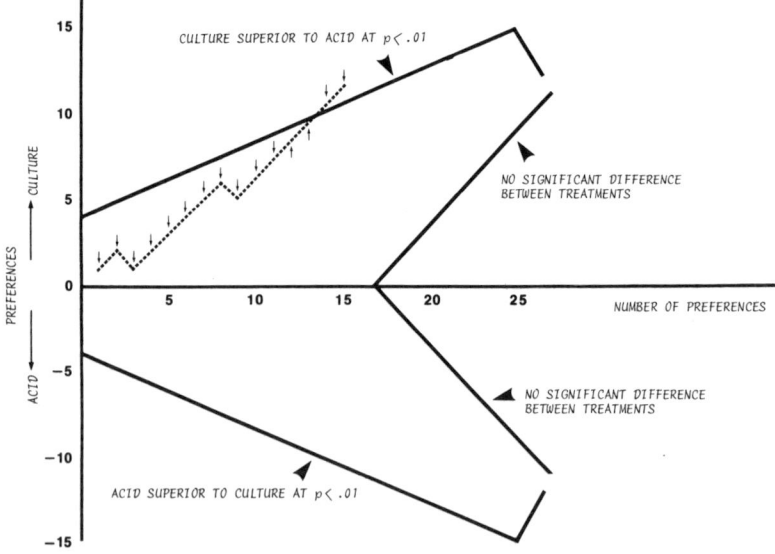

Figure 3. Preferences between valeric acid and placental culture for covert exhibitionist behaviors, regardless of extent, before reaching criterion of a 75 percent reduction in covert behaviors.

subject pairs were tested, thus proving at the .01 level of probability that this preference for culture did not occur by chance.

Figure 4 similarly shows odor preferences in overt exhibitionist behaviors, with culture again proving to be superior. Figure 5 shows the greatest difference in treatments, requiring only 9 subject pairs to prove a stronger subjective aversion to culture than to acid; no subject judged acid more noxious than culture.

Discussion

These results verify what our patients had been telling us all along: valeric acid was putrid but the placental culture reached heights of nausea difficult to describe. Indeed, among the first 22 patients exposed to the placental culture's odor, 8 vomited at some point during the combination of scenes and odor in the office sessions, 6 of them on 2 different occasions and 2 of them also during

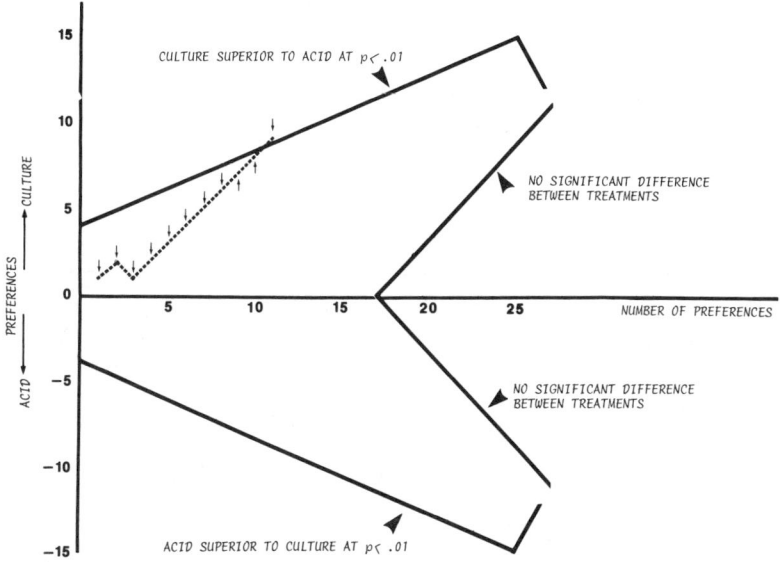

Figure 4. Preferences between valeric acid and placental culture for overt exhibitionist behaviors, regardless of extent, before reaching criterion of a 75 percent reduction in overt behaviors.

home practice sessions. We were sufficiently convinced to add several sessions with culture to supplement 3 acid-treated patients who had had a less than optimal response.

A fault of this type of statistical analysis is the failure to specify the margins of difference between culture and acid. A separate analysis using a standard t-test to compare all subjects verified that the differences were significant at the .05 level at the end of treatment.

After treating 38 exhibitionists, we thus were reasonably convinced of the efficacy of ACS. Fully 33 of these patients reported complete freedom from exhibitionist urges and behaviors. Of the remaining patients one had completely dropped out of treatment, 2 were referred for more traditional modes of therapy, and 3 continued a combination of therapies (to be described later) with eventual,

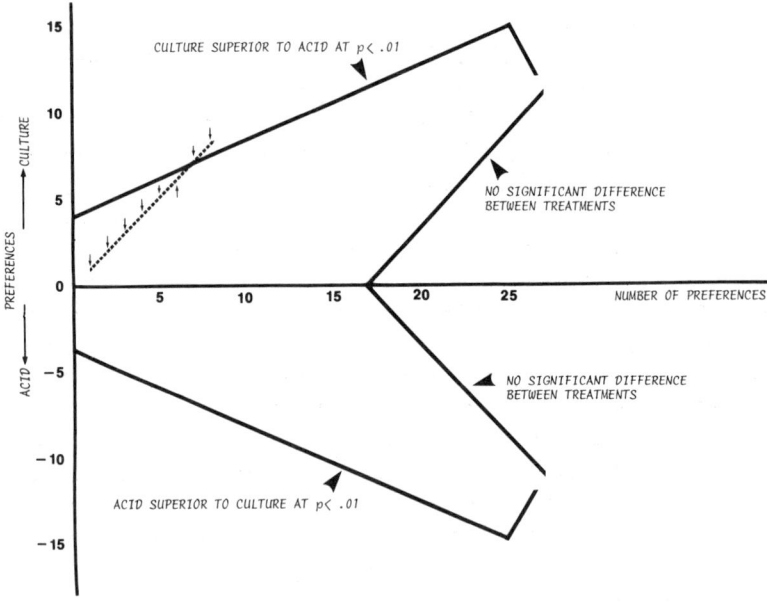

Figure 5. Preferences between valeric acid and placental culture for subjective ratings of aversion, regardless of extent.

although partial, improvement. Despite its apparent success, one glaring failure of this early research was its lack of objective verification. Could an exhibitionist's report be trusted? We had no alternative but to examine that indicator of male sexual arousal, the erection.

Experiment 3

Although some researchers have questioned the absolute trust placed in the penile plethysmograph (Henson & Rubin, 1971; Laws & Rubin, 1969; Rooth & Marks, 1974; Rosen, 1976), this instrument continues to be the favorite assessment tool of most sexual investigators. Data collected from a host of laboratories attest to its apparent reliability, though measurements of its validity are more difficult to assess. While some authors question the plethysmograph's validity on the grounds that some men can voluntarily inhibit an erection (Rooth &

Marks, 1974; Rosen, 1976), the instrument appears to register changes in penile volume so slight as to theoretically preclude conscious manipulation (Barlow, Becker, Leitenberg, & Agras, 1970).

Of more immediate significance is the question of how changes in penile volume are clinically relevant. We have treated exhibitionists who claimed significant improvement, but their plethysmograph records still demonstrated an increase in tumescence response to exhibitionist scenes. Some of these patients, whose frequency data, legal records, and even temptation test results all bespoke improvement, admitted to some continuing sexual enjoyment from listening to or fantasizing about exhibitionist scenes. It is of interest in this regard that a number of our homosexual patients have continued to manifest positive plethysmograph records when viewing homosexual slides, despite clear evidence of a decrease in or absence of homosexual behavior and a consequent increase in heterosexual behavior, including erectile changes in the plethysmograph records when viewing heterosexual slides. Although Barlow et al. (1970) noted a decrease in penile volume in heterosexual men who viewed homosexual slides, we have recorded the opposite: many of our heterosexual men showed slight, but definite, increases in tumescence when viewing homosexual slides, and several admitted to some conscious experience of pleasure.

The homosexual and exhibitionist literature is further confounded by several important studies that eliminated from their sample population individuals who failed to demonstrate an increasing tumescence when viewing homosexual or exhibitionist slides (Callahan & Leitenberg, 1973). It might have been of interest to include those subjects, but analyze data for them separately.

Purpose

The present study was designed to discover whether ACS could produce plethysmograph changes in the expected direction in order to verify patient reports and legal records. Temptation tests were not used as they were believed to be an unnecessary entrapment and superfluous when plethysmograph records were available.

Methods

Subjects. Twenty patients formed the population of Experiment 3. Their demographic data are not presented, but did not offer any striking differences from data collected previously.

Treatment procedures. All patients received a program of ACS as outlined in Experiment 1 and presented in Table 3.

Assessment. Frequency data for covert and overt exhibitionist behaviors were collected as in Experiment 1. Legal records also were collected as previously described. Penile plethysmograph records were obtained at 5-week intervals to 15 weeks and then at 3, 6, and 12 month follow-up periods, on the Grass Model 7 polygraph via a penile transducer, and with data recorded as described by Barlow, et al. (1970). These records were expressed as percentage of erections given resting base-line and full tumescence values obtained by Callahan and Leitenberg's (1973) method of having the subject imagine exposing to a desired object until full and stable tumescence had been achieved and maintained for 30 seconds. Long-term data for most of these patients are presented in Experiment 7.

Results

Frequency records. Mean frequency data for covert and overt exhibitionist behaviors are depicted graphically in Figure 6. Mean changes in both covert and overt behaviors from the beginning of treatment to its termination are highly significant ($p < .01$), despite the fact that 4 of the 20 subjects failed to show any major changes.

Legal records. Results of the legal records are not depicted. Only two reports of exposing occurred during treatment, although four reports occurred in the first 6 months after treatment. All reports were for 3 of the 4 subjects who failed to show improvement in their frequency data.

Plethysmograph records. Mean changes in plethysmograph recordings are presented in Figure 7 as percentage of erections. Significant decreases in tumescence can be seen both at the end of treatment and at 6-month follow-up ($p < .01$), although of slightly lesser magnitude on the latter occasion. Data on an individual basis are not presented; however, patients spanned a continuum of percentage change values, with the 4 treatment failures clustered at the lower end.

Of greater significance is the correlation between plethysmograph changes and degree of change in patients' recorded frequency records. A significant positive correlation was found (Rho = 0.79). If

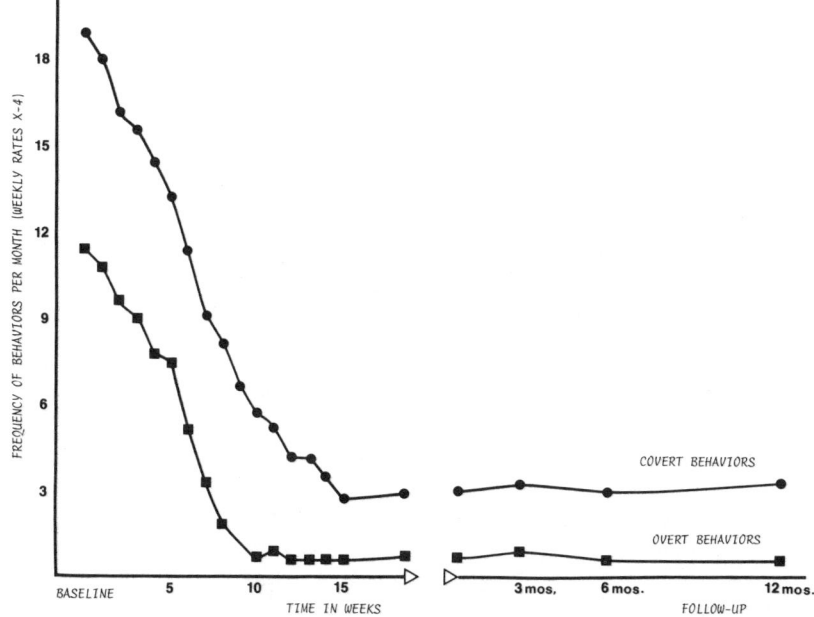

Figure 6. Mean frequencies of covert and overt exhibitionist behaviors during treatment and follow-up.

one were to judge the results solely from the patient's own reports, one would be correct (as defined by plethysmograph records) the vast majority of the time.

Hidden in the averaged data is an interesting statistic: of 20 subjects, 6 (or 30 percent) showed either paltry or absent responses to exhibitionist fantasies on their initial plethysmograph records. Just one of these 6 subjects subsequently failed to improve, and the remaining 5 contributed the majority of what little scattering was seen in the correlation between plethysmograph recordings and frequency reports. It thus appears that patients should not be denied treatment merely because they do not obtain an erection when presented with exhibitionist images or other materials. To underscore this point, a different statistic was prepared by correlating the percentage change in plethysmograph records as a function of absolute initial erection measured with exposure to the two highest-ranking exhibitionist scenes. In this instance, there was no significant relationship (Rho = .12).

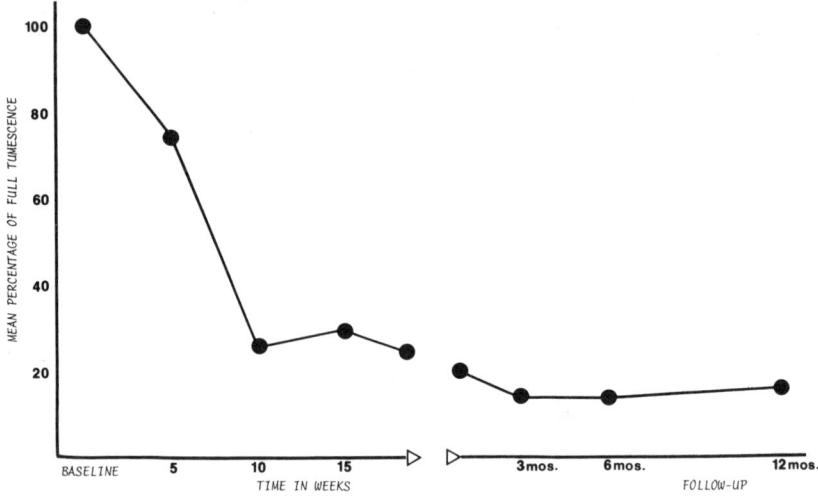

Figure 7. Mean percentage of full tumescence in plethysmograph recordings during treatment and follow-up.

Discussion

Experiment 3 demonstrated that patients' frequency records matched the penile plethysmograph records well, thus verifying earlier work (Brownell, Hayes, & Barlow, 1977). Both kinds of records offer encouraging evidence that ACS markedly reduced exhibitionist covert and overt behaviors. However, several of our observations reinforced the notion proposed by Laws and Rubin (1969) that the plethysmograph is not a phallic lie detector, especially in its use in research environments. In this study, its demonstrated errors were in two directions: some patients continued to experience erections but plainly did not expose or even want to do so; others rarely experienced erections and yet continued to expose. We chose to treat the individuals in these cases—not the plethysmographs.

Have we learned anything new from the introduction of the penile plethysmograph? Probably not. Strength of erection was neither a predictor of subsequent treatment response at base-line nor an indicator of permanency of remission at follow-up, as is better demonstrated in Experiment 7. It must not be overlooked, however, that this instrument can be used to provide therapeutic feedback in conditioning trials (Laws & Rubin, 1969).

We had the opportunity to examine the validity of plethysmograph recordings further in a brief study of 5 homosexual men from whom detailed histories were obtained. In that study, strength of erections was not well correlated with Kinsey ratings (Kinsey, Pomeroy, & Martin, 1948), thus raising the possibility that the plethysmograph may be but one of several parameters necessary to measure sexual response. In the future, perhaps the plethysmograph will be coupled with other measures of physiologic arousal such as GSR, pulse and blood pressure measurements (Rosen, 1976), or even localized electroencephalographic changes.

Experiment 4

The 4 experiments reported to this point were intended to answer questions about the ability of ACS to diminish the exhibitionist response. Even though ACS had been shown to be an effective treatment for exhibitionism, was it the most effective? Also, regardless of comparative efficacy, was ACS feasible in terms of therapist training and the economics of patient care? A comparative treatment study could help to answer these questions.

One behavior therapy for exhibitionism mentioned previously is "unassisted" covert sensitization (CS), performed without the use of an odor to boost its effect. As Cautela (1966) predicted, covert sensitization has become a behavior therapy standard (Little & Curran, 1978). Indeed, Callahan's (1973) results indicate that it may be slightly more effective than shock for maladaptive sexual approach behaviors. Fensterheim (1974) gave a detailed report of an exhibitionist who was treated with CS with moderate success. Burdick (1974) treated 6 exhibitionists with CS and concluded that all were "improved," as judged by self-reports of covert and overt behaviors. However, none were completely rid of covert urges to expose, and the author concluded that their prognosis was guarded. Hayes, Brownell, & Barlow (1978) have even reported a successful case of self-administered CS in an exhibitionist patient.

Electric shock aversion (ESA) has been employed against maladaptive sexual approach behaviors for many years (Feldman & MacCulloch, 1972; MacCulloch & Feldman, 1967; MacDonough, 1972;

McConaghy, 1970; Miller & Haney, 1976; Thorpe, 1972). As an example, Abel, Levis, and Clancy (1970) treated 3 exhibitionists with shock contingent on taped, individualized scenes, and reported decreases in plethysmograph measurements after treatment in all 3 patients. In one of the few comparative studies in this area, Callahan & Leitenberg (1973) treated an exhibitionist and 2 homosexuals first with ESA, and then with CS. The investigators showed patients slides of nude females and instructed them to imagine exposing to them, with electric shock applied, and randomly interspersed slides of nude females and instructions to imagine intercourse with them, without shock. CS was found to be slightly superior to ESA, especially in regard to patients' reports of exhibitionist urges. In another comparative study, Rooth and Marks (1974) treated 12 exhibitionists with a rotation of three techniques: ESA, self-regulation (a mèlange of rehearsing competing behaviors, self-administered CS, and exposure to oneself in a mirror), and relaxation control. ESA produced the greatest change in the course of exposing behaviors, and self-regulation was also found significantly superior to the use of relaxation control alone. In conclusion, the authors advised a combination of aversive and self-regulatory techniques. Clearly ESA has been demonstrated to be effective against exhibitionist behaviors, although long-term follow-up studies are pending. No extensive trials of the more complicated anticipatory avoidance shock procedures have been completed for exhibitionists, as opposed to homosexuals.

One of the most novel and elegantly simple treatments of a maladaptive sexual approach disorder is the treatment originally called "shame aversion therapy." Serber, an early advocate, developed the technique after trying to take pictures of a transvestite cross-dressing: the patient was so anxious about being watched that he could not proceed. In 1970, Serber reported on eight patients made to commit their sexual misbehaviors in two or three sessions in front of observers who merely watched without comment. Only one of Serber's patients was an exhibitionist, but the author was impressed with this technique. Stephenson and Jones (1972) and Reitz and Keil (1971) describe the successful treatment of exhibitionists by having them expose to clinical treatment personnel, including women. The ingenious work of Wickramasekera (1976) with this technique, which he terms aversive behavior rehearsal (ABR), has also demonstrated success.

Purpose

Clearly, CS, ESA, and ABR are three treatments of proven merit for exhibitionism. The purpose of Experiment 4 was to compare ACS directly with CS, ESA, and ABR to determine their relative efficacies. The use of a placebo relaxation-control group was deemed unnecessary and unethical because of the lack of effect seen with controls in this research and the demonstrated efficacy of the behavioral treatments employed (Rooth & Marks, 1974; Little & Curran, 1978).

Methods

Subjects. Forty patients were prospectively entered into this study in order of referral. As patients were referred, they were alternately assigned to one of four treatment groups of 10 patients each: CS, ESA, ABR, or ACS. Procedures of informed consent were used and any patient not responding to his treatment was thereafter assigned a different treatment. Demographic variables again are not presented (but see Experiment 7). The only significant difference between groups occurred between the CS and ABR groups, with the CS group being younger; this was not felt to be a determining factor.

Treatment procedures

Covert sensitization. The method described by Cautela (1967) was employed. Five exhibitionist scenes were followed by individually chosen noxious images in 10 30-minute sessions.

Electric shock aversion. The method and equipment described by Abel, Levis, and Clancy (1970) were employed, in which shock was made contingent upon taped scenes of an individual's exhibitionist behavior. There were three segments to each scene. The electric stimulus was delivered during sessions 1 to 4 after the final segment of the scene, in sessions 5 to 7 after the second segment of the scene, and in sessions 8 to 10 after the first segment. Thus punishment was given at earlier segments in accordance with a chain theory of sexual approach behavior. It was deemed desirable to decondition as many segments of the chain as possible.

Aversive behavioral rehearsal. The method described by Reitz and Keil (1971) was employed. A patient was required to expose in his usual way (usually by unzipping his fly, pulling out his penis, and masturbating) for 3 minutes in front of three to five treatment personnel in the same room. These personnel always included at least two women. No comments or behaviors were exhibited by the observers. Ten ABR sessions of 30 minutes each were held.

Assisted covert sensitization. The method previously described in Experiment 1 and presented in Table 3 was employed in 10 30-minute sessions. The only distinguishing feature of ACS as opposed to CS was the inclusion of an actual aversive stimulus—the foul odor of a placental culture.

Each group received the appropriate treatment from four therapists familiar with, and skilled in, each of the behavioral methods. The therapists randomly rotated among the four treatments so that therapist bias could be adequately controlled.

Assessment. Frequency data for covert and overt exhibitionist behaviors were collected as in Experiment 1. Legal records were also collected as previously described. Penile plethysmograph records were taken before treatment, at 5-week intervals during treatment, and at 3, 6, and 12-month follow-ups in the same manner as reported in Experiment 3.

Results

Frequency records. Figure 8 depicts mean reported frequencies of covert exhibitionist behaviors before and after treatment and at 6-month follow-up. Overt behaviors correlated well with covert behaviors and are omitted for ease of presentation. It can be seen that while each active treatment produced improvement, the order of treatment effects was ACS>ESA=ABR>CS, with significant differences occurring only between each treatment and CS. Among ACS, ESA, and ABR, there were no significant differences, although the superiority of ACS over ABR approached significance ($p<.10$). The difference might have been more significant with greater numbers of subjects. ESA and ABR appeared to take longer for noticeable

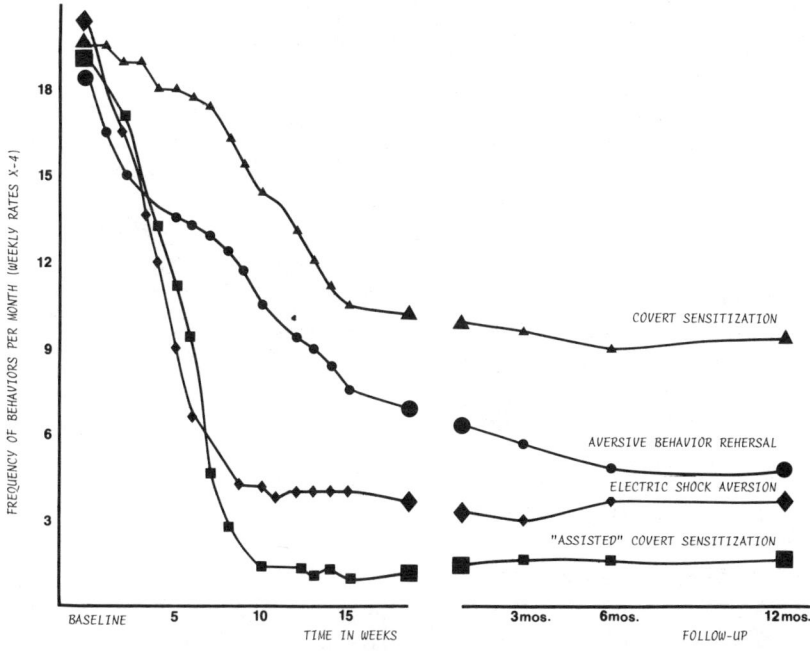

Figure 8. Mean frequencies of covert exhibitionist behaviors during treatment and follow-up for covert sensitization, electric shock aversion, aversive behavior rehearsal, and assisted covert sensitization.

treatment effects than ACS to begin but, after 12 weeks of treatment, no significant differences emerged among the three treatments.

Legal records. Due to the low number of patients within each treatment group and the small number of reported violations, no significant differences emerged. Each group averaged between 1.2 and 2.0 arrests or suspicions during treatment and follow-up period.

Plethysmograph records. Table 6 shows the mean percentage of erection changes as a function of type of treatment offered. With this measurement, ACS = ABR > ESA > CS. Significant differences at 12-

Table 6. Mean Percentage of Full Tumescence in Plethysmograph Recordings during Treatment and Follow-up within Each Treatment Group

TIME OF ASSESSMENT	TYPE OF TREATMENT			
	Covert Sensitization	Electric Shock Aversion	Aversive Behavioral Rehearsal	Assisted Covert Sensitization
Baseline	100	100	100	100
5 weeks	68.9	80.7	87.1	72.5
10 weeks	61.9	76.5	63.2	47.8
15 weeks	74.5	32.5	28.5	21.7
3 months	73.9	37.7	20.2	15.9
6 months	70.5	33.4	24.4	18.6
12 months	75.0[a]	39.4	20.2[a]	12.4[a]

[a]Differences significant at the .01 level.

month follow-up occurred only between ACS and CS ($p < .01$) and between ABR and CS ($p < .01$). Again, correlations between frequency ratings and plethysmograph readings were high ($r = +.72$).

Discussion

When deciding upon a treatment option, the clinician must judge not only the probability of success, but also the cost in terms of time and money, and the acceptability of the procedure to the client.

Regarding efficacy, ACS appears to merit first choice among the four behavioral alternatives tested in Experiment 4. This conclusion may be limited by the omission in these studies of variations on a behavioral theme; for example, the aversion relief and anticipatory avoidance techniques, or the use of operant conditioning methods.

The choice of treatment method is made perplexing when the clinician takes into account issues of cost, time, and acceptability. Cost and time required are usually, but not invariably, connected. In this regard, ABR may claim a distinct advantage. If the claims of its early proponents are verified by greater numbers of patients treated, ABR may well be the speediest of any behavioral treatment yet devised. Several cases have been described as being resolved after only one session (Wickramasekera, 1976)—a remarkable example of single trial learning.

Even if ABR can result in such dramatic improvements, other techniques might still be useful. Many patients object to one treatment or another and these objections can impede treatment progress unless options are made available. For example, across all studies, of 30 patients offered ABR, 22 refused it, and 22 of 32 patients who were offered ESA refused that method. On the other hand, just one out of 20 patients refused ACS when it was offered, and none of 34 refused CS. In clinical practice it is best to be able to offer at least two effective modalities for any maladaptive sexual approach behavior. Experiment 4 demonstrates that ACS is an effective treatment technique for exhibitionism when compared with other behavioral treatments, and it enjoys good patient acceptability.

Experiment 5

Our initial technique in presenting aversive odors was simply to place an open jar (of valeric acid or cultured placenta) under the noses of our patients. This mode of presentation seemed unscientific as the aversive stimulus could not be objectively measured (nor could the patient's response). Several studies have similarly employed odor presentations which could not be quantified, though Weitzel, Horan, and Addis (1977) have reported on an apparatus to measure doses of pleasant or unpleasant odors. As we gained experience, we tried various techniques of odor presentation, including the use of a squeeze bottle and a more complicated electrical air-pump method.

Purpose

Experiment 5 tried to compare, although in retrospective fashion, three means of presenting a noxious odor to determine if an optimum method of presentation could be found.

Methods

Subjects. Records of 30 subjects were chosen with the use of a random numbers table and allocated to one of three treatment groups: open bottle (group 1), squeeze bottle (group 2), and electrical air pump (group 3). The use of all three techniques was ongoing as we treated our clients. Several patients had received two or even three different modes of odor presentation, and they were eliminated from consideration in this project. Thus all patients within the experimental group who had received just one mode of odor presentation were listed in order of referral, and the random numbers table was used to pick 10 persons within each category. Groups did not differ significantly in terms of age, duration of exposing history, or number of legal difficulties.

Treatment procedures. All subjects, regardless of group, had received an identical paradigm of treatment with ACS as detailed in Experiment 1 and Table 3. The sole difference between the three groups was the method of presenting the odor. *Group 1* had the foul odor presented merely by having the therapist hold an open bottle of placental culture directly under the patient's nose, as close as possible without touching him, at the appropriate points during scene presentations. The odor was removed as escape elements were introduced in the scene. *Group 2* had the foul odor presented via a squeeze-bottle apparatus. A piece of cultured placenta and its liquor were placed in a plastic squeeze bottle with a nasal tube attached at top. At appropriate points during scene presentations, the therapist positioned the bottle so that the tube entered the patient's nostril, and squeezed the bottle once every two seconds. The therapist removed the tube when escape elements were introduced into the scene. *Group 3* had the foul odor delivered by means of an electrical air pump exactly as described by Weitzel et al. (1977). As escape occurred in the scene, fresh air was substituted for the placental culture.

Assessment. Frequency data for covert and overt exhibitionist behaviors were collected as in Experiment 1. Legal records were collected as previously described. Plethysmograph records were collected and recorded as described in Experiment 3. Records were available for five subjects (two in group 1, one in group 2, and two in group 3). These records showed excellent correlation with frequency data and thus are not presented here.

Results

Frequency records for each of the three odor presentations revealed no significant differences.

Discussion

Despite the small number of subjects and the retrospective nature of the data collection, these results confirmed our clinical impression that exact control of odor presentation via sophisticated equipment was not a prerequisite to beneficial outcome. Nonetheless, electrical air pump equipment can help to answer questions of optimum strength and duration of odor in a fashion equivalent to electronic equipment with ESA.

ACS requires the patient to focus on an evolving scenario in his imagination. Perhaps the ability to present an odor and extend it over a portion of this evolving scene enhances therapeutic effect. Electric shock is rarely administered over a time period exceeding half a second and it may be most effective with brief images, such as slides, pictures, or sexually related words. The slower evolution of fantasied images might best lend itself to a longer, more flexible aversive stimulus presentation as can be accomplished in ACS, whether produced with a bottle held inelegantly under the nose, squeezed from a snifter bottle, or accurately measured with an electric air pump wafting doses of stench to the patient's waiting nostrils.

Experiment 6

Aversion therapy is relatively young, a child of the burgeoning behavior therapies first published and promoted in the last decade. Long-term follow-up studies of patients treated with aversive techniques are not common and it is hoped are still in the making. We are thus quite often unsure how permanent our effects at intervention will be.

The advisability of booster sessions was recognized early (Wolpe, 1969). Nonetheless, few studies have systematically examined whether behavioral treatments offer a permanent or a temporary improvement. In our work with exhibitionists, we noticed that booster sessions were needed at increasing intervals to perpetuate the benefits of treatment (Maletzky, 1977). Occasionally a patient would encounter too enticing a situation and begin to expose again. Often this would occur several months to years after active therapy had ended. A few booster sessions then helped to eliminate exhibitionist urges. Although patients could have produced their own boosters at home via audio tape and smell, sessions in the office were felt to be more powerful and more certain to induce behavior change.

Purpose

This study attempted to determine if booster sessions of ACS were necessary to produce continued abstinence from exhibitionism.

Methods

Subjects. Twenty-five patients were prospectively chosen for this follow-up study from the middle phases of our work with exhibitionists.

Treatment procedures

1. Active treatment with 10 to 12 bi-monthly conditioning sessions of ACS.
2. Twelve months of no active conditioning. To control partially for the supportive effects of active therapy, monthly follow-up sessions were held to collect data, promote life-style change, and offer encouragement.
3. Booster sessions monthly for 12 months; concomitantly, home use of tapes and foul odor once each month for 12 months.
4. Continuous follow-up by telephone contact monthly for another 12 months. Patients identified as having an increase in exhibitionist urges or behaviors were treated by being instructed to listen to their tapes and use the odor weekly for 6 months. In addition, ACS sessions were administered to these individuals once every other month for 6 months.

Assessment. Frequency data for covert and overt exhibitionist behaviors were collected as previously reported in Experiment 1. Legal records also were collected as previously described. Plethysmograph records were collected and recorded as described in Experiment 3.

Results

Figure 9 demonstrates the average monthly frequency of covert and overt exhibitionist behaviors in each of the four treatment phases. Figure 10 shows average plethysmograph changes expressed as percentage of full erection during these treatment phases. On both records it appears that exhibitionist tendencies could reappear and require additional, although infrequent, reconditioning. Yet the averaged data obscure the fact that many patients did *not* require boosters. The increase in frequency data and plethysmograph records were attributable to just 7 of the 25 patients. The rest remained free of exhibitionist behaviors and showed significant decreases in

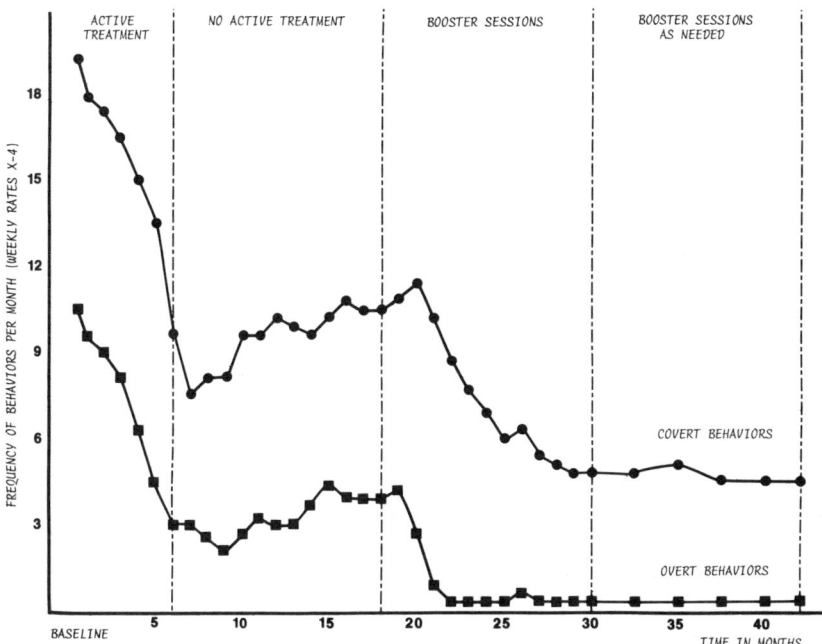

Figure 9. Mean monthly frequencies of covert and overt exhibitionist behaviors in active treatment, no active treatment, booster session, and variable booster session conditions.

the plethysmograph records at all points of testing during a 54-month period, despite the lack of boosters in phases 2 and 4. It must be remembered that during the two years of follow-up in phase 4, no boosters, whether at home or in the treatment setting, were required.

Discussion

For some exhibitionists, boosters were necessary to maintain the effects of aversive conditioning. Most of these patients described a reawakening of exhibitionist urges and fantasies in the presence of a particularly provocative stimulus. Once a single exhibitionist behavior occurred, it was easier for similar behaviors to follow in less enticing settings. Yet for most exhibitionists, no such boosters were required. In comparing the characteristics of patients requiring

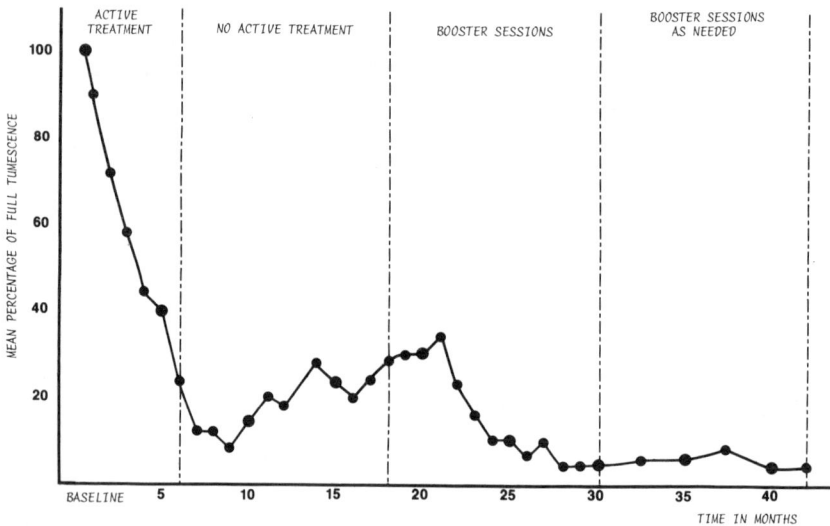

Figure 10. Mean percentage of full tumescence in plethysmograph recordings in active treatment, no active treatment, booster session, and variable booster session conditions.

boosters with those who had not required them, there were no distinguishing features to help predict who would falter later on. It appeared, however, that many of those not requiring boosters had been able, by themselves or through therapy, to rearrange their environments in such a manner as to decrease their entry into especially provocative situations.

If some exhibitionists require boosters, how long should such treatment continue? Based on the present research, it would be safe to offer boosters for at least three years. With the aid of tape recorders and home practice, it should be possible to program boosters at infrequent intervals for many years after active therapy has ended. The patient is given, via home practice, the means to carry on treatment whenever he feels the need. Treatment is thus viewed as an ongoing learning process rather than as a time-limited procedure controlled by treatment personnel. Perhaps aversive conditioning, at least as it is employed in ACS, can be successful in initiating a process of change which must then be pursued either by continued aversive conditioning (boosters), environmental change, or preferably both. To insure that the effects of conditioning continue, our standard practice currently is to extend boosters over at least a two-year period and urge the patient to continue his own booster sessions at home once every two to three months indefinitely, or as he feels the need. It would be of interest, however, to determine how long some patients can continue without any booster sessions.

Experiment 7

We have the good fortune to have been able to treat over 150 men who exposed. These patients were usually referred through the legal system, but many also were referred by doctors, relatives, and friends. Nonetheless, the sample described here may be quite biased as clinicians only encounter one form of this condition. Some exhibitionists are not apprehended and these individuals, perhaps more fortunate or more discreet, may never come to treatment (Bastani, 1976). Several of our patients described many years during which they never exposed but engaged in sexual fantasies of doing so. Are these latent exhibitionists? It seems safe to assume that, of all exhibitionists, those with the most exposing incidents generally come to treatment. Many of these individuals already have their lives in disarray: marriages broken, jobs lost, self-esteem pitifully low. Although the clinician may face many tasks in helping the exhibitionist, he often must first deal with the exhibitionism itself, either by court demand or by the pressing need to prevent another exposure before the exhibitionist is apprehended and imprisoned.

Purpose

The purpose of the following "experiment," actually a collection of data already at hand, was to review and characterize outcome data from all exhibitionists treated with ACS, asking the following questions:

1. Can a successful treatment package be developed for exhibitionism using ACS?
2. Can specific components of this package be sufficiently isolated so as to ferret out the critical elements of therapy?

Methods

Subjects. To spare the reader a lengthy table enumerating characteristics of each of the many subjects treated, demographic data is summarized here. Of 155 subjects treated thus far, 64 were referred from defense attorneys, 18 from prosecuting attorneys, 20 from judges, 21 from police, 19 from other physicians, 7 from relatives, and 6 from friends. These men were surprisingly young, with an average age of 28.2 (range 18–57). They had been exposing for 1.27 years at a rate of 1.4 exposures per month. They were singularly unlucky: for every 7.3 exposures there was one apprehension, though certain individuals were either lucky or devious enough to escape detection, perhaps because of their exposing styles. At any rate, other evidence indicates a high re-arrest rate for exhibitionists (Mohr, Turner, & Jerry, 1964). One exhibitionist exposed only to very young girls unlikely to report the incident or later identify him, and avoided detection for 23 years during which an estimated 400 exposing incidents occurred.

We saw no female exhibitionists: their reports in the literature (Eber, 1977; Hollander, Brown, & Roback, 1977) seem to describe narcissistic women who obtain attention from men through partial exposure. We know of no cases in which a man exposed to another man or boy. Of 155 patients treated, 93 were treated with ACS alone, 5 with CS alone, 7 with ESA alone, 7 with ABR alone, 5 with ACS and CS, 3 with ACS and ESA, and 3 with ACS and ABR. To date, an additional 32 patients have been treated with ACS and a combination of techniques, including some of those just mentioned and others to be described. These last 32 represent our latest patients: hence they have received our utmost attention in developing an exhibitionism treatment package. In 21 patients, exhibitionism was only one of several maladaptive sexual approach behaviors occurring: 9 of these patients fondled women inappropriately and 9 fondled young girls. For many patients, exhibitionism was one step in a chain leading (at least occasionally) to molestation. In addition, 3 patients had committed rape after exposing. The latter has not been previously reported and must be considered rare (Rooth & Marks, 1974).

Treatment procedures. The treatment of exhibitionism with ACS has already been described. Because our task increasingly has become treating patients rather than constructing research paradigms, many of our recent patients have been treated with a combination of methods outside the rigorous definition of ACS. These methods did not constitute, in our thinking, major additions to ACS but were relatively minor aids. Fortunately, several patients were treated with a combination of the aids first, and we were partially able to assess the strength of their effects without ACS. We will divide the data into two groups: patients treated purely with ACS, and those treated with ACS aided by the techniques to be described.

Approximately 50 percent of these subjects were treated by psychiatric personnel without professional degrees but having extensive training in behavioral methods, including ACS and the other therapies to be described. The remaining 50 percent were treated by professionals: 11 percent by several psychologists and social workers and 39 percent by the author.

1. *Self-monitoring procedures.* Recording a behavior can sometimes have an effect upon its frequency (Maletzky, 1974b). For treatment as well as for observational purposes, then, most patients were asked to record urges to expose and the provoking stimuli, if any. Some patients, however (N = 15), were asked not to keep records so that the treatment effects of such monitoring behavior of itself could be studied.

2. *Thought-changing procedures.* A good number of patients (97) were instructed in thought-stopping and thought-changing procedures (Fensterheim, 1974; Meichenbaum, 1974). Whenever an urge to expose occurred, these patients were asked to continue looking at the stimulus, if any, for several seconds while imagining an "antisexual" thought; examples included being arrested, having their family learn of exposing incidents, or imagining the foul odor and vomiting. Thereafter the patient was instructed to turn away physically from the provoking stimulus and leave the situation.

3. *Fantasy change.* Several authors have commented upon the importance of masturbatory conditioning in promoting deviant sexuality (Brownell, Hayes, & Barlow, 1977; Fensterheim, 1974; McGuire, Carlisle, & Young, 1965). A number of our patients (approximately 30 percent) masturbated or had intercourse to fantasies of exhibitionism. Many of these individuals (24) were asked to switch their fantasies from exhibitionism to regular sexual activity just before orgasm. They were then given the challenging task of trying to make

this switch earlier and earlier in their sexual fantasies until they were ideally beginning masturbation or intercourse with fantasies of regular sexual activity.
4. *Environmental control.* If exhibitionism was the end result of a chain of behaviors, it should theoretically be easier to stop the chain at its instigation rather than near its conclusion. Hence 47 patients were asked to review what stimuli initiated urges to expose and then to avoid placing themselves in such settings. One patient, for example, always exposed in his car to women riding in buses alongside him. By changing his route home, this part of his exhibitionism ceased. Another patient exposed from his back porch to girls leaving a nearby school. By switching to an evening shift at work, he was tempted far less often.
5. *ABR.* This technique has been described in Experiment 4. Twelve patients besides those described also underwent this technique. All patients undergoing this procedure had exactly 10 ABR trials. Four of them permitted video tapes to be made of their ABR trials to show to patients and staff. These patients then viewed their tapes with other staff present.
6. *Thioridazine.* Twelve patients were given thioridazine (trade name Mellaril®), an antischizophrenic medication, in doses ranging from 25 mg to 100 mg at bedtime. This medication produces diminished libido and relative erectile failure in 70 to 80 percent of men ingesting it (Bernstein, 1978). It was used to decrease the chance of exposure at the initiation of treatment in cases where the exhibitionist was at grave risk to expose and hence be arrested, and could not exert adequate controls. In no case was thioridazine continued beyond the first 12 weeks of treatment with ACS.
7. *Miscellaneous.* Besides actually exposing to neutral others as in the ABR technique, certain subjects (14) were asked to expose in front of their mirrors—to themselves, so to speak. Homework assignments had the patient actually seek out exposing situations (after several office ACS sessions) but engage in other responses to exhibitionist stimuli. For example, frequently the patient was asked to smell his vial of putrid odor while looking at a potential victim. At other times he was advised to take a photograph of the "victim." These photographs were then used in the office and at home in association with the foul odor and fantasies of exposing.

Although we considered the use of any of these 7 categories to be adjunctive, we had an opportunity to test whether combinations of these techniques without ACS would be effective. We treated 21 subjects with several of these additional measures in weekly visits for a 12-week period without combining them with ACS. The patients were treated with a combination of self-monitoring, thought-turning, environmental control, and fantasy-changing techniques. ABR had been tested in Experiment 4 and was not included in our recomputation of data for the sample.

Assessment. In reviewing data collected over nine years on 155 subjects, it was no surprise that assessment techniques were quite variable. For all 155, however, the following records were available: frequency data for covert and overt exhibitionist behaviors were collected as in Experiment 1; legal records were collected as previously described; for 54 subjects, data were collected using penile plethysmograph records which were produced and recorded as described in Experiment 3; for 10 early subjects, data were additionally available from the temptation test.

Results

Data are presented first for all subjects treated with ACS, regardless of adjunctive techniques used, and then for subjects treated with ACS alone.

Data for all subjects. Data summarized in Table 7 show base-line, post-treatment, 6-month, and one-year follow-ups for all assessment techniques, for all subjects measured by the technique, and without regard to adjunctive techniques employed. No significant differences emerged when data were separated by individual treatment personnel or by their classification (e.g., social worker, physician, or technician); hence data are not presented separately by type of treatment personnel. It is clear that ACS produced vastly significant decreases in covert and overt exhibitionist behavior, legal reports of exposures, penile plethysmograph records, and successes on the temptation test. Patients improving on one measure generally improved on all measures used. Of the 155 patients treated with ACS, 135—or 87 percent—improved to the extent of eliminating all overt exhibitionist behaviors. An "all or none" response usually was seen: only 8 percent of those who improved did so partially. Ninety-two percent of the

Table 7. Mean Treatment Results for All Subjects with ACS across All Measures: Overt and Covert Exhibitionist Behavior Frequencies, Legal Records, Plethysmograph Records, and the Temptation Test

MEASURE EMPLOYED	TIME OF ASSESSMENT				
	Base-line	15 wk	6 mo	12 mo	24 mo
Frequency data (N = 155) in monthly frequencies					
Covert behaviors	27.3	2.7	2.1	2.3	1.1
Overt behaviors	8.7	1.1	.7	.6	.7
Legal records (N = 155) in numbers of charges per 6-month period	2.1	.9	.5	.5	.2
Plethysmograph records (N = 54) in percentage of full tumescence	100	37.2	22.4	23.0	22.9
Temptation test (N = 10) in percentage passing the test	—	90	—	100	—

Note. Differences between baseline and each succeeding evaluation period are significant at least at the .05 level for frequency data, legal records, and plethysmomograph recordings.

rest, or 80 percent of the entire sample, were apparently cured: they reported not even slight urges to expose, regardless of provoking situation. It is of major significance that none of these 135 patients has been charged or arrested for exhibitionism since termination of active treatment. This statement holds true in all cases, even though many of the men have been out of active treatment for eight or nine years.

Data for subjects by adjunctive technique employed. Table 8 demonstrates treatment assessed at each measurement interval with and without various adjunctive techniques, and using only covert exposing behaviors as the measurement; the other assessment techniques were either too widely dispersed to be of value, or they correlated highly with covert exposing frequencies (such as overt

Table 8. Mean Monthly Covert Exhibitionist Behavior Frequencies for All Subjects with ACS Alone or in Combination with Adjunctive Techniques

TREATMENT METHOD (ACS)	TIME OF ASSESSMENT				
	Base-line	15 wk	6 mo	12 mo	24 mo
Alone[a] (N = 62)	28.7	2.7	3.2	2.9	2.9
With thought changing (N = 78)	26.2	2.9	3.2	2.2	2.6
With fantasy changing (N = 21)	21.9	3.3	2.9	2.9	2.9
With environmental control (N = 32)	32.4	3.5	3.5	3.2	3.0
With aversive behavior rehearsal (N = 10)	28.3	2.9	2.8	2.6	2.2
With thioridazine (N = 10)	27.6	2.5	1.9	2.0	1.9
With thought and fantasy changing (N = 19)	19.0	3.1	3.1	2.9	2.8
With thought changing and environmental control (N = 7)	22.9	2.9	2.5	3.0	3.1
With thought and fantasy changing, and aversive behavior rehearsal (N = 7)	25.2	2.2	2.6	2.2	2.3
With all adjunctive techniques, except aversive behavior rehearsal and thioridazine (N = 21)	22.0	2.5	2.2	2.0	2.3

Note. No significant differences were present among any treatment methods; all treatment differences were significant over time.

[a]The only addition was self-monitoring procedures.

frequencies and plethysmograph records). No clearly significant differences emerged upon analyzing these results, though a slight trend developed favoring the inclusion of some of these techniques; in other words, we could make no firm conclusions about which adjunctive techniques were most helpful or whether any additional technique contributed significant power to the aversive conditioning employed. Although results gathered from the treatment of 21 subjects over a 12-week period using a combination of self-monitoring, thought change, fantasy change, and environmental control procedures revealed no significant treatment changes, slight trends in a positive direction were seen: covert exhibitionist behaviors were reduced by 9 percent ($p>.10$) and overt behaviors by 17 percent ($p>.10$). With the addition of ACS, significant differences began to emerge after the twelfth week of treatment, and by 24 weeks of treatment, these patients showed significant changes from base-line. Covert behaviors by that time had been reduced by 92 percent ($p<.001$) and overt behaviors by 97 percent ($p<.001$). Data for 15 patients who were asked not to keep self-monitoring records showed no primary effect from that procedure. These results, while not strictly controlled, indicate that the adjunctive techniques were not sufficient of themselves to produce desired behavior change.

Discussion

ACS did not work for every patient, but it worked for most. Our longest post-treatment follow-ups have now been nine years. Although many patients continue to return for booster sessions, most do not; yet at follow-up only a small difference has been found between those attending boosters and those who do not. Successful treatment for many of these patients might have initiated a chain of positive developments, including freedom from urges to expose, enhancement of normal sexual relationships, improved marital communications, and a lessening of guilt. These in turn might have helped the exhibitionist further to avoid exposing, thus perpetuating a positive behavior cycle.

Using adjunctive techniques with ACS did not seem to contribute to its effectiveness. However, the responsibility for following through with many of these treatments was in the hands of the patients, some of whom might not have completed their assignments at home thoroughly. Moreover, many patients reported help with adjunctive techniques. It is probably best at present to treat patients with a relatively full therapeutic repertoire. Hence, we have combined ACS with self-monitoring, thought changing, fantasy changing, and environmental control techniques in treating our last 32 patients. For 2 patients, the effects of this combination needed to be bolstered by ABR; for 2 other patients, thioridazine was required at first to lessen the severity of exhibitionist urges. This presently constitutes our treatment package. We honestly believe that its flexible use will eliminate exhibitionism in over 90 percent of exposing offenders.

Experiment 8

Of the 155 patients already described, 20 clearly did not benefit from treatment. Of these, 9 did not complete treatment for unknown reasons and 4 did not keep appointments consistently. When contacted, 3 of the 13 men were incarcerated for subsequent exposing incidents. All of these patients—whether incarcerated, reporting exposing urges and incidents or not—were counted as treatment failures.

Outcome data for these 20 patients indicated poor response across all treatment options afforded. The treatment failures could be clearly differentiated from the remaining 135 patients, raising the question of whether they shared any characteristics that could have helped us predict treatment failure. Also of interest was the question of what happens to those who fail in treatment.

Purpose

The purposes of the present study were to examine demographic variables, exposing behavior, legal records, and treatment responses to other forms of therapy for patients who did not benefit from ACS, with the goal of trying to characterize the nonresponder.

Methods

Subjects. Characteristics of the 20 patients will be discussed in the results section.

Treatment procedures. Treatment offered for the 20 failing patients followed the original procedure described in Experiment 1. Therapy for the 7 patients who left treatment early was terminated at scattered points over the course of treatment and generally occurred before the midpoint.

Assessment

> During treatment frequency records for covert and overt exhibitionist behaviors were collected as in Experiment 1. Penile plethysmograph records were available for 12 of the 20 failing subjects and were produced and recorded as described in Experiment 3.

At six-month follow-up attempts were made to reach each of the 20 treatment failures. We were successful in contacting 16 of the men, 14 of whom agreed to a follow-up visit and to keep frequency records for one week prior to the visit. During the visit, penile plethysmograph records were made to the patient's original scenes and the frequency records were reviewed. Legal records were available for all 14 of these men.

Results

Demographic and treatment characteristics of the 20 patients for whom therapy clearly failed to produce a treatment response were compared to the 135 patients who showed a good treatment response. Parameters such as duration of exposing, number of incidents, prior legal record, time of entry into the treatment program, or presence of adjunctive techniques were not correlated with treatment response. Several factors, however, did tend to distinguish between failing and succeeding subjects. For one thing, the failing subjects were younger, with an average age of 22.1 as opposed to 28.4 years for the men who succeeded in the program. For another, these subjects were usually disgruntled about lack of immediate success. Thus we computed another measure: velocity of change. This measure was computed by summing weekly changes in frequency data from the first four treatment weeks and then averaging the changes. For 135 successful patients, this figure was 6.2 for covert and 4.1 for overt behaviors; for the 20 failing patients, the figures were 2.7 and 1.4 respectively, both significant differences ($p < .05$).

Of the 20 failing subjects, we were able to determine that 4 had subsequently entered alternate treatment programs. Two entered a group for exhibitionists, one entered individual psychodynamic therapy, and one was sent to a state hospital program for sexual offenders. Of the 3 in outpatient therapy, 2 subsequently exposed and are now incarcerated.

Discussion

Unfortunately, these data do not help us predict exactly which individuals will or will not benefit from ACS. But there is some significance to be gleaned. Many of the patients failing ACS dropped out of treatment because of no immediately obvious response. Examination of their charts revealed expressions of frustration and pessimism. Based upon these impressions, it would seem prudent to be alert for such patients, especially those in younger age groups, and to design treatment programs with more frequent early contact, more demonstrable positive feedback, and more initial environmental support. Such a program might include visits two to three times a week but of brief duration, the use of graphs and charts along with initial easily demonstrable treatment goals, much verbal reinforcement, and several sessions with family members to garner their help in supporting the patient through the early phases of treatment. We now routinely incorporate these procedures when we identify an easily frustrated, younger patient.

These data also underscore the fact that exhibitionism is not a self-limited condition. Exhibitionists who left treatment or for whom treatment was not successful evidently got arrested with much greater frequency than those who completed treatment successfully (Bastani, 1976; Mohr, Turner, & Jerry, 1964). The effects of previous arrests and incarcerations, fractured marriages, job losses, and ruined friendships may all be too weak in lessening the compulsion to expose and in reducing the anticipation of sexual pleasure associated with genital display.

SYNTHESIS OF RESULTS

Comparative Efficacy of Assisted Covert Sensitization[2]

The experiments described here were carried out over a period of years (1970–1978) and in a variety of clinical settings but with a general consistency of treatment approach. Data analyzed separately by place of treatment (clinic, private practice, or medical school) or type of treatment personnel (technician versus professional) were not significantly different. A variety of clinical research assessment techniques demonstrated the efficacy of assisted covert sensitization, as applied to most exhibitionist patients, without the unwanted effects of a decrease in other heterosexual behaviors or an increase in anxiety or aggression.

However, as our results indicate and several other chapters in this book demonstrate, alternate behavioral approaches also are effective in the treatment of exhibitionism. Two major forms of behavior therapy for exhibitionism are electroshock aversion (ESA) and aversive behavioral rehearsal (ABR). Why choose ACS?

The use of electric shock in behavior therapy has an honorable history (Abel, Levis, & Clancy, 1970; Fookes, 1969; Marks & Gelder, 1967; Marks, Gelder, & Bancroft, 1970; McConaghy, 1970). It undoubtedly is the most widely employed aversive stimulus today, although not all reports are favorable (James, 1978; James, Orwin, & Turner, 1977; MacDonough, 1972). In our presently reported series of 155 patients, ESA was offered to 34 patients: to 20 patients, it was offered as the only treatment and to 14 it was offered within a combination of treatments, including ACS and ABR. Of the 32 men to whom it was offered, 22 refused to consider shock. Fourteen of these patients were offered only the use of ESA, and 8 were offered shock along with other therapies. Many of our patients had heard of electric shock and refused it on the basis of prejudice or misinformation. As one patient said, "nobody's going to use electricity on me!" Several patients confused ESA with electroconvulsive therapy. These reactions were not systematically studied and certainly our bias could have affected patients' responses adversely, but for many of the patients we were trying to use a combination of techniques and very much wanted them to accept our suggestions.

One of the difficulties we have experienced in the use of electric shock aversion is the issue of timing. In most imagery techniques, no one moment in time can be isolated precisely as the crucial instant to present the aversive stimulus. In scene presentations with ACS, a conglomeration of exhibitionist elements is presented to a patient over a 10 to 45-second interval and *all during that time* an aversive stimulus (foul odor) is presented so that a variety of elements within each scene can be associated with the noxious stimulus. It is difficult to administer an electric shock over a long period of time. By presenting, quickly removing, and then re-presenting the electric stimulus, one could actually reinforce (by escape) exhibitionist elements within the scene; hence its use may best be reserved for short-term stimuli such as pictures or slides (MacDonough, 1972). A foul odor may have an advantage because of its flexibility of duration; it can be presented for exactly the length of time required within each scene. After-odors have never been a problem, as the patient easily habituates to the background odor of the foul preparation and yet never adapts to the odor presented under his nose or administered by a "snifter." The odor does not escape the room in which it is being used and traces of it are undetectable 10 minutes after treatment has ended.

Duration of aversive stimulus also may be important for practice at home and on the street, as patients can easily carry small vials of the odiferous substance for use "in vivo." Our attempts to build and then have patients employ an in-pocket, battery-powered electric shock apparatus have not been uniformly successful. In addition, we have encountered other disturbing side-effects with ESA. Often a patient is shocked out of imagining a scene. Patients also tend not to use shock apparatuses for practice at home. Thus, in our experience, ESA is best used with the presentation of discrete stimuli such as pictures or slides rather than imagined scenes.

There has been some comment on the tendency for ESA to produce an increase in aggressive behaviors (Rachman & Teasdale, 1969). We have only rarely observed this phenomenon. All of these impressions obviously are anecdotal and biased at best. Comparative trials of patient acceptance and compliance would be of interest.

One inescapable obstacle usually in the way of all therapies is the cost of treatment. The equipment necessary to produce safe, reliable electric aversive stimuli and to provide out-of-office electric aversion is often costly. Equipment necessary to present slides and to automate their presentation with shock, or to produce shock escape or avoidance, is even more costly. Foul odors, and equipment (if any) used to present them, usually are easily at hand at nominal expense.

Length of treatment is also an important economic consideration in devising feasible, effective therapy. In this regard the early reports employing ABR are especially appealing as so few sessions are evidently required. Although our comparisons of ABR with ACS seem to favor the latter, our bias may have been showing. Moreover, we were struck with the occasional patient who responded dramatically with ABR. Unfortunately, we could not foretell who might exhibit such a response.

ABR is a powerful technique (Jones & Frei, 1977; Serber, 1970; Wickramasekera, 1976). In our experience it was usually a frightening one as well. Of 35 individuals offered the technique, 22 at first refused it, even before they knew options existed and even though many had been ordered into treatment as a condition of probation or parole. Studies on ABR may have reported only the "best" patients, as only these may consent to undergo the treatment. ABR was not, in some instances, inexpensive since fees for psychiatric staff and facilities were charged to many of the patients directly. Nor was ABR without adverse effect. Seven of the 22 patients who finally completed the procedure complained of anxiety, insomnia, and depression for several weeks thereafter. This was thought to be a small price, however, for the beneficial effect. ABR is unquestionably an innovative and powerful treatment for exhibitionism (and perhaps for other conditions such as alcoholism as well) in selected patients.

Present Treatment Program

Clinicians are seemingly embarrassed with riches in the treatment of exhibitionism. Potent and ingenious therapies have been devised and, as hinted before, the diverse approaches can be categorized and presented to the patient and therapist for each to pick and choose a blend of selections from this menu to please every palate and pocketbook. No matter how pure or prejudiced any therapist is, it is difficult not to sample a bit of this and that in concocting a feast of therapies.

We too have been unable to resist this temptation and routinely order up a smorgasbord of therapies sufficient to make a pure researcher retch. Clinically, however, these combinations seem to work. Our approximate present paradigm, mentioned briefly at the end of Experiment 7 and presented in Table 9, should be taken as only one of a number of variations on three general themes: ACS with adjunctive techniques, ACS with ESA paired with slides and photographs of "victims," or ACS paired with ABR. These themes are chosen more by patient acceptance than by any ability, as yet, to predict who will do better with what.

As has been seen, a number of adjunctive techniques are usually added. Several of the most recently helpful have been frequency recording; thought-stopping and thought-changing procedures; masturbatory fantasy change; explanations of behavior chaining with instructions of how to avoid early, rather than late, behavioral elements; environmental change (for example, asking the exhibitionist who exposes to school girls from his car to take a different route home); exposing to a mirror; exposing to wives, girlfriends, or parents; videotaping exhibitionist acts and having the patient view the tape with girlfriend or relatives; having the patient view other men exposing; having the patient view videotapes of other men exposing;

photographing scenes which would have elicited exposing and using the pictures with a foul odor or electric shock; plus the predictable homework assignments of associating the foul odor with unzipping one's fly, being tempted by an exposing situation, or having urges to expose. Some concern has been voiced about the exclusive use of punishment techniques (Sansweet, 1975; Yates, 1975): thus we occasionally include measures designed to increase socially acceptable heterosexual behaviors such as assertive training (Herson, Eisler, & Miller, 1973), social skills training (Goldsmith & McFall, 1975; Lutzker, 1973) and desensitization to fearful heterosexual stimuli (Curran, 1975). This list is long but not exhaustive. Further work might include asking the exhibitionist to meet and get to know, as individuals, those to whom he exposes. His actions are usually so devoid of personal contact that he might be changed if he were to regard his victim as another human being. Group behavior therapy also would be of interest.

Since completing work with these 155 patients, we have had the opportunity to treat an additional 31 patients employing the paradigms shown in Table 9 and the newer adjunctive techniques just described. All but 3 patients markedly reduced both overt and covert exhibitionist behaviors, not only according to self-reports, but to observer reports, legal records, and plethysmograph records as well. We have no hesitation in recommending that exhibitionist offenders be offered a fair trial of such therapies and, if legally restricted, be allowed relative freedom when at least halfway through that trial.

Rationale

Why does aversive therapy work for exhibitionism? As evidence accumulates for the efficacy of these techniques, are we any closer to a theory of aversive conditioning in humans? The patient knows he will not have to smell a foul odor or receive a shock if he chooses to expose outside the treatment setting. Aversive conditioning obviously has little to do with cognitive knowledge as it is now understood.

It has been surmised that a class of behaviors termed "consummatory" are peculiarly responsive to malodorous aversion therapies (Bandura, 1969; Little & Curran, 1978; Maletzky, 1973; Maletzky, 1974a). Such responses include ingestion of foods and beverages and indulgences in sexual behavior. There is some evidence to support this view, though at best it is underwhelming (Maletzky, 1973; Maletzky, 1974a). Still, it is a seductive notion that putrefying odors

Table 9. Approximation of Present Treatment Paradigm for Exhibitionism

DESCRIPTION	TREATMENT PHASE	AVERAGE FREQUENCY AND DURATION
1. History taking	Self-explanatory	¾ of the first hour
2. Education	Explanation of exhibitionism as a learned response, not a manifestation of a deviant personality	¼ of the first hour
3. Treatment explanation	Description of treatment techniques, provision of reading materials	¼ of the second hour
4. Data collection	Explanation of how to self-monitor covert and overt exhibitionist behavior	¼ of the second hour
5. Relaxation training		
a. With therapist	Explanation of relaxation technique and introduction to patient in office	½ of the second hour
b. Without therapist	Listening to relaxation tape at home every night	12 minutes nightly for two weeks
c. With pleasant imagery	Listening to relaxation tape at home every night followed by one minute of concentrating on an idiosyncratic pleasant scene	13 minutes nightly for one week
6. Scene collection	Collection and revision of exhibitionist and noxious scenes	All of the third hour
7. Sensitization		
a. With therapist	Scene visualizations under relaxation, with placental culture, and performed by therapist; recording tapes of scenes	30 minutes weekly for an average of 12.7 sessions

Table 9 (Continued).

DESCRIPTION	TREATMENT PHASE	AVERAGE FREQUENCY AND DURATION
b. Without therapist	Scene visualizations under relaxation, with placental culture, and performed by patient at home (or in office) listening to tape, without therapist present	30 minutes, 3 times weekly, for an average of 19.7 weeks
8. Use of adjunctive techniques		
a. Thought-changing	Substituting noxious images for exhibitionist urges and fantasies	Introduced during the first 2 sensitization sessions
b. Fantasy-changing	Changing masturbation fantasies from exhibitionist to normal heterosexual ones increasingly early during masturbation	Introduced during the second 2 sensitization sessions
c. Environmental control	Changing external stimuli previously triggering exhibitionist behaviors	Introduced during the first 2 sensitization sessions
d. Aversive behavior rehearsal	Exposing to hospital nursing staff; reviewing videotape of procedure with significant others	5 exposing sessions spaced 2 weeks apart, during active sensitization treatment; viewing videotape of 2 such sessions with significant others 3 days after that session
e. Electric shock aversion	Pairing pictures of potential victims and fantasies of exposing to them with an electric shock	10 sessions of 10 pairings each, randomly alternated with active sensitization treatment

Table 9 (Continued).

DESCRIPTION	TREATMENT PHASE	AVERAGE FREQUENCY AND DURATION
f. Thioridazine	An antischizophrenic medicine usually producing diminished libido and erectile failure	25–100 mg at bedtime for the first 4–12 weeks, in cases where urges will almost certainly eventuate in overt behaviors and arrests before treatment can be effective
9. Sensitization "in vivo"	Smelling placental culture in situations previously triggering exhibitionist behaviors	All situations are encountered, all during active sensitization treatment; approximately 20 weeks
10. Covert sensitization without therapist	Imagining exposing with bad consequences (being arrested, getting sick) or imagining exposing to unattractive victims (parents, police, the elderly, hospital staff)	Nightly for 12–15 weeks during active sensitization treatment
11. Booster sessions		
a. With therapist	Same as 7a	30 minutes, in office, at 3-, 6-, and 12-month intervals following active sensitization treatment
b. Without therapist	Same as 7b	Whenever the patient feels it is necessary; average of 7 such sessions over a one-year period following active sensitization treatment

have some special power in overcoming appetitive responses. It is said that dogs fed contaminated chow will never eat from the same bowl again, and it seems self-evident that there is strong survival value attached to being repelled by rotting meat. Two of the foulest smelling chemicals known, valeric acid and butyric acid, are produced in nature by the action of bacteria upon animal tissues.

Our patients almost uniformly deny nausea when confronted by previously provocative situations (cf. Reitz & Keil, 1971); rather, they describe an absence of exhibitionist urges. Are they simply unaware of subliminal feelings of nausea, or are they in fact "normalized" so that exhibitionism holds no pleasure for them? A tantalizing clue exists in a recent brief and uncontrolled observation we have made. Among nonexhibitionist men exposed to exhibitionist scenes, penile plethysmograph recordings reflected a mild trend toward increased penile volume. Among exhibitionists successfully treated with ACS, however, a mild trend toward a decreasing penile volume was found.

Maladaptive sexual approach behaviors may also be well suited for deconditioning with covert techniques because of the importance imagery plays in sexual response (Little & Curran, 1978). These findings point the way to further study: Are exhibitionists merely quantitatively, as opposed to qualitatively, different than "normal" men? Do exhibitionists treated with ESA, ABR, group therapy, or psychoanalysis also show a decrease in sexual responses to exhibitionist stimuli? What factors can help us to predict which type of treatment will be best for each patient? Do some exhibitionists only want to masturbate when viewing women, or are all exhibitionists interested in having the women *see* their genitals? In trying to understand exhibitionism, can we also understand the anthropological significance our clothing serves? Is exhibitionism merely a sexual response occurring inappropriately early in the sexual chain? Or is exhibitionism a completely vicarious sexual enjoyment, a sort of coward's rape?

Other less theoretical questions abound. Which treatment is most economical, and which is most acceptable? What is the optimal timing of trials—can they be done in one exhaustive day, or is spacing of trials important (Sambrooks, MacCulloch, & Waddington, 1978)? Are there seasonal differences in the frequency of exhibitionism (our data show an increase in spring and summer) and does time of day make a difference? If so, can this knowledge help our prevention or treatment of exhibitionism? What percentage of exhibitionists get erections when exposing and what percentage climax? Does this make a difference in treatment results? It is exciting to think that effective treatments for exhibitionism are at hand and answers to these questions may not be far behind.

SUMMARY

Eight experiments have been described, most of which attempted to answer a variety of questions regarding the efficacy of assisted covert sensitization (ACS), a technique that pairs scenes of exposing behavior with a putrid odor. Several foul odors have been compared, as have various techniques for presenting the odors. A number of assessment techniques have been employed, including subject and observer reports, reviews of legal records, a temptation test, and penile plethysmograph records. The technique has been compared to covert sensitization, electric shock aversion, and aversive behavior rehearsal. Long-term follow-ups have demonstrated that ACS produces long-lasting changes, but the need for booster sessions in certain patients has been documented. Finally, a rationale for ACS has been presented and questions raised which remain to intrigue future researchers.

The academic and clinical worlds of behavior therapy are not so disparate as to preclude helping us to answer these questions. In the practice of psychiatry, for example, the clinical discovery that an element of nature as simple as lithium could prevent acute episodes of manic-depressive illness led to increasingly elegant studies of the relationship between biochemistry and the mystery of man's moods. Exhibitionism is an eminently treatable maladaptive sexual approach behavior. In its treatment, we may discover its causes. Who knows, when the lions of clinical practice lie down with the lambs of academia, what brain children they may hatch?

ACKNOWLEDGMENTS

The author is indebted to the medical and psychiatric staffs of Lyster Army Hospital, Ft. Rucker, Alabama; the residents and faculty of the Department of Psychiatry, the University of Oregon Health Sciences Center, Portland, Oregon; and the staff of Woodland Park Mental Health Center, Portland, Oregon for assisting in the conception, design, and implementation of the projects described herein.

NOTES

1. The author is indebted to Donald Molde, M.D., for the suggestion of valeric acid as a malodorous substance.
2. Attempts will be made in the future to avoid this obvious misnomer, and to apply the more appropriate term "aversive imagery."

REFERENCES

Abel, G. G., Levis, D. J., & Clancy, J. Aversion therapy applied to taped sequences of deviant behavior and exhibitionism and other sexual deviations: A preliminary report. *Journal of Behavior Therapy and Experimental Psychiatry,* 1970, *1,* 59–68.

Armitage, P. Sequential medical trials. Springfield, Ill.: Charles C Thomas, 1960, pp. 34–40.

Ashem, B., & Donner, L. Covert sensitization with alcoholics: A controlled replication. *Behavior Research and Therapy,* 1968, *6,* 7–12.

Bancroft, J. H. J., & Matthews, A. M. Penile plethysmography: Its physiologic base and clinical application. *Proceedings of the 7th European Conference on Psychosomatic Medicine, Acta Medica Psychosomatica,* 1967, *7,* 475–480.

Bandura, A. *Principles of behavior modification.* New York: Holt, Rinehart & Winston, 1969, pp. 507–508.

Barlow, D. H., Becker, R., Leitenberg, H., & Agras, W. S. A mechanical strain gauge for recording penile circumference change. *Journal of Applied Behavior Analysis,* 1970, *3,* 72.

Bastani, J. B. Treatment of male genital exhibitionism. *Comprehensive Psychiatry,* 1976, *17,* 769–774.

Bernstein, J. G. Chemotherapy of psychosis. In J. G. Bernstein (Ed.), *Clinical psychopharmacology.* Littleton, Mass.: PSG Medical Books, 1978.

Bross, I. Sequential medical plans. *Biometrics,* 1952, *8,* 188–205.

Brownell, K. D., Hayes, S. C., & Barlow, B. A. Patterns of appropriate and deviant sexual arousal: The behavioral treatment of multiple sexual deviations. *Journal of Consulting and Clinical Psychology,* 1977, *45,* 1144–1155.

Burdick, W. R. Exploration of the aversion therapy technique of covert sensitization with selected patients of exhibitionism. Doctoral thesis, University of Minnesota, 1972. Order No.: 72–32, 282. *Psychology Abstracts,* 1974.

Callahan, E. J., & Leitenberg, H. Aversion therapy for sexual deviation: Contingent shock and covert sensitization. *Journal of Abnormal Psychology,* 1973, *81,* 60–73.

Cautela, J. R. Treatment of compulsive behavior by covert sensitization. *Psychological Review*, 1966, *16*, 33–41.

Cautela, J. R. Covert sensitization. *Psychological Reports*, 1967, *20*, 459–468.

Colson, C. E. Olfactory aversion therapy for homosexual behavior. *Journal of Behavior Therapy and Experimental Psychiatry*, 1972, *3*, 185–187.

Curran, J. P. Skills training as an approach to the treatment of heterosexual/social anxiety. *Psychological Bulletin*, 1977, *84*, 140–157.

Davison, G. C. Elimination of a sadistic fantasy by client-controlled counterconditioning techniques: A case study. *Journal of Abnormal Psychology*, 1968, *73*, 84–90.

Diamet, C., & Wilson, G. T. An experimental investigation of the effects of covert sensitization in an analogue eating situation. *Behavior Therapy*, 1975, *4*, 499–509.

Eber, M. Exhibitionism or narcissism? Letter to the editor. *American Journal of Psychiatry*, 1977, *134*–153.

Emmelkamp, P. M. G., & Walta, C. Effects of therapy set on electrical aversion therapy and covert sensitization. *Behavior Therapy*, 1978, *9*, 185–188.

Ewalt, J. R., & Farnsworth, E. L. *Text book of psychiatry*. New York: Blakiston, 1963.

Feldman, M. P., & MacCulloch, M. J. Avoidance conditioning for homosexuals: A reply to MacDonough's critique. *Behavior Therapy*, 1972, *3*, 430–436.

Fensterheim, H. Behavior therapy of the sexual variations. *Journal of Sex and Marital Therapy*, 1974, *1*, 16–28.

Fookes, B. H. Some experiences in the use of aversion therapy in male homosexuality, exhibitionism and fetishism-transvestism. *British Journal of Psychiatry*, 1969, *115*, 339–341.

Foreyt, J. P., & Hagan, R. L. Covert sensitization: Conditioning or suggestion? *Journal of Abnormal Psychology*, 1973, *82*, 17–23.

Foreyt, J. P., & Kennedy, W. Treatment of overweight by aversion therapy. *Behavior Research and Therapy*, 1971, *9*, 29–34.

Franks, C., Fried, R., & Ashem, B. An improved apparatus for the aversive conditioning of cigarette smoking. *Behavior Research and Therapy*, 1966, *4*, 301–308.

Freund, K. Some problems in the treatment of homosexuality. In H. J. Eysenck (Ed.), *Behavior therapy and the neuroses*. Oxford: Pergamon Press, 1960, pp. 326–331.

Goldsmith, J. B., & McFall, R. M. Development and evaluation of an interpersonal skill-training program for psychiatric patients. *Journal of Abnormal Psychology*, 1975, *54*, 51–58.

Hackett, T. P. The psychotherapy of exhibitionists in a court clinic setting. In J. Masserman (Ed.), *Seminars in psychiatry* (Vol. 3). New York: Grune & Stratton, 1971, pp. 297–306.

Hayes, S. C., Brownell, K. D., & Barlow, D. H. The use of self-administered covert sensitization in the treatment of exhibitionism and sadism. *Behavior Therapy*, 1978, 9, 283–289.

Henderson, D. K., & Batchelor, I. R. C. *Text book of psychiatry for students and practitioners*. London: Oxford University Press, 1969.

Henson, D. E., & Rubin, H. B. Voluntary control of eroticism. *Journal of Applied Behavioral Analysis*, 1971, 4, 37–44.

Herson, M., Eisler, R. M., & Miller, P. M. Development of assertive responses: Clinical measurement and research considerations. *Behavior Research and Therapy*, 1973, 11, 505–521.

Hollander, M. H., Brown, C. W., & Roback, H. B. Genital exhibitionism in women. *American Journal of Psychiatry*, 1977, 134, 436–438.

James, S. Treatment of homosexuality (Part II): Superiority of desensitization/arousal as compared with anticipatory avoidance conditioning: Results of a controlled trial. *Behavior Therapy*, 1978, 9, 28–36.

James, S., Orwin, A., & Turner, R. K. Treatment of homosexuality (Part I): Analysis of failure following a trial of anticipatory avoidance conditioning and the development of an alternative treatment system. *Behavior Therapy*, 1977, 8, 840–848.

Janda, L. H., & Rimm, D. C. Covert sensitization in the treatment of obesity. *Journal of Abnormal Psychology*, 1972, 80, 37–42.

Jones, I. H., & Frei, D. Provoked anxiety as a treatment of exhibitionism. *British Journal of Psychiatry*, 1977, 131, 213–215.

Kennedy, W. A., & Foreyt, J. Control of eating behavior in obese patients by avoidance conditioning. *Psychological Reports*, 1968, 23, 571–573.

Kinsey, N., Pomeroy, W. B., & Martin, C. E. *Sexual behavior in the human male*. Philadelphia: Saunders, 1948.

Laws, D. R., & Rubin, H. B. Voluntary control of eroticism. *Journal of Applied Behavioral Analysis*, 1969, 2, 93–99.

Liechtenstein, E., & Keutzer, C. S. Investigation of diverse techniques to modify smoking: A follow-up report. *Behavior Research and Therapy*, 1969, 7, 139–140.

Little, L. M., & Curran, J. P. Covert sensitization: A clinical procedure in need of some explanation. *Psychological Bulletin*, 1978, 85, 513–531.

Lutzker, J. R. Reinforcement control of exhibitionism in a profoundly retarded adult. *Proceedings of the 81st Annual Convention of the American Psychological Association*, 1973, 8, 931–932.

MacCulloch, M. J., & Feldman, M. P. Aversion therapy in the management of 43 homosexuals. *British Medical Journal*, 1967, *2*, 594–597.

MacDonough, T. S. A critique of the first Feldman & MacCulloch avoidance conditioning treatment for homosexuals. *Behavior Therapy*, 1972, *3*, 104–111.

Maletzky, B. M. Assisted covert sensitization: A preliminary report. *Behavior Therapy*, 1973, *7*, 139–140.

Maletzky, B. M. "Assisted" covert sensitization for drug abuse. *International Journal of Addictions*, 1974a, *9*, 411–429.

Maletzky, B. M. Behavior recording as treatment. *Behavior Therapy*, 1974b, *5*, 107–111.

Maletzky, B. M. "Booster" sessions in aversion therapy: The permanency of treatment. *Behavior Therapy*, 1977, *8*, 460–463.

Maletzky, B. M., & George, F. S. The treatment of homosexuality by "assisted" covert sensitization. *Behavior Research and Therapy*, 1973, *11*, 655–657.

Maletzky, B. M., & Klotter, J. K. Episodic dyscontrol: A controlled replication. *Diseases of the Nervous System*, 1974a, *35*, 175–179.

Maletzky, B. M., & Klotter, J. K. Dexedrine and delinquency: Hyperkinesis persisting? *Diseases of the Nervous System*, 1974b, *35*, 543–547.

Mathis, J. L., & Collins, M. Mandatory group therapy for exhibitionists. *American Journal of Psychiatry*, 1970, *126*, 162–167.

Mathis, J. L., & Collins, M. Enforced treatment of exhibitionists. *Current Psychiatric Therapy*, 1971, *7*, 139–145.

Marks, I., & Gelder, A. M. Transvestism and fetishism: Clinical and psychological changes during faradic aversion. *British Journal of Psychiatry*, 1967, *113*, 711–729.

Marks, I., Gelder, A. M., & Bancroft, J. H. J. Sexual deviants two years after electric aversion. *British Journal of Psychiatry*, 1970, *117*, 173–185.

McConaghy, M. Subjective and penile plethysmograph responses to aversion therapy for homosexuality: A follow-up study. *British Journal of Psychiatry*, 1970, *117*, 555–560.

McGuire, R. L., Carlisle, J. M., & Young, B. G. Sexual deviations as conditioned behavior: A hypothesis. *Behavior Research and Therapy*, 1965, *2*, 185–190.

Meichenbaum, D. *Cognitive behavior modification*. Morristown, N.J.: General Learning Press, 1974.

Miller, H. L., & Haney, J. R. Behavior and traditional therapy applied to pedophiliac exhibitionism: A case study. *Psychological Reports*, 1976, *39*, 1119–1124.

Mohr, J. W., Turner, R. E., & Jerry, M. B. *Pedophilia and exhibitionism.* Toronto: University of Toronto Press, 1964.

Morgenstern, K. Cigarette smoking as a noxious stimulus and self-managed aversion therapy for compulsive eating. *Behavior Therapy,* 1974, 2, 255–260.

Rachman, A. J., & Teasdale, J. Aversion therapy: An appraisal. In C. M. Franks (Ed.), *Behavior therapy: Appraisal and status.* New York: McGraw-Hill, 1969.

Reitz, W. E., & Keil, W. B. Behavioral treatment of an exhibitionist. *Journal of Behavior Therapy and Experimental Psychiatry,* 1971, 2, 839–841.

Rickels, M. K. *Exhibitionism.* Philadelphia: Lippincott, 1950.

Rooth, F. G., & Marks, I. M. Persistent exhibitionism: Short-term response to aversion, self-regulation, and relaxation treatments. *Archives of Sexual Behavior,* 1974, 3, 227–248.

Rosen, R. C. Genital blood flow measurement: Feedback applications in sexual therapy. *Journal of Sex and Marital Therapy,* 1976, 2, 184–196.

Sambrooks, J. E., MacCulloch, M. J., & Waddington, J. L. Incubation of sexual attitude change between sessions of instrumental aversion therapy: Two case studies. *Behavior Therapy,* 1978, 9, 477–485.

Sansweet, S. J. *The punishment cure: How aversion therapy is being used to eliminate smoking, drinking, obesity, homosexuality . . . and practically anything else.* New York: Mason/Charter, 1975.

Serber, M. Shame aversion therapy. *Journal of Behavior Therapy & Experimental Psychiatry,* 1970, 1, 213–215.

Smith, T. E. Correction treatment of the sexual deviant. *American Journal of Psychiatry,* 1968, 125, 615–621.

Stephenson, J., & Jones, I. A. Behavior therapy techniques for exhibitionism. *Archives of General Psychiatry,* 1972, 27, 839–841.

Thorpe, G. L. Learning paradigms in the anticipatory avoidance technique: A comment on the controversy between MacDonough & Feldman. *Behavior Therapy,* 1972, 3, 614–618.

Weitzel, W. B., Horan, J. J., & Addis, J. W. A new olfactory aversion apparatus. *Behavior Therapy,* 1977, 8, 83–88.

Wickramasekera, I. Aversion behavioral rehearsal for sexual exhibitionism. *Behavior Therapy,* 1976, 7, 167–176.

Wolpe, J. *The practice of behavior therapy.* New York: Pergamon Press, 1969.

Yates, A. *Theory and practice in behavior therapy.* New York: Wiley, 1975.

9

AN EXTENDED CASE REPORT:
The Nuts and Bolts of Treating an Exhibitionist

Reid J. Daitzman
Daniel J. Cox

B. was a 31-year-old married engineer who was self-referred for exhibitionism after being arrested and charged. He was raised by an alcoholic father after his mother died when he was six. B. greatly resented his mother's "abandoning" him and an older sister's mothering of the younger siblings but not him. He first exposed six months after marrying a high school girlfriend who "forced him to marry her" at age 20. Exposure incidents periodically occurred every six months. Exposure occurred during stressful times produced by conflicts with wife, in-laws, and employment. B. had sought psychotherapy 2½ years earlier but terminated after 15 sessions because, "he thought he could handle it." On one occasion the patient attempted suicide because of guilt over compulsive exposure and fear that

---

Names, dates, and places have been changed to protect the client's identity.

family members would find out. Over his 11-year history of exposure, he had been arrested on four occasions. Five days before contacting the clinic, he had exposed three times to both older and younger females. On the day of these exposures, he had experienced significant stress at work and school, and his in-laws were visiting to celebrate his daughter's birthday. The three months prior to this incident had been filled with multiple stresses: taking on a new job, moving to a new city, buying a house, and enrolling in college.

For this patient, exhibitionism produced both positive and negative reinforcement. It was positively reinforced by orgasm, gratifying fantasies ~~of sexual prowess~~, and a sense of thrilling challenge with legal authorities. It was negatively reinforced by the great reduction of tension and stress which followed exhibiting, in his own words, "Its like throwing a metal pole into the spokes of a wheel, everything comes to a grinding stop."

At the time of the initial contact, the patient's marriage was in serious jeopardy due to his repeated arrests and continued exhibitionism. The wife was so afraid of stressing the patient and triggering an exposure incident that she avoided confiding any potentially stressful material to him. Consequently, marital communication was gradually deteriorating. However, B. reported a gratifying sexual relationship with his wife, with intercourse occurring approximately four times a week. He denied masturbation except when exposing.

Letter to former therapist from authors

> B., who reports being a patient of yours, is recently charged with exhibitionism. He is being evaluated for possible treatment here at our clinic. In order to complete our evaluation for therapeutic and legal purposes, we would appreciate receiving a summary of your therapeutic efforts and your prognosis. Thank you for your time and efforts.

Therapist response

> I am saddened to hear that B. is in trouble again. I originally saw him as a legal requirement. B. was only in treatment with me for a very short period of time—less than 15 sessions. I definitely saw him as neurotic and in need of treatment, but his true motivation at that time was not significant except in a legal sense. I hope that you can work toward a more successful conclusion with B.

BEHAVIORAL ANALYSIS OF EXHIBITIONISM

The first few treatment sessions should be oriented toward the clarification of previous exhibitionistic episodes. All episodes should be included, not just those which came to the attention of the legal system. Since many exhibitionists have a loss of memory during the actual exhibiting event, the construction of previous events is usually time consuming and frustrating for both patient and therapist. It is strongly recommended that this analysis be completed in three parts. Part 1 is simply a listing of remembered events, and is usually incomplete. Part 2 is an in-depth reconstruction of the antecedents and consequences of the events mentioned in part 1. As therapy sessions progress, the completion of parts 1 and 2 becomes easier. In order to facilitate these reconstructions, the therapist should request that the more recent episodes be listed first. These reconstructions can take place both during and between sessions.

Part 1

B. listed eleven episodes for part 1:

1. January 1968: Philadelphia, Pa. Stopped, but not arrested. Passed out, taken to the hospital, examined, and released. Told that I was stopped for a routine check. Was told that I might be a diabetic.
2. September 1968: Pittsburgh, Pa. I exposed myself about three different times. No incident.
3. April 1969: Pittsburgh. Same as above.
4. April 1970: Pittsburgh. I was arrested and charged. The charge was reduced to disturbing the peace.
5. November 1971: Scranton, Pa. I exposed myself four or five times at different times. No incident.
6. September 1972: Wilkes Barre, Pa. I was arrested and charged, but the court released me with the understanding that I would seek help. (B. saw a therapist for about six months.)
7. April 1973: Westchester, Pa. I was arrested and charged, but the charges were null-processed.
8. July 1973: New York City. I was stopped and I passed out just as I had in Philadelphia.

9. May 1974: Westchester. I was arrested and charged. I don't know what happened in court, but I was released.
10. March 1975: Wilkes Barre. I was stopped and I passed out. My wife was called and they did not arrest me.
11. October 1976: Charlottesville, Va. I was arrested and charged and now I am here. (B. made no mention of the exposing incidents, only the arrest.)

Part 2

B. was subsequently asked to expand upon his listing of remembered events.

1. January 1968: Philadelphia. I had just completed a navy training program. It was a work-study type of program in which you were required to work as a power plant operator for six hours a day and then spend an additional six hours a day in supervised or unsupervised study. I got up that morning and took Diane to work, which was in downtown Philadelphia. On the way home, as I was sitting at a busy intersection, I unbuckled my pants, opened my zipper, took out my penis, and exposed myself. I then drove through the intersection like this. At the next traffic light I came to my senses and put myself back together.
2. September 1968: Pittsburgh. I exposed myself by driving around a shopping center with my pants down around my knees. I finally came to my senses and drove home.
3. April 1969: Pittsburgh. I exposed myself in the same manner just described. I don't remember what was going on just prior to each of these times.
4. April 1970: Pittsburgh. I exposed myself in the public library. I had been in the library looking for a book and noticed this girl was glancing at me now and then. I decided to expose myself to her and did so by taking my penis out of my pants and letting her get a glimpse of me with my penis exposed.
5. November 1971. We had just moved to Pennsylvania, where I had just started working. I was out shopping and exposed myself by pulling my pants down and driving around a shopping center. I did this in two different shopping centers. I finally got hold of myself and drove home.

6. September 1972: Wilkes Barre. On Labor Day weekend, I exposed myself by driving around the mid-city shopping center. I never really picked out anyone in particular to expose myself to, but just drove slowly around the shopping center with my pants down. I finally stopped and started to drive home.
7. April 1973. I was at a university for the purpose of using the library. When I left the library, I started driving around the campus with my pants down. I finally came to my senses and drove home.
8. July 1973. We were in New York City to celebrate our anniversary. The day before our anniversary, I was out shopping and started driving around some stores with my pants down.
9. May 1974. Diane was pregnant with Tracy and we were out shopping. I had both Diane and Jim with me. We were in a department store shopping for various things and Diane took Jim and they went off together to look for something. I was wandering around the store and started exposing myself. I walked between the racks of dresses, took my penis out, and let the women working in the area and those shopping get a glimpse of me. Then I walked to another area.

Part 3

Upon completion of part 2, B.'s memory considerably improved and he was requested to elaborate further on parts 1 and 2.

Labor Day Weekend 1972: Wilkes Barre

It was Saturday and I had this weekend off and things at work were starting to slow down. We had been working extremely long days in the process of getting our plant operating. The plant was now at 100 percent efficiency and the tension was off. This was the first weekend anyone at the power plant had had off all summer. I had to do work on my blue Volkswagen Beetle. I got up early and left the apartment to work on the car. Diane was still sleeping. We had planned on going out that evening and Diane didn't want me to work on the car, but to spend the day with her. We had been looking at a lot of houses and Diane was really on my case about buying a house, so we had finally decided to buy one of the houses which we had looked at. After completing the work on the car, I drove into Wilkes Barre and began staring at the women and having sex fantasies. I was wearing a T-shirt and cut-off dungarees. I began driving through the mid-city shopping center with my pants down and playing with myself. I was tense and mad at myself; I knew that Diane was home worrying because she had been upset when I told her I had to work on the car. I really hadn't lost my senses completely and probably would have pulled my pants up and gone home because the shopping center was very crowded and I hadn't picked out any particular girl to expose myself to. The cars were moving slowly around the parking lot and, as I sat amid the traffic in the main lane in front of the stores, I noticed that a good-looking girl working in a store was watching me. I got really excited and erect and drove around again and pulled up in front of the store and sat there masturbating while she watched me. After ejaculating I started for home but was stopped and arrested.

April 1973: Westchester State College

I had left work and gone with a fellow employee to help him pick up some lawn and garden materials. We had left after 8 hours of work, which was early because we were working 12-hour days at the time. After helping Larry, I drove to the library. When I left the library, I started driving around the campus fantasizing sexual relations with a lot of good-looking women. I was in my 67 Chevy with the windows down and it was a warm spring evening. I pulled my pants down and drove slowly around thinking about screwing some of the women I was seeing. I was very tense and unsettled, my stomach was tight, and I was feeling extremely shook up. I masturbated to ejaculation while watching the co-eds and then pulled myself together and drove off feeling like a real piece of shit.

July 1973: New York City

We had gone to New York City in order to leave Jim with Diane's parents. Our wedding anniversary is July 10th and we wanted to spend it alone together, without Jim. Shortly after we got to New York City, I decided to go out and see if I could find a book that I had been looking for. As I drove by some stores, I saw a lot of good-looking females walking around in their scanty summer clothing and I started having sexual fantasies. I got extremely tense and keyed up and pulled my pants (bermuda shorts) down and started playing with myself. I was in my 67 Chevy and had the windows down so that it was easy to see inside. I was extremely tense and scared but couldn't talk myself out of driving slowly down the fire lane with my genitals exposed. I continued this for about 10 minutes and finally stopped after exposing myself to a particularly good-looking woman as she got out of her car. I never really had a complete erection and was very shook up throughout the entire ordeal. After exposing myself to this woman, who reacted with disbelief and disdain, I put myself back together and started to leave. As I was driving across the parking lot, a police car came into the driveway through which I was going to exit. The officer motioned for me to pull over and came over to my car. He asked me to get out of the car and as I did, I passed out. When I awoke I was in the emergency room and Diane and her dad were there.

May 1974: Westchester

I had been working quite a bit—usually 12 hours a day, 7 days a week—so Diane and I hadn't spent much time together. We had made plans to go over to Westchester and do some shopping. When I came home I didn't really want to go but Diane did, and she told me that both Jim and I needed haircuts and we could get that done at the same time. Diane talked me into going and was feeling badly about it, so she did a whole lot of idle chattering while we were driving over to Westchester. I was in a bad mood about work, I guess, and really didn't say much. Diane was about six months pregnant with Tracy at this time and I think she was worried that I was reacting negatively to the idea of another child. Jim and I got haircuts and Diane shopped, and then we went shopping together. I bought a pair of pants and was looking around at various things while trying to take care of Jim, who was being bad.

Diane decided to take Jim and go off and leave me to wander around by myself, probably to pacify me because she was still worried that I was upset with her. I started wandering around the store looking at the women in their light, early summer outfits. I began to think about how I would like to screw some of the foxy chicks in the tight-fitting shorts. I was in the women's clothing section of the store and looking at two foxy chicks. One in particular had on tight white shorts and you could see the outline of her bikini panties under the shorts. I started taking my penis out at various times as I followed these two girls around and fantasized fucking the real foxy one in the white shorts. I was extremely tense and nervous and completely forgot about being in a bad mood. I suddenly realized what I was doing and stopped. I started to leave the store and go wait in the car for Diane and Jim. When I stepped outside the store, the store security officer approached me.

March 1975: Wilkes Barre

We were participating in the Lenten Program of our church. Diane was not particularly enthused because I had volunteered our help and she was doing all that we were supposed to do together because I didn't have the time. Diane's parents called on Good Friday evening to say that they would be visiting us for Easter. Diane had invited them previously but they were not sure if they could make it. Diane was really working hard getting ready for having friends over after Mass on Saturday night, and things were pretty hectic. On Saturday morning I took Jim and Tracy shopping so that no one would be in Diane's way. Later in the afternoon Jim and Tracy and I came home and everything was pretty well taken care of. We still had a couple of hours before we expected Diane's parents to arrive and I decided to go over to the local shopping center and pick up some things. I got into my Volkswagen and drove over to the shopping center.

I saw a lot of good-looking females walking around in their spring outfits and I started having sexual fantasies. I pulled my pants down and started driving slowly around the shopping center while masturbating. I don't remember anyone seeing me, but I was pretty keyed up and very tense. I pulled up my pants and was just pulling myself back together when a police car pulled up behind me in the shopping center and motioned for me to pull over. I pulled over and, as I opened the door and got out of the car, I saw police cars coming from every direction as if someone had robbed the bank. At this point I passed out. When I woke up, Diane was there and I was released to her.

Events Prior to Incident of October 1, 1976

We had been in the transitional stage of moving from Wilkes Barre to Virginia since June. There had been belated, unexpected financial problems related to the move. The house which we bought in Virginia was in need of plenty of repair work. Diane was worried about being able to afford entertaining all of the guests that we were expecting. By the end of July we had moved and were in the process of unpacking. By October we had accomplished only about 50 percent of the things that we had expected to complete by the end of August. My sisters and their children had visited us and Diane's grandmother had spent two weeks with us. Diane's parents had already been to visit us a few times. Diane was anxious for me to accomplish more of the repair, maintenance, and typical work needed on the new house since we also were expecting a visit from her brother.

October 1, 1976: Virginia

Diane and Jim had shopped for a gift for Tracy's birthday the day before and were excited about it. Because of my schedule with school and work, we couldn't have Tracy's party on her birthday, which was September 30. Diane asked me to put a toy together, but ended up doing it herself. As I was leaving for school, Diane asked me what time I would be home and then told me to be sure not to be late or Jim would be very upset if we had to postpone Tracy's party again. Diane's brother also was arriving that evening.

I had just left school and probably noticed a few good-looking girls. I got into my yellow station wagon and decided to drive into Virginia and locate the golf course so that Diane's brother and I could go golfing on Saturday. I left Peidmont and drove in on Route 20. I hadn't driven into Virginia this way before and was surprised to find the downtown area. I saw some good-looking women and started having sexual fantasies. I pulled my pants down and started driving around the downtown mall playing with myself while I looked at the women. I was tense and upset at the same time and arguing with myself mentally, but I continued to play with myself. As I turned down the next street, which was next to a small park, I saw a nice-looking woman about 45 years old walking through the park toward the street which I was on. I pulled up to the intersection and positioned the car so that she could see me. As she approached the intersection, she walked right up to the corner, at which point she should have had no trouble glancing into the car and seeing my exposed genitals. She gave no indication that she had seen anything unusual, and walked across the street in front of me and kept on going. I pulled away from the intersection and as I drove down the next street, I pulled my pants up and drove out of the downtown area and over to the Route 250 bypass where I had remembered seeing a golf course. While looking for the golf course, I came across a high school and the previous process started all over again. I drove around the block a couple of times with my pants down, never really getting a good opportunity to expose myself. Just as I was pulling up to an intersection, I saw two girls walking toward me and I decided to sit there and expose myself to them. I continued to play with myself and tried to get an erection, but I was too nervous and upset. As the girls got close, they looked into the car when I yelled, "Hey, you want to fuck?"

When they saw me exposing myself, one of the girls screamed and then I drove off feeling extremely rotten and depressed but at the same time relieved. I drove around for a bit trying to figure out just why I had exposed myself. I started to drive home but figured the police would be looking for me. Not knowing whether or not the girls had given the police a good description of the car, I drove back to the area of the high school where a policeman stopped me.

OVERVIEW OF TREATMENT

Therapy lasted 22 sessions, spanning six months. Sessions 1 to 4 consisted of history taking and a detailed behavioral analysis of B.'s past exposure incidents. Electromyographic (EMG) biofeedback and relaxation exercises were conducted during sessions 5 to 7 as a general coping strategy for his anxieties and suspicions. Because of his "secret deviancy," the patient was continually defensive and suspicious that others might know of his "hideous behavior."

Hierarchy construction consumed sessions 8 through 10. Although the hierarchy ranged in subjective units of discomfort from minimally (10 Suds) to maximally (100 Suds) arousing, the sequential steps also reflected the chain of events that led up to orgasmic exposure, with the earlier links being less arousing than the later sequences. Hierarchy construction was difficult but therapeutic for the patient. It required him to explore his "hideous behavior" which he had previously avoided thinking about. In identifying the functional relationship between exposure and stresses, the patient saw himself as personally responsible for a behavior that he had avoided considering and which he thought to be "automatic."

Sessions 11 through 21 involved the active ACS process, incorporating punishment and avoidance paradigms. During assisted covert sensitization (ACS), the patient was instructed to relax, given guided imagery of a gratifying heterosexual scene involving his wife for discriminant learning purposes, and then presented with the deviant scene. Each hierarchical scene typically was presented three times. Each successive presentation involved introducing the aversive element earlier in the scene, followed by imagined self-control and relief.

Aversive elements consisted of imagining nausea and vomit concurrently with smelling the foul odor of valeric acid. B. was also asked to imagine being discovered in the act of exposing himself by family members as he simultaneously viewed their photographs.

At home the patient was instructed to listen to a recording of the previous session's ACS and self-administer the valeric acid. His wife was very supportive of this "homework." Beginning session 15, she became the "home therapist" and introduced the valeric acid as her husband listened to the tape. This had the positive effect of making the taboo subject of exhibitionism nonthreatening, and allowing her to be less anxious with the knowledge that she could do something to assist in the control of her husband's exhibitionism. Subsequently, the wife became much more communicative and comfortable in asserting her opinions and feelings with B. In addition to home practice, the patient listened to the tape and used the valeric acid while driving, the situation in which most exposure events had occurred.

Relaxation and Biofeedback Training

In anticipation of the administration of ACS, biofeedback-assisted deep muscle relaxation began during session 5. B. was asked to chart his levels of relaxation between sessions. He was given a take-home sheet and asked to plot his relative relaxation on a 5-point scale. He was asked to record his sensations, images, thoughts, and conditions of relaxation. Deep muscle relaxation was achieved after four training sessions. Average μV (microvolt) levels after relaxation decreased from $4.5\,\mu$V to $2.1\,\mu$V.

After extensive practice and developing a sense of control, the patient was instructed to drive through shopping centers and begin to fantasize exposure while engaging in aversive imagery and the use of photographs or valeric acid.

To ensure maintenance of treatment gains following termination and to reduce extended therapist contact for booster sessions, the patient and his wife were instructed to employ ACS on a weekly basis for three months while listening to tapes of previous sessions.

Following this procedure, they were to conduct ACS on a monthly basis for the next nine months. To provide motivation for such self-directed treatment, B. deposited $10 into the "booster kitty" for each home session he completed. These monies were to be "cashed in" for the couple's personal use for items that they otherwise would not purchase.

ASSISTED COVERT SENSITIZATION

We relied heavily upon parts 1, 2, and 3 for leads as to the most effective imagery with which to administer ACS. Sessions 5 through 8 were used to construct (1) the actual scenes used during the assisted covert sensitization, (2) heterosexually arousing scenes which would precede the exhibitionistic imagery, and (3) the negative and aversive scenes which would follow the exhibitionistic imagery.

The Construction of Scenes Used During Covert Sensitization

Ten scenes were constructed. At first, all scenes were in the second person, for example, "You are in your car, driving some place." Later they were modified for first-person presentation, as in "I am in my car driving someplace." The use of first person personalized the account and contributed to its overall effectiveness.

These scenes had to be constantly reiterated and modified. It was important to be flexible during hierarchy construction. For example, scene 7 (SUD= 85) was originally written as follows, and later changed to version 2.

Version 1. You are driving around a college campus. It's a beautiful day and there are lots of good-looking girls walking around. It's just about dusk and you are driving around, exposing yourself. Your pants are pulled down and you have an erection while playing with yourself and thinking of how you'd like to screw some of those foxy girls. As you are driving, you are getting more aroused, thinking more and more of all those sexy women. You don't know if anyone has seen you yet. You are getting more aroused as you continue to drive, play with yourself, and think about encountering one of those women. Tension continues to build in your abdomen, your genitals, and throughout your entire body. You feel an ejaculation coming on deep in your genitals. In an uncontrolled manner you are so aroused that you finally ejaculate with a surge of relief, as your semen pulsates out.

Version 2. I am driving around a college campus. It's a beautiful day and there are lots of good-looking girls walking around. It's just about dusk and I am driving around exposing myself. My pants are pulled down and I have an erection while playing with myself and thinking of how I'd like to screw some of those foxy girls. As I am driving, I am getting more and more aroused, thinking more and more of all those sexy women. I don't know if anyone has seen me yet. I am getting more aroused as I continue to drive, play with myself, and think about encountering one of those women. Tension continues to build in my abdomen, my genitals, and throughout my entire body. I feel an ejaculation coming on deep in my genitals. In an uncontrolled manner I am so aroused that I finally ejaculate with a surge of relief, as my semen pulsates out. I drive off in this totally disrupted state feeling very low about myself.

The ACS Hierarchy

Scene 1: Subjective units of arousal = 10. You are in your car driving someplace. You have thoughts of things to be accomplished. You pull up to a stop light and you see some girls in short skirts with extremely attractive legs, nice figures, and very pleasant and attractive facial features. You begin to think of how you might have an encounter with them and how that encounter could lead to your disrobing them, climbing into bed with them, and having them suck you off and then having relations. The light turns green and you drive further down the street, becoming more involved in your fantasy. As you pull up to the next stop light, you pull your pants down and continue fantasizing having relations with one of the girls as you play with yourself. There's a shopping center up ahead and you decide that you will expose yourself. But at the same time you have great qualms of guilt and you don't know if you should. The light turns green and you pull ahead. As you drive into the shopping center, you have feelings of both wanting to expose yourself and not wanting to expose yourself. You drive through the shopping center rather quickly and do not stop in order to prevent exposure. As you reach the end of the shopping center, you stop, feel stupid, pull your pants up, and regain your senses.

Scene 2: SUA = 20. It's a nice summer day and you are driving through a new town. No one knows you there. You are looking around to see what's in the city. You start to expose yourself. You drive past a library and in a little park you see a very attractive but elderly lady walking through the park. You think you'll expose to her. You drive around the park to a stop light and position yourself so she'll see you. You get excited thinking that she will react with shock. You begin to fantasize meeting her and having sexual play with her as she approaches the car. You don't have an erection but you are playing with yourself. Your pants are down to your knees, you are bare, and she should be able to see you. You are looking at her legs as she walks in front of the car. She doesn't seem to notice you. She walks away without any noticeable display of shock.

Scene 3: SUA = 35. You are in your car with your pants down. You have one hand down on your penis as you play with yourself and drive slowly around a shopping center with the intent to expose yourself. You are thinking to yourself that you would like to see a good-looking girl and shock the hell out of her with your dick. You see this good-looking girl with extremely attractive legs in a short skirt. She has a very sexy body and long hair, and is very neatly dressed. You really get keyed up. She is starting to walk toward you. You pull the car out to expose yourself. All the while, you are thinking the fantasy that you'll meet her, she'll fall in love with you, and you'll have a very exciting physical sexual experience.

Scene 4: SUA = 45. You are in downtown Portsmouth and are just coming out of a stationery store. You get in your car and start to drive home. As you approach the downtown area, you come to an intersection where you consider the possibility of either going home or going downtown to expose yourself. As you continue to think about exposing yourself, you get more and more aroused. Suddenly you say, "The hell with it, I'm going to expose myself." You turn downtown. When you come to the next stop light you pull your pants down and begin to play with yourself. As you do so, you become more and more aroused. As you look out onto the streets you see a very attractive woman walking there.

Scene 5: SUA = 50. It's a nice day and you are driving in a downtown section. You've pulled the car up in front of a store with a large window. You have your pants down and are masturbating. Your penis is hard and you are becoming more and more keyed up as you continue to stroke and play with yourself. The car is situated so that a female clerk in the store can see you. You look at the female clerk while you masturbate and think of her reaction if she saw you. You are becoming more and more aroused as you sit there fantasizing and hoping that she will look.

Scene 6: SUA = 60. You are driving around a shopping center very slowly. You are thinking that you want to find an attractive woman to see you. Your pants are down and you are playing with yourself. Then you see a good-looking girl pull up in a parking place. You drive up behind her and see her get out of the car and show a lot of leg. As she gets out of the car, you watch the sway of her body. You begin to think that if she only saw you, you could establish a relationship with her. As you continue to fantasize about having relations with her, you play more vigorously with your penis. You hope that she sees you. She is walking past your car toward the store. Possibly she sees you expose yourself, but you are not sure.

Scene 7: SUA = 75. It's a beautiful summer day. The sky is blue and the sun feels warm. You are in the car, driving to the shopping center. You are playing with yourself and enjoying it but you don't have an erection. All of a sudden, you see an attractive 30-year-old woman looking at you with great shock. She is speechless and covers her face with her hands as she runs away. You feel this surge in your penis as you have an ejaculation without an erection.

Scene 8: SUA = 85. You are driving around a college campus. It's a beautiful day and there are lots of good-looking girls walking around. It's just about dusk and you are driving around exposing yourself. Your pants are pulled down and you have an erection while playing with yourself and thinking of how you'd like to screw some of those foxy girls. As you are driving, you are getting more aroused, thinking more and more of all those sexy women. You don't know if anyone has seen you yet. You are getting more aroused as you continue to drive, play with yourself, and think about encountering one of those women. Tension continues to build in your abdomen, your genitals, and throughout your entire body. You feel an ejaculation coming on deep in your genitals. In an uncontrolled manner you are so aroused that you finally ejaculate with a surge of relief, as your semen pulsates out.

Scene 9: SUA = 92. You are sitting in the car in front of a store with a large window, situated so that you can look into the store and see a sexy-looking female clerk. And she is looking out the window and watching you expose and masturbate. Instead of getting shocked, she seems to get a kick out of this. As she is looking at you while you stroke your penis and become more and more aroused, your fantasies carry you away. You think that she wants you. You continue to masturbate and your penis swells with excitement as your whole body fills with mounting tension. As your fantasy builds, you come to the thought of intercourse. At that point, you have this tremendous surge deep in your genitals as you ejaculate. You drive away.

Scene 10: SUA = 100. It's late afternoon in the summer and you're driving around the shopping center, exposing yourself. You're sitting in your car with an erection and playing with yourself. You see this sharp-looking lady with a short skirt and great-looking legs walking to a store. You begin to think of getting close to her, getting in bed with her, having her caress you. You pull the car up closer in a position where she will be sure to see you. As she approaches the car, she gives you this flirty glance and you get more and more excited. As she walks around the car, you continue to fantasize exhilarating activities with her. You continue to watch her body and her good-looking legs. As she walks around the car, your excitement mounts even further and you play with your erected penis. She turns around, sees you, and is shocked. She is speechless, covers her face, and turns. With that expression, you have a relieving ejaculation.

Problems in Constructing the ACS Hierarchy

Many of these scenes are sexually explicit. It is important for the therapist to desensitize himself to the verbalization of these images. As in other therapies dealing with sexually explicit materials and behavior (e.g., sex therapy), the patient will notice any anxieties on the therapist's part during treatment. It is also important during interviewing and assessment that relevant questions be asked. For example, it is important to ascertain all the details of the sexual response cycle as it pertains to heterosexual, homosexual, and exhibitionist behaviors. During behavior analysis, the therapist can pretend that a motion picture was taken during the patient's most recent exhibitionistic episode. It is the therapist's responsibility to fill in the details, frame by frame.

The Construction of Heterosexual Arousal Scenes

If the patient is married or "going with someone," this step becomes much easier. However, if the person lacks the social skills necessary for mutually satisfactory heterosexual experiences, it may be difficult to formulate the appropriate images. In this case social skills training may be appropriate. Any socially acceptable heterosexual image is appropriate, including masturbation fantasy. The following scenes are outlines of the erotic imagery presented after relaxation induction.

Tips in constructing the heterosexual scenes. In order to facilitate the construction of these scenes, the therapist can ask the patient to free associate after deep muscle relaxation in the office. The therapist should determine whether a partial erection occurs or if there are other indices of arousal. Increased heartbeat, shallow breathing, perspiration, or difficulties in maintaining relaxation give hints as to the adequacy of these images. In addition, it may be helpful to have the patient remember particularly pleasing heterosexual experiences with his wife or somebody else. It is probably better that these scenes be realistic and "socially acceptable." For example, it would be less efficient to use a surrogate image such as a recent affair or earlier girlfriend. This is especially crucial if the wife will later participate as a home surrogate behavior therapist. She will certainly be aware of the content of the images, and it would be antitherapeutic to have her listening to her husband becoming sexually aroused "with another woman."

Heterosexual Arousal Scenes

It's after dinner and my wife and I are cleaning up. The kids are in the other room watching TV and I am walking around generally getting in her way. I'm pecking on her neck and fondling her from time to time and she is jokingly resisting me but can't do much because her hands are in the dish water. We both start to get a little aroused. After the dishes, she goes on and puts the kids to bed and I go into the spare bedroom and study.

1. After the kids are in bed, my wife comes into where I'm studying and she starts kissing me and playing around. I say, "the heck with the books," and sit Diane on my lap. We proceed to kiss and pet more heavily. We both get more and more excited. My penis is erect and we're partially unrobed. Finally Diane says, "let's go into the bedroom." We go to the bedroom and I take her clothes off. We get into bed and continue to pet, kiss, and caress, and maybe have oral sex. Then we begin an extended period of intercourse in which we both become extremely excited and more, until reaching orgasm. We go limp and feel quite content. We continue to lie there in each other's embrace.

2. After the kids are in bed, Diane goes to another room and does her needlework. I start to get horney and I decide to put down my books and go to her. I go into the other room and start to kid with Diane. I begin to kiss her and stroke her. Eventually she puts her work down and begins to get excited too. Our hands are in each other's clothes and my penis is erect. We get even more excited and I want to do it on the floor. Diane says, "let's go to the bedroom." When we get there, I take off all her clothes and she takes off mine. We get into bed and under the covers. I feel our two warm bodies touch and entwine as we caress and kiss and pet. We engage in much varied foreplay.

We begin to have sex. For ten minutes we go at it, getting further and further aroused. We both come to climax and go limp. We continue to lie there holding each other and feeling content.

We are both in bed in the morning. We are just lying there enjoying the warm bed, the touch of each other, and the silence. I wake up to an erection. I start playing around with Diane and she gets excited as she lies there. She becomes lubricated as she just passively lies there enjoying it. She's in a state of semiconsciousness. I roll over and penetrate her and begin intercourse. We both get more and more excited very quickly. I ejaculate. Afterwards, we just lie there for a couple of minutes, just enjoying ourselves, not wanting to get up.

The verbal presentation of these scenes should take anywhere from 5 to 10 minutes. It is recommended that they be tape recorded and the re-used during the week as homework.

Aversive Imagery Scenes

The next part of therapy involved the construction of aversive imagery items. They are highly idiosyncratic and some care should be taken during their construction. The assisted part of ACS involved modifying these basic aversive scenes. In this case we used valeric acid, a particularly obnoxious olfactory stimuli. We strongly recommend that if valeric acid is used, other members of the staff or clinic be aware of its use. It has a lingering smell which can be devastating to other clients. Make sure the office is well aired and that none of it spills on the carpet or furniture. Valeric acid is also slightly toxic (independent of what the label says) and its lingering odor can produce chronic coughing to those exposed to it over a period of a week.

We also had B. bring in a series of photographs of his family and friends. They gave us information as to who his friends were and the physical characteristics of his family. In turn, this information made some of our presentations more realistic to the patient when we suggested he was discovered by them. Finally, it maximized transfer to the home situation.

Typical Aversive Scenes (all not used)

1. There is a big, fat secretary at work. She's pearlike, with short, black, irregularly cut hair. I see her put her finger up her nose and pick it, then put it in her mouth.
2. As I expose myself, Jim walks by and sees me and just stands there in unbelievable shock.

    As I expose myself, Diane walks by and sees me and just stands there in unbelievable shock.

    As I expose myself, my sister walks by and sees me and just stands there in unbelievable shock.
3. I feel my stomach become uneasy. I feel as though I'm going to vomit. I feel my stomach contract and feel the puke surge up my throat. I can taste it as it rises in my throat. I feel it in my mouth and around my teeth as I try to hold it back. The smell is putrid and the taste makes me even sicker. I can't hold it in any more and I proceed to vomit all over myself. I can feel and smell the warm sticky stuff run out of my mouth, down my face and into my lap.

4. There is this man at work who is all hot and clammy, and he stinks. He's just thrown up and he's gagging. I have to give him mouth-to-mouth resuscitation. I bend over him and start to feel nauseated. I reach for his head.

SELECTED THERAPY NOTES

Session 4

The majority of this session was spent going over the hierarchical sexually arousing scenes that B. had written down since our last session. Though they were somewhat scanty, it was possible to beef them up with further details upon discussion. It is interesting to note that during this discussion he explained his typical fantasy as one not of initial gross sex, but of meeting a woman who becomes rapidly infatuated with him in a very emotional manner, which subsequently leads to going to bed and her performing fellatio on him, concluding with intercourse. We also discussed how his behaviors—including stimulus, thought, intent, and action—are a sequential chain of behaviors that progressively get stronger and typically culminate in exposing. He appeared to be quite intrigued by the idea of a chain of responses.

It is interesting to note that B. has difficulty "appreciating a good-looking girl" now because, upon doing this, he reflects on the therapy sessions and how uncomfortable he feels when disclosing his exposures. At this point, shame therapy as well as its rationale was explained to him, though no commitment to offer such a therapeutic approach was made. B. also voiced the concern that this difficulty in appreciating a good-looking woman would be all-pervasive and he would lose some of his sex drive. He did note that he had had only minimal sexual contact with his wife since the detailed construction of the sexual hierarchy began. It was explained to him that the process of discrimination learning would allow him to isolate the therapeutic effect to only inappropriate sexual behavior.

Session 5

B. continued to discuss his concern that treatment would generalize to the suppression of all of his sexual behavior, as it had done initially. To counter this, hierarchical scenes of normal sexual relations will be incorporated which will not be paired with any aversive consequence, but will culminate in fantasized gratifying sexual arousal and relief.

Some concern is surfacing as to whether the wife should be brought in and informed thoroughly of the treatment rationale. However, she reports not wanting to know and resists the idea.

In exploring the gratification of exposing, two additional clarifications have come up. In addition to the physical sexual arousal, there is a "keyed up," "hyped up" general gratifying feeling and a thrill involved with the idea of "getting away with something you shouldn't do," e.g., seducing a girl in her parent's home.

The majority of the session was spent in expanding the hierarchical paragraphs. Though this is a very aversive experience for B., the clarity of his memory and the insight into his feelings seem to improve as this exploration continues.

Session 7

In further discussing the thrill of exposing, a new dimension surfaced, i.e., besides sexual arousal there is a tension relief component from doing something wrong (illegal) and getting away with it. This new dimension will be incorporated in the hierarchy scenes.

The remainder of the session was spent on developing "normal" heterosexual scenes and nauseating scenes.

Session 8

This was the second ACS session. B. reported that during the last session and throughout the last week, he had been able to relax better than ever. While doing the home ACS with the tape, he reported feeling nausea in the form of a tight stomach and a knot in his throat. However, he still felt sexually aroused to the scenes. After practicing the home sessions, he reported needing to eat or drink something in order to eliminate the sense of nausea.

In today's session, the normal scenes were presented only twice; once before the 10-point scene and once before the 20-point scene. B. reported being able to visualize the scenes but not becoming aroused to them. This may be attributed to the fact that imaginary and chemical nausea were introduced along with the suggestion to fantasize arousal. Throughout the session, he reported difficulty in relaxing his stomach and chest because of the nausea scene.

A fan is generally needed to clear the air.

Session 10

B. entered the session very agitated and upset, reporting that he had practiced the relaxation exercises and the CS scenes only once. Apparently after leaving the last session, he found himself working with a demanding, perfectionist, critical female as a lab partner. This was quite frustrating to B. since he lost control of what was happening ("she wouldn't do what I told her"). They had to stay late, the lab work wasn't finished, and he felt as if he had to give in and play the "dummy . . . the monkey role." That evening and each successive evening, his relations with his boss progressively deteriorated. B. feels that they are equally trained and should work cooperatively instead of "me just being his paper pusher." Consequently, B. felt "uptight and irritable" all week. At one point his wife asked him if he was going to expose himself. It became clear to B. that conditions were prime for exposure because it is after such exposure that he can "unwind and start all over again."

Also during the week, the patient got into a heated argument with his female psychology teacher.

Generally there was a lot of agitation, irritability, projection of responsibility, inability to relax and cope, and a potential, though never acted upon, condition for exposure. Patient attributes the fact that he did not expose himself as being due to the therapy.

No CS took place in this session, only biofeedback-assisted relaxation training, history taking, and ventilation. The patient was given last week's CS tape and a bottle of valeric acid for home practice and for use when experiencing exhibitionistic urges.

Session 13

In the last few weeks B. has been under considerable pressure. They are the types of pressure that in the past led to his exhibitionism. In spite of them, he has not had the urge to expose himself and is feeling very good about this.

His wife has been very supportive of the whole therapeutic endeavor and has encouraged him to carry the valeric acid in the glove compartment of his car. During the last few weeks he has practiced at home in a state of relaxation and while listening to the tape recording of the previous session.

Today we continued with (1) relaxation induction, (2) heterosexual arousal using guided in vivo imagery, and (3) covert negative sensitization. We tape-recorded the session and gave it to B. to listen to at home. He was concerned about the long-term effects of the present therapy and was assured that his wife would help in future interactions. His court hearing is in May and both therapists feel that his treatment for exhibitionism is going according to plan. Assisted covert sensitization will continue next week.

B. successfully completed another scene that he had constructed earlier in therapy. He went through deep muscle relaxation, and then was read a heterosexually arousing story which was paired with a prepared exhibitionism scene. Aversive cognitive and chemical elements were delivered contingent upon his successful self-control of exhibitionism. He will continue to listen to the tape once daily at home while self-delivering the noxious olfactory stimulation. His wife may begin to participate, especially because of her concern about the long-term effects of the treatment.

B. is feeling better than last week: he has apparently resolved some conflict with his boss at work as well as been relieved from the midterm pressures of examination.

Session 15

We continued with assisted covert sensitization, completing the SUD 60 exhibitionism item. Again, the items were tape-recorded and B. was asked to practice daily. His wife continues to be an important adjunct therapist. She is very supportive and helps him during his relaxation and tape sessions at home.

B. mentioned that he likes to listen to the recorded tapes late at night while driving in his car. This is his one chance to be alone and relax, and it also contributes to an active fantasy life on his part.

The patient was asked to write a check for $8.40 to the present therapist as reimbursement for the valeric acid. He will be seen next week at the same time. We anticipate four or five more sessions and termination around the time of his court hearing at the beginning of May.

Session 17

B. came in stating that everything was "okay." He had been able to avoid or ignore the aversive boss. B. reports that he and his wife have practiced the tape daily, with her presenting the valeric acid at appropriate times. He reported using the tape on three occasions while driving home from work at 1:30 A.M. He reported that this experience was qualitatively different from practice at home, i.e., more realistic. B. was encouraged to use the valeric acid in vivo; i.e., he was advised to drive through town and force himself to fantasize and become aroused while viewing females, at the same time inhaling valeric acid. B. voiced some reservations over this "acid test" but decided to try it.

The patient reported that three to four weeks ago, "I just reached over while in my car and sniffed the acid a couple of times. I told myself it was just to see if it was leaking, but maybe I was suppressing an impulse."

This session was spent on item 10 with SUD = 92. The aversive element was again suggested, with the additional suggestion that his son, Jim, saw him. This possibility was quite shocking to him because "he sees me as the perfect dad." This "perfect dad" image is promoted by B. and is a reflection of how he negatively perceived his own father as a child.

Since there is only one remaining hierarchy item, it was suggested that his wife attend the next session to discuss treatment and booster issues.

B. continues to replay the prior week's tape at home. His wife has become an efficient behavior therapist and has been a motivating influence for the patient. B. also continues to play the tape in his car, which produces maximum transfer between his exhibitionistic episodes and his behavior therapy.

Particularly disturbing to B. was the fantasy of his son seeing him exhibit. This shame therapy produced high emotional arousal and was quite aversive. In some ways it is analogous to implosive therapy, and it has deviated from our usual interval scaling of positive and negative scenes.

In today's session SUD = 85, which involved walking around a college campus, was presented. Rather than having B. read a heterosexually arousing scene with his wife, he was simply asked to imagine such a scene for two minutes. Then, after a state of arousal, he was asked to shift to the exhibitionist episode. At the end of this episode, his wife viewed him ejaculating and vomiting. This scene was presented twice.

One more scene will be presented, and his wife will be coming into therapy next week. At this point, she will be informed about the progress of therapy and her own role as a booster therapist.

Because B. has become very disturbed about some of the shame aspects of the aversive imagery, the therapists have decided to continue general supportive psychotherapy until the termination of his behavior therapy for exhibitionism. We feel that this man needs continued supportive therapy for his self-concept and low self-esteem.

Session 19

B.'s wife attended today's session. She had many questions concerning her role in treatment and how she can facilitate maximum therapeutic gain. She was especially concerned about her role as therapist and her lack of objectivity in this role. At first she did not like listening to the home tapes, but she has since gotten very used to it. She also questioned why her husband exhibits himself and how this relates to their marital relationship. She stated that since his last exhibitionistic episode, the frequency of sexual intercourse has decreased. We talked about their changed relationship and how both of them would like to understand why the exhibitionism occurs.

The patient failed to practice the in vivo homework. However, both therapists feel that he should not be encouraged too much to actually participate in these behaviors. Theoretically, we might not be doing the patient any good; and empirically, he might be observed, which could get him into legal trouble. Thus we encouraged him only to drive around and if he did become aroused to turn off those feelings voluntarily with the aids he has learned in therapy.

The problem of booster sessions arose. It was decided that the couple would pick specific future dates and have a system of rewards when they actually participate in these booster sessions. Thus, if they deposit $10 into their "booster kitty," they will buy each other a gift or go to a restaurant as a reward for their successful therapeutic gains.

The next two sessions will terminate the assisted covert sensitization aspects of the therapy. At that point, the couple will be seen again together and the judge will be informed as to the results of the therapy.

Today's session overviewed B.'s treatment of the last few months. B. brought in an outline of his reactions to therapy as well as his behavior during the "test phase" of his treatment. His wife also wrote down some of her own impressions of B.'s course of therapy and her continued psychological involvement in treatment. We have one more scene to complete next session. Very shortly a letter will be sent to the defense attorney outlining B.'s course of treatment. In the letter it will be recommended that he be put on probation.

This past week the patient actually went to a shopping center and performed certain response sequences. He began to play with himself and then proceeded to expose. He then voluntarily inhibited this response sequence and drove away after pairing the sequence with valeric acid.

Future booster sessions and incentives were discussed, and an appointment was scheduled for the next session.

We terminated active treatment for B.'s exhibitionism. He was exposed to the last scene (100 Sud). This information was taped and repeated three times. B. will continue to listen to the tape and be assisted by his wife in future sessions. He was given the MMPI to return by mail.

Recontact of Lawyer

The therapist should make sure that he is aware of the hearing date. By the time ACS is begun, the therapist should have some idea of both treatment frequency and duration. At least three to four months should be allowed for completion of the ACS paradigm. Upon determining a tentative end-date for treatment, the client's lawyer should be contacted to make sure that there is enough time to complete the treatment program.

Assuming that treatment is successful, the following points should be considered in the follow-up letter. The therapist may mention that the patient cooperated fully, the treatment was effective, the treatment has been concluded (active phase), follow-up will be maintained, and there is an extremely low probability of reoccurrence. *Never say* that the behavior will never occur again.

Example of a follow-up letter

> For approximately the last six months, I have been seeing B. for treatment of exhibitionism. B. has been highly cooperative in all treatment regimens. My professional opinion is that he has benefited from treatment. As mentioned in my first letter, B.'s treatment has been behavior oriented, with the goal of treatment to eliminate the possibility of future exhibitionistic episodes. In my opinion, his active treatment for exhibitionism was terminated as of _____. From this point on, B. and his wife will see

Dr. _____ for booster sessions. This phase of treatment is part of the overall treatment plan.

In my best judgment, there is an extremely low probability of recurrence of B.'s exhibitionistic behavior. I strongly recommend that this young man be given the opportunity to remain working and to continue with his education.

If you have any other questions concerning B., please do not hesitate to call me at _____.

Legal Outcome of This Case

B. was found guilty of the exhibitionism charge. He was given a one-year probation contingent upon further psychiatric treatment. In a telephone call with B.'s lawyer, he mentioned that B.'s prior exhibitionistic behavior necessitated the guilty verdict. Although B. was disturbed about having a criminal record, he felt that the decision was "fair."

B.'s SELF-DESCRIPTION OF REHEARSAL SELF-EXPOSURE

Second and Third Time

I got out my bottle of acid and placed it on the seat of the car right beside me. I did this typically when I was leaving school at about 1:00 P.M. in the afternoon.

I drove to a shopping center and started looking at the women and trying to fantasize all sorts of sexual encounters. I drove slowly through the shopping center, trying to get turned on by some woman or women. I wasn't having very much luck with this method so I pulled into a parking place and just sat there trying to tell myself that I just had to get into this thing.

As I was sitting in the parked car and trying to put things in the proper perspective, a really foxy-looking girl came walking across the parking lot and got into her car. As I watched her, I started getting in the right frame of mind to try out my smell (acid). She got into the car and drove off, but I continued to sit there and imagined myself seducing her and having sex with her and playing with myself as I imagined these things. At this point I reached for the acid and took a long whiff. As the tension was already there, the smell of puke just sort of capped things and left me feeling rather low.

I put the acid away and started the car. I drove home feeling very unsettled (upset) about having to go through what I had just done. After getting home and talking to Diane about things, I felt a little better, but still not settled.

Fourth Time

The next time I just went to a shopping center parking lot and parked. I went through a 15-minute relaxing session in which I let my mind relax and also my body. I usually let the replay of the therapy sessions run through my mind while relaxing.

When I felt really relaxed, I sat up, opened my eyes, and just watched the people moving about while daydreaming. When I saw a good-looking girl, I let my mind wander, and soon I had my penis out and was playing with it. As I was playing with myself and looking at one or more of the women, I saw an ideal situation for exposing myself. When this thought came into my mind, I reached for the acid and took a good whiff. The putrid smell sent thoughts of our therapy sessions through my mind and I stopped playing with myself and sat there for a while trying to relax and telling myself that I should feel good about having controlled my impulse to expose myself.

My feelings and private thoughts about the therapy are very interlaced and I am not sure if I should try to separate them. The first time I went through an exposure rehearsal sequence, I was extremely upset about having to do it and therefore did not do a very good job. I drove into a shopping center, looked around at a few women, let some sexual thoughts run through my mind, and took a whiff of the acid. The smell of vomit definitely changed my train of thought, but I don't think that I was really concentrating on exposure thoughts to begin with.

After the first time, I was still upset but more determined. The upset feeling I referred to was a tightness of the stomach (just mild) and a kind of clammy, uneasy feeling. I was feeling this was because I had my doubts as to whether this part of the therapy was really necessary. After being reassured that it was necessary and then doing a better job of actually getting into the exposure sequence, I came to realize that it definitely was necessary because it taught me that I could maintain control.

I also was having uneasy feelings about purposely going out to look at other women and letting my mind wander to sexual thoughts about them. This feeling came from Diane's expressed feelings that she didn't even like to think that I could have thoughts or desires about other women. After talking with her when I came home, we came to a better understanding about this. I am quite sure that we both agree an idle sexual thought about another woman is in no way an act of infidelity. I do feel that my exposing myself was possibly connected in that I was daring her to get mad at me for being unfaithful and also begging her to forgive me and show how much she loves me.

The changes as just mentioned and my feelings and thoughts are all intermingled in this way. I feel it best to just write down what comes out.

My feelings after the first few times I went through an exposure sequence were those of a depressed person. I should mention my feelings while engrossed in the exposure rehearsal. Although I was always fully aware that I was just making a dry run at things, I was very much able to let myself go and have some really sexy fantasies about the women I was watching. While having these fantasies, however, the tightness in my stomach seemed to dampen them and to help inhibit me. I found that I was more aware of both my mental and physical feelings and sure that I could control them.

The "downer" that seemed to come with the culmination of things was stemming from my low opinion about what I was doing. I have dealt with this by likening it to unclogging a stopped-up commode. It is a very distasteful job, but one which must be done if you wish to flush the shit down the drain. I am not trying to be funny with this comment; it is simply my honest thoughts on the subject. I guess that the therapy has caused or forced me to think about things and to face the fact that I dislike much of my own personality and especially the part associated with exposing myself.

B.'s Private Thoughts About The Therapy

I'm not sure that I have any private thoughts. It seems as though my mind has really been picked clean on the subject. When I first started, I was very doubtful as to how successful I would be, but I knew I had everything to gain and very little to lose. Looking back now, I feel that I had nothing to lose. I was afraid of being programmed. My great fears of being programmed were that whenever I started having erotic thoughts about a woman, I would get sick and have to run off and vomit somewhere. As I look at things now, I don't feel programmed at all. I feel quite the contrary: I am much more aware of my feelings and thoughts now than before treatment. I feel that Diane and I are much more aware of each other's needs and desires. My thoughts also wander less and I see this as an improvement.

The therapy has brought about many of the changes already mentioned and also others. One change for the better is my sexual relationship with Diane. This change is not just sexual, but includes our total awareness of each other. Prior to therapy, Diane was constantly trying to tune in to my needs, feelings, and desires and I was putting up a barrier and refusing to admit it. I was not even concerned with whether I was tuning into Diane, but was taking her very much for granted. As I have already pointed out, all of this is out in the open now and our relationship seems to have started freshly.

The one negative change has been my performance at work and school. I have definitely declined in both places and am now doing average work. I seem to have more self-confidence, however, and feel that this will aid me in gradually getting back to my previous standard.

B.'s Wife's Reflections on Her Own Role in Treatment

I have often thought about what I would say if asked how I feel, but it's hard to put my thoughts in writing. At this point, I would say that I am guardedly optimistic. I feel that my husband's therapy has gone well and he thinks so too. Of course B. has felt this way before, but the exposure problem hadn't been solved. So I'm afraid really to "believe" again. I don't think that I will be able to relax and be confident for a long time. I think that B. and I have come a long way since this therapy began. When B. and I first tried to discuss his problem openly, we always ended up arguing, or worse, silent. Now we talk freely and can even laugh about some aspects of the problem.

I'm really glad to be included in B.'s treatment and I think he is glad about it too. I always thought I shouldn't ask about it, and B. thought I didn't want to know about it. So, as I said, our relationship in regard to B.'s problem has definitely improved.

I'm a little worried about continuing the therapy at home. I wonder if the tape will become routine after a few times and lose its effect. The idea sounds good and I know that we will continue on a regular schedule.

From my point of view, our relationship in regard to other aspects of our marriage is not what it was. I really don't feel that I can count on B. I'm afraid to make plans of any kind and, when I do, I worry that B. will expose himself and get arrested. I hope that in time these feelings will pass. I've also found that I try to keep all my problems to myself (big and small) so that I won't put any more burden on B. Lots of times this results in some depressing moods for me. Then I feel as if I'm not being fair to our children because I don't give them enough attention. I'm usually very careful to keep these moods a secret when B. is around. This sounds very silly as I'm writing it, but I'm worried about myself. I seem to have a very hard time controlling my emotions now.

Anyway, I am hopeful that everything will work out for us. One thing I haven't mentioned is that I do care very much about B., our marriage, and our family. I want very much for us to stay together. I've thought of what I'd feel like if we separated and I really can't imagine it—I know I'd be miserable.

FOLLOW-UP AT 18 MONTHS

Follow-up of this patient spanned 18 months. Over this period there was a complete absence of exhibitionistic urges, fantasies, and acts as reported by both patient and wife. In addition to the elimination of this symptom, the MMPI at termination and at 12-month follow-up, as well as patient and spouse reports, indicated a dramatic reduction in depression, anxiety, paranoia, alienation, and defensiveness. At post-treatment only one scale was above 70 T, compared with eight scales at pretreatment evaluation. Verbal reports also indicated a marked improvement in marital communication, wife's assertiveness, and general marital happiness. During the fourth month of follow-up, the patient's police record was uncovered by a routine character check at work. Despite the stress provoked by this threat to his job security, there was no indication of any regression. At 12-month follow-up, the patient assumed a new position involving a vertical promotion with a different firm. This promotion necessitated selling their home, relocating 2,000 miles away, and purchasing a new home. Instead of this change being stressful, the patient perceived it as a challenge, and again there was no evidence of therapeutic regression.

PATIENT'S SELF-REPORT AT 24 MONTHS

My new job is working out great and Diane and the kids seem to have adjusted to our new home. I am especially pleased with Diane's adjustment and our relationship since moving out here. Diane has been more outgoing and has already made new friends.

We have been doing a lot more things together as a family. My new job has been a 40-hour week that has allowed me to play sports and get involved with my son's soccer and basketball teams. I haven't started school yet, but I know that when I do the course load I take will be small enough to insure that I will have time to spend with my family. I will probably be putting in longer days during the coming year as construction of the plant nears completion, but I feel confident that no insurmountable problems will arise.

Diane and I have been very open with each other and talk things out when we need to. We have also been talking a great deal more about anything that either of us wants to, and I feel that we are both listening more to each other. I am not trying to say that we don't have disagreements, but right now things couldn't be better.

I am writing this letter on a Saturday afternoon while babysitting the kids. We just came home from our son's basketball game and dropped Diane off at a friend's house on the way home. I think I have just described a typical Saturday and should probably go through the whole week. Monday—basketball, Tuesday—bowling, Wednesday—free, Thursday—basketball, Friday—bowling, Saturday—basketball and whatever, Sunday—church and relax. We also have set up a reading schedule so that we sit down as a family five days a week and read together for a half-hour.

I am happy to say that I have no exhibitionism to report. I have really had an upbeat frame of mind since we last saw each other. Diane and I have talked about my past exhibitionism but we have not used the tapes or valeric acid. Our talks have indicated to me that Diane feels more at ease now than she has in the past six years. I do feel that it will be a while before either of us feels free of the past, but I also have a feeling of well-being and purpose right now.

COMMENT

Assisted covert sensitization was used to eliminate arousal to exhibitionistic stimuli and fantasies. The aversive element consisted of noxious imagery, foul odors, and the shame component of being discovered in the act by family members. These aversive components were all quite flexible and portable, allowing easy modification for patient idiosyncrasies and in vivo application. The use of fantasized discovery along with photographs of family members allowed a blending of traditional covert sensitization with the more recent shame aversion therapy.

In addition to eliminating exhibitionistic arousal with aversive conditioning, significant changes occurred to allow more adequate coping under stress. With the development of new mechanisms for coping with both stress and exhibitionistic urges, the patient now relaxed instead of tensed, the marital relationship became a support instead of an exacerbating factor, and he no longer felt helpless and depressed.

The patient was not dependent upon the therapist for booster sessions. Instead, it became the responsibility of the patient and his wife. This procedure is in marked contrast to previous research in which stable follow-up evaluation occurred in the context of ongoing therapist-conducted booster sessions. Although this is a single-case report, it adds evidence to the position that ACS can produce stable treatment gains without continued therapist-conducted booster sessions.

Finally, on the basis of the patient's MMPI and self-report, this case documents how a symptomatic treatment focus can have positive effects in other significant areas of the patient's life.

POSTSCRIPT

In July 1979 the patient re-exposed himself at a shopping center after having attended a party and drinking heavily. He stated that he became "sidetracked" after drinking beer and drove to a shopping center. He exposed his penis to a 35-year-old "attractive woman" leaving a food store. After seeing her react to the exposure, he drove away. The woman made a complaint and recorded his license. The police investigated but did not press charges after contacting the patient's current therapist. His therapist has been instructed (after the client's request) to perform booster sessions with the client and his wife and to have the client carry valeric acid in the glove compartment of his car.

SECTION FOUR
CONCLUDING COMMENTS

10	Victims of Exhibitionism	289
11	Theoretical and Therapeutic Integration	295
12	Working between the Legal System and the Therapist	311
13	Future Research Issues	339

10

VICTIMS OF EXHIBITIONISM

Daniel J. Cox
Barry M. Maletzky

The implicit assumption in much of the literature on exhibitionism is that indecent exposure is a harmless and victimless nuisance. The only victim of the compulsive behavior is thought to be the exhibitionist himself, who frequently suffers social and familial rejection. This chapter reviews the available, although scarce literature on the victims to evaluate the legitimacy of this assumption.

One of the major difficulties in doing research about the effect of exhibitionism on its victims is the difficulty in identifying the women involved. As Cox and MacMahon (in press) and Gittleson, Eacott, and Mehta (1978) point out, only 17 percent of the women victimized make statements to the police. Not only does this represent a small proportion of the total number of victims, but it probably reflects a very biased sample—that is, women assertive enough to make such reports.

FREQUENCY

Though we know that exhibitionism accounts for one-third of all reported sexual offenses and it is the second most common sexual deviancy presenting itself at mental health facilities (Cox & Daitzman, 1979), this data does not indicate how frequently the act of indecent exposure occurs in the natural environment. Because only 17 percent of the exposure incidences are ever reported to the police and the subsequent conviction rate bears an unknown relationship to police reports, it would be grossly unreliable to estimate the frequency of exhibitionism on the basis of the criminal records. It appears that the only accurate way to estimate how frequently indecent exposure occurs is to ask a random sample of women whether or not it has happened to them. Gittleson et al. (1978) reported an informal survey of British female medical students in which approximately one-third reported that they had witnessed exhibitionism. In a more formal survey of 100 British psychiatric nurses, with a mean age of 33, 44 percent reported that they had been victims of exhibitionism outside their work situation. Of these victims, 34 percent had been exposed to more than once.

Cox and MacMahon (1978) surveyed 405 college females who were taking general psychology courses. To correct for possible sampling bias, responses were obtained for different geographic areas of the United States from women who were attending the University of Louisville (Kentucky), the University of Montana, Portland State University (Oregon), Indiana State University, and North Texas State University. The mean age of the respondents was 20 and their mean estimated family income was $19,000. Of this sample, 32 percent reported that they had been victims of exhibitionism. Of these victims, 37 percent had been exposed to more than once.

The British and United States survey results are strikingly similar. If we were to extrapolate these findings to an estimated United States female population of 110 million, it would mean that 35,200 million have been victimized by exhibitionism. Even this number is probably an underestimate since the mean age of the Cox and MacMahon (1978) sample was only 20 years. We would assume that, up to a point, the older the woman is, the more likely she is to be exposed to.

AGE OF VICTIMS

Gittleson et al.'s (1978) nursing sample indicated that 57 percent of the victims were first exposed to before they were 16 years of age.

Only 19 percent of the victims were 21 years or older at the time of their first exposure experience.

Similarly, Cox and MacMahon (1978) found that 66 percent of the college women who reported being first exposed to were 16 years of age or younger. This figure is probably somewhat inflated due to the youthfulness of the Cox and MacMahon sample. These data confirm Rooth's (1971) view that the most likely victim is a girl at or about the age of puberty. Given this critical age, it is essential to explore what psychological impact indecent exposure might have on the victims.

PSYCHOLOGICAL EFFECT

From 37 names of women exposed to and listed on police records, Maletzky (submitted for publication) interviewed and administered psychological tests to 15. Ten were excluded from the study due to their youth (12 years and younger), and 12 refused to participate. Assessment occurred from 31 to 127 (mean of 63) days after the exposure incidents. A standard interview was administered to both the victim and a significant other, and the victim alone was administered the MMPI and the Hamilton Anxiety Scale.

Exhibitionists in this study chose to expose to predominantly young (average age 22.7), attractive, single women. Exposing incidents clustered in warmer weather and in daylight hours. Just one of the 15 victims knew the exhibitionist before the exposing episode. None of the victims believed that they had contributed to the episode by acting or dressing seductively. Three of these women had been exposed to twice and one woman had been exposed to three times, though none of these four had been exposed to more than once by the same man.

Almost all of the victims (13 of 15) judged that the experience had produced negative effects upon them, but none could specify the effects in behavioral terms. Often the victim expressed the feeling that "it was a bad sort of thing . . . it really shocked me" but there was no demonstrable subsequent effect on school, job, or housewife functions, nor any change in quality of their relationships with others, including husbands and boyfriends. Victims often cited subsequent verbal examinations by police and attorneys, and testimony in court, as the most damaging aspects of their experience.

A significant other for each victim was located for 14 of the 15 women involved in the study. Two were husbands, 5 were boyfriends, 4 were mothers, 2 were fathers, and one was a grandmother. Each had daily contact with the victim. Twelve of the 14 (7 of the 9 males and all of the females) thought emotional trauma had occurred to the victims because of the incident. None could point to a specific behavioral abnormality or a decline in function, except for a short-term (one to two week) increase in anxiety and insomnia.

Lack of preexposure testing precluded comparison, but the average MMPI score showed no significant elevation except for occasional mild elevations of the Hysteria (HYS) scale. No increase above normal limits was seen on the average results of the Hamilton Anxiety Scale, although several test scores exceeded normal ranges.

Since these data are only based on 41 percent of the victims who reported the incident in cases where the exhibitionist was arrested, generalization of these findings is unwarranted until larger, better controlled studies are done.

Gittleson et al. (1978) reported a number of emotional responses to indecent exposure. Fifty-seven percent recalled fear, 30 percent disgust, 9 percent anger, 15 percent curiosity, 12 percent amusement, 6 percent pity, and one percent embarrassment. Of the 43 percent of exhibitionistic incidents reported to be upsetting, 37 percent of the victims reported that this effect passed within a month's time. Thirty percent of the exposing incidents were reported to affect the victims when they were subsequently walking outside, and 6 percent reported that it had affected them sexually. Similarly, Davis and Davis (1976), in an interview report of 25 victims of indecent exposure, indicated that many women began avoiding the areas where the exhibitionistic act had occurred. Thus they felt limited in their freedom to move about within their own environment. In concurrence with Maletzky, these researchers found no serious psychological problems resulting from the incidents, but many victims attributed blame to themselves for the exposure and felt that the act had had a negative effect on their own self-concept.

Fifty-nine percent of the Cox and MacMahon sample rated their exposure experience as either "not at all" or "slightly" distressing, though 15 percent rated the experience as "severely" or "very severely" distressing. Similarly, 14 percent rated the exposure as "severely" or "very severely" affecting their attitudes toward men or sex, and 9 percent equally described its adverse effect on their attitudes toward themselves as women.

CONCLUSION

It is obvious from this review that indecent exposure is a significant problem, even if one only considers the huge number of women involuntarily involved in the act. The significance of the problem is highlighted by the fact that the majority of victims when first exposed to are under 17 years of age. In addition, a few exhibitionists use the act as a first step toward molestation although this progression is rare.

In accord with Gunn (1976) and Gittleson et al. (1978), it must be concluded that, for the majority of victims, the long-term effects of exhibitionism are minimal. There is evidence, however, that a minority of victims may be significantly traumatized by the event. Although this minority represents only a small percentage of all the victims, in absolute numbers it represents thousands of females.

Considering these findings and the data from Chapter 1, it appears that exhibitionism is not a victimless crime; it takes a toll both in terms of its perpetrators and its victims. It is hoped that these findings will encourage mental health and legal professionals to take a more active look at the treatment of both exhibitionists and their victims. The paucity of relevant studies in the scientific and legal literatures demonstrates that this has not yet been accomplished.

REFERENCES

Cox, D. J., & Daitzman, R. Behavioral theory, research and treatment of male exhibitionism. In M. Hersen, R. M. Eisler, & P. M. Miller (Eds.), *Progress in behavior modification* (Vol. 7). New York: Academic Press, 1979.

Cox, D. J., & MacMahon, B. Incidence of male exhibitionism in the United States as reported by victimized female college students. *National Journal of Law and Psychiatry,* 1978, 1, 453–457.

Davis, S. K., & Davis, P. W. Meaning and process in erotic offensiveness: An exposé of exposées. *Urban Life,* 1976, 5, 377–396.

Gittleson, N. L., Eacott, S. E., and Mehta, B. M. Victims of indecent exposure. *British Journal of Psychiatry,* 1978, 132, 61–66.

Gunn, J. Sexual offenders. *British Journal of Hospital Medicine,* 1976, 15, 57–65.

Maletzky, B. Impact of exhibitionism on its victims. Manuscript submitted for publication, 1979.

Rooth, F. G. Indecent exposure and exhibitionism. *British Journal of Hospital Medicine,* 1971, 5, 521–533.

11

THEORETICAL AND THERAPEUTIC INTEGRATION

John M. Rhoads

There was a young fellow called Rex
With diminutive organs of sex
When charged with exposure
He said with composure
"De minimis non curat lex!"

This limerick succinctly catches many of the characteristics of the syndrome of exhibitionism: the narcissism of the exposer; his feelings of inferiority; the act of exposing; and his calm, almost triumphant demeanor when caught and brought to trial. Lasègue (1877) and Krafft-Ebing (1900), who described exhibitionism in 1877 and 1886 respectively, noted that he (there is considerable argument over whether women are or can be exhibitionists) rarely approaches or touches his victim, that the act seems devoid of sexual or logical motives, and that with certain exceptions mental illness in the usual sense is not in evidence. To these characteristics one might add some observations by Hackett (1971) based on his examinations of 214 persons, 37 of whom he was able to treat—a discouraging figure. Of the 37 patients, 30 exposed with a flaccid or semierect penis. Of the 7 who exposed with erections, 4 masturbated during the exposure. Most were married, but had a frequency of copulation lower than that of the general population. All authors agree that the exhibitionist seeks a strong emotional response from the victim. These observations must be taken into account when theorizing about or treating an exhibitionist.

ANALYTIC APPROACH TO EXHIBITIONISM

How can one best explain these observations and from them formulate a treatment plan? The limerick delineates one of the major problems of treatment; namely, the fact that almost no exhibitionists seek treatment except under duress from family or the law. In the past, as is apparent from Hackett's figures, few remained in treatment to a successful conclusion. Nevertheless, until the 1960s nearly all theoretical formulations were made by psychoanalysts, and based on examinations of a number of exhibitionists and the treatment of a few. Allen (Chapter 4, this volume) has reviewed the psychoanalytic ideas on the subject and so there is no need to repeat them, other than note a few ideas especially relevant to this discussion.

In Sperling's (1947) case report of an exhibitionist, she noted that the greatest technical problem was the analysis of the patient's narcissistic resistances. She concluded that her patient had identified with his mother as an outgrowth of sibling rivalry. Feeling that she had neglected him for subsequent children, when under stress in later life he would exhibit, thereby teasing and frustrating his victim as he felt his mother had done to him.

The hostility noted by Sperling is the core of Stoller's (1975) view of perversions. He defines perversion as

> the result of an essential interplay between hostility and sexual desire. . . . Perversion, the erotic form of hatred, is a fantasy usually acted out but occasionally restricted to a daydream (either self-produced or packaged by others, i.e. pornography). It is a habitual, preferred aberration necessary for one's full satisfaction, primarily motivated by hostility. By "hostility" I mean a state in which one wishes to harm an object. . . . The hostility and perversion take form in a fantasy of revenge hidden in the actions that make up the perversion and serves to convert childhood trauma to adult triumph. To create the greatest excitement, the perversion must also portray itself as an act of risk taking.

He believes, unlike many learning theorists and analysts, that the trauma of childhood actually took place and is memorialized in the details of the perversion. Thus he sees the perversion as a reliving of an actual historical trauma aimed at one's sex or gender identity. The "pervert," by deviant means, manages to convert the defeat of childhood into victory as an adult: by showing his penis and obtaining a reaction, he proves that he has not been unmanned.

Other psychoanalytic writers (A. Reich, 1951) have noted the importance of masturbation fantasies and their direct causal relationship to behavior. Marmor (1978) defines the deviant individual as someone who has difficulty in achieving satisfactory sexual relations with a mature partner. Deviant practices represent alternative ways of attempting to achieve gratification and are seen as a displacement phenomenon. Marmor holds that the deviation represents a compromise expressed in symbolic fashion by an individual who fears a mature relationship but has not given up the desire to relate.

Allen (see Chapter 4, this volume) remarks that exhibitionism is more apt to occur in the male because, unlike his sisters, he is likely to have experienced a relatively sudden shutting-off from the mother's bathroom or dressing room. He also states that what serves as antecedent behavior for the compulsive exhibitionist is often neither sexual deprivation nor a need for contact, "but rather a narcissistic or emotional hurt, a rejection by someone significant, or a failure in work related or male role related achievements. . . . The exhibitionist is unable to assert himself with other men, and when his functioning as a normal male is threatened, he asserts himself in a more primitive way." This point of view agrees with Hackett, who states that in his large series of cases, most often the precipitating event was an unsatisfactory experience with a supervisor or with male peers which made the exhibitionist feel hurt and angry. He believes that exhibitionists "lack mechanisms for expression of anger, and often can't even recognize that they are angry."

Allen's case study (see pp. 69–76) serves as an excellent illustration of Stoller's thesis of the hostility inherent in perversion. P.'s dissatisfaction with exhibiting at a nudist beach was solved when he found that he could stand naked next to the public beach where people were wearing swimsuits; and by masturbating with an erection at that spot, he could shock people at the clothed beach as well as young girls entering the nudist beach, without fear of arrest.

Fenichel (1945) stated that the erogenous pleasure of exhibiting is always connected with an increase in self-esteem which is anticipated or actually gained by the fact that others look at the subject. He related this increase in self-esteem to a need for reassurance against the fear of castration, expressing in libido theory what Stoller later put in terms of ego psychology as threats against sex gender identity. Both ways of looking at the syndrome may help to explain the sexual component of exhibitionism.

Rickles (1942) notes that many exhibitionists are actually pleased to be arrested, as arrests prove they are capable of doing something that classes them as a criminal—thereby confirming their masculinity. He also stresses the importance of the "overly close relationship to the mother continuing unchanged into adult life, at best displaced to the spouse." Often the mother saw the son as a grandiose phallic extension of herself. The limerick catches this aspect in the exhibitionist's name.

Adler (see Ansbacher & Ansbacher, 1956) saw exhibitionism as the result of organ inferiority, with the exposures aiming to restore a sense of adequacy. Adler noted both the trauma to the exhibitionist's self-esteem and the exhibitionist's hostility to his victim. He stated, "the fight against the norms of society is always present. The inclination to frighten and harm children by exposing oneself and to disparage others by exposing to them, assigns to this perversion a place close to sadism." Adler noted that the exhibitionist seeks a condition of uncontested superiority over the victim.

An important issue is whether exhibitionism is culture-bound. Adler commented on the antisocietal aspect of the act, and Allen referred to the differential between boys and girls in child-rearing practices. Rooth (1973) surveyed a number of psychiatrists in 24 non-European, non-North American countries, none of whom had ever seen a case of exhibitionism. I have talked with several African psychiatrists who know of its existence but doubt that it occurs in their countries. Cox (personal communication, 1978) points out the flaw in this method, which is that psychiatrists see only a small portion of reported cases and it is potential victims who should be canvassed. Certainly anyone who has travelled in the Caribbean, Central America, or southern Europe is quickly made aware of the lack of shame in those areas about normal acts of elimination. Further cross-cultural research is in order to clarify this issue.

Psychoanalytic explanations of the data are summarized here. Sperling and Fenichel note the narcissism of the exhibitor. Rickles (1942) notes the mother's narcissism which is handed on to the exhibitionist. Marmor delineates the immaturity of the patient's efforts to achieve gratification via a symbolic displacement; the neurotic compromise of an individual who has not given up the struggle to achieve a mature relationship despite his fears of it. All authors stress the importance of fantasy, including Reich, Marmor, Sperling (who saw the act as teasing a victim), and Stoller (who sees it as the reenactment of a childhood trauma). Stoller believes that hostility is the basis of all perversion. A number of writers base the etiology on trauma: Stoller on a childhood trauma aimed at sexual identity; and Sperling as displacement from maternal nurture by siblings. Allen and Hackett see the current precipitating event as frequently being a narcissistic injury due to failure to compete with male peers. All agree that the exhibitionist seeks to build self-esteem by evoking a response of awe or fear in the victim or even by arrest (Rickles, 1942). Adler called attention to the fact that the exhibitionist's hostility is also directed against society.

ANALYTIC VERSUS BEHAVIORAL TREATMENT

One notes that the number of actual cases reported by analysts is small in number and many of the communications do not cite cases at all, but rather state theoretical conclusions. The behavioral literature, however, lists large numbers of cases, frequently with rigidly controlled studies of efficacy. Allen (Chapter 4, this volume) notes that the analytic method is probably ill-suited to the exhibitionist. With the psychoanalytic method, the exhibitionist is confronted with a mirror image of himself, certainly not the response he is looking for. In fact, mirror-imaging has served as the basis for a type of aversive conditioning by Serber (1970). The lack of success of the analytic method undoubtedly accounts for the sparseness of cases reported in the analytic literature. In contrast, the results of behavior therapy seem quite good. This is true after a relatively few sessions, and certainly in contrast to the length of an average psychoanalysis. Compared to the analysts, who have formulated theories after intensive observation of a few cases, behaviorists are sparse on theory after successfully treating many cases. Behaviorists are, after all, quite pragmatic and perhaps there is less need for involved theory. It is interesting to note, however, that as a result of careful long-term follow-ups and as multifaceted behavioral approaches have evolved, behaviorists tend to sound somewhat like analysts in their theorizing.

Both Brownell (Chapter 7, this volume) and Cox and Xavier (unpublished manuscript) have done superb reviews of the behavioral literature. Their extensive surveys will not be duplicated here, but certain features of importance will be singled out for discussion. Behavioral treatments basically have comprised one or a combination of the following methods: aversive conditioning, desensitization, or retraining the ego to develop newer and more desirable sexual potentials. Most methods have concentrated on either blocking the behavior by aversive methods, or interfering with, altering, or promoting new fantasies. In 1945 Eidelberg observed that changes occurring in masturbation fantasies during treatment indicated successful progress of the treatment. As indicated by Abel (1974), behaviorists have carried this observation several steps further to the point where they recognize that fantasy determines behavior, and if the fantasy can be altered then the behavior also will be altered.

Brownell (Chapter 7, this volume) states that exhibitionism consists of a group of sexual and nonsexual behaviors which have been learned from the individual's interaction with the internal and external world. These behaviors originate in the child's early years, when he observed how males and females acted toward him and modeled himself after certain specific persons. This is close to Allen's view (1974) that the parents' response to looking–exhibiting behaviors will condition the later uses of looking, showing, and concealing.

McGuire, Carlyle, and Young (1965) suggest that the symptom or behavior is learned at some time in the past and can be changed by learning a new pattern of behavior. They quote Jaspers to the effect that perversion arises through accidents of the first experience; that is, an early sexual experience is remembered and forms the basis for subsequent sexual activity, rather much like Stoller's idea of the original trauma. McGuire, however, feels that it does not simply happen due to a simultaneous association with a past experience; since, as he points out, many are exposed but most do not develop a perversion. He postulates that learning takes place *after* the initial experience which plays a part only in supplying a fantasy for later masturbation. He asks, why masturbate to that particular fantasy? His answer is that it was the first real sexual experience, as opposed to stories, guesses, rumors, or books. An important part of Mc-

Guire's theory is that subsequent masturbation reinforces the initial experience. Fantasy alters the original experience and elaborates a new fantasy which, through repeated reinforcement by masturbation, becomes more and more dominant. This mechanism may determine the specific displacement discussed by analysts. The fantasy then determines subsequent behavior. He cites as an example a 14-year-old boy who observed a girl in her underwear through a window. The boy masturbated to that memory, but with time the memory of the girl faded and his memory was distorted by numerous shop displays and ads for women's underwear which became the stronger cue. Ultimately he had no interest in girls, but was stimulated by feminine underwear.

Fensterheim (1974) writing on the behavior therapy of sexual variation notes that behaviorists do not really offer a developmental formulation. He cites Rachman and Hodgson's experiment which demonstrated that via Pavlovian conditioning of pictures of sexy women with boots, a sexual response could be obtained to boots. He states, "My own clinical experience suggests that whatever the genesis, these variant behaviors at some point become autonomous. Such a formulation at once explains the lack of success of the psychoanalytic methods and the great success of the behavioral approaches with these behaviors. All the evidence indicates that rapid and successful treatment occurs only when they are treated as if they were autonomous manifestations." This observation is of great theoretical and practical importance, as it explains another aspect of the persistence of symptoms and their resistance to extinction in addition to the ego-syntonic aspects discussed previously. The shift from pictures to boots would appear to be similar in concept to Marmor's idea of symbolic displacement.

COMBINED APPROACHES TO TREATMENT

Brownell, Hayes, and Barlow (1977) stress that the removal of deviant behavior will not necessarily or spontaneously lead to the development of normal behavior. Stated otherwise, the interference with deviant arousal patterns alone will not necessarily lead to the spontaneous development of heterosexual arousal. The authors quite accurately point out that therapists for years made the assumption that if the deviant arousal pattern was interfered with, desired behavior would immediately replace it. As they point out, individuals may have multiple deviant patterns, each of which must be treated, and in addition the individual may lack mechanisms for alternative expression. Multifaceted behavioral therapy aims to provide some of these mechanisms. They cite Barlow's classes of components of sexual functioning: heterosexual arousal, heterosocial skills, deviant arousal, and gender role deviation. Any or all of these components may play a part in a given case and require separate therapy.

Hackett's (1971) psychotherapy had two aims: 1) to demonstrate that anger was the problem and the basis for the act of exhibitionism, and 2) to teach better modes of expression. Brownell et al. utilized this principle in the use of covert sensitization for interference with multiple deviant arousal patterns plus orgasmic reconditioning to heterosexual stimuli, in order to introduce new and desired types of behavior. Marquis (1970) pioneered the technique of orgasmic reconditioning which utilized the principle of initiating masturbation with the usual deviant fantasy, and at the point of inevitability shifting to the desired fantasy. Davison (1968) reported treating a client with a problem of sadism with both Marquis's method of orgasmic retraining and a covert aversive treatment of the sadistic fantasy. Herman, Barlow, and Agras (1974) reported on the instigation of heterosexual responsiveness during the treatment of sexual deviation by utilizing film clips of a nude seductive female as a means of education and retraining. They felt re-education was necessary and theorized that when aversion works it is not only because of the suppression of the deviant arousal, but also because heterosexual responses were made possible. Brownell (Chapter 7) stresses the need for development of heterosocial skills. His case report illustrates a multifaceted behavioral approach to the treatment of exhibitionism. He stresses assessment of the patient's sexual and social behaviors leading to specific treatment goals, measurement of heterosexual behavior and arousal, and the need for the treatment program to consist of "a number of procedures aimed at remedying excesses and deficits in particular problem areas."

A few authors have attempted to combine psychoanalytic theory and psychodynamic therapy with behavior modification. Rhoads and Feather (1974) describe cases in which a psychodynamic formulation served as the basis for prescribing behavioral techniques. These cases include the report of treatment of a transvestite by reversal of a masochistic masturbation fantasy through the use of a sadistic counter-fantasy.

Annon (1973) reported on the alteration of masturbation fantasies as well as the environment in which they were used. Following successful fantasy alteration with the use of aversive techniques, the subject practiced masturbatory techniques similar to those he would actually use in intercourse. This amounts to fantasy retraining or education.

Lazarus in 1968 reported on the treatment of a case of pseudonecrophilia utilizing a method of desensitization to shape and alter the qualitative aspect of the patient's masturbatory fantasies. The patient was presented with verbal images which progressed from imagining intercourse with a female corpse, to an unconscious female, to an inattentive female, and finally to a responding female. He noted that behavioral change followed upon successfully changing the fantasy; the patient ultimately was able to be aroused by the normal scene, and his behavior followed suit. This case has important implications for exhibitionism: it demonstrates that the change of fantasies is possible by means other than aversion, and that with a change of fantasy, change in behavior may be expected to follow.

Rhoads (1978) reports cases in which behavior modification was used as the initial approach. With its partial success a weakening of resistances occurred and disclosure of psychodynamically important material followed, to be subsequently dealt with by analytically oriented therapy. Segraves and Smith (1976) also reported on concurrent psychotherapy and behavior therapy, in which a patient in analytically oriented therapy was referred for the behavioral treatment of certain target symptoms. Behavioral confrontation led to certain transference reactions and ultimately to a decreased resistance to the psychodynamic therapy. D'Alessio in 1968 reported on the concurrent use of behavior modification and psychotherapy. He reported three cases and stated that therapy could go either way; that is, starting with behavior modification and shifting to traditional psychotherapy, or starting with traditional psychotherapy and later introducing behavioral therapy aimed at the removal of specific symptoms. In one case he began with individual psychotherapy, later introduced a desensitization procedure, and ended up with sessions divided between the two methods. In another case he introduced relaxation, encountered resistances, switched to an insight-oriented therapy, and ultimately returned to desensitizing the patient. Though none of his cases involved exhibitionism, his case reports do demonstrate an innovative and imaginative application of mixed therapies.

Mathis and Collins (1970) used group therapy to develop increased ego abilities in order to lessen the intensity and frequency of narcissistic injuries and to improve methods of coping with life stresses. Birk, Huddleston, Miller, and Cohler (1971) devised a combination of group therapy, aversive conditioning, and heterosexual reconditioning for the treatment of homosexuals seeking to change. Birk states:

> We emphasize the importance of concomitant psychotherapy because a conditioning procedure of this kind is dependent on punishment and response suppression. It cannot be expected to lead to extinction of homosexual responses, but only to their suppression through punishment. It can be expected to work even behaviorally only if punishment is continued, as by booster treatment, or much better if during the period of response suppression some stable gratifying response system can successfully compete with and eventually supplant the homosexual response patterns. Heterosexual modes of reinforcement must be opened up, either through psychotherapy or by favorable life circumstances if a durable improvement is to occur.

The psychotherapy component was aimed at understanding and reducing the patient's heterosexual fears, furnishing group support, and reinforcing heterosexual experimentation.

CASE STUDY

As an illustration of using both insight and behavior therapy, it may be relevant here to cite the case of a 50-year-old lawyer who referred himself at the insistence of the court. He had been arrested for exhibiting to young boys, and convicted and placed on indefinite probation. His past history indicated that nudity had been common in his early family life, his mother walking about nude until the patient reached puberty. He was very close to his mother but he saw his father as aloof and forbidding. He had been married for 18 years. He had had exhibitionistic fantasies throughout much of his adult life, and these were accentuated if he had been drinking. At such times he was "apt to allow the bathing suit to slip off." He was treated with

Maletzky's (1974) method, which seemed to block most of his impulses to exhibit. He also was instructed to keep a record of impulses and acts, and after about a dozen treatments the rate dropped to near-zero. It was at this time that he began to talk spontaneously about feelings of inferiority which dated back to boyhood, particularly when he compared the size of his penis to that of his father. He commented that if he were in a locker room he had no compunction about walking around in the nude if there were young boys; but if there were grown men present, he kept his back to them so that he would not be shown up as inadequate and inferior. This was interpreted as the reason for the pedophilic part of his exhibitionism, inasmuch as he felt he could compete with young boys at an advantage. The patient continued to practice covert sensitization twice daily. When he reported several abortive exhibitionist episodes, he was able to relate them to sudden drops in self-esteem resulting mainly from his work situation. When things were not going well and he felt that he was not demonstrating his worthwhileness or superiority, temptation would arise. He recalled that the series of episodes for which he was arrested had begun after he was put in a governmental post of administrative responsibility with no actual casework to do. This was an unfamiliar situation for him and he found himself unable to cope with the politics inherent in the situation. His self-esteem was damaged, he became angry at "the authorities," and he began to act on the exhibitionistic fantasies which had been latent for most of his adult life. These apparently had originated in the general nudity, exposure, and seduction that took place in his household as a child.

He was followed-up for a period of three years and, since the original behavioral treatment, there were only several abortive episodes of exhibitionism—with none in the past two years.

This case demonstrates the successful use of an aversive technique aimed at gaining immediate control of the symptom. When the patient learned that he could control the urge, he was able to admit to the therapist—and more importantly to himself—his feelings of inferiority and inadequacy. Having made this admission, he could take steps either to avoid future traumas or to cope with situations more satisfactorily.

The essence of these methods appears to be that they make use of certain principles discovered in the psychoanalytic investigations of exhibitionists, the observations of a number of clinicians, and the outcome studies by behaviorists documenting scientifically which methods work and which do not. Of special note are the following observations, whether looked at from the standpoint of learning theory or psychoanalytic theory. (1) Exhibitionists were exposed to experiences in childhood that warped their heterosexual responsiveness. (2) When subjected to certain specific stresses in adult life (most authors agree that this trauma or threat is to the individual's self-esteem and particularly to his sense of manhood and masculinity), the exhibitionist regresses to a symbolic means of rehabilitating his self-esteem. While most psychoanalytic authors think in terms of a problem with his mother, Allen (Chapter 4, this volume) and Hackett relate it to competitive difficulties with peers. (3) Exhibitionism with its inherent risks is basically a hostile act toward the victim who symbolically represents someone else. The exhibitionist seeks a response of fright, awe, or shock to reassure himself of his manhood. (4) Since the experience is pleasurable and even necessary (e.g., for the avoidance of depression), exhibitionists generally resist treatment. As Marmor points out, the exhibitionist is unwilling to trade a positive experience for nothing. Birk points out that "no patient wants to be 'successfully' treated and left without a sexual outlet." (5) Since the response of the victim is a necessary part of the exhibitionistic act, exhibitionists often must linger in order to savor it. This increases the risk of arrest. In some instances, the arrest itself serves a reinforcing function since it proves that the exhibitionist is a potent individual. Perhaps one solution will be a change in social attitudes, with different responses to the sight of genitals. A former secretary of mine was accosted by an exhibitionist in the gardens adjoining the hospital, but missed the whole show because she wasn't wearing her glasses. He fled from the scene, according to witnesses, after having failed to elicit the desired reaction.

CONCLUSION

Brownell and Cox's reports, plus Allen's and my own experience, confirm that psychoanalysis is rarely of value as therapy, but that behavior modification is effective. One could combine some psychoanalytic insights with behavioral methods by appropriate evaluation of the case and selection of target behaviors or attitudes for extinction, reinforcement, introduction, or interpretation. Many exhibitionists are deficient in heterosexual arousal and general ego functions, and find it difficult to be appropriately assertive. Because exhibitionism gratifies their needs to express hostility and erotic arousal while building self-esteem, it is difficult to extinguish. Therapy must therefore be aimed at extinction not only of the undesirable behavior, but also at building better methods for coping with stress and rehabilitating self-esteem. As noted previously, a vacuum cannot exist in a personality: if one takes away a method of adaptation, however poor, unsatisfactory, and dangerous it may be, it must be replaced. As one patient remarked, "Doctor, it's nice to have all this insight, but what in hell can I do with it?" If the patient is unable to develop new behaviors on his own, and the therapist does not suggest or provide acceptable alternatives, the patient will continue in the "tried and true" method.

As noted by Frank, most patients come for therapy with an attitude of hopelessness and helplessness. Exhibitionists, on the contrary, come with the feeling that they have no need to see a psychiatrist and are there only under duress. This constitutes a major resistance to alteration of the pathological behavior. Introduction to treatment by behavioral assessment and treatment methods is the best initial move, since it demonstrates quickly to the patient that it is possible for him to control his symptomatic behavior. At this point new fantasies may be introduced, new training may be given to overcome the patient's lack of confidence or to provide the inner resources that are lacking, or a psychodynamic type of therapy may be initiated. I have found that patients often come to a first appointment with little to say and denying all psychological or emotional problems. Once behavior therapy opens up the possibility that new and better options exist, a relationship of trust develops and they begin to talk spontaneously about their problems with living. Then the therapist must decide whether to proceed with further behavioral approaches, switch to a psychotherapeutic method with the aim of providing usable insight, or combine the two by using the insights as the basis for specific training to remedy immaturities or ego defects. The last option may be done through counseling, role playing, directed fantasy, desensitization, assertive training, group therapy, and ultimately in vivo trials.

REFERENCES

Abel, G. G., & Blanchard, E. B. The role of fantasy in the treatment of deviation. *Archives of General Psychiatry*, 1974, *30*, 467–475.

Allen, D. W. *The fear of looking or scopophilic-exhibitionist conflicts.* Charlottesville: University of Virginia Press, 1974.

Annon, J. S. The therapeutic use of masturbation in the treatment of sexual disorders. In R. D. Rubin, J. P. Brady, & J. D. Henderson (Eds.), *Advances in behavior therapy* (Vol. 4). New York: Academic Press, 1973.

Ansbacher, H. L., & Ansbacher, R. R. (Eds.). *The individual psychology of Alfred Adler.* New York: Basic Books, 1956, p. 427.

Birk, L., Huddleston, W., Miller, E., & Cohler, B. Avoidance conditioning for homosexuality. *Achives of General Psychiatry*, 1971, *25*, 314–323.

Brownell, K. D., Hayes, S. C., & Barlow, D. H. Patterns of appropriate and deviant sexual arousal: The behavioral treatment of multiple sexual deviances. *Journal of Consulting and Clinical Psychology*, 1977, *45*, 1144–1155.

Cox, D. J., & Xavier, N. S. *Behavioral treatment of male exhibitionism.* Unpublished manuscript, University of Virginia Medical School, 1979.

D'Alessio, G. R. The concurrent use of behavior modification and psychotherapy. *Psychotherapy: Theory, Research and Practice*, 1968, *5*, 154–159.

Davison, G. Elimination of a sadistic fantasy by client-controlled counterconditioning technique. *Journal of Abnormal Psychology*, 1968, *73*, 84–90.

Eidelberg, L. A contribution to the study of masturbation fantasy. *International Journal of Psychoanalysis*, 1945, *26*, 127–137.

Fenichel, O. *The psychoanalytic theory of neurosis.* New York: Norton, 1945, p. 72.

Fensterheim, H. Behavior therapy of the sexual variations. *Journal of Sex and Marital Therapy*, 1974, *1*, 16–28.

Hackett, T. P. The psychotherapy of exhibitionists in a court clinic setting. *Seminars in Psychiatry*, 1971, *3*, 297–306.

Herman, S. H., Barlow, D. H., & Agras, W. S. An experimental analysis of exposure to "explicit" heterosexual stimuli as an effective variable in changing arousal patterns of homosexuals. *Behaviour Research and Therapy*, 1974, *12*, 335–345.

Lasègue, C. Les exhibitionistes. *L'Union Médicale*, 1877, *23*, 703.

Lazarus, A. A case of pseudonecrophilia treated by behavior therapy. *Journal of Clinical Psychology*, 1968, *24*, 113–115.

Maletzky, B. M. "Assisted" covert sensitization in the treatment of exhibitionism. *Journal of Consulting and Clinical Psychology*, 1974, *42*, 34–40.

Marmor, J. Sexual Deviancy: Part I. *Journal of Continuing Education in Psychiatry*, 1978, *39*, 23–32.

Marquis, J. N. Orgasmic reconditioning: Changing sexual object choice through controlling masturbation fantasies. *Journal of Behavior Therapy and Experimental Psychiatry*, 1970, *1*, 263–271.

Mathis, J. L., & Collins, M. Mandatory group therapy for exhibitionists. *American Journal of Psychiatry*, 1970, *126*, 1162–1167.

McGuire, R. J., Carlisle, J. M., & Young, B. G. Sexual deviations as conditioned behavior: A hypothesis. *Behaviour Research and Therapy*, 1965, *2*, 185–190.

Rachman, S., & Hodgson, R. J. Experimentally induced sexual fetishism: Replication and development. *Psychological Record*, 1968, *18*, 25–27.

Reich, A. A discussion of 1912 on masturbation and our present-day views. *Psychoanalytic Study of the Child*, 1951, *6*, 80–94.

Rhoads, J. M. Psychomatic illness: A behavioral approach. *Psychosomatics*, 1978, *19*, 601–607.

Rhoads, J. M., & Feather, B. W. The application of psychodynamics to behavior therapy. *American Journal of Psychiatry*, 1974, *131*, 17–20.

Rickles, N. K. Exhibitionism. *Journal of Nervous and Mental Disease*, 1942, *95*, 11–17.

Rooth, G. Exhibitionism outside Europe and America. *Archives of Sexual Behavior*, 1973, *2*, 351–363.

Segraves, R. T., & Smith, R. C. Concurrent psychotherapy and behavior therapy. *Archives of General Psychiatry*, 1976, *33*, 756–763.

Serber, M. Shame aversion therapy. *Journal of Behavior Therapy and Experimental Psychiatry*, 1970, *1*, 213–215.

Sperling, M. The analysis of an exhibitionist. *International Journal of Psychoanalysis*, 1947, *28*, 32–45.

Stoller, R. J. *Perversion*. New York: Pantheon, 1975.

von Krafft-Ebing, R. *Psychopathia sexualis*. New York: Putnam, 1965.

12
WORKINGS BETWEEN THE LEGAL SYSTEM AND THE THERAPIST

Steven R. Smith
Robert G. Meyer

Psychotherapists are deeply involved with the legal system in the assessment and treatment of exhibitionists. Studies of exhibitionists in Canada by Gigeroff et al. (1968) indicate that 67 percent of exhibitionists were ordered by courts to receive psychiatric assistance as a condition of probation. In addition, other exhibitionists were referred to psychotherapists by probation officers. In all, three out of four exhibitionists on probation were seen by psychotherapists. Exhibitionists as a group represented the highest percentage of sex offenders referred for psychotherapy.

Exhibitionists account for more than one-third of all sex offenders, making exhibitionists the largest single group of apprehended sex offenders. As a group they also have the highest rate of recidivism. Forty-six percent, in one study, had more than four convictions for activity related to exhibitionism (Gebhard et al., 1965). Because the act seems to be truly compulsive, repeated exposures are likely, and the exposure is often in a place identified with the exhibitionist (such as an automobile or home), arrest of the exhibitionist is probable in about one-third of the reported cases of indecent exposure (Smukler & Schiebel, 1975). The likelihood of arrest, the tendency toward recidivism, and the frequency with which exhibitionists are referred to a psychotherapist make it clear that a large number of exhibitionists are seen by psychotherapists. It is essential, therefore, that the psychotherapist who treats exhibitionists be aware of the laws to which the exhibitionist may be subject. In particular, indecent exposure laws, related statutes such as lewd conduct and disorderly conduct laws, and sexual psychopath laws are relevant. These laws are considered more thoroughly in Chapter 2 of this volume. In this chapter we will examine the roles that the psychotherapist may play in the assessment, sentencing, and treatment of exhibitionists. Then we will look at several of the psycho-legal problems of importance in the legal system's handling of exhibitionists. Finally, we will consider several matters that a psychotherapist should keep in mind in working with exhibitionists in the legal system.

LEGAL ENVIRONMENT

The psychotherapist may play a number of different roles in the legal system's handling of exhibitionists or those charged with indecent or lewd exposure. The therapist may be asked to evaluate a criminal defendant or potential criminal defendant and to report the evaluation to an attorney or the court; the therapist may be involved in treatment ordered by or under the general supervision of a court; or the therapist may advise legislative bodies or courts concerning the general nature of exhibitionism and the proper legal response to it. These roles require that the psychotherapist react to and interact with the legal system in unique ways. Following an examination of each of the roles that a psychotherapist may have, issues relating to all three roles will be considered.

EVALUATION

Psychotherapists may be asked by the defense counsel, the prosecutor, the court or one of the agencies of the court, or a corrections agency such as a parole board to evaluate someone who is or may be charged with indecent exposure or a similar crime. The services a psychotherapist will be expected to provide will vary, depending on the point in the proceedings that he or she is contacted and the person or group seeking the evaluation.

Preindictment Evaluation

Only rarely would a psychotherapist be contacted concerning a defendant before charges were formally placed against the defendant. It is possible, however, that the defense attorney might request a delay in officially charging a defendant pending an examination by a psychotherapist. It is also possible that a prosecutor might wish to have an initial evaluation before formal charges are preferred.

The most likely situation in which this very early evaluation would be requested is when a person of some note is involved as a defendant or where there is grave doubt that the defendant was capable of the crime. Usually the early evaluation would be aimed at preventing someone, such as a person of some note, from unfairly being charged with a sex offense. Charging a well-known person—particularly a politician—with a sex crime obviously would seriously and irreparably damage him. Even if the person did in fact expose himself, the prosecutor may be faced with a choice of charging the defendant with an offense such as disturbing the peace or with indecent exposure. The defense attorney may request the evaluation to demonstrate to the prosecutor that a charge without the stigma of being a sex offense should be used. Under such circumstances, the parties will most likely be interested in ascertaining whether the defendant is truly a sex offender. If the defendant is not a true exhibitionist, the prosecutor may feel freer to charge the defendant with an offense not carrying a serious stigma, or not to charge the defendant with any crime at all.

When an evaluation is requested before formal charges have been lodged, the situation the psychotherapist faces is likely to be extremely delicate. The psychotherapist must be extraordinarily circumspect in the language he or she uses to report findings and conclusions to the court and to attorneys. The report may become public, particularly if it involves a public official. Anything in the report that points to a mental illness or appears to the prosecutor to suggest sexual perversion may put considerable pressure on the prosecutor to charge the defendant with indecent exposure rather than a nonsexual crime. The psychotherapist should particularly avoid language in such a report that would appear to the press or the public to suggest sexual perversion unfairly. (The problems associated with using the jargon of psychology and psychiatry in communicating with attorneys and officers of the court are considered in greater detail later in this chapter.)

Pretrial Evaluation

A therapist may be contacted by either the prosecution or the defense after formal charges have been filed against the defendant to prepare general background information for trial, or to arrange for the therapist's own direct testimony at the trial. The defense attorney may also contact a psychotherapist for information which will provide the basis for plea bargaining with the prosecutor.

Evaluation of defendants with an eye toward testimony at trial is considered in the next section. Evaluation done to provide information as a basis for plea bargaining involves many of the same principles as preindictment evaluation. Although more common than preindictment evaluations, these pretrial evaluations directed toward plea bargaining are still relatively unusual.

It is particularly helpful to the parties in a pretrial evaluation to have assessment of the dangerousness of the defendant in terms of the likelihood that he will repeat the exposure or move on to more dangerous sex crimes, and in terms of the likelihood that his exposure will harm the victims. It may also be helpful to have information concerning the treatment which would be effective in dealing with any serious psychological problems that led to the exposure.

Because the purpose of the pretrial evaluation may vary, it is important that the psychotherapist carefully review the purpose, intended use, and possible distribution of any evaluation which is done. The necessity for close communication between the psychotherapist and the party requesting the evaluation is a recurrent theme throughout this chapter: without such communication, the evaluation will be of limited value to the party requesting it and the experience may be rather frustrating for the therapist.

In some jurisdictions there are sexual psychopath laws which may begin to operate before the trial. In these jurisdictions, a psychotherapist may be called upon to provide evidence concerning the dangerousness of the defendant or to evaluate the defendant in other ways even before a trial is held. (These matters are discussed more fully in the section of this chapter dealing with evaluations persuant to sexual psychopath laws.)

Evaluation for Trial

Considering the level of involvement of psychotherapists following the conviction of an exhibitionist for indecent exposure, it is somewhat surprising that psychotherapists are not more involved in indecent exposure trials. The reason for this is primarily that the issues to be decided at trial are typically not those which require or are clarified by the testimony of psychotherapists. The issues at trial are whether the defendant's conduct fell within the legal definition of indecent exposure in that jurisdiction; for example, whether the defendant exposed his genitals where he should have known that he was likely to be viewed by members of the public. Psychotherapists may be called upon to testify on collateral issues such as the mental ability of a defendant to form a specific intent required by the statute. Particularly in jurisdictions in which the jury is involved in sentencing, a psychotherapist may be called to testify concerning the mental or emotional condition of the defendant and the probable effect of certain forms of punishment.

If the psychotherapist is to testify at a trial, it is absolutely essential that he or she discuss with the attorney who will call the therapist as a witness (1) specifically, the purpose of the testimony, and (2) courtroom process and procedure.

Psychotherapists testifying at trials are subject to cross-examination. For many expert witnesses, including psychotherapists, this is the most difficult part of a courtroom appearance. The potential issues and problems which will be involved in cross-examination are another subject which should be directly discussed with the attorney who is planning to call the psychotherapist as a witness. The difficulties that a psychotherapist may encounter in cross-examination are graphically portrayed by Ziskin (1975).

Presentence Evaluation

Presentence evaluations are far more common than preindictment or pretrial evaluations or testimony at trial. Typically a presentence investigation is conducted after the defendant has been found guilty. The purpose of a psychological evaluation at this stage is to assist the court in determining the appropriate disposition (punishment) for the defendant. It is particularly important for the psychotherapist to remember that a wide variety of offenders may be convicted under indecent exposure statutes. It is important for the therapist to identify clearly the nature of the indecent exposure; that is, whether the defendant is a true exhibitionist or, for example, a naked sunbather. The possibility of treating any significant mental condition of the patient should also be considered. The dangerousness of the defendant may be an issue.

A presentence evaluation may be done for the prosecutor, the defense, or the court. Regardless of the person for whom the evaluation is conducted and before the evaluation begins, the therapist should clarify with the appointing parties what information he or she is expected to provide.

At this level of the proceedings, the defense attorney will undoubtedly be trying to avoid imprisonment of the defendant. Prosecutors will probably be most anxious to eliminate recidivism and to insure that a dangerous sexual criminal will not be released to circulate at large. Many persons convicted of indecent exposure receive only a fine. Defendants with a history of repeated convictions of indecent exposure, however, may well be subject to a jail or prison sentence. A proposal for a treatment plan that stands some reasonable chance of success will provide a great service in suggesting a way of returning the defendant to society without requiring prison, and at the same time provide some prospect of protecting society from being subjected to repeated episodes of the defendant's behavior. A suggestion of alternative forms of treatment thus may be particularly valuable in a presentence evaluation (Hackett, 1971; Mathis & Collins, 1970).

Parole and Probation Evaluations

Beyond an initial parole or probation evaluation, which is used to determine whether parole or probation should be granted and is essentially the same as a presentence evaluation, the psychotherapist may be asked to provide periodic review of the defendant's progress. These progress reports may be a part of court-ordered therapy or conducted by a psychotherapist not directly involved in the treatment of the defendant.

Sexual Psychopath Laws

In some jurisdictions, persons convicted of or charged with indecent exposure or lewd conduct may be subject to the sexual psychopath laws. These laws provide for the civil commitment of sexually dangerous persons. Psychotherapists typically play a major role in sexual psychopath hearings. Generally they are expected to report on the mental or emotional condition of the patient and to inform the court whether or not the person is dangerous. Persuant to sexual psychopath laws, courts typically depend very heavily on the expert testimony of psychotherapists in determining whether to commit a person.

Diagnostic Tests and Exhibitionism

Since different personality types are manifested in exhibitionism, psychological tests and other diagnostic devices can be of help. Lester (1975) asserts that the MMPI and the Rorschach are useful in assessing exhibitionists. Exner's (1978) work with Rorschach signs that predict dangerousness can be particularly useful to the psychologist. His rather complex array of signs show promise of substantial predictive value across an array of dangerous persons, and could be particularly useful in determining which exhibitionists are dangerous.

Graham (1977) has noted the usefulness of certain MMPI code types in assessing acting-out potential and Rader (1977) also has studied this in detail. The 4-8/8-4 and the 4-9/9-4 code types are typically indicative of the characterological type of exhibitionist. Scale 4 of the MMPI is labeled the Psychopathic deviate scale; scale 8 is the mania scale. A combination of these scales is usually considered to be indicative of a sociopathic value system with the potential for acting out against others. Elevation on scales 1 (hysteria), 2 (depression), and 3 (hypochondriasis) would be more characteristic of the neurotic categories. As Graham notes, a number of recently developed MMPI subscales have been related to aggressive acting out. These subscales have not yet been specifically applied to categorizing exhibitionists, but there is every reason to believe that they could be helpful in that regard.

Psychotherapist–Defendant Relationship

Regardless of the time at which a psychotherapist interviews or evaluates a patient or for whom the evaluation is conducted, the therapist should inform the patient of the conditions under which the evaluation is being conducted. In particular, the defendant should be informed of the person or group for whom the evaluation is being done and whether or not the ordinary psychotherapist–patient confidentiality will not apply to the relationship.

TREATMENT

Many persons brought into the legal system on a charge related to indecent exposure are sent for or seek some form of psychotherapy. A psychotherapist is, in fact, more likely to be used to provide treatment for the individual charged with indecent exposure than to simply evaluate the defendant.

The reasons for the heavy dependence upon psychotherapy for the indecent exposure defendant as compared to other criminal defendants is not entirely clear. In part, the emphasis on psychotherapy probably relates to the fact that the crime of indecent exposure appears to a lay person (judge or attorney) as such bizarre behavior that it clearly must represent some form of mental illness. In addition there is the feeling that exhibitionism, while not in itself a violent crime, is a prelude to more serious sex offenses including rape. It is, therefore, necessary to do something about the exhibitionist before he becomes a serious sex offender.

A rather heavy reliance upon therapy for exhibitionists, as opposed to others who may be charged with indecent exposure, probably makes a good deal of sense. Given the highly impulsive nature of the exhibitionist act, imprisonment is not likely to be effective in deterring the exhibitionist; nor is his removal from society through imprisonment likely to help the defendant in developing necessary interpersonal skills which may be weak. Removal from his family and loss of employment may rather seriously injure the defendant. With or without imprisonment there is a rather high likelihood of recidivism. Without treatment, the exhibitionist is likely to repeat the exposure. It is, therefore, in the interest of both the defendant and society to provide some form of therapy for the defendant.

Stages at which Referral May Occur

An indecent exposure defendant may be referred to a psychotherapist for treatment at roughly the stages described previously concerning evaluation. For the purposes of discussion, these may be divided into two areas: referral prior to trial and referral after trial.

Treatment before Trial

A defendant may be referred to a therapist before he is charged with a crime, or after he is officially charged but before trial. In such circumstances the defendant's attorney and the prosecutor have usually reached an agreement that formal prosecution of the defendant would serve no purpose and would in fact be harmful. The defendant will therefore apparently be voluntarily attending therapy, but this voluntary attendance may in fact be coerced and be viewed by him as punishment.

The effort to work out an agreement for the defendant to enter therapy prior to formal charges has the advantage that he will not have a sex offense charge on his criminal record. Avoiding a conviction for a sex offense is important enough that many defendants agree to enter therapy to avoid such a conviction. There is, in addition, the suggestion that many exhibitionists in fact wish to be caught so as to go into therapy or be punished.

Referral prior to conviction so that the referral is not pursuant to a court order has advantages to the therapist in that the therapist is likely to have a little greater flexibility in dealing with the defendant. The absence of a court order or court direction of therapy means that the court will not be overseeing treatment. Therefore the therapist usually will not be required to provide as many and as thorough reports on the progress of therapy as might be required when it is done pursuant to a court order.

Treatment after Trial

Treatment which is begun after a trial has started or after the defendant has pleaded guilty is usually undertaken pursuant to a court order or under the authority of the court. Such treatment may be begun after a formal finding of guilt, in which case it may take the form of a condition of parole or may be done while the court holds formal sentencing in abeyance with the understanding that, if the defendant successfully completes treatment, the court will not sentence him. If he does not complete the treatment, however, the sentence—usually involving prison—will be imposed. In a few cases, treatment may begin before there is a formal finding of guilt by the court. This alternative is particularly attractive for many defendants in that it may provide a way of avoiding conviction for a stigmatizing sex offense.

Regardless of the time at which therapy is ordered, it is essential that the psychotherapist understand what is expected in terms of treatment; that is, what the court will require to be accomplished before the patient is "released" from therapy. It makes a real difference as to whether the therapist is expected to continue treatment until the defendant is "cured," is unlikely to perform further acts of exhibitionism, has received the "usual" course of therapy for exhibitionism, or would receive no further benefit from therapy. Often courts will expect psychotherapists to indicate that there is little likelihood the defendant will engage in exhibitionist behavior again. It is very desirable to identify the goals of therapy clearly before the therapist agrees to direct the therapy or before the therapy actually begins.

The psychotherapist should understand that certain methods of treatment generally available for use with exhibitionists may not be available when the treatment is conducted pursuant to a court order or as part of the criminal justice system. Therapy conducted in these situations will be subject to the constitutional guarantee against cruel and unusual punishment contained in the Eighth Amendment to the Constitution. Certain extremely aversive therapies, for example, may be prohibited by the Constitution. (These matters are discussed more fully in the section of this chapter dealing with cruel and unusual punishment.)

Coercion and Therapy

In addition to these forms of entry into therapy which to one degree or another involve a voluntary decision on the part of the defendant (although the defendant may be volunteering in the face of a jail sentence), there are a few other circumstances in which the defendant's participation is in no real sense voluntary. These circumstances include when the patient is committed to a mental hospital or is sentenced to prison where the therapy takes place. Under such circumstances, the therapy will occur in an institutional setting and will be subject to the rules of the institution as well as to constitutional limitations.

To some degree almost any psychotherapy for an exhibitionist facing charges or convicted of indecent exposure is coerced. There has been serious debate concerning whether therapy which is coerced or court-ordered can be effective. There is at least some reason to believe that the system which seems to be evolving and which encourages psychotherapy instead of imprisonment for the exhibitionist, even if the psychotherapy must be coerced, may be effective. Kaslow (1976) has suggested that obligatory therapy can work if it is interpreted and really viewed as what it is, i.e., an expression of society's concern for its members: "They may be mandated, they may resist, they will test you out and they will battle you. But if you hang in there and they know you give a damn, they come back" (p. 362).

Reports of Progress

Whether a psychotherapist is consulted by one of the parties or the court either for an evaluation or for treatment of the defendant, the therapist will be expected to provide some form of report to the court. The usual rules regarding confidentiality and psychotherapist–patient privilege will not apply to the examination and treatment of the defendant if conducted for one of the parties or the court with an eye toward litigation or conducted pursuant to a court order. (Issues relating to confidentiality are described in more detail later in this chapter.) The therapist should inform the defendant that the usual rules regarding confidentiality will not apply and that the therapist will be expected to make periodic reports to the court. While such a process may make a patient initially more reluctant to discuss matters with the therapist, in the long run it may provide for a greater level of trust between the therapist and the patient. If the therapist believes that it would be difficult to establish any form of serious trust and communication with the defendant if confidentiality were to be breached in any serious way, then he or she should speak with the judge in the case before seeing the defendant. There should be definite agreement, usually presented in writing via a letter, or better yet in a court order, concerning the obligation of the therapist to report to the court. Even with such an agreement, it may be impossible for the therapist and patient to be assured that additional information cannot be obtained from the therapist in a court proceeding at a later time.

The therapist should also determine the persons or groups who may have access to any reports. The therapist and the party requesting the evaluation may wish to avoid certain areas or certain language if the evaluation report will be available to the other party or to the public.

Correct Classification and Reports to the Court

Whether a psychotherapist is doing an evaluation of a person charged with or convicted of indecent exposure, or providing treatment in connection with such a charge, the nature of the report and suggestions to the prosecutor, defense attorney, or court should depend on the classification of the defendant. Persons charged with indecent exposure and sent to psychotherapists for evaluation or treatment include nonexhibitionists, primary exhibitionists (compulsive exposers), and secondary exhibitionists (those whose exposure is incidental to a more serious mental problem).

As we have noted, some persons charged with indecent exposure are not exhibitionists at all. This group may include nude sunbathers, burlesque stars, "streakers," and drunks (typically engaged in public urination). It is not particularly unusual for teenagers charged with indecent exposure to be referred to a psychotherapist even though they were clearly engaging in activity which was not related to true exhibitionism. When the therapist is satisfied that this is the case, it is important to report that the defendant is in fact not a true exhibitionist and he (or she) does not pose a serious threat to society, and perhaps to suggest any professional assistance the person needs to deal with problems he (or she) is having. Often in such cases, of course, no treatment is really called for and this should be explained clearly to the court, the prosecutor, or the defense attorney. Some of the persons classified as not being true exhibitionists may nonetheless be prone to repeat episodes of indecent exposure. For example, drunks charged with indecent exposure because of urinating in public may engage in the same conduct again when intoxicated. This fact should be revealed to the court and it should also be noted that the problem is not one of exhibitionism, but of intoxication. Thus intoxication is the problem that needs to be dealt with and the usual treatment for exhibitionism would be ineffective in dealing with the defendant's indecent exposure.

Primary exhibitionists are compulsive exposers. This group is almost exclusively limited to men. They typically have a history of poor heterosexual adjustment; they tend to be lonely; and even under situations of extreme provocation, they have difficulty in recognizing their feelings of anger (Gebhard et al., 1965; Smuckler & Schiebel, 1975). These persons have an extremely high rate of recidivism and without treatment are likely to continue engaging in exhibitionist behavior. Treatment programs as described in other chapters may be suggested to help the primary exhibitionist. Courts and people involved with the defendant's welfare should be informed of this fact. In addition, the court might also be informed that exhibitionists are generally young, ranging in age from adolescence to the mid-thirties. The number of charges for indecent exposure peaks at about the age of 25. Therefore the likelihood of continued episodes of indecent exposure decreases as a defendant passes 25 years of age and often disappears after his mid-thirties (Gigeroff et al., 1968). Particularly for older defendants, this information should be relayed to the court.

Secondary exhibitionists include the mentally deficient, schizophrenics, and individuals with organic brain disease. The exposure of these people is incidental to a more serious mental problem and courts, prosecutors, and the defense should be informed that treatment for exhibitionism is not likely to be effective. The serious mental problems that these patients have are not likely to be solved by imprisonment. In many cases referral to a psychotherapist for treatment does make sense. In other cases it is appropriate for legal measures other than the indecent exposure laws to be used. In some cases, these persons may be candidates for a declaration of incompetency or involuntary civil commitment.

The classification of individuals who may be charged with indecent exposure is considered further in the section of this chapter dealing with dangerousness (page 327).

Deception

A major problem in treating exhibitionists is deception. Since many exhibitionists who enter therapy are under coercion of some kind and must continue therapy until they have been determined to be "cured," there is an incentive for some defendants to falsify reports or otherwise deceive the therapist in order to be allowed to terminate therapy or probation. Bogan (1975) refers to this problem of "dissimulation . . . concealing facts, intentions or feelings under some pretense; putting on a false appearance" (p. 20). Dissimulation is often difficult to spot and in part is cited as a failure of therapeutic programs within correctional systems.

Other therapists have noted the difficulty in dealing with deception in treating the exhibitionist. Rosen and Kopel (1977), for example, reported treating a transvestite exhibitionist using biofeedback techniques. After two years of apparently successful treatment, the patient reported that he had been cured, but the patient's wife disclosed that he had resumed indecent exposure. The patient had in fact been deceiving the therapist during the greater part of the two years in which he had undergone therapy.

Sadoff et al. (1971) have noted that individuals who reported that they had benefited from group therapy were later arrested more often than those who complained about the therapy. They also found that a psychotherapist who examined the defendant was significantly less successful in predicting future criminal behavior than the therapist who had conducted the group therapy in which the defendant participated.

These and other studies indicate the importance of recognizing the opportunity for deception, and they suggest that the therapist who conducted treatment with a patient is more likely than the clinician doing a diagnostic evaluation to predict future criminal behavior. In either case, the possibility that deception exists might well be revealed to the court or other organizations requiring reports from the therapist.

Diagnosticians should consider utilizing tests such as the MMPI and the Cattell 16 Personality Factor Test, since they incorporate scales for faking good and bad results. Specific scales such as the Marlowe-Crowne Social Desirability Scale could also be useful. The problem with deception suggests the value of including psychologists in the diagnostic process. Other mental health professionals usually receive limited training in the use of psychodiagnostic tests, and the interview is particularly vulnerable to manipulation by deception.

It has also been recommended that other measures which could be related to deception be incorporated in therapy. For example, observation of pupillary dilation and voice changes as well as the more traditional physiological measures of the polygraph offer promise of detecting deception. Reported changes in sexual orientation verified by penile plethysmography are also a possible means of detection, although there are obvious problems with invasion of privacy, not to mention the irony of using this procedure with the exhibitionist.

Some therapists have suggested that it is necessary to resort to temptation in order to establish a clear understanding of whether the patient has been cured. A temptation test has been proposed by Maletzky (1974) whereby an attractive female associate of the therapist stations herself in a place likely to elicit exposure by the defendant. Presumably only those who successfully resisted the temptation would be considered cured. Temptation tests which go beyond this rather mild invitation to exhibitionism might give the courts some problems. At some point "temptation" could be claimed to be entrapment. The use of more accepted psychological measures of "cure" as suggested by Serber and Wolpe (1972) are likely to be considerably more palatable to courts. If tests which appear to involve serious trickery or unusual methods of assessment are to be used, the therapist should communicate this in confidence to the court to avoid future confrontation concerning such methods.

Treatment and Sexual Psychopath Laws

Sexual psychopath laws typically provide for the civil commitment of certain sex offenders, generally sex offenders who are determined to be dangerous. Although sexual psychopath statutes vary among jurisdictions and not all jurisdictions even have sexual psychopath laws, it is possible that an exhibitionist may be subject to sexual psychopath laws in some states. The psychotherapist plays a major role in determining whether a patient is a sexual psychopath under the state statute, in treating sexual psychopaths committed to mental facilities, and in releasing sexual psychopaths once they are "cured" or no longer dangerous.

The prediction of dangerousness is particularly important in cases involving sexual psychopath commitment. Because true exhibitionists are not generally dangerous, the psychotherapist should make it clear that if the court is dealing merely with an exhibitionist he is not likely to be dangerous to other persons.

Problems with the Current Treatment Approach

Despite the many gains in the treatment of exhibitionists and the trend toward treating exhibitionists rather than imprisoning them, there are many problems in the current system of evaluation and treatment (Austin and Utne, 1977). The following problems have been noted:

1. Treatment labels the defendant as sick. This labeling is harmful.
2. Psychotherapists, in fact, cannot reliably classify criminals so as to predict their future activities or to be able to treat them adequately.

3. The overcrowding and brutality in prisons and the overcrowding of treatment facilities make genuine rehabilitation extremely difficult.
4. Much of what passes for treatment is punishment.
5. Because of high rates of recidivism, there is little reason to believe that most exhibitionists are rehabilitated.
6. Some forms of treatment rely on methods which are of dubious legality.
7. "Treatment" emphasizes individual pathology rather than the societal causes of crime.
8. Treatment programs allow for too much discretion and too much opportunity for treating similar defendants very differently.
9. Coerced treatment is inherently distasteful and is possibly only partially effective.
10. Exhibitionists can deceive therapists concerning progress in therapy so that it is difficult to determine whether therapy has in fact been successful.

Although each of these difficulties concerning the treatment approach to exhibitionism contains an element of truth, they represent areas in which improvement can be made through continued efforts by psychotherapists. For many defendants, treatment still appears to be a more attractive alternative than incarceration without rehabilitation therapy.

Alternatives to the present system should continue to be examined by psychotherapists and attorneys. One proposal would take account of the fact that indecent exposure is generally a nuisance offense rather than an offense of violence and would provide for the release of exhibitionists on probation or after payment of a small fine. Psychotherapy would then be available to these persons on a voluntary basis ("Pedophilia, Exhibitionism and Voyeurism," 1969). Such alternatives should continue to be studied.

THE THERAPIST IN THE LEGISLATIVE PROCESS

Beyond providing evaluation and treatment as part of the legal process, psychotherapists can perform a valuable function by becoming involved in the legislative process relative to crimes such as indecent exposure. Unfortunately mental health professionals have not traditionally been involved with legislative bodies in the development of the law regarding sex crimes. Increasingly, however, lawmakers are becoming aware that psychotherapists can play a useful role in the legislative process.

A psychotherapist might expect to be questioned concerning the threat that an exhibitionist poses to the mental health of other people, particularly children. Legislators also undoubtedly will want to know about the dangerousness of the exhibitionist, whether he is likely to become violent, or whether exhibitionism is one step on the way toward becoming a rapist. The therapist also can provide valuable information concerning the disposition of those found guilty of indecent exposure. He can play an important role in helping lawmakers understand that fundamentally different persons commit the crime of indecent exposure and need to be treated differently. He could also explain the compulsive nature of indecent exposure and that prison terms may not be effective in dealing with the exhibitionist. Methods of treatment available for the exhibitionist should also be explained to legislators by psychotherapists. Because so many states have sexual psychopath laws, the dangerousness of the exhibitionist takes on an especially important dimension in determining whether it is rational to classify exhibitionists with violent sex offenders, and particularly whether it is rational to include exhibitionists under the sexual psychopath laws.

DANGEROUSNESS OF EXHIBITIONISTS

The issue of the dangerousness of a person charged with or convicted of indecent exposure appears in one form or another repeatedly in the legal system. There is some feeling that those viewing the indecent exposure may be emotionally harmed and exhibitionism may be one step on the road toward violent sexual offenses. Exhibitionists may even be subject to lengthy civil commitment through sexual psychopath laws because they are thought to be dangerous.

It was noted earlier that many persons convicted of indecent exposure are neither primary nor secondary exhibitionists. Most of the nonexhibitionists convicted of indecent exposure are probably not dangerous. Even many primary and secondary exhibitionists are generally not dangerous.

The fact that most exhibitionists are not dangerous is inherent in the psychological definition of exhibitionism which typically assumes that the act of exhibiting represents the "final sexual gratification without any intention of further sexual contact" (Hackett, 1971, p. 297). Of course there is evidence that this is not always the case, and there is an increasing awareness that dangerousness is in the eye of the beholder. While it may generally be agreed that one who seriously threatens the life or physical well-being of another is dangerous, there is not agreement as to whether one who threatens the emotional security of another should be considered dangerous. In recent times there has been a definite movement toward narrowing the concept of dangerousness to situations where physical injury or very serious emotional injury is involved. Modern clinical studies generally characterize indecent exposure or lewd conduct as a social nuisance rather than as dangerous activity. The harm to the victim is described as minimal (cited in Blair, 1976). This was particularly evident in Millard v. Harris (1968), wherein the civil commitment of an exhibitionist was held to be illegal in the absence of demonstrated dangerousness. Judge Bazelon stated:

> There was not evidence of any actual harm to adult women from appellant's past exhibitionism. . . . Very seclusive, withdrawn, shy, sensitive women are in a minority. While the law must and does protect them like other citizens, there are limits on the extent to which the law can sweep the streets clean of all possible sources of occasional distress to women (cited in detail in Robitscher, 1972, p. 15).

There seems to be a general agreement (Lester, 1975; Hendrix & Meyer, 1976; Rader, 1977; Smukler & Schiebel, 1975) that the exhibitionist is typically passive-dependent and obsessive in his personality functioning. In fact, he is often quite schizoid. All of these traits predict a lack of dangerousness, and this is borne out by most of the data.

For example, MacDonald's (1973) data show that only about 4 percent of 200 exhibitionists used force to gain the attention of their victims, or were aggressive in any other way. Lester's (1975) own observations agree with this. MacDonald makes another related observation: the exhibitionist act is most likely to occur on a weekday from 8 to 9 A.M., or from 3 to 5 P.M. This shows a total lack of correlation with the peak occurrence of any of the standard violent crimes.

Though exhibitionists are not particularly dangerous in any one incident, there are occasions when aggression does occur, and this takes on greater importance since in absolute numbers exhibitionists are the largest single group of sexual offenders. Except for Sturup (1967), who assessed that 93 percent of exhibitionists did not repeat, most researchers (Gebhard et al., 1965; Lester, 1975; MacDonald, 1973) feel that the recidivism rate is approximately 30 to 45 percent. The junior author's own experience (Hendrix & Meyer, 1976) would certainly support the latter data. Also, as MacDonald notes, approximately 25 percent of the exhibitionists which he studied had been convicted for prior sexual offenses, and 55 percent admitted that they had been involved in many undetected acts.

Although the exhibitionist is often passive-dependent and possibly schizoid, there are other personality types involved. Many different categorizations (Lester, 1975; Rader, 1977; Smukler and Schiebel, 1975) have been defined. The following list is a distillation of personality types of individuals who may be involved in exhibitionism. It demonstrates the diversity of disorders leading to exhibitionism and possible charges of indecent exposure.

1. *Neurotic impulsive.* This person is sexually confused, tense, anxious, and neurotically driven, and the act probably involves less premeditation than by any other type.
2. *Neurotic inadequate.* This person is shy and introverted, has few if any adequate social relationships, and appears to use the act as a means toward desired socialization and as a pathetic attempt at sexual and ego affirmation.
3. *Unaware.* The exhibitionism in these cases is a secondary result of mental retardation, organic brain disorder, senility, or extreme alcoholic intoxication.
4. *Characterological.* Here sexual arousal per se is the prime motivation, and the exhibitionism is often used as a lead-in to further sexual involvement. There is often a hostile attitude toward the victim, and in many ways the act is a "passive rape." Most important, there is little or no guilt about the behavior.

The first two groups are seldom aggressive and the third group may only be dangerous in an incidental fashion. Though the fourth group is apparently small in terms of percentage, it does pose a small threat of aggression to the victim; and because of the high absolute number of exhibitionists, some social concern is warranted.

It is, of course, important that the psychotherapist identify the personality type of the exhibitionist and his potential dangerousness.

LIMITATIONS ON THERAPY

Limitations on the use of certain types of therapy with exhibitionists may be imposed by courts, state or federal statute, or by state or federal constitution. Certain types of treatment may be prohibited by the cruel and unusual punishment provision of the Eighth Amendment to the Constitution. If the treatment of a person in the criminal justice system becomes so rough as to "shock the conscience," it may run afoul of the due-process provisions of the Fourteenth Amendment.

The constitutional limits on therapy imposed by the doctrine of cruel and unusual punishment are not clear. Courts have not made extensive use of the prohibition on cruel and unusual punishment, so that it is not well defined ("The Cruel and Unusual Punishment Clause," 1966). For the purposes of the Eighth Amendment, some forms of treatment may be considered punishment. Therefore some forms of treatment conducted through the legal system may violate the Eighth Amendment. Generally punishment is considered cruel and unusual if it is disproportionate to the crime that has been committed, excessive in that it goes beyond what is necessary to achieve a legitimate penal goal, or "offends the contemporary sense of decency" (Rubin, 1976).

Although the cruel and unusual punishment limitation has been used only sparingly, two noteworthy cases have involved indecent exposure. In one case it was used to knock down a statute permitting felony life sentences for those convicted twice of indecent exposure,[1] and in another instance to eliminate the civil commitment of exhibitionists without direct demonstration of dangerousness.[2]

Most forms of treatment of exhibitionism, of course, would not run afoul of these tests of cruel and unusual punishment. Some forms of aversive therapy have, however, been determined to be cruel and unusual ("Aversion Therapy," 1974). Aversive therapy employing great physical discomfort may run afoul of the Eighth

Amendment. Some forms of shame aversive therapy in which the defendant must engage in exhibitionism in front of a known audience may offend the contemporary sense of decency. Certainly castration as a form of punishment or compulsory treatment for exhibitionism may be considered cruel and unusual.

If a proposed treatment for exhibitionism is not excessively intrusive, painful, or embarrassing, and yet provides potential for a claim that it represents cruel and unusual punishment, the therapist should pay particular attention to obtaining a full and—to the extent possible—uncoerced, informed consent before engaging in the therapy. In addition, if serious question concerning the legal propriety of the therapy may be raised, the therapist should inform the court of the treatment plan before it is begun.

Except for the most aversive or shame-producing of therapies and for castration, the current definitions of cruel and unusual punishment do not appear to limit seriously the treatments which may be employed for exhibitionism.

ISSUES RELATING TO CONFIDENTIALITY

Many psychotherapists have noted the importance of confidentiality for effective therapy. Virtually all psychotherapists have an ethical obligation to maintain the confidences of their patients. In some states confidentiality is further protected by a psychotherapist–patient privilege which limits the power of courts to order a therapist to reveal the confidences disclosed by his patients in therapy.

The treatment of an exhibitionist on a voluntary basis, with no thoughts of any charge of indecent exposure (or similar charges), and not pursuant to a court order would be subject to the psychotherapist's professional obligation to keep the patient's secrets and might also be protected under a psychotherapist–patient privilege if one was available in the state. Inasmuch as an exhibitionist is seldom dangerous to others, the circumstances in which the psychotherapist would be forced to breach confidentiality outside of court without the permission of the patient are fairly limited. Since many states do not have a psychotherapist–patient privilege, or have a privilege that is extraordinarily limited (Meyer & Smith, 1977), the therapist cannot count on being able to maintain the patient's confidences if an issue related to the patient's mental condition is raised in court.

Evaluations or treatment conducted as part of the legal process are subject to considerably different rules concerning confidentiality. The purposes of these evaluations or the nature of the treatment require that periodic reports be made and forwarded to other persons. In some cases, as when the assessment is done for the defense attorney, the protection of the attorney–client privilege may help protect the communications from being released in court. More typically, however, the information and conclusions of the therapist will be subject to review by the courts and may become public knowledge. Unless it is protected as part of the attorney–client privilege (as when the therapist is doing an assessment for the defense attorney), the information revealed by the patient in therapy will probably not be privileged and may be subject to disclosure in cases unrelated to the indecent exposure charge.

Since the rules relating to confidentiality are so different when the patient is being evaluated or treated in connection with a charge such as indecent exposure, the therapist should carefully explain the limits on the protection of confidentiality before evaluation or treatment is started.

POTENTIAL LIABILITY

There has been a significant increase in the number of claims of malpractice filed against professionals. Although psychotherapists have not traditionally been subject to as many claims as other professionals, malpractice claims against psychotherapists are no longer as infrequent as they once were. Psychotherapists evaluating or treating an exhibitionist do not run a particularly significant risk of facing malpractice claims. An examination of the areas in which malpractice claims may arise against psychotherapists indicates that there are potential malpractice problems in dealing with exhibitionists and suggests ways of limiting the risk of malpractice.

Probably the most common claim for malpractice in psychotherapy results from the negligent administration of treatment, particularly treatment involving some physical component, most often electroconvulsive therapy. The administration of certain forms of aversive therapy and the administration of drugs carry a limited potential for liability if the therapist administers them in a careless or a reckless manner. Similarly, the failure to make an adequate examination on which to base a diagnosis might lead to a claim of negligence.

It has proven to be very difficult to sue a psychotherapist successfully for improperly administering therapy without this physical component. It is difficult to prove what injuries were the result of improper therapy; and because there is no single accepted method of treatment, it is sometimes difficult to determine what constitutes improper therapy. A psychotherapist is not expected to provide perfect therapy, but only such therapy as a reasonable practitioner would provide. A psychotherapist who takes unfair advantage of a patient (typically makes unprofessional sexual advances toward the patient) during therapy would be subject to liability for improper treatment.

The legal system has put increasing emphasis on the necessity for informed consent in treatment. To the extent that there are dangers or discomforts associated with the treatment proposed for an exhibitionist, these dangers and discomforts should be explained to the patient unless it would be dangerous to do so or a serious emergency exists which prevents the explanation. Particularly when an aversive therapy or therapy involving shame is anticipated, it is important that informed consent be obtained. Under ordinary circumstances a therapist who unethically violates the confidences of a patient may be subject to liability through negligence or invasion of privacy.

The psychotherapist–patient relationship is fundamentally altered when the psychotherapist must make reports to a court, the prosecutor, or defense counsel. To the extent that a psychotherapist goes beyond the obligation to report and makes information about the patient available to members of the general public, potential liability for breaching confidentiality exists. A therapist, for example, who publishes a book identifying his patient and revealing secrets of the patient is engaging in unethical conduct which is subject to liability.

There is generally limited liability for testimony presented in court. Unless a psychotherapist has perjured himself, liability for testimony is very limited. Statements made to courts are generally immune from the operation of the laws of libel and slander. Unless a psychotherapist at a trial or hearing has made a statement maliciously or knowing that it was false, the commitment or other confinement of an exhibitionist based on that testimony is not likely to be the basis of a successful suit against the therapist.

PRACTICAL CONSIDERATIONS

In evaluating or treating exhibitionists in cooperation with the legal system, the psychotherapist will be more productive and find the work more rewarding if he or she is attentive to several important matters.

The psychotherapist should clearly understand who the client is and what the therapist's role will be. The therapist may be conducting an evaluation for the prosecution, for the defense, or for the court. This evaluation may be aimed at a trial or sentencing, or at settling the case by agreement or through plea bargaining before going to trial. It is important for the therapist to know whether he or she ultimately will be expected to provide an evaluation that the parties will accept or discuss between themselves or whether he will be expected to provide testimony in court.

The psychotherapist should meet with and have a serious discussion with the party employing him, i.e., the attorney for the defense, the prosecution, or the judge. From this discussion, the therapist should clearly understand what he is expected to do, the law that will be applied in the case, and what testimony, if any, will be expected from the therapist. The laws concerning indecent exposure and sexual psychopath commitment vary considerably from state to state. It is important, therefore, that the psychotherapist understand what criteria are relevant in his evaluation of a defendant. In providing treatment, a therapist needs to know what limits, if any, will be applied to the treatment choices available. He also must understand what reports will be expected by the court or others and at what point treatment of the exhibitionist is expected to be terminated.

If the therapist will be expected to testify at a hearing or trial, a discussion should be held with the defense attorney to consider the therapist's testimony and cross-examination. Many expert witnesses are frustrated, confused, and frightened by cross-examination. Many of the problems with cross-examination can be avoided by a thorough discussion of what to expect on cross-examination. In some cases a mock cross-examination in which an attorney in a practice session asks the therapist questions which may be asked at trial may be helpful. Before any other proceeding (hearing, deposition, etc.) in which the therapist will participate, the attorney and the therapist should meet to discuss what will be expected of the therapist.

The psychotherapist should deal frankly with the issue of the fee that will be charged for his services. This discussion should include an understanding of the rate of compensation and the person or organization which will be responsible for payment. If the defendant in a criminal action is to pay the therapist for the service, the therapist may wish to have a written understanding with the defendant or a prepayment for the services. (It is nearly a cliché among criminal defense attorneys that an attorney should get the money "up front.")

In making reports to attorneys or courts, a psychotherapist should generally deal with the issue of dangerousness. Because there is a general feeling that exhibitionists are or at any time may become dangerous, it may be necessary for the therapist to emphasize that the vast majority of exhibitionists are not dangerous and exhibitionism is not the first step on the road to becoming a rapist.

Psychotherapists should exercise caution in the language that they use in making reports to or testifying before attorneys and courts. Technical language may mean something quite different to those untrained in psychotherapy than it does to therapists. For example, the statement that "Because his victims are often children and young women, it is often considered that the exhibitionist is at least very similar to the pedophile. The dynamics of the disorders bear several similarities," may cause a lay person to assume that the exhibitionist is or is likely to become a pedophile (child molester). Such a conclusion by a judge or jury may have very serious consequences for an exhibitionist charged with indecent exposure, including a jail term or civil commitment under a sexual psychopath law. The therapist should be aware of the danger that the jargon of psychotherapy may be misinterpreted and take pains to avoid language which may be misunderstood.

SUMMARY

Psychotherapists play an important role in the legal system in the evaluation and treatment of persons charged with indecent exposure. In working with the legal system, therapists should remember that not all persons charged with or convicted of indecent exposure are exhibitionists. Indecent exposure in some states includes the behavior of naked sunbathers, burlesque stars, and drunks. The therapist should recognize the differences among the types of persons who are charged with indecent exposure and in proper cases inform the court, the defense counsel, or the prosecutor that the defendant is not a true exhibitionist.

An individual who has exposed himself may be sent to a psychotherapist for evaluation before formal charges are initiated, at some point before trial, after trial but before sentencing, or after sentencing. A psychotherapist may also be asked to participate in a commitment hearing pursuant to a sexual psychopath law.

Psychotherapists may also be involved with providing therapy to persons charged with indecent exposure. A variety of treatment approaches have been suggested. Many defendants enter therapy under some form of coercion. The therapist should recognize this and be prepared to deal with it as well as with the possibility that the patient may falsely report a cure so that he will be permitted to discontinue therapy. The Eighth and Fourteenth Amendments may not permit the use of certain extreme kinds of treatment if it has been court-ordered or supervised. If a therapist is concerned that a form of treatment might not be within the limits of the law, he should contact the court and explain the proposed treatment.

Regardless of the point at which therapists evaluate or treat someone convicted of indecent exposure, they should understand that the usual rules regarding confidentiality do not apply. Therapists will be expected to make reports to the defense counsel, the prosecution, or the court. Some of this information may become public. Therapists should clearly understand who will have access to information in reports they make, and they should explain this to the patient.

Psychotherapists may also become involved in the legislative process. Therapists are likely to be asked about the dangerousness of exhibitionists and about the treatment available for exhibitionism. They can make major contributions to improving the laws dealing with exhibitionists. Very few exhibitionists are dangerous. There is considerable evidence that they should be treated under nuisance laws rather than as a serious threat.

Psychotherapists who deal with exhibitionists are not subjecting themselves to a particularly significant risk of encountering malpractice claims. Therapists should, however, obtain informed consent—particularly for any kind of treatment involving significant physical contact such as aversive therapies or the use of drugs, or a significant invasion of privacy as is used in some shame therapies.

As a practical matter, psychotherapists should be attentive to several matters when dealing with exhibitionists in the legal system: (1) therapists should clearly understand who the client is and what the therapist's role is in the case; (2) therapists should meet with the proper parties to understand what will be expected of them, and the law that they will be expected to apply; (3) if they are expected to testify in court, therapists should discuss their testimony and cross-examination with the party who will call them; (4) therapists should have a clear understanding of the compensation they will receive; (5) since there is often a general feeling that exhibitionists are dangerous, psychotherapists should deal directly with the dangerousness issue; and (6) psychotherapists should be careful not to use technical language which courts and attorneys may misunderstand.

NOTES

1. In re Lynch, 8 Cal. 3d 410, 503 P. 2d 921, 105 Cal. Rptr. 217 (1972).
2. Millard v. Harris, 406 F.2d 964 (D.C. Cir. 1968).

REFERENCES

American Civil Liberties Union. *The rights of gay people.* New York: Avon Books, 1975.

Austin, W., & Utne, M. Sentencing: Discretion and justice in judicial decision-making. In B. Sales (ed.), *Psychology in the legal process.* Jamaica, N.Y.: Spectrum Publications, 1977.

Aversion therapy and the involuntarily confined: Rehabilitation or retribution? *University of Florida Law Review,* 1974, 27, 224.

Blair, J. Sex offender registration for section 647 disorderly conduct convictions in cruel and unusual punishment. *San Diego Law Review* 1976, 13, 391.

Bogan, J. Client dissimulation: A key problem in correctional treatment. *Federal Probation,* 1975, 39, 20.

The cruel and unusual punishment clause and the substantive criminal law. *Harvard Law Review,* 1966, 79, 635.

Exner, J. *The rorschach: A comprehensive system* (vol. II). New York: Wiley, 1978.

Gebhard, P., Gagnon, J., Pomeroy, W., & Christenson, C. *Sex offenders: An analysis of types.* New York: Harper & Row, 1965.

Gigeroff, A., Mohr, J., & Turner, R. Sex offenders on probation. *Federal Probation,* 1968, *32,* 18.

Graham, J. *The MMPI: A practical guide.* New York: Oxford University Press, 1977.

Hackett, T. The psychotherapy of exhibitionists in a court/clinic setting. *Seminars in psychiatry,* 1971, *3,* 297.

Hendrix, E., & Meyer, R. Toward more comprehensive and durable client changes: A case report. *Psychotherapy: Theory, Research and Practice,* 1976, *13,* 263.

Kaslow, F. Panel workshop: Court-mandated treatment—obstacle or opportunity. *Contemporary Drug Problems,* 1976, *5,* 321.

Lester, D. *Unusual sexual deviations: The standard deviations.* Springfield, Ill.: Charles C Thomas, 1975.

MacDonald, J. *Indecent exposure.* Springfield, Ill.: Charles C Thomas, 1973.

Maletzky, B. "Assisted" covert sensitization in the treatment of exhibitionism. *Journal of Consulting and Clinical Psychology,* 1974, *42,* 34.

Mathis, J., & Collins, M. Mandatory group therapy for exhibitionists. *American Journal of Psychiatry,* 1970, *126,* 1162.

Meyer, R., & Smith, S. A crisis in group therapy. *American Psychologist,* 1977, *32,* 638.

Pedophilia, exhibitionism and voyeurism: Legal problems in the deviant society. *Georgia Law Review,* 1969, *4,* 149.

Rader, C. MMPI profile types of exposers, rapists and assaulters in a court services population. *Journal of Consulting and Clinical Psychology,* 1977, *45,* 61.

Robitscher, J. Statutes, law enforcement and the judicial process. In H. Resnick & H. Wolfgang (Eds.), *Sexual behavior: Social, clinical and legal aspects.* Boston: Little Brown, 1972.

Rosen, R., & Kopel, S. Penile plethysmography and biofeedback in the treatment of a transvestite-exhibitionist. *Journal of Consulting and Clinical Psychology,* 1977, *45,* 908.

Sadoff, R., Roether, H., & Peters, J. Clinical measures of enforced group psychotherapy. *American Journal of Psychotherapy,* 1971, *128,* 224.

Smukler, A., & Schiebel, D. Personality characteristics of exhibitionists. *Diseases of the Nervous System,* 1975, *36,* 600.

Sturup, G. Dare we release them? *International Journal of Offender Therapy,* 1967, *11,* 2.

Ziskin, J. *Coping with psychiatric and psychological testimony.* Beverly Hills, Ca.: Law and Psychology Press, 1975.

13

FUTURE RESEARCH ISSUES

William D. Murphy
Gene G. Abel
Judith V. Becker

In reviewing the literature relating to exhibitionism, one finds numerous clinical descriptions and case studies outlining treatment approaches, but little in terms of well controlled, clinical research. This lack of controlled investigation is regrettable, given the high frequency and the relatively high recidivism rate of the disorder. Hackett (1971), for example, in presenting data reported by Mohr, Turner, and Jerry (1964), indicates that exhibitionism is the second most common sexual offense in the United States and Canada. Furthermore, recidivism rates tend to be greater than other sexual offenses. Frisbie and Dondis (1965) report a five-year recidivism rate of 40.7 percent for treated exhibitionists, with the recidivism rate increasing to 71 percent for exhibitionists with a history of previous sexual and nonsexual offenses (Gray & Mohr, 1965).

The lack of controlled studies is also unfortunate because of the effect exhibitionism has on the life of the patient, i.e., job losses, family and marital discord, and the further consequences of incarceration. These patients are also a cost to society as a result of

---

Preparation of this chapter was supported in part by USPHS GR MH 28051 awarded to Gene G. Abel by the Center for the Control and Prevention of Rape, Rockville, Maryland.

attempts at social disposition, i.e., frequent court procedures, prison sentences, and hospitalization.

For these reasons, a more empirical approach to the problem of exhibitionism is needed to understand this deviation and provide the most efficient and effective therapeutic modalities in the least restrictive environment. The specific goals of this chapter are (1) to review research questions felt to be relevant to exhibitionists, including the process of clinical research, the areas of deficit and excess in exhibitionists, and appropriate dependent variables which can be used to evaluate these excesses and deficits; and (2) to discuss the ethical issues which arise when doing research with a population that has a high probability of being involved with the legal system.

RESEARCH DESIGN ISSUES

As an introduction to research issues, first we will provide an overview of various levels of scientific investigation for readers not familiar with applied social science research and to detail our experiences in applying various research designs in the evaluation of exhibitionists. It is hoped that the section will assist applied clinicians in taking a clear look at ways they could more systematically collect information on their subject population. It is our belief that much clinical practice could become applied clinical research with some attention to the standardization of data collection procedures. Clinical research and clinical practice have for too long been separate endeavors when, in fact, we feel that attention to the details of applied clinical research will lead to improved clinical practice.

Abel, Blanchard, and Becker (1976), in reviewing the literature relating to the psychological treatment of rapists, outline three levels of scientific investigation based on the descriptions of Bergin (1971), Bergin and Strupp (1972), and Strupp and Bergin (1969). They include uncontrolled case reports, single-case experimental designs, and controlled group-outcome studies. These three approaches to scientific inquiry, plus quasi-experimental designs, are outlined below.

Case Reports

The case report is the most common type of report about exhibitionism found in the literature, and it represents the therapist's uncontrolled impressions of the treatment process and outcome.

Since such reports are completely uncontrolled, the validity of any conclusions drawn from them must only be accepted with caution.

An example of such a case report is the description given by Bond and Hutchinson (1960) of a 25-year-old exhibitionist treated with systematic desensitization. Although the initial report indicated that the case was successful (a later case study by Quirk (1974) reports the relapse of this case), one cannot conclude that systematic desensitization was the only active ingredient of treatment since many other uncontrolled variables could have been responsible for the patient's initial, apparent improvements. Readers are referred to Campbell and Stanley's (1966) and Neale and Liebert's (1973) excellent reviews which outline the factors confounding interpretation of case studies. Nonetheless, case studies are important in initial therapeutic attempts, and they provide information that can later be investigated with appropriately controlled designs.

Single-Case Experimental Design

The single-case experimental designs derived from operant conditioning (Sidman, 1960) are the sine qua non of the behavior therapy literature. (See Barlow & Hersen, 1973; Hersen and Barlow, 1976; and Leitenberg, 1973 for further details.) The most classic of these designs is some form of the reversal design, in which the dependent variable is precisely specified. For example, penile responses to exhibitionistic and nonexhibitionistic stimuli are collected during a no-treatment base-line phase. When a stable base-line has been achieved, a specific treatment is introduced, then withdrawn, and finally reintroduced. If the specific treatment applied is the one effective variable, then changes will be observed in the dependent variable only when that treatment is in effect.

Although reversal designs are quite common in basic operant research, they are more difficult to apply with sexual deviations, where ethical considerations may preclude withdrawing treatment or where the effects of treatment may be permanent and not subject to reversal. For this reason, two other single-case designs, the multiple base-line across behaviors and the multiple base-line across subjects, may be more appropriate for use with exhibitionists.

These designs can be best described by using examples from the literature. Brownell, Hayes, and Barlow (1977), used a multiple base-line design across behaviors to treat five patients who had multiple sexual deviations. Three of the subjects were exhibitionists in addition to having a second deviation. In this design, base-line data (card sorts and/or penile responses) were collected separately for each deviation. Treatment (covert sensitization) was introduced sequentially, first to one deviation and then to the second. Results indicated that changes in the dependent variable only occurred when the specific treatment was applied to the specific deviation, thus strongly suggesting that covert sensitization was responsible for the change in arousal to each separate sexual deviation.

Although these designs are quite useful in demonstrating the effectiveness of specific treatments, we feel that they have limited application in the empirical investigation of exhibitionists. The reasons for their limited use are the small number of exhibitionists with more than one active deviation, and the problem of correlated base-lines (Kazdin & Kopel, 1975). The second problem, and the one that is more serious from a scientific standpoint, is outlined in Figure 1. The subject, who demonstrated arousal to thoughts of raping an adult female, thoughts of incest, and thoughts of exhibitionism, evidenced decreased arousal to measured deviations of both incest and rape when treatment (covert sensitization) was applied to only one behavior (incest). Since arousal to both incest and rape decreased even though only incest was treated, no statement can be made concerning the effectiveness of covert sensitization in this case. We have repeatedly encountered this difficulty in applying multiple base-line designs across deviations or behavior, as have other investigators (Levin, Murphy, Barry, & Wolfinsohn, 1977; Webster, Sanders, & Alford, 1978). The reason for such difficulty with the designs as compared to Brownell et al. is unclear at this time. Differences in subjects' expectations for change could account for these differences, or cases in which correlated base-lines occur may simply not be published. Further research is needed to investigate this issue.

For these two reasons, a second multiple base-line design, the multiple base-line across subjects, may have wider applicability with exhibitionists. The crucial element of this design is the collection of base-lines of various lengths across subjects. For example, if penile measures were being used to evaluate the effectiveness of shame aversion for four exhibitionistic subjects, the following design might be employed. Subject 1 would receive two pretreatment base-line sessions and then treatment would be introduced. Subject 2 would receive four base-line sessions prior to treatment, and Subjects 3 and 4 would receive six and eight base-line sessions respectively. If

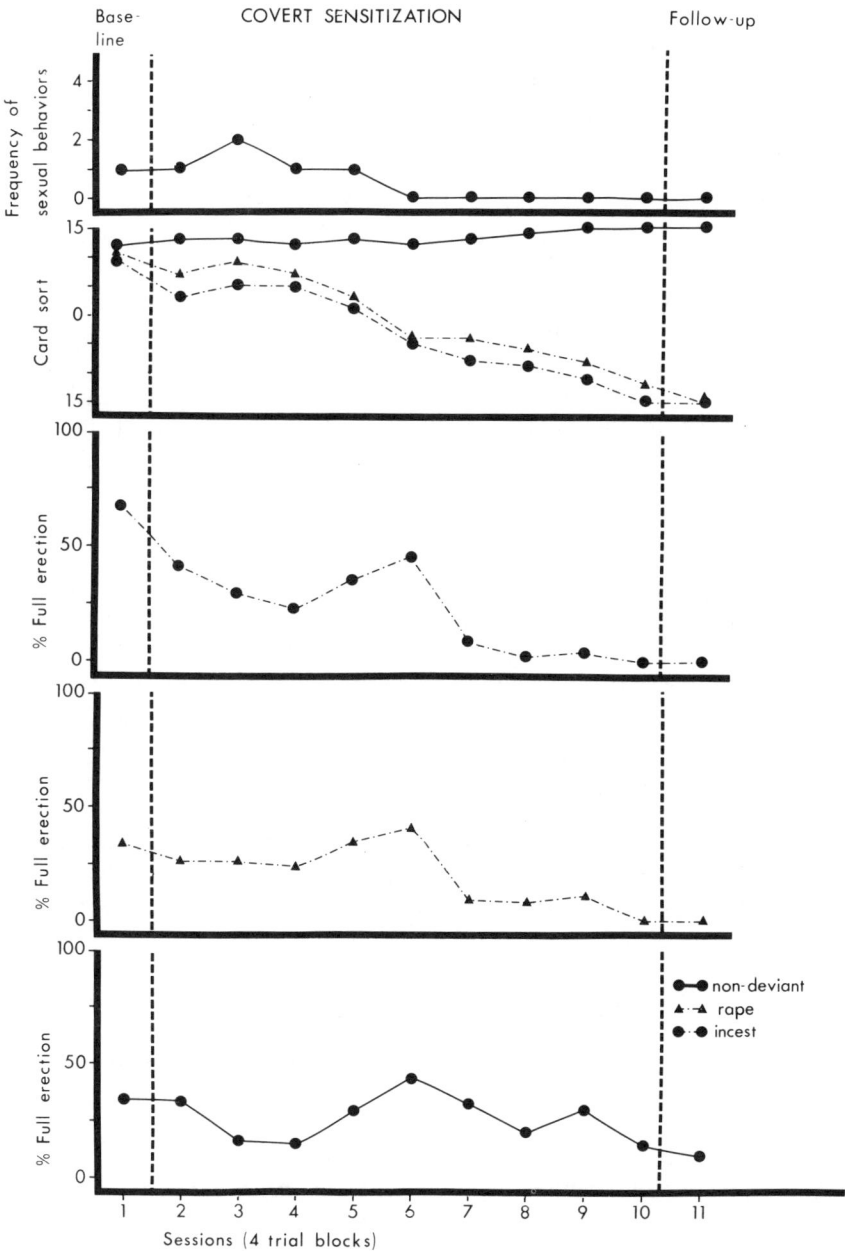

Figure 1. Erection responses and self-report measures for a subject undergoing covert sensitization treatment targeting incest stimuli.

change occurred only when treatment was introduced, then we could say with some empirical justification that the change was due to the specific treatment applied.

Normally the results from such multiple base-line designs are interpreted empirically by "eyeballing" the data. However, there are currently statistical procedures available, such as time-series analyses and nonparametric procedures (Kazdin, 1976), which allow statistical analyses of the designs. A second advantage of the multiple base-line design across subjects is that it may be more appropriate to nonbehavioral investigations than other operant designs. By attending to data collection, for example, the same design outlined in Figure 2 could be applied to the evaluation of group therapy (Mathis & Collins, 1970a, b) or individual therapy (Hacket, 1971) for exhibitionism if appropriate attention were paid to the length of the base-lines needed.

The major difficulty we have found with the multiple base-line design across subjects, especially in the case of exhibitionists, is in maintaining sexual arousal throughout the base-line if erection responses are used as the major dependent variable. This problem will be addressed in greater detail in the section of this chapter devoted to penile recording.

Controlled Group Outcomes

A third class of designs which are most appropriate for comparing subclasses of patients or various treatment modalities is the controlled group-outcome study. Only a few of these studies have appeared in the literature dealing with exhibitionists. The crux of the controlled group-outcome study is random assignment of subjects to groups (or matching subjects in groups) and direct manipulation of the independent variables by the investigators (Campbell & Stanley, 1966; Kiesler, 1971; Kerlinger, 1973; Neale & Liebert, 1973). Differences between groups provide a valid test of the investigators' hypotheses.

Although the true controlled group-outcome study may be a goal for research on exhibitionism, there are other designs that are more appropriate for the applied researcher in situations where the requirements of the controlled group-outcome studies cannot be met. For example, Campbell and Stanley (1966) have outlined various quasi-experimental designs for use when

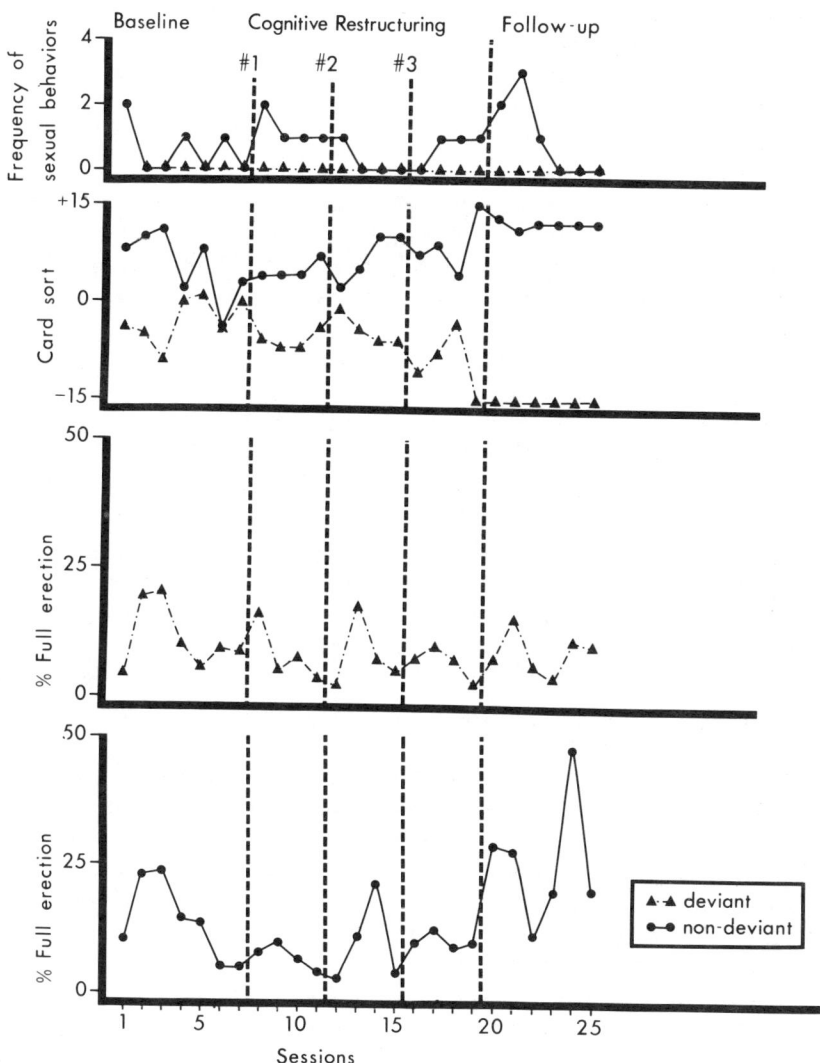

Figure 2. Erection responses and self-report measures of an exhibitionist being treated with a cognitive restructuring technique (shame aversion).

the research person can introduce something like experimental design into his scheduling of data collection procedures (e.g., the where and to whom of measurement), even though he lacks the full control over the scheduling of experimental stimuli (the when and to whom of exposure and the ability to randomize exposures) which make a true experimental design.

In a similar vein, Kiesler (1971) has outlined correlational-naturalistic designs in which ongoing, naturally occurring processes are investigated rather than direct manipulation of the independent variable. An example of this design is Evans's (1968) study comparing the differential responsiveness of exhibitionists with and without deviant masturbatory fantasies to electrical aversion treatment. The subjects for this investigation were 10 exhibitionists, 5 with deviant masturbatory fantasies and 5 without deviant fantasies. Results indicated that the subjects without deviant masturbatory fantasies deconditioned faster in an aversive conditioning paradigm than those having deviant fantasies. This study is correlational in the sense that the investigator did not directly manipulate deviant fantasies. For this reason, no statement can be made concerning causation. According to Kiesler, however, this type of design does "provide interesting leads and permits certain predictions."

These designs have limitations in validity and interpretation as outlined by the authors just cited (see also Neale & Liebert, 1973). Given the limited amount of research in the area of exhibitionism, however, clinical research could benefit from adoption of some of these less than "pure" research designs. Framing research questions realistically, given the clinical situation, may help in providing the initial data base for understanding and treating exhibitionists. In addition to the design used, an equally critical research problem is the collection of reliable and valid data without which even the most sophisticated design becomes meaningless. The following section is devoted to this issue.

ASSESSMENT AND DEPENDENT VARIABLES

Although the collection of reliable and valid dependent measures is important, one must determine relevant areas in the population to assess. In making this determination, the investigator is influenced by his or her theoretical orientation as to the cause of human behavior. The present authors are no exception to this rule and the reader quickly will become aware that many of the assessment procedures outlined here appear behavioral in nature. However, we would strongly like to point out that our orientation does not mean the procedures cannot be employed effectively by investigators of other theoretical orientations. In our work with sexual aggressiveness, we have used these assessment procedures to evaluate the effectiveness of dynamically oriented psychotherapy and have found that the measures are sensitive to and reflect changes occurring in this type of treatment.

Abel, Blanchard, and Becker (1976, 1978) and Barlow and Abel (1976) have outlined a theoretical approach to studying excesses and deficits in sexual deviates. Table 1 presents an update of these areas and the type of measurement procedures currently employed in their project. In inspecting Table 1, the reader will notice that the assessment procedures in general are derived from empirical behavioral approaches. That is, an attempt is made to observe samples of the actual behavior that the therapy procedures are attempting to change. The connection between assessment and treatment is a major tenant of behavioral assessment.

If the left side of the table is inspected, it is clear that the areas outlined are not necessarily idiosyncratic to a behavioral or learning

Table 1. Problem Areas of Exhibitionism and Suggested Measurement Procedures

	EXCESSES AND DEFICITS	MEASUREMENT PROCEDURE
AROUSAL PROBLEMS	Excessive arousal to deviant stimuli Deficient arousal to non-deviant stimuli	Penile recordings and self-report
SOCIAL SKILLS PROBLEMS	Heterosocial skills Assertiveness skills Empathy skills Gender motor behavior	Video-tape ratings, therapist ratings, and self-report
SEXUAL PERFORMANCE PROBLEMS	Sexual dysfunctions Sexual knowledge	Self-report inventories and sex education test

conceptualization of exhibitionism or sexual deviation. In fact, these areas have been derived from reviews of the literature (Abel et al., 1976, 1978), suggesting that many are dealt with in other programs treating sexual deviation. For example, Abel, et al. (1976), in reviewing the literature on the psychological treatment of rapists, found that excessive arousal to deviant stimuli, deficient arousal to nondeviant stimuli, and heterosocial/heterosexual skills training were consistently components of treatment programs ranging in orientation from analytic to behavioral. In reviewing the literature on exhibitionism, one also is struck by the numerous clinical descriptions which suggest that exhibitionists are inadequate in heterosocial/ heterosexual relationships, have difficulty expressing anger, or have specific sexual dysfunctions (Hackett, 1971; Hadden, 1973; Mathis & Collins, 1970a; Vera, 1976). These are specifically the behaviors measured when we measure assertiveness, heterosocial skills, and sexual dysfunction. For this reason, the empirical procedures enumerated here are not limited to assessment of behavioral treatments, but are quite applicable to treatment approaches of various theoretical orientations.

The model of deviant sexual behavior presented in Table 1 is derived from past research and clinical experience in treating a large number of sexual deviates having a wide variety of deviations (Abel, 1976; Abel & Blanchard, 1976; Abel, Blanchard, & Becker, 1976, 1978). The details of the assessment procedures are outlined in another section of this chapter (see pp. 353–376). For readers unfamiliar with the model, the components in relationship to exhibitionists follow next.

The first component of the model is excessive arousal to deviant stimuli. By definition, exhibitionists display excessive sexual arousal to appropriate stimuli (e.g., children) or inappropriate interactions with the sexual object (i.e., the act of exhibiting; Bancroft, 1974). Since one component of exhibitionist behavior is excessive arousal, a component of treatment would be aimed at the suppression or elimination of this arousal.

The second component, deficient arousal to nondeviant sexual stimuli, may or may not be associated with deviant sexual stimuli. Some exhibitionists display adequate heterosexual relationships with a wife or partner. However, for exhibitionists who are deficient in heterosexual arousal, whether secondary to anxiety or resulting from inadequate experience, specific treatment for this problem is needed.

Although decreasing inappropriate arousal and increasing appropriate arousal are necessary, they are insufficient if the patient does not have the social skills for meeting, interacting with, and dating appropriate partners. These specific social behaviors are outlined in Table 1 as heterosocial, assertive, and empathy skills. If a subject is deficient in one or more of these areas, then a third specific treatment component must be directed at the remediation of social skills problems.

The fourth skills area is gender motor problems, i.e., the adoption of opposite-sex role behaviors. We have not found this to be a major problem with exhibitionists; it is more likely to be found in transvestites or transsexuals.

The final area to be considered in a comprehensive treatment program is a possible deficit in sexual performance with appropriate partners. Treatments include sex education and sexual dysfunction therapies (Annon, 1974, 1975).

The Process of Data Collection

The previous section outlined specific treatment areas and introduced measurement procedures to be used as dependent variables. Before elaborating on the specific measurement procedures, however, we will deal with some general procedures which are important in doing applied research and outline how the data collection procedure operates.

Our first major recommendation for doing applied clinical research with exhibitionists is that the investigator develop a standardized initial assessment procedure and then devise specific assessments as dictated by each case. We employ the assessment procedures listed in Table 1 in addition to paper-and-pencil measures of personality, intelligence, and sexual function. For example, the MMPI, Eysenck Personality Inventory, Otis Quick Scoring Intelligence Test, Freund Gender Identity Scales (Freund, Nagler, Langevin, Zajac, & Steiner, 1974), Sexual Orientation Method (Feldman, Mellor, & Pinchof, 1966), Bem Androgny Scale (Bem, 1974), and McHugh's Sex Knowledge Inventory (McHugh, 1968) are routinely collected.

This standardized initial assessment allows the investigator to collect a data pool which is consistent across subjects, regardless of the subject's specific deviation or presenting complaint. It allows us to have similar data on various types of sexual deviates and on subjects who have been successful and unsuccessful in treatment. Applied clinical research, unlike laboratory research, is not a one-shot endeavor. In laboratory or academic research, one usually develops a hypothesis and then designs an appropriate research strategy to test the hypothesis. In clinical research, however, many hypotheses only occur in the process of treating patients. By having available a standardized set of data, the clinical researcher is able to do retrospective studies as he develops hypotheses about the subject population. These retrospective investigations can serve as pilot studies to determine whether large-scale prospective studies are feasible.

Many clinicians have probably had the experience, after working with a large number of patients over a number of years, of gaining insight into some of the variables affecting the problem. In reviewing their notes however, they realize that the data collected varies across subjects and they are therefore unable to provide any support for their observations. By standardizing the initial assessment procedure, one can avoid this loss of data. Much of the literature on exhibitionism seems to suffer from this problem and therefore is reduced to clinical descriptions and therapists' perceptions of what the crucial variables are without any type of adequate data.

A second procedure recommended to the applied researcher is multivariate rather than univariate data collection (Bergin, 1971; Kiesler, 1971; and Campbell & Stanley, 1966). This means that (1) we assess across the areas outlined in Table 1; and (2) we attempt, where possible, to provide more than one assessment procedure per area. Multiple assessment across areas arises from the belief supported by personality research (Mischel, 1968) that generalized trait approaches to personality are not predictive of human behavior and are not an adequate means of assessing patient progress. Our experience clearly indicates that exhibitionists differ in their areas of excesses and deficits. For example, some patients may be deficit in all the areas outlined in Table 1 and others may show deficits in only one or two of the areas. Treatment programs that focus on only one area (i.e., aversion therapy for excessive arousal) are in many instances doomed to failure, and those that attempt to provide treatment in all areas are very inefficient in terms of cost effectiveness.

Multiple assessments within areas arise from a lack of knowledge regarding the most reliable and valid means of clinical assessment. In addition, by using multiple assessments one can begin to develop validity data by making comparisons of the various assessment procedures. For example, as will be detailed later, we routinely collect behavioral ratings of heterosocial skills along with the therapists' rating of them. By doing this, we are able to determine whether our specific behavioral ratings reflect an overall perception of heterosocial skills by the therapists. This type of social validity research has been outlined in detail by Wolf (1978).

The third recommendation for those involved in clinical research is to collect frequent repeated observations throughout treatment (Kiesler, 1971). In our own project, this results in two types of repeated assessment procedures. The first, which is similar to Cronbach's (1970) idea of narrow band–high fidelity assessment, is to gather frequent measures on the specific variable expected to change during treatment. For example, an exhibitionist being given treatment to reduce deviant arousal would be measured frequently during treatment with penile responses to deviant and nondeviant stimuli. Thus there is a specific tracking of progress throughout treatment. Second, the initial assessment is repeated after each component of the treatment program. For example, when the patient completed cognitive restructuring therapy (shame aversion), he would be reassessed with the penile recordings and in addition would receive a reassessment of the social skills areas outlined in Table 1. If he was found to be deficit in a social skills area, a specific treatment would be provided and frequent measures of that area would be made throughout treatment. Following the second treatment component, he would receive the initial assessment battery again and decisions would be made as to whether further treatment was necessary. This two-pronged approach to repeated measurement was adopted mainly as an efficiency measure. Although in a perfect world we would like to have repeated measures on all the variables throughout treatment, this is an impossibility, given the limitations on both professional and patient time. Therefore we feel that our approach is an adequate compromise between the ideal world of research and the realities of a clinical situation.

To summarize, the data collection procedure that is employed by our project and which seems applicable to many clinical and research settings, regardless of theoretical orientation and specific dependent variables adopted, is to:

1. Provide an initial standardized assessment of all patients.
2. Make the assessment multivariate rather than univariate to maximize the understanding of exhibitionism and the use of limited-subject pools.

3. Make repeated observations throughout treatment and follow-up.

The following case represents an example of our data collection procedure.

Case 1

The patient was a 35-year-old male who voluntarily presented himself for evaluation and treatment of exhibitionism and pedophilia. He had a rather long history of both deviations, being involved in exhibitionist behavior for 21 years and pedophilia for the last 8 years. According to his own report, he had been involved with at least 600 children and had approached another 300, although no sexual contact had occurred. Upon entering the project, the patient received a standardized initial assessment which consisted of penile recordings to various types of deviant stimuli, including exhibitionism to young children and rape, in addition to recordings of his arousal to nondeviant stimuli (mutually consenting intercourse with an adult woman). He also received assessment of his heterosocial, assertiveness, and empathy skills. These assessments were conducted by video taping the patient role-playing various situations with a confederate from the project and then having these video tapes rated for the skills just described. In addition, he received the paper-and-pencil tests which were a part of the program, including a sexual dysfunction packet and a sex education test. The patient also received two separate clinical interviews. The results of this initial assessment indicated that the patient did show deviant arousal to young children and to stimuli depicting exhibitionism. He was not deficient in either heterosexual arousal or any of the social skills outlined in Table 1. His personality assessment suggested that he was above average in intelligence and had no severe psychopathology such as psychosis or severe depression; although there was a strong tendency for the patient to rationalize and intellectualize his problem.

After this initial assessment, base-line measurements were collected to determine the patient's level of arousal both to young females and exhibitionistic stimuli prior to treatment. There were also daily collections of the patient's self-report variables. These included a frequency count of the patient's deviant behavior and nondeviant fantasies. It should be noted that, in counting frequency, masturbation was defined as deviant or nondeviant depending on the fantasies used. The second type of ongoing self-report measure was a card-sort measure to deviant and nondeviant descriptions of sexual behavior. The patient rated each of the descriptions on a −3 (aversive) to a +3 (highly arousing) scale.

Following these four base-line probes, the first treatment introduced was covert sensitization directed at young females. Erection measures and self-report data were collected after each treatment session for both exhibitionistic and pedophilic stimuli. In addition, after every 12 treatment sessions of covert sensitization, a clinical interview was held with one of the treatment staff not involved directly in the patient's treatment. It has been found that these periodic clinical interviews, although subjective, provide a good deal of information about the process of therapy and the patient's perception of the effective elements in treatment. Following covert sensitization treatment targeted at young females, reassessment was begun as outlined previously. Again, probes were made on the patient's sexual arousal to various sexual stimuli and a reassessment was done of his social skills. The results of this second assessment indicated that the patient showed decreased arousal to young females and somewhat decreased arousal to exhibitionistic stimuli. In addition, his social skills remained above average and it appeared that he needed no treatment in this area. Although the patient's arousal to exhibitionism was not high, it was felt that it might be best to provide some specific treatment in this area since he was from out of state and was leaving the project. For that reason, two cognitive restructuring (shame aversion) sessions were provided specifically for exhibitionism.

THE CLINICAL INTERVIEW AS A SOURCE OF DATA

As "behavior therapists" who are known to champion the value of penile measures of sexual arousal and behavioral role-playing assessment of social skills, we are tempted to begin this section by expounding on the virtues of the plethysmograph and video tape as sources of data. However, in an attempt to provide a framework for clinical research based in reality, we will begin our discussion where most clinical researchers (as well as most clinicians) begin—that is, with the clinical interview.

In the area of exhibitionism, the interview and the therapist's impression of treatment dynamics have been the major data for published reports (Evans, 1970; Hackett, 1971; Karpman, 1948; Zechnich, 1971). Even in the area of behavioral assessment, more attention is paid to the clinical interview (Linehan, 1977; Morganstern, 1976). Linehan has pointed out the value of the clinical interview in terms of efficiency and flexibility in initial data collection, and in terms of establishing an interpersonal relationship. For the clinical researcher, however, the initial interview also should be the point at which to begin structured data collection. As an example, Table 2 represents the structured interview component of our treatment program for sexual deviates. Most of the variables in this table are self-explanatory and consist of items which both the literature and clinical experience suggest are relevant to treatment outcomes (Bancroft, 1974; Evans, 1970) and to the severity of the problem (i.e., ability to control). Item 5 may be somewhat unclear: it is rated positive if the patient displays an hysterical or antisocial personality, or is psychotic or retarded. Items 11 and 14 are specified for rapists (R) or pedophiles (P), but can be adapted for exhibitionists. This structured component of the clinical interview (other information is also collected) serves as one source of data for our project. As outlined in the previous section, the structured interview is repeated at various points throughout treatment and during follow-up.

The advantage of such a procedure is that a standard set of data is collected for all subjects prior to treatment, during treatment, and throughout the follow-up period. The problem of realizing after one-year follow-up that there are certain variables the interviewer forgot to collect at some point during contact with the research subject is avoided. A second advantage of the structured interview is that the variables collected allow one to define the population with which one is working. If the same variables were collected by various researchers, comparison across studies would be improved.

It should be pointed out that the information included in Table 2 at the present time seems relevant to clinical outcome in sexual deviation as well as to defining the severity of the problem. Further research is needed across settings and with larger populations to determine both the validity of these specific variables with exhibitionists and other variables which may be relevant to clinical outcome. For example, the number of arrests for sexual and nonsexual crimes may be an important predictor of recidivism (Gray & Mohr, 1965), as might marital adjustment (Rooth, 1974).

Table 2. Items From a Structured Clinical Interview

ITEMS:

1. Current percent of deviant masturbatory fantasies
2. Duration of deviant behavior (number of months)
3. Current frequency of deviant behavior per week
4. History of no significant heterosexual interest
5. Moderate or severe evidence of weak ego or emotional instability
6. Gender motor behavior: Extremely feminine/Extremely masculine   −3   −2   −1   0   +1   +2   +3
7. Current ability to control deviant behavior: zero percent (absolute control)–100 percent (no control)
8. First real sexual experience in detail
9. Diagnosis (If mixed deviances, what are the percentages?)
10. Kinsey rating (circle one):
    Exclusively heterosexual / Bisexual / Exclusively homosexual
       0   1   2   3   4   5   6
11. Aggression rating:
    rape (R)   0 (nonrapist)   1 (no physical)   2 (physical)   3 (excessive physical)
    pedophilia (P)   0 (no coercion)   1 (no physical)   2 (physical)   3 (excessive physical)
12. Effects of alcohol/drugs on sexual arousal
13. Skills rating: Poor   Average   Excellent
    social skills   1   2   3   4   5
    assertiveness skills   1   2   3   4   5
    empathy skills   1   2   3   4   5
14. Extent of rape and pedophilia:
    R   Attempted   Completed   Number of victims
    P

In addition to the need for research on the validity of self-report variables, the question of the reliability of the subject's self-report cannot be avoided. Clinicians working with exhibitionists realize that the exhibitionist's tendency to deny the severity of his problem is a more than rare occurrence. (See Rosen & Kopel, 1977 for an excellent clinical example.) There are no secret answers to this problem, but a number of procedures may help to increase the reliability of information collected from the subjects.

The first procedure is to conduct two independent clinical interviews separated by four to seven days. This approach is especially useful for subjects with a long history of exhibitionism, since part of their unreliability is due to poor memory rather than deliberate faking. After the first interview, the subject usually spends time thinking about the content of the interview and on many occasions remembers further details by the time of the second interview. In addition, the delay between interviews gives the subject increased contact with project staff as he progresses through the remainder of the assessment. With this increased contact, the beginning of a therapeutic and research relationship is usually established. By the second interview, the patient has begun to trust members of the project and on many occasions will divulge information withheld during the initial interview. A second approach is to collect collateral information wherever possible. This includes clinical interviews with significant others initially and throughout treatment and follow-up, collection of police reports, past hospital reports, and reports from other therapists with whom the subject may have been involved. The final and probably most important approach is to rely on objective data in addition to self-report measures. Although certain important variables are only available through the patient's self-report, (i.e., frequency of deviant masturbatory fantasies), total reliance on these types of measure and the patient's own report of his ability to control his deviant behavior can lead to inaccurate evaluation of treatment outcome. The following case study is an example of this problem:

Case 2

The subject was a 22-year-old single male. He had a 2-year history of exhibitionism and was exposing himself approximately every other day. He had been arrested three times and was expelled from the university he was attending following his third arrest.

Assessment included seven base-line sessions during which the subject's penile response was measured to stimulus material including slides, fantasies, and video tapes of both deviant and nondeviant stimuli. The subject also completed a card sort and frequency count. Following assessment, he received three cognitive restructuring (shame aversion) sessions. During these sessions the patient exposed himself to a female target while a four-member audience observed. The patient was asked to verbalize his fantasies and thoughts while exposing himself and to ask the target and the audience for feedback on his behavior. The patient was then seen for eight follow-up sessions which covered a period of four months. It was at this point that he started breaking appointments. Following the cognitive restructuring, the patient reported that he had been helped by these sessions and had neither deviant arousal nor exhibitionistic behavior. His card sort was rated as negative for all of the deviant items and positive for the nondeviant items. He indicated that during the treatment sessions he had learned things about himself. He stated that the most effective component was when one of the black members of the audience gave him feedback about how demeaning his behavior was to the black race.

Throughout the treatment, it had been the impression of the treatment staff that the individual was very well defended and it was questionable whether or not the cognitive restructuring actually had any effect on him.

As mentioned previously, the subject discontinued his contact with us. He received several letters as well as phone calls encouraging him to return for follow-up. Six weeks after his last follow-up session, we received a call from the subject. He had been arrested for exhibitionism and was requesting an appointment. When he was seen for follow-up, the patient reported that he had indeed exposed himself while he was in therapy, apparently right after the second treatment. He reported that his urges had been strong and he was not able to control them. When asked why he did not relate this information to the treatment staff, he reported that he "didn't know how to tell them," and he also felt he would have let them down. He expressed concern that further treatment would have been implemented and he was not interested in continuing treatment.

The patient reported that he had not played the audio tape of the sessions which had been given to him to use when he had an urge to exhibit. He felt that the sessions had been helpful to him. In essence, he reported that the professional staff had done all they could to help him, but he had not been really interested in helping himself. He described the cognitive restructuring sessions "wearing out," his urges increasing in frequency, and going on a "rampage of exhibitionism." He described himself as being very defensive in the treatment sessions and being "too cool" to integrate any of the feedback that had been given to him.

The patient felt that it would take something much more severe like imprisonment to stop him from exposing himself. He was, in fact, arrested for exposing himself and served 24 hours in jail, which he found very aversive. He related that the experience was so aversive to him that he would never expose himself again.

Because of the project's plans to relocate, this subject was referred to a mental health center in his home town for further treatment. The subject was to receive therapy as a condition of his probation. He agreed to continue in therapy but again assured the staff that he would never expose himself again as he had "learned his lesson."

The following week, we received a phone call from the therapist who had been assigned to treat the patient in his home town. She reported that in the course of history taking, the patient had exposed himself to her.

Conclusion. This case demonstrates the nonreliability of self-report data. In his erection measures (Figure 2), he had experienced a return to prebase-line levels of deviant arousal following his second shame session. At two other points during follow-up, his deviant arousal had returned to base-line levels. The subject denied penile arousal as well as any deviant urges or behaviors. Had we relied solely on his erection measures and discounted his verbal report, we would have had a more accurate description of his behavior.

PENILE RECORDING

The first two areas outlined in Table 1 refer to excessive arousal to deviant stimuli and deficits in arousal to nondeviant stimuli. As pointed out, exhibitionists by definition show excessive deviant arousal and, in some but not all cases, deficits in nondeviant sexual arousal. Assuming that excesses and deficits in sexual arousal are areas of concern with exhibitionism, the next step is determining appropriate dependent variables to assess these areas. Although self-monitoring of the behavior (for example, frequency counts of deviant and nondeviant behaviors) or attitudinal measures (card sorts) have their place in the measurement, total reliance on these subjective reports leads to the difficulties observed in the case history reported earlier. To date, the most objective measure of sexual arousal is direct recording of penile tumescence (Zuckerman, 1971). The specifics of this technology and its application to sexual deviations have been reviewed extensively by Abel and his colleagues (Abel, 1976; Abel & Blanchard, 1976; Barlow & Abel, 1976).

For those unfamiliar with penile recording, we will briefly outline the procedure here. In general, most investigators employ circumferential measure of penile responses using either a mercury-in-rubber strain gauge (Bancroft, Jones, & Pullman, 1966) or a metal band strain gauge (Barlow, Becker, Leitenberg, & Agras, 1970). Both devices are small and fairly comfortable for the subject to wear. Both are fairly sensitive to penile arousal and have similar response characteristics (Laws, 1977). Currently both types of gauges are commercially available. A more sensitive device is the volumetric transducer (Freund, 1957, 1961, 1963; McConagy, 1974) which encloses most of the penis. These devices are more cumbersome and probably less applicable to clinical research (Abel & Blanchard, 1976).

Once the subject has the penile gauge on, he is exposed to relatively brief (usually two minutes) sexual stimuli through slides, fantasy, audio tapes, or video tapes. Responses to these sexual stimuli are scored for maximum deflection which is converted to percent of full erection to allow comparison across subjects. Recently another component of the response, i.e., area under the curve which takes into account both time and amplitude, has been investigated (Abel, Blanchard, Becker, et al., in press; Quinsey & Harris, 1976). However, both reports suggest that maximum amplitude is the most appropriate measure. Little data is currently available on other components of the penile response, such as time to maximum erection (recruitment) or time to detumescence (recovery). Nor is there information on alternative measures of genital arousal such as penile pulse amplitude, a psychophysiologic measure related to dilation and constriction of blood vessels. Heiman (1977), for example, found this measure to be more sensitive to sexual arousal than circumferential measures in normal males. Although erection responses are the most sensitive measure of sexual arousal to date, data is still needed on the basic parameters of this response.

The remainder of this section deals with using penile responses as a dependent measure with exhibitionists and discusses some basic validity questions.

Stimulus Material

The major types of stimulus used for assessing sexual deviates, as mentioned, are video tapes, audio tapes, slides, and subject-generated fantasy. Data comparing these stimuli have been reviewed by Abel and Blanchard (1976). The data indicate that video stimuli generate

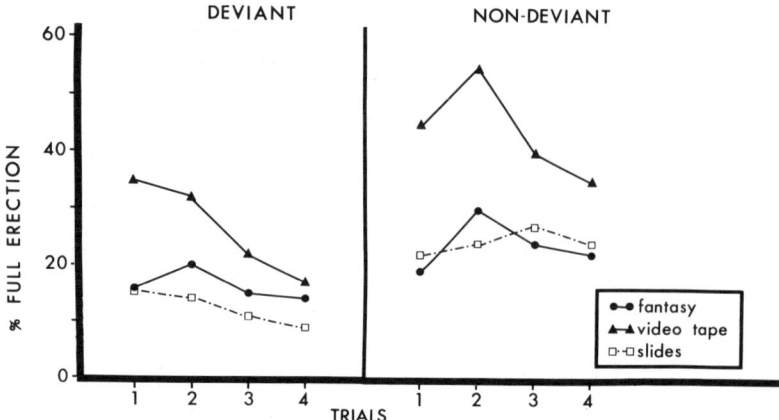

Figure 3. Mean base-line erection responses of 16 exhibitionists to deviant and nondeviant stimuli across three stimulus modalities.

the greatest erection response across diagnostic categories, including exhibitionism (Kolarsky & Madlafousek, 1972).

In our own project, exhibitionists' responses to deviant and nondeviant stimuli are assessed using video tapes, slides, and free fantasy. Figure 3 presents the data for 16 exhibitionists who received four base-line measures prior to treatment. Analysis of variance performed separately for deviant and nondeviant stimuli indicates a significant stimulus effect for deviant ($F = 19.77$, $df = 2, 165$, $p < .001$) and nondeviant ($F = 43.70$, $df = 2, 165$, $p < .001$) behaviors, with significant trial effects for both categories ($F = 5.15$ deviant, and 4.99 nondeviant, $df = 3, 165$, $p < .01$). Interactions were nonsignificant. The stimulus effect is consistent with past research and suggests that video stimuli produce the largest erection responses. As evidenced in Figure 3, there is a decrease in deviant sexual arousal across base-line sessions for deviant stimuli. This is fairly consistent across the three stimulus categories and is supported by a significant linear trend ($F = 10.04$, $df = 1, 165$, $p < .01$). For nondeviant stimuli, the linear trend is nonsignificant and the quadratic trend is significant ($F = 13.06$, $df = 1, 165$, $p < .01$). This suggests, for nondeviant stimuli, some initial suppression during the first base-line session, possibly due to novelty or apprehension, followed by dishabituation during the second base-line session and then a gradual return to initial levels.

This decrease in base-line sexual arousal for deviant stimuli makes it extremely difficult to evaluate treatment effects appropriately. Changes during treatment cannot be attributed to the specific intervention employed when the dependent variable is already decreasing prior to the introduction of treatment. Attempts to extend the number of base-line periods have likewise been fruitless in that continued decreases usually have been observed. The reasons for this difficulty in maintaining deviant arousal with exhibitionists is not clear. One obvious explanation would be that the exhibitionist is suppressing his erection to deviant stimuli.

In regard to differences between subjects who maintained arousal ($n = 5$) and those not maintaining arousal ($n = 11$) on the items outlined in Table 2, the subjects maintaining arousal rated their control to be less ($x = 76$ percent, 0 = perfect control, 100 = no control) than those not maintaining arousal ($x = 33$ percent) and had a longer history of exhibitionism (17.4 years versus 11 years). Other variables showed little difference. These differences in rated control lend some indirect support to the idea of voluntary suppression. That is, the subjects who could exert voluntary control did so in the laboratory. However, because of the small sample size for subjects maintaining arousal, no meaningful statistical comparison can be made.

Although there is indirect evidence for the idea of voluntary suppression, we are not at this point in time completely satisfied with that explanation. The major reason is that we do not find this difficulty to the same extent in other diagnostic categories which have been investigated. It is uncertain why exhibitionists would be the only group in which widespread difficulties in maintaining arousal are observed.

What is clear is that additional research is needed to develop appropriate stimulus materials for exhibitionists. The value of audio tapes with exhibitionists should be investigated (Abel, Blanchard, Barlow, et al., 1975; Abel, Levis, & Clancey, 1970) as well as studies using variations on instructional sets (i.e., becoming aroused versus suppressing erection) as reported by Abel, Barlow, Blanchard, et al. (1975) with homosexuals. This type of initial comparison between arousal and suppression instructions should provide the experimenter with some basic information regarding the subject's ability to suppress and control his erection response independent of self-reports.

In addition, formal comparisons between exhibitionists and other sexual deviations are needed. Rooth and Marks (1974) have suggested that erection measures may be inappropriate with exhibitionists since many expose with a flaccid penis and do not use deviant masturbatory fantasies. In relation to Rooth and Marks' (1974) observations, we do have the percentage of deviant fantasies used during masturbation for all of our subjects. In comparing those subjects who maintained arousal with those who did not, we found no difference between groups (x = 46 percent in each group). However, we need a larger sample size to determine if the data are reliable. Data also are needed regarding the effect that erectile state during actual exhibitionistic acts has on laboratory measures of erections. It should also be clear that in investigating stimulus modalities, more than one or two measurement sessions are necessary to determine the value of each modality for use with exhibitionists.

Validity of Penile Measures

Validity is a rather complex question (Anatasi, 1968) and only a few of the issues where there is a need for immediate research will be discussed. The first of these issues is whether arousal to cues defined as exhibitionist in actuality reflect exhibitionistic arousal or more general heterosexual arousal. The question is whether nonexhibitionist sex offenders and normal individuals would respond any differently than exhibitionists to the same stimuli. In the area of homosexuality (Mavissakalian, Blanchard, Abel, & Barlow, 1975), rape (Abel, Barlow, Blanchard, & Guild, 1977; Abel, Blanchard, Becker, & Djenderedjian, 1978), and pedophilia (Quinsey, Steinman, Bergersen, & Holmes, 1975), this type of contrasted group validity is becoming available and suggests that penile measurement reliably separates deviates from nondeviates. However, in the area of exhibitionism, these types of group comparison have not been made. To determine the validity of exhibitionistic stimuli, we must determine whether it is specific to exhibitionists.

A second aspect of the validity problem in the use of penile circumference measures with sexual deviates is the lack of data available on the ability to fake erection response. Problems in this area were eluded to in the previous section which discussed the difficulty in maintaining arousal with exhibitionists. This data is extremely important if penile measures are to be used in the area of exhibitionism. Early data (Freund, 1961, 1963), indicated that subjects did attempt to alter their erection responses. Later data demonstrated that normal subjects (Laws & Rubin, 1969) and homosexuals (Abel, Barlow, Blanchard, & Mavissakalian, 1975) could suppress erection responses on instruction. However, even with this early data, there was little direct research on the ability to fake erection responses until recently (Laws & Holmen, 1978; Quinsey & Bergersen, 1976; Quinsey & Carrigan, 1978).

Quinsey and his colleagues have investigated the ability of normal subjects to fake sexual arousal to stimuli depicting young children. Monetary incentives ($5.00) were provided to subjects who could appropriately fake response patterns. In the first study (Quinsey & Bergersen, 1976) two of five normal subjects altered their erection responses to slides so that they appeared to be pedophiliac. In the second study, which was basically the same, some of the slides were accompanied by auditory fantasy material. The rationale was that subjects might have more difficulty faking with the addition of auditory material. In this investigation, seven of nine normals were able to fake their sexual arousal patterns and show maximum arousal to pedophiliac cues. The addition of the auditory material did not significantly affect the subjects' ability to fake their responses. Differences between the two studies were attributed by the authors to sampling differences.

The problem in this study of course, was that normal populations were used and attempts were made to fake increased sexual arousal, which may be more difficult to fake than suppression of arousal (Laws & Rubin, 1969). Quinsey & Carrigan (1978) point out that their pedophiliac subjects seem to have more difficulty controlling their responses than normal subjects. However, even with these limitations, it should be clear that attention must be paid to the intentional alteration of erection responses.

A final recent study of ability to falsify response (Laws & Holmen, 1978), is an excellent example of how a case report can generate extremely useful information. This report presents a single subject (a pedophile) who appeared to be extremely adept at faking. The subject was able to alter his sexual arousal through both cognitive and physical means. The authors point out that physical manipulations of the transducer are sometimes easy to detect if the investigator is familiar with his subject's typical response pattern. However, cognitive manipulations are impossible to detect. For example, the subject in this experiment could verbalize about an adult female while observing the slide of an adult female, but at the same time be fantasizing a child. Both the erection produced by the subject and his audio-taped verbal fantasies were impossible to detect as false. Given these difficulties Laws and Holmen suggest:

> We *should* continue to use penile erections as the main primary dependent measure because, despite its amendability to influence, it remains the single best index of sexual arousal. What we should *not* do is continue to treat it reverentially as a truly objective measure.

In the area of exhibitionism, where penile measurement has received little attention, the problem of faking response has received no attention. If investigators adopt the penile response as a dependent variable in this area, attention should be paid from the start to the problem of response alteration. In addition, we need to investigate the subject's motivation to falsify response. Although legal problems may be significant in and of themselves, our own hopes of treatment effectiveness may be communicated to the subject and contribute to the problem (Rosen & Kopel, 1977; Laws & Holmen, 1978). Until more data is available on the problem of faking, we should realize, as pointed out by Abel and Blanchard (1976), that the value of erection responses is in their presence and not in their absence. That is, we can say little about a subject's sexual arousal pattern when no response occurs.

Social Skills

In a previous section of this chapter, areas of possible deficit in exhibitionists were outlined, including social skills. These are behaviors related to effective interpersonal relationships that many writers of various theoretical orientations (Hackett, 1971; Hadden, 1973; Mathis, 1975; Rickels, 1968; Rooth, 1971) have outlined as being problems for sexual deviates, including exhibitionists. *Heterosocial skills* refers to the ability of the individual to initiate and follow through contacts with opposite-sex partners. *Assertiveness skills* (Eisler, Miller, & Hersen, 1973) are the individual's ability to express both positive and negative feelings and to request changes in the behavior of others. Assertiveness was added to our overall assessment package as we noticed more and more deviates whose exhibitionism seemed to follow their inability to express their anger to significant others. Hackett (1971) indicates that significant others include family members, but in addition interactions with peers and employers also should be considered. *Empathy skills,* which are needed to identify and relate to the problems of others, were added when we observed that many sexual deviates were rather cold in their interpersonal relationships and did not attend to the effects their behavior had on others.

The assertiveness assessment procedure currently employed is based on the Behavioral Assertiveness Test developed by Eisler, Miller, and Hersen (1973) and revised by Eisler, Hersen, Miller, and Blanchard (1975). This role-played assessment procedure has been used to investigate deficits and treatment progress in schizophrenics (Bellack, Hersen, and Turner, 1978; Hersen & Bellack, 1976) and explosive personalities (Frederiksen, Jenkins, Foy, & Eisler, 1976). Basic psychometric data related to assertiveness are also beginning to appear in the literature (Bellack, Hersen, & Turner, 1978; Pachman, Foy, Massey, & Eisler, 1978). The literature in the area of assertiveness training has been reviewed recently by Rich and Schroeder (1976).

The Behavioral Assertiveness Test is designed for rating videotaped, role-played situations. The ratings include both verbal and nonverbal components (see Eisler, Miller, & Hersen, 1973 for details). Our adaptation of the procedure is to have the subject role-play four scenes. These include the expression of tender feelings, anger, depression, and a request for new behaviors. The psychometric properties of the scale are in the process of being analyzed but the data is presently incomplete. We have employed the scale to evaluate assertiveness training in sexual deviates and have found that the scale reliably changes as the patient improves clinically in assertiveness. We have also found in certain individuals that assertiveness is independent of heterosocial and empathy skills (Becker, Abel, Blanchard, Murphy & Coleman, 1978) which tends to indicate the specificity of each of these social skills.

The components of empathy skills assessment, developed from Truax and Charkhuff (1967), is presented in Table 3. In this assessment procedure, subjects are asked to role-play four 2½-minute scenes in which a confederate presents a problem (i.e., unmarried and pregnant). The video-tape is then rated in 30-second blocks for the occurrence or nonoccurrence of empathetic behavior (see Table 3). If

Table 3. Components of the Empathy Skills Checklist

Verbalizes partner's feelings.
Accurately verbalizes partner's feelings.
Explores partner's feelings further.
Subject's affect consistent with empathy.
Attaches partner's feelings to situation.
Accurately attaches partner's feelings to situation.

the subject is found to be deficient in empathy skills, a standard social-skills training program of modeling, behavioral rehearsal, video-tape feedback, and social reinforcement is employed. The empathy skills assessment procedure is the latest addition to the assessment package and little data is currently available. Again, in single-case application (Becker et al., 1978) the scale reflected change during empathy skills training and was independent of assertiveness or heterosocial skills.

The heterosocial behavioral checklist (Barlow, Abel, Blanchard, Bristow, & Young, 1977) is currently employed to evaluate heterosocial skills. (See Table 4.) To complete a heterosocial rating, each subject is video taped in three 2½-minute scenes. The scenes increase in intimacy from an initial meeting to an interaction in which the subject attempts to convey very close feelings to a female with whom he is well acquainted. These behaviors are then rated on the scale outlined in Table 4 in 30-second blocks. In addition to the objective ratings, the subject is rated by the therapist during the initial interview on a 1 (very poor skills) to 5 (very good skills) scale of heterosocial skills. The clinical rating is done blind to the objective ratings. We currently have initial assessment data on 67 deviates. The data specifically includes 21 pedophiles, 9 rapists, 9 exhibitionists, and 28 "others" including mainly voyeurs, homosexuals, transvestites, and transsexuals.

Two questions initially looked at were whether there were any differences between categories of deviates and between the three scenes of increasing intimacy. In terms of the three scenes, there was very little difference. For voice, form of conversation, and affect, the appropriate mean percent was slightly lower on scene 3 than scene 1. However, a t-test performed between scene 1 and scene 3 was not significant. The maximum mean difference between scenes for any

Table 4. Components of the Heterosocial Skills Checklist

VOICE	FORM OF CONVERSATION
Loudness	Initiation
Pitch	Follow-up
Inflection	Flow
No special dramatic effect	Interest
AFFECT	MOTOR BEHAVIOR
Facial expression	Buttocks
Eye contact	Legs crossed
Laughter	Legs uncrossed
	Arm movements
	Hand movements
	Firm wrist

of the categories was .08. For motor behavior, the maximum difference was even less (.02). Since few differences were observed across scenes, the majority of data presented in this section are the means collapsed across all three scenes.

In terms of group differences, Table 5 presents the mean percent appropriate for each group across the four components of the scale along with the means for the entire sample. One-way analysis of variances were performed separately for each of the components, and these F values and probability levels also are presented in Table 5. It should be realized that because of large differences in cell size across groups in this and other analyses to be presented, the data must be considered tentative. Because of small cell sizes in some groups, post hoc tests have been avoided. Inspection of Table 5 indicates that for our sample rapists appear to be poorest in all of the components except motor behavior, where no group differences were observed. The means for the remainder of the subjects are similar, although much lower than for the socially skilled groups reported by Barlow et al. with the exception of the voice component for exhibitionists. This suggests that the present sample is weighed heavily with subjects having poor heterosocial skills. Since the 67 subjects were consecutive referrals and not preselected by the therapist for social skills deficits, it is obvious that difficulties in heterosocial situations are frequent problems for sexual deviates, including exhibitionists.

Table 5. Mean Percent Appropriate for Various Diagnostic Groups for Each of the Heterosocial Skills Components

Groups	Voice	Form of conversation	Affect	Motor behavior	n
Pedophile	83	61	67	64	21
Rapist	45	26	28	66	9
Exhibitionist	96	79	74	80	9
Others	84	64	68	58	28
F value	3.35**	4.14**	3.90*	1.34	
X total	80	60	63	64	

*$p < .05$
**$p < .01$

Special caution should be taken in interpreting the results from the voice category. These data are likely a result of the scoring procedure adopted. Many of the poorly skilled individuals did not talk during the role-played situation. The procedure to date has been to give these individuals a zero-percent rating in the voice category. Individuals with low scores in this category are rated as deficient in the specific behaviors composing the category, which is not necessarily the case. To correct this scoring problem, the research confederate initiates conversation during a fourth role-playing scene so that a voice sample can be obtained for rating purposes. Since this procedure has just been instituted, adequate data to determine whether the voice category is a general problem in exhibitionists is not yet available.

A third question concerning the use of the heterosocial skills checklist is whether there are differences in subjects across therapists' ratings of skills. This is a question of the validity of the objective skills rating. Table 6 outlines this data along with F values. As can be seen, the objective ratings tend to increase across the 1 to 5 ratings assigned by the therapist. This suggests, within the limitations of the current data, some match between therapists' ratings and the role-played assessment.

In relationship to the same question of validity is the correlation between therapists' ratings and the various skills components. As can be seen from Table 7, voice, form of conversation, and affect are all moderately and significantly related to the therapists' social skills ratings. Although these correlations are highly significant, the mod-

Table 6. Mean Percent Appropriate for Each
Heterosocial Skills Component across Therapist Ratings

Components	THERAPIST RATINGS					F value
	1	2	3	4	5	
Voice	59	75	81	97	99	2.74*
Form of conversation	27	52	58	85	93	6.29**
Affect	27	54	66	90	95	8.24**
Motor behavior	60	65	56	73	64	.954
n	9	23	17	14	4	

*$p < .05$
**$p < .001$

erate size of the coefficients suggests that there were other variables being assessed by the clinicians which were not measured by the objective assessment procedure. In fact, multiple regression analysis performed with clinician ratings as the dependent variable resulted in only one variable (affect) being entered in the equation with an overall multiple R of .577, thus suggesting that a large portion of the variance was unexplained. The data presented in Table 6 and the correlations in Table 7 lend support to the value of the scale in terms of initial validity. However, further research is needed to delineate other heterosocial variables which are not tapped by the present scale. In this context, Marshall and Gordon (1977) have analyzed heterosocial interactions in terms of sequencing of verbalizations. It is possible that a combination of this type of sequencing analysis and Barlow et al.'s (1977) scale may lead to a more accurate analysis of heterosocial deficits.

The final set of analyses was designed to look at both the inner correlation among various components and the actual structure of the scale. Table 8 correlates each specific behavior with a subcomponent of the scale: e.g., the correlations of loudness, pitch, inflection, and dramatic effect with voice; the correlations of initiation, follow-up, flow, and interest with form of conversation; and so on.

The sample size varies across specific behaviors (e.g., loudness, pitch), since for some subjects certain behaviors could not be rated. For example, if the subject did not talk during the 2½-minute scene, it was impossible to rate interest; although initiation was rated as zero percent and the overall category, form of conversation, also received

Table. 7. Correlations between Therapist Rating and Heterosocial Skills Components, and the Intercorrelations between Components

	THERAPIST RATING	VOICE	FORM OF CONVERSATION	AFFECT	MOTOR BEHAVIOR
Therapist rating	—	.38*	.52**	.58**	.08
Voice		—	.81**	.80**	-.13
Form of conversation			—	.84**	.01
Affect				—	
Motor behavior					—

*$p < .01$
**$p < .001$

Note. $n = 67$

Table 8. Correlation of Specific Heterosocial Behaviors with Total Component Scores

VOICE		FORM OF CONVERSATION		AFFECT		MOTOR BEHAVIOR	
Loudness	.89	Initiation	.95	Facial	.71	Buttocks	.73
Pitch	.78	Follow-up	.56	Eye contact	.91	Crossed legs	.72
Inflection	.31	Flow	.88	Laughter[b]	.42	Uncrossed legs	.76
Dramatic effect	.02[a]	Interest	.92			Arm movements	.32
						Hand movements	.39
						Firm wrist	.44

[a]Based on one scene
[b]Based on two scenes

Note. See text for comments on significance.

a rating of zero. Because of this variation in sample size and for easier comprehension, the correlations presented in Table 6 consist of the means of the individual correlations calculated separately in each of the three scenes. For dramatic effect and laughter, the means are based on less than three scenes because in some scenes the mean appropriate percent was 100 (perfect). This lack of variability precluded calculation of the correlation coefficient.

In terms of significance, loudness and pitch were significantly correlated with voice in all three scenes; inflection was significantly correlated with voice in two of the three scenes; and the correlation coefficient involving dramatic effect was not significant in the one scene in which calculations were possible. For form of conversation, all specific behaviors (initiation, follow-up, flow, and interest) showed significant correlations in all three scenes. In the affect category, facial expression and eye contact were significantly correlated with affect in all three scenes; and laughter showed a significant correlation in one scene, an insignificant correlation in the second, and could not be calculated in the third. Buttocks, crossed legs, and uncrossed legs were correlated with the overall subcomponent in all three scenes, arm and hand movement showed significant correlations in two of the scenes, and the firm wrist category showed significant correlations in only one scene.

Table 7 presents the intercorrelations among the overall categories and Table 9 presents a factor analysis using the four components in each scene as variables. As can be seen from Table 7, the variables are highly interrelated except for motor behavior. This is also evident from the factor analysis, which produced two factors. The first is an overall social skills factor having high loadings for all variables except motor behavior, which loaded on the second factor, a pure motor behavior factor. Factor one accounts for 55.5 percent of the total variance and factor two accounts for 19.7 percent of the total variance, for a cummulative percentage of 75.2 percent. It should be noted that these are unrotated factors as rotation created no substantial changes in factor structure.

Summary of Heterosocial Skills Assessment

The data on heterosocial skills have been presented in rather lengthy detail as a model for the type of analysis or research needed in this area to improve the methodology of measuring complex social be-

Table 9. Factor Analysis of the Components of the Heterosocial Skill Checklist across Three Scenes

COMPONENT	SCENE #	FACTOR 1	FACTOR 2
Voice	1	.7705	.0378
Form of conversation	1	.9063	.1075
Affect	1	.7642	.1124
Motor behavior	1	−.0745	.7692
Voice	2	.7536	−.1680
Form of conversation	2	.9304	.0499
Affect	2	.8247	.0199
Motor behavior	2	−.0983	.9471
Voice	3	.8303	−.1256
Form of conversation	3	.8963	.0832
Affect	3	.8814	.0389
Motor behavior	3	.0053	.6961

havior. Similar data is beginning to appear for assertiveness (Bellack, Hersen, & Turner, 1978; Pachman et al., 1978). The areas outlined here as social skills seem to be crucial for exhibitionists, as noted previously. In addition, this data has not previously appeared for the objective heterosocial skills checklist developed by Barlow et al.

This data is as incomplete and inadequate as the data currently available for assertiveness and empathy. One basic inadequacy is in the area of validity. The use of clinical ratings as validity measures involve many problems. A major problem is our own potential bias. Although the ratings are blind to the actual result of the role-played assessment, our staff is familiar with the content of the scales used in the objective assessment. What is needed in the area of heterosocial skills (and other social skills) are independent ratings of social skills by individuals unfamiliar with the objective ratings (Bellack, Hersen, & Turner, 1978; Wolf, 1978). We also need blind ratings for heterosocial skills and assertiveness at various points throughout treatment to determine if the changes observed in objective measurement are reflected in other ratings of the individual's overall heterosocial or assertiveness development.

A second major problem involves basic psychometric properties. This type of analysis has begun on intercorrelations and factor analysis, but much more information is needed. From the data presented, it is clear that some of the variables employed do not relate well to subcomponent scores (i.e., dramatic effect, laughter, arm movement, hand movement, and firm wrist). The rather high correlations among subscales (i.e., voice, affect, form of conversation) also suggest a good deal of redundancy in the scale. Similar moderate correlations have been found between the behavioral components of assertiveness and global ratings (Pachman, et al., 1978). In addition, motor behavior does not seem sensitive to differences in clinical ratings in the population studied. Since rating the video tapes is a rather lengthy process, investigators may want to drop the motor behavior scale unless they are dealing specifically with patients having potential gender motor problems (i.e., transsexuals or transvestites).

Further data also is needed in terms of the reliability of the scale. Behavior therapists have attended to interrater reliability in the social skills area, but have given little attention to the reliability of the scale across time. We are currently in the process of collecting this type of reliability in the areas of heterosocial skills, assertiveness, and empathy.

A third potential problem is racial differences and socioeconomic class differences in the social skills areas. The problem was touched on by Barlow et al. in the initial development of the heterosocial skills checklist, but has received very little further investigation. Since exhibitionists come from a variety of socioeconomic levels, it should be determined if the behaviors being measured are appropriate across these classes.

A final important area is generalizability of the data outside the laboratory assessment procedure. Recent data by Bellack, Hersen, and Turner (1978) showed disappointing generalizability for assertiveness training in hospitalized psychiatric patients. This type of data appears nonexistent for exhibitionism and other sexual deviations. For the objective measurement of all social skills to be valuable, it must reflect patient performance outside the laboratory.

It appears that many of the procedures for objectively measuring important social skills have been developed by behavior therapists who reject traditional psychological assessment for many good reasons. However, given the state of the literature, they also seem to have rejected traditional psychometrics. Some refocusing on basic issues in psychometrics such as reliability, validity, and the internal consistency of the scales is necessary for the development of adequate objective measures in the complex area of social skills.

Sexual Dysfunctions and Sexual Knowledge

Although literature on the brief treatment of sexual dysfunction is flourishing (Annon, 1974, 1975; Kaplan, 1974; Masters & Johnson, 1970), adequate data to assess the effectiveness of these treatments are lacking (Kinder & Blakeney, 1977; Reynolds, 1977; Sotile & Kilman, 1977). In the area of exhibitionism, problems with premature ejaculation, impotency, and sexual inhibition have been reported (Hackett, 1971; Mathis, 1975; Rooth, 1971; Vera, 1976). What is lacking with exhibitionists in the general area of sexual dysfunction is adequate definition and assessment procedures.

In our own project, a self-report inventory composed of attitudinal measures of sexual arousability and frequency counts of various nondeviant sexual behaviors, along with satisfaction ratings for these sexual behaviors, is employed. We also use McHugh's (1968) Sex Knowledge Inventory for the determination of general sexual knowledge.

The value of these scales with exhibitionists and other sexual deviates is yet to be determined. Penile measures may have limited usefulness in this area, since impotence may be situational and subjects suffering from premature ejaculation in general do not experience difficulty with having erections. Clinically, we do see sexual dysfunction problems in our subjects and their partners. In some cases, the exhibitionistic behavior appears highly related to the sexual problems. For example, the wife of one subject with a long history of exhibitionism had limited interest in sexual activity. Part of her lack of interest was secondary to her anger regarding his deviant sexual behavior, but at the same time her lack of interest seemed to increase his urges to expose himself. By the time the patient entered the project, this vicious cycle was well established in their sexual relationship. Adequate treatment required involvement of the subject and his wife in sexual dysfunction and marital counseling.

Research is needed to establish adequate definitions of various sexual dysfunctions and to develop reliable and valid dependent measures for use in this area. For a better understanding of exhibitionists and better planning of treatment programs, data is needed regarding the frequency of sexual dysfunction in exhibitionists and their role in the etiology and maintenance of exhibitionistic behavior. Our experience to date suggests that when sexual dysfunctions occur in exhibitionists, whether of primary etiological significance or secondary to marital discord, the problem must be attended to if successful rehabilitation is to be expected.

Recidivism

Recently Reppucci and Clingempeel (1978) outlined various problems in using recidivism as either a dependent or independent variable. The first major problem presented is the "behavior/system discretion confound." The authors point out that throughout the levels of the criminal justice system, decisions are made in terms of initial arrest, prosecution, and sentencing. These decisions cannot be separated from the actual criminal behavior, as they may reflect administrative policy rather than the occurrence or nonoccurrence of criminal behavior.

Additional problems arise when subjects are hospitalized rather than incarcerated, die, or move to other states where their behavior reoccurs (Reppucci and Clingempeel, 1978). As suggested by the authors, these problems are related to how and from where recidivism data are gathered. In their review of methodology in corrections, they have found that most investigators use only one source of information. We have encountered exhibitionists who have been arrested and incarcerated in three different states in widely separated parts of the country. If only local sources of information were used, this specific patient's recidivism rate would be only one-third of the actual reoccurrence. We have also seen a subject who was arrested in two different, adjacent counties in the same state within the same month and neither jurisdiction was aware of the other incident.

Another problem with exhibitionism and other sexual deviations is that the behavior occurs at a much higher rate than arrests. For example, one treated subject may be arrested after 50 exhibitionistic acts while another may be arrested after 1 or 2. Frequency of arrest would not, in these cases, clearly represent the response to treatment. One subject from our project had a pretreatment rate of exposure of 2 to 3 times per week, and in the year following treatment, he exposed himself only 4 or 5 times. If recidivism rates are looked at in a yes/no fashion, this subject would be counted the same as subjects whose post-treatment rate is the same as their pretreatment rate.

Reppucci and Clingempeel suggest that gradations of recidivism should be employed and attempts should be made to use multiple sources of data in determining recidivism. We concur with these suggestions but also recommend that, in the area of sexual deviation and exhibitionism, plethysmography be used as an additional source of data.

PREDICTIONS OF TREATMENT SUCCESS

Another area which has received little attention is the prediction of which subjects will respond to treatment. Witzig (1968) has indicated from clinical experience that subjects with the diagnosis of sociopathy are poor treatment candidates. Evans (1970) examined a number of subjective variables related to success (no recidivism for six months following treatment) in subjects treated with electrical aversion for exhibitionism. Results indicated that the failure group had a higher frequency of deviant masturbatory fantasies, a higher frequency of exposing themselves, and a longer history of exhibitionism; and within the aversion therapy treatment, unsuccessful clients took more trials to end their exhibiting behavior and to cease having urges to expose themselves. There were no differences between groups in terms of age, education, marital status, frequency of masturbation, and frequency of intercourse.

The age of the target has also been found to relate to recidivism rate. Frisbee and Dondis (1965) have found that exhibitionists with children as their victims have a higher recidivism rate than exhibitionists with adult targets.

It has also been suggested that continuation in therapy is predictive of eventual outcome (Hackett, 1971; Mathis & Collins, 1970a; Witzig, 1968). This is not a surprising finding but it has lead some authors to suggest that mandatory therapy is necessary (Hackett, 1971; Mathis & Collins, 1970a). However, because of the ethical considerations in mandatory treatment, controlled studies addressing this issue are needed. Ethical considerations in applied research will be addressed in the final section of this chapter.

Another suggestion is that, in addition to investigating patient variables related to success, a harder look is taken at the adequacy of current treatment programs. It is our contention that adequate treatment must at least include treatments aimed at the deficits and excesses outlined in Table 1. Treatment failures may result from our failure as clinicians to assess adequately and treat the relevant areas outlined, and in our lack of knowledge about areas yet undefined.

Rather than only searching for the personality characteristics of our failures, we should learn from them what treatment needs we have failed to consider. Table 1 is surely incomplete in terms of deficit areas in exhibitionists and other sexual deviates. Only a systematic approach will determine what additional areas need assessment and treatment.

PREDICTION OF DANGEROUSNESS

Although exhibitionists are usually considered nondangerous in terms of physical harm to their victims, a recent review by Rooth (1973) suggests that about 10 to 12 percent of exhibitionists go on to more serious sex crimes. Frisbee and Dondis (1965) have evidence suggesting that approximately 11 percent of individuals first arrested for exhibitionism will later be arrested for pedophilia or sexual assault. Gebhard, Gangnon, Pomeroy, and Christenson (1965) examined the later offenses of individuals first arrested for exhibitionism. They found that 72 percent of second offenses and approximately 65 percent of third and later offenses were exhibitionistic acts. The remainder of the second, third, and later offenses were scattered across various diagnostic categories. For pedophilic incidents, the rate was 5 percent for second offenses, and it increased to 9 percent for third and later offenses. In terms of heterosexual aggression, 5 percent of the exhibitionists had second offenses in this category, which increased to 9 percent for third and later offenses. Rooth's own data on 30 exhibitionists suggests a low frequency of violent sexual behavior but rather large incidences of pedophilia, hebephilia (arousal to adolescents), and incest.

Attempts at predicting dangerousness are currently rather unpopular among mental health professionals in view of their poor success rate in the past. Ignoring the problem however, will not make it go away. Current data suggest that at least 10 percent of exhibitionistic patients will commit or have already committed more serious sexual offenses. As both clinicians and researchers, we must deal with this problem. One possible means (although still in the experimental stage) is to measure penile responses to aggressive and pedophiliac stimuli. We are currently collecting this data on all exhibitionists in the project and have found that, for subjects presenting histories of rape and pedophilia in addition to exhibitionism, their erection responses indicate arousal in both areas. Data from the project for rapists clearly indicates that rapists respond to stimuli depicting rape, while nonrapist sex offenders (Abel, Barlow, Blanchard, & Guild, 1977) and nonsex offenders (Abel, Blanchard, & Becker, 1978) do not. However, further data is needed before we can determine if erection measures are predictive of exhibitionists likely to commit more serious sexual offenses.

TREATMENT CONSIDERATIONS

The focus of the chapter has been on the process of applied research and the dependent variables relevant to the problem of exhibitionism. Treatment has been reviewed in other chapters of this volume; therefore the comments in this area will be rather brief.

The research into treatment effectiveness in exhibitionism has been almost nonexistent to date. Studies comparing the effectiveness of the treatments outlined in this book are needed. For example, research is needed that compares behavioral procedures to group and individual therapy approaches. As alluded throughout this chapter, assessment of treatment outcome must be multivariate. The most important question in treatment research may not be what type of treatment is most effective, but what type of treatment (behavioral, individual, or group) is most effective in correcting excesses and deficits. By using multivariate assessment we may begin to determine the unique contribution that each type of treatment has to offer to the remediation of exhibitionism. Only when the data are available can rational treatments be designed using the most effective combination of treatment modalities.

A final problem in treatment research and assessment is the ethical problem in working with subjects involved with the law or having a high likelihood of such involvement.

Ethical Issues

Numerous ethical and research guidelines have been published, including guidelines for behavior therapists (Association for the Advancement of Behavior Therapy, 1977), psychologists (Ethical Principles, 1973), and psychologists working in the criminal justice system (Task Force on the Role of Psychology, 1978); federal guidelines

(U.S. Department of Health, Education, and Welfare, 1975; National Commission for the Protection of Human Subjects, 1977); and Law Enforcement Assistance Administration (1976) guidelines regarding confidentiality of data. The problem among clinical researchers may not be a lack of guidelines, but an understanding of how to implement these guidelines in an applied clinical research project. For this reason, rather than reviewing governmental and professional organization guidelines, we present a system here that has been applied and been found acceptable by both federal funding agents and local research committees.

There are four interrelated areas that must be considered by the applied researcher. The first is to guarantee that the proposed project has had external review and been approved by a committee of knowledgeable professionals outside the research project. The second issue is in regard to guaranteeing the informed consent of participating subjects, and the third issue is to determine the benefits-to-risks ratio. Finally, the clinical researcher must have a means of guaranteeing confidentiality of the research data or making any limitations on confidentiality clear, and initially conveying this to the research subject.

An external review has become almost standard in universities and research settings that receive federal funding. For applied researchers working in other areas or where funding is not from federal sources, it is strongly recommended that efforts be made to develop a patient-participation committee of knowledgeable professionals who would review all projects. In our own project, in addition to this external review we have a patient advocate and a patient advocate committee made up of local citizens from various backgrounds. At the current time the patient advocate is paid by our project, but the patient advocate committee to which the advocate reports is comprised of volunteers. It is the purpose of the committee and the patient advocate to review each subject who presents himself to the project and to determine his acceptability. This guarantees that both the overall project and each subject entering the project will be reviewed by an external committee, therefore decreasing the risk of ethical abuse. A second advantage of the advocacy committee is that, by inclusion of local citizens, it helps to guarantee public support for the research/treatment project—especially when one is dealing with rather unpopular areas such as the treatment of sexual deviations.

A second major issue relates to adequately informed consent. The first step is to prepare a thorough consent form. This consent form should include a detailed description of the procedures to be employed and should outline the possible benefits and risks to the patient. In an applied research program, the consent form should also outline alternative treatments available to the subject. It has even been suggested that, on the issue of alternative procedures, individuals who are experts in these alternative procedures be called upon to explain these treatments to the patient (Slovenko, 1975). The consent form shown here (Figure 4) represents the type of consent we use in cognitive restructuring, a treatment that could have possible risks to the patient. In addition, a policy has recently been adopted that research subjects re-sign the consent form midway through treatment, guaranteeing that the original consent form has been followed by the investigators thus far. The subject also signs the consent form at the end of treatment and makes any comments about variations between the content of the consent form and his actual experience. The preparation of this type of consent form is a rather easy procedure, but does not answer all of the problems involved in obtaining informed consent. This is especially true when there are subtle forms of coercion for the patient to enter the research project, when he is under age, or when his mental status leaves doubts about his ability to give voluntary informed consent. Our research project's procedure for dealing with coercion is to accept only patients not involved in the legal system. Even here, however, we sometimes find attempts at coercion such as patients who are referred by the local police and instructed that charges may be dropped if they "volunteer" for the project.

Our second procedure is to allow the patient advocate and the patient advocate committee to determine if the subject is acceptable and can give truly voluntary and knowledgeable informed consent. A special procedure used with juveniles is to have both the guardian and the subject sign separate informed consents. The guardian's informed consent is similar to the one signed by the subject, but it also indicates that no data will be released to the guardian without permission of the subject. That is, we explain in detail what types of evaluation and treatment the subject will receive, but make it clear initially that the results of the evaluation or treatment will not be released without permission from the subject.

Special problems arise in informed consent for investigators working with incarcerated sex offenders. Currently there are federal guidelines (1977) outlining the procedures necessary for research to occur with prisoners. In addition, Klockars (1974) in a review of the problem suggests a rather unique solution. He recommends that prisoner unions be developed to negotiate with professional re-

Figure 4. Consent form for cognitive restructuring (shame aversions).

I, _____, understand that I am being offered a new treatment for exhibitionism called cognitive restructuring. The treatment is designed to stop me from exposing myself by associating guilty feelings with the actual act of exposing myself. During the treatment, I will be expected to expose myself as I've done in the past, but I will be observed by others. An audience of males or females will watch me carry out my exposing myself. I can expect to get very anxious, nervous, emotionally upset, depressed, develop a fast heart rate, perspire, and in general feel very uncomfortable during this treatment. The reason I will feel these bad feelings during the treatment is so that bad feelings can be associated with the very behavior I am trying to control—exhibiting myself.

There are other forms of treatment for exhibitionism, which include talking with a therapist, family therapy and various forms of aversion such as electrical aversion, covert sensitization, odor aversion and chemical aversion. All of these aversive techniques associate aversive events with the act of exposing myself.

The reason my therapist is suggesting cognitive restructuring is that it is much more powerful than the other forms of treatment and therefore success can be brought about with fewer hours of therapy.

The side effects described above may persist for days to weeks and possibly months after my treatment, depending upon the amount of discomfort I feel during the actual treatment session. I can also expect that a treatment session will reduce my erection responses. In some cases, patients have developed impotency due to the treatment. In most cases this has cleared up relatively fast. Should it occur in my case, it will be treated by my therapist or I will be referred to the appropriate treatment center to receive treatment. If at any time during any portion in my treatment I would like to discontinue my consent and participation in the treatment, this is perfectly acceptable to my therapist. My signature below indicates that I've read and understood this treatment and agreed to participate in same. If I have any questions about this consent form, I have written them in the space indicated below.

Figure 4. (Continued).

Patient's Name _____

Patient's Therapist _____

Date _____

Witness _____

To insure that the therapy was indeed as described above, I have indicated below any deleterious effects of the therapy that have occured to me.

Patient's Name _____

Date _____

---

searchers both for wages for research participation and determining whether the research project is acceptable. Although the federal guidelines and the article by Klockars may be helpful to the researcher working with incarcerated individuals, it is still a very difficult area and final solutions are yet to be achieved.

The third issue is the benefits-to-risks ratio. Federal policy (National Commission for the Protection of Human Subjects, 1977) mandates that the rights and welfare of the subject are to be adequately protected, with the benefits outweighing the possible risks to the subject. However, Stoltz (1974) notes, "Judgments about subject protection procedures would be simple indeed to make, if the risk/benefit ratio could be quantified, or even if all of us could just agree on what the risks and potential benefits are for a given study." Stoltz also comments that the situation is further complicated by changing customs, changes in definitions of risks and benefits, and changes in knowledge and value over time. The use of external review committees and patient advocate committees, along with detailed consent forms explaining risks and benefits, is one step in dealing with this problem. However, as in working with incarcerated offenders, there is no one clear solution for determining risk/benefit ratios.

The final issue in applied research is the means of protecting the confidentiality of the data. The Law Enforcement Assistance Administration (1976) has published guidelines for the protection of human subject data in investigations funded by that agency. Our own approach has been to code all subject data by number and to insure that no identifying information is included in the subject's file. In addition, the match between the subject's number and name is held by a colleague outside of the country. Therefore, the only individuals who know the number are the patient and the collaborater who holds the match between the names and numbers. We clearly inform the subject of this arrangement and inform him that if he releases his number to anyone, he is also releasing the contents of the information in his files.

In terms of incarcerated sexual offenders, the APA task force on psychologists within the criminal justice system has recommended that confidentiality in the prison setting should be the same as that in voluntary noninstitutional settings, and all parties should be informed of the confidentiality arrangements.

The final aspect of the confidentiality problem is in terms of having information related to possible dangerous acts the client may engage in or already have engaged in. This has become especially relevant since the Tarasoff decision which, if upheld and generalized to other states, may make it necessary for the therapist to inform the patient's potential victim if his or her name is known to the therapist.[1] Decisions such as Tarasoff place the clinical researcher in a very dangerous position in that during the process of evaluation and treatment he may gain information which by law must be reported to the authorities. The subject who is voluntarily seeking treatment is also in an extremely unenviable position. If the subject divulges too much information, he may be risking his freedom. Our approach to this problem has been to be completely honest with the subject. We explain state laws regarding patient–psychologist or physician confidentiality. In addition, we explain the Tarasoff decision and the ramifications this law could have for the subject if it were generalized to the state in which we are working. Decisions regarding what information to divulge is then left up to the patient and this right is respected by the research team.

A final issue is subject recruitment. This issue is not necessarily related to ethical issues, but failure to consider the recruitment procedure and to maintain public support may disrupt a research project before it begins. One procedure which has been fairly successful is to begin subject recruitment by communicating only with other mental health professionals through discussions with local psychiatric, psychological, and social work associations and presentations at local mental health delivery systems. Attempts are made to detail the research program to mental health professionals working in both the private and public sectors. Once these presentations have been made to mental health professionals and have received no negative publicity, the next move is to present the project to key community leaders. This involves presentations to local government, lawyers' associations, local religious leaders, and individuals or groups who appear to have key leadership roles in the community. Only after presentations to the community leaders and after we have answered the questions they raise, is any type of public announcement made regarding the research program. At this point, newspaper articles and appearances on local TV programs may be appropriate. This procedure has been used effectively and with no adverse public reaction, even though our project encompasses not only exhibitionists, but also rapists and pedophiles.

Special problems may arise when subjects are recruited from the justice system. If an investigator is to see court-referred subjects, it is suggested that a clear contractual arrangement be negotiated with the legal system, outlining the type of information that will be released and any limitations on the access of the justice system to the data. This contractual arrangement should be made clear to every subject entering the project.

In terms of request for information, our policy is that we will only prepare a report which is given directly to the patient. This report states clearly that the subject should read it thoroughly and then determine whether he wishes to forward it to the requesting agency. Information is not forwarded to any party other than the subject. This policy was adopted in response to incidences in which reports were forwarded to a subject's lawyer (with written and signed release-of-information forms), who then used the reports in a way unacceptable to the subject. The subjects on occasion directed their subsequent anger at us. To avoid this problem, reports are given only to the subject and he takes the responsibility for its use.

The previous discussion has certainly not exhausted all the ethical problems a clinical researcher faces, but it is hoped that these general guidelines and specific procedures will be of help.

NOTE

1. Tarasoff v. Regents of the University of California et al., 118 Calif. Rpts. 129, 529 P 2d 533 (California 1974). The Tarasoff decision was made by the supreme court of California in a case filed by the parents of a girl who was murdered by her ex-boyfriend. The boyfriend had been under psychological care at the student counseling center at the University of California. The patient's therapist, believing the individual to be dangerous, notified the police who did not detain the patient. The court ruling indicated that the therapist should not only have informed the police but also the potential victim since the victim's name was known to the therapist.

REFERENCES

Abel, G. G. Assessment of sexual deviation in the male. In M. Hersen and A. S. Bellack (Eds.), *Behavioral assessment: A practical handbook.* New York: Pergamon Press, 1976.

Abel, G. G., Barlow, D. H., Blanchard, E. B., & Guild, D. The components of rapists' sexual arousal. *Archives of General Psychiatry,* 1977, *34,* 895–903.

Abel, G. G., Barlow, D. H., Blanchard, E. B., & Mavissakalian, M. Measurement of sexual arousal in male homosexuals: Effects of instructions and stimulus modality. *Archives of Sexual Behavior,* 1975, *4,* 623–629.

Abel, G. G., & Blanchard, E. B. The measurement and generation of sexual arousal in male sexual deviates. In M. Hersen, R. Eisler, & P. M. Miller (Eds.), *Progress in behavior modification* (Vol. 2). New York: Academic Press, 1976.

Abel, G. G., Blanchard, E. B., Barlow, D. H., & Mavissakalian, M. Identifying specific erotic cues in sexual deviations by audiotaped descriptions. *Journal of Applied Behavior Analysis,* 1975, *8,* 247–260.

Abel, G. G., Blanchard, E. B., & Becker, J. V. Psychological treatment for rapists. In M. Walker & S. Brodsky (Eds.), *Sexual assault.* Lexington, Ma.: Lexington Books, 1976.

Abel, G. G., Blanchard, E. B., & Becker, J. V. An integrated treatment program for the rapist. In R. T. Rada (Ed.), *Clinical aspects of the rapist.* New York: Grune & Stratton, 1978.

Abel, G. G., Blanchard, E. B., Becker, J. V., & Djenderedjian, A. Differentiating sexual aggressiveness with penile measures. *Criminal Justice and Behavior,* 1978, *5,* 315–332.

Abel, G. G., Blanchard, E. B., Murphy, W. D., Becker, J. V., & Djenderedjian, A. Two methods of measuring penile response. *Behavior Therapy*, in press.

Abel, G. G., Levis, D. J., & Clancy, J. Aversion therapy applied to taped sequences of deviant behavior in exhibitionism and other sexual deviations: A preliminary report. *Journal of Behavior Therapy and Experimental Psychiatry*, 1970, *1*, 59–66.

Anastasi, A. *Psychological testing* (3rd ed.). London: MacMillan, 1968.

Annon, J. S. *The behavioral treatment of sexual problems: Brief therapy* (Vol. 1). Honolulu: Enabling Systems, 1974.

Annon, J. S. *The behavioral treatment of sexual problems: Intensive therapy* (Vol. 2). Honolulu: Enabling Systems, 1975.

Association for the Advancement of Behavior Therapy. Ethical issues for human services. *Behavior Therapy*, 1977, *8*, v–vi.

Bancroft, J. *Deviant sexual behavior: Modification and assessment*. Oxford, England: Clarendon, 1974.

Bancroft, J., Jones, H. C., & Pullman, B. P. A simple transducer for measuring penile erections with comments on its use in the treatment of sexual disorders. *Behavior Research and Therapy*, 1966, *4*, 239–241.

Barlow, D. H., & Able, G. G. Recent developments in assessment and treatment of sexual deviation. In W. E. Craighead, A. E. Kazdin, & M. J. Mahoney (Eds.), *Behavior modification: Principles, issues and applications*. Boston: Houghton Mifflin, 1976.

Barlow, D. H., Abel, G. G., Blanchard, E. B., Bristow, A. R., & Young, L. D. A heterosocial skills checklist for males. *Behavior Therapy*, 1977, *8*, 229–239.

Barlow, D. H., Becker, J., Leitenberg, H., & Agras, W. S. Mechanical strain gauge recording penile circumference change. *Journal of Applied Behavior Analysis*, 1970, *3*, 73–76.

Barlow, D. H., & Hersen, M. Single case experimental designs: Uses in applied clinical research. *Archives of General Psychiatry*, 1973, *29*, 319–325.

Becker, J. V., Abel, G. G., Blanchard, E. B., Murphy, W. D., & Coleman, E. Evaluating social skills of sexual aggressives. *Criminal Justice and Behavior*, 1978, *5*, 357–367.

Bellack, A. S., Hersen, M., & Turner, S. M. Role-play tests for assessing social skills: Are they valid? *Behavior Therapy*, 1978, *9*, 448–461.

Bem, S. The measurement of psychological androgyny. *Journal of Consulting and Clinical Psychology*, 1974, *42*, 155–162.

Bergin, A. E. The evaluation of therapeutic outcomes. In A. E. Bergin & S. L. Garfield (Eds.), *Handbook of psychotherapy and behavior change: An empirical analysis*. New York: Wiley, 1971.

Bergin, A., & Strupp, H. *Changing frontiers in the science of psychotherapy.* Chicago: Aldine & Atherton, 1972.

Bond, I. M., & Hutchinson, H. C. Application of reciprocal inhibition therapy to exhibitionism. *Canadian Medical Association Journal,* 1960, *83,* 23–25.

Brownell, K. D., Hayes, S. C., & Barlow, D. H. Patterns of appropriate and deviant sexual arousal: The behavioral treatment of multiple sexual deviations. *Journal of Consulting and Clinical Psychology,* 1977, *45,* 1144–1155.

Campbell, D. T., & Stanley, J. C. *Experimental and quasi-experimental designs for research.* Chicago: Rand McNally, 1966.

Cronbach, L. J. *Essentials of psychological testing* (3rd ed.). New York: Harper & Row, 1970.

Eisler, R. M., Hersen, M., Miller, P. M., & Blanchard, E. B. Situational determinants of assertive behaviors. *Journal of Consulting and Clinical Psychology,* 1975, *43,* 330–340.

Eisler, R. M., Miller, P. M., & Hersen, M. Components of assertive behavior. *Journal of Clinical Psychology,* 1973, *29,* 295–299.

Ethical principles in the conduct of research with human participants. Washington, D.C.: American Psychological Association, 1973.

Evans, D. R. Masturbatory fantasy and sexual deviation. *Behaviour Research and Therapy,* 1968, *6,* 17–19.

Evans, D. R. Subjective variables and treatment effects in aversion therapy. *Behavior Research and Therapy,* 1970, *8,* 147–152.

Feldman, M. P., Mellor, V., & Pinchof, J. M. The application of anticipatory avoidance learning to the treatment of homosexuality. Ill: The sexual orientation method. *Behaviour Research and Therapy,* 1966, *4,* 289–299.

Frederiksen, L. W., Jenkins, J. O., Foy, D. W., & Eisler, R. M. Social-skills training to modify abusive verbal outbursts in adults. *Journal of Applied Behavior Analysis,* 1976, *9,* 117–125.

Freund, K. Diagnostika homosexuality u nuvu. *Czechoslovak Psychiatrie,* 1957, *53,* 382–393.

Freund, K. Laboratory differential diagnosis of homo- and heterosexuality: An experiment with faking. *Review of Czechoslovak Medicine,* 1961, *7,* 20–31.

Freund, K. A laboratory method of diagnosing predominance of homo- or hetero-erotic interest in the male. *Behaviour Research and Therapy,* 1963, *1,* 85–93.

Freund, K., Nagler, E., Langevin, R., Zajac, A., & Steiner, B. Measuring feminine gender identity in homosexual males. *Archives of Sexual Behavior,* 1974, *3,* 249–259.

Frisbee, L. V., & Dondis, E. H. *Recidivism among treated sex offenders* (California mental health research monograph no. 5). Sacramento, Ca.: Department of Mental Hygiene, 1965.

Gebhard, P. H., Gagnon, J. H., Pomeroy, W. B., & Christenson, C. V. *Sex offenders.* New York: Harper & Row, 1965.

Gray, K. G., & Mohr, J. W. Follow-up of male sexual offenders. In R. Slovenko (Ed.), *Sexual behavior and the law.* Springfield, Ill.: Charles C Thomas, 1965.

Hackett, T. P. The psychotherapy of exhibitionists in a court clinic setting. *Seminars in Psychiatry,* 1971, *3,* 297–306.

Hadden, S. B. Exhibitionism. *Psychiatric Annals,* 1973, *3,* 23–32.

Heiman, J. R. A psychophysiological exploration of sexual arousal patterns in females and males. *Psychophysiology,* 1977, *14,* 266–274.

Hersen, M., & Barlow, D. H. *Single case experimental designs: Strategies for studying behavior change.* New York: Pergamon Press, 1976.

Hersen, M., & Bellack, A. S. A multiple-base-line analysis of social-skills training in chronic schizophrenics. *Journal of Applied Behavior Analysis,* 1976, *9,* 239–245.

Kaplan, H. S. *The new sex therapy.* New York: Brunner/Mazel, 1974.

Karpman, B. The psychopathology of exhibitionism: A review of the literature. *Journal of Clinical Psychopathology,* 1948, *9,* 179–225.

Kazdin, A. E. Statistical analyses for single-case experimental designs. In M. Hersen & D. H. Barlow (Eds.), *Single case experimental designs.* New York: Pergamon Press, 1976.

Kazdin, A. E., & Kopel, S. A. On resolving ambiguities of the multiple base-line design: Problems and recommendations. *Behavior Therapy,* 1975, *6,* 601–608.

Kerlinger, F. N. *Foundations of behavioral research.* New York: Holt, Rinehart & Winston, 1973.

Kiesler, D. J. Experimental designs in psychotherapy research. In A. E. Bergin & S. L. Garfield (Eds.), *Handbook of psychotherapy and behavior change: An empirical analysis.* New York: Wiley, 1971.

Kinder, B. N., & Blakeney, P. Treatment of sexual dysfunction: A review of outcome studies. *Journal of Clinical Psychology,* 1977, *33,* 523–530.

Klockars, C. B. Professional researchers and prisoner subjects: Some ethical problems and practical solutions. *The Prison Journal,* 1974, *2,* 34–42.

Kolarsky, A., & Madlafousek, J. Female behavior and sexual arousal in heterosexual male deviant offenders: An experimental study. *Journal of Nervous and Mental Disease,* 1972, *155,* 110–118.

Law Enforcement Assistance Administration. *Confidentiality of Research and Statistical Data.* Washington, D.C.: U.S. Department of Justice, 1976.

Laws, D. R. A comparison of the measurement characteristics of two circumferential penile transducers. *Archives of Sexual Behavior,* 1977, *6,* 45–51.

Laws, D. R., & Holmen, M. L. Sexual response faking by pedophiles. *Criminal Justice and Behavior,* 1978, *5,* 343–356.

Laws, D. R., & Rubin, H. H. Instructional control of an autonomic sexual response. *Journal of Applied Behavior Analysis,* 1969, *2,* 93–99.

Leitenberg, H. The use of single-case methodology in psychotherapy research. *Journal of Abnormal Psychology,* 1973, *82,* 87–101.

Levin, S. M., Murphy, W. D., Barry, S. M., & Wolfinsohn, L. The use of psychologically aversive imagery in covert sensitization. Unpublished manuscript, 1977.

Linehan, M. M. Issues in behavioral interviewing. In J. D. Cone & R. P. Hawkins (Eds.), *Behavioral assessment: New directions in clinical psychology.* New York: Bruner/Mazel, 1977.

Marshall, W. L., & Gordon, A. *Assessment of sexual-aggressive social competence.* Paper presented at the First Annual Conference on the Evaluation and Treatment of Sexual Aggressives, Memphis, April 1977.

Masters, W. H., & Johnson, V. E. *Human sexual inadequacy.* Boston: Little Brown, 1970.

Mathis, H. I. Instating sexual adequacy in a disabled exhibitionist. *Psychotherapy: Theory, Research and Practice,* 1975, *12,* 97–100.

Mathis, J. L., & Collins, M. Mandatory group therapy for exhibitionists. *American Journal of Psychiatry,* 1970a, *126,* 1162–1166.

Mathis, J. L., & Collins, M. Progressive phases in group therapy of exhibitionists. *International Journal of Group Psychotherapy,* 1970b, *20,* 163–169.

Mavissakalian, M., Blanchard, E. B., Abel, G. G., & Barlow, D. H. Responses to complex erotic stimuli in homosexual and heterosexual males. *British Journal of Psychiatry,* 1975, *126,* 252–257.

McConaghy, N. Measurements of change in penile dimensions. *Archives of Sexual Behavior,* 1974, *3,* 381–388.

McHugh, G. *Sex knowledge inventory: Form X.* Soluda, N.C.: Family Life Publications, 1968.

Mischel, W. *Personality and assessment.* New York: Wiley, 1968.

Mohr, M. W., Turner, R. E., & Jerry, M. B. *Pedophilia and exhibitionism: A handbook.* Toronto: University of Toronto Press, 1964.

Morganstern, M. P. Behavioral interviewing: The initial stages of assessment. In M. Hersen & A. S. Bellack (Eds.), *Behavioral assessment: A practical handbook.* New York: Pergamon Press, 1976.

National Commission for the Protection of Human Subjects in Biomedical and Behavioral Research, Department of Health, Education and Welfare. Protection of human subjects: Research involving prisoners—Report and recommendations. *Federal Register,* 1977, *42,* 3075–3091.

Neale, J. M., & Liebert, R. M. *Science and behavior: An introduction to methods of research.* Englewood Cliffs, N.J.: Prentice-Hall, 1973.

Pachman, J. S., Foy, D. W., Massey, F., & Eisler, R. M. A factor analysis of assertive behavior. *Journal of Consulting and Clinical Psychology,* 1978, *46,* 347.

Quinsey, V. L., & Bergersen, S. G. Instructional control of penile circumference in assessments of sexual preference. *Behavior Therapy,* 1976, *7,* 489–493.

Quinsey, V. L., & Carrigan, W. F. Instructional control of penile responses to visual stimuli with and without auditory sexual fantasy correlates. *Criminal Justice and Behavior,* 1978, *5,* 333–342.

Quinsey, V. L., & Harris, G. A comparison of two methods of scoring the penile circumference response: Magnitude and area. *Behavior Therapy,* 1976, *7,* 702–704.

Quinsey, V. L., Steinman, C. M., Bergersen, S. G., & Holmes, T. F. Penile circumference, skin conductance and ranking responses of child molesters and "normals" to sexual and nonsexual visual stimuli. *Behavior Therapy,* 1975, *6,* 213–219.

Quirk, D. A. A follow-up on the Bond-Hutchison case of systematic desensitization with an exhibitionist. *Behavior Therapy,* 1974, *5,* 428–431.

Reppucci, N. D., & Clingempeel, W. G. Methodological issues in research with correctional populations. *Journal of Consulting and Clinical Psychology,* 1978, *46,* 727–746.

Reynolds, B. S. Psychological treatment models and outcome results for erectible dysfunctions: A critical review. *Psychological Bulletin,* 1977, *84,* 1218–1238.

Rich, R. A., & Schroeder, H. E. Research issues in assertiveness training. *Psychological Bulletin,* 1976, *83,* 1081–1096.

Rickles, N. R. Exhibitionism updated. *Corrective Psychiatry and the Journal of Social Therapy,* 1968, *14,* 200–208.

Rooth. F. G. Exhibitionism, sexual violence, and paedophilia. *British Journal of Psychiatry,* 1973, *122,* 705–710.

Rooth, F. G. Indecent exposure and exhibitionism. *British Journal of Hospital Medicine,* 1971, *9,* 521–534.

Rooth, F. G., & Marks, I. M. Persistent exhibitionism: Short-term response to self-regulation and relaxation treatment. *Archives of Sexual Behavior,* 1974, *4,* 43–52.

Rosen, R. C., & Kopel, S. A. Penile plethysmography and biofeedback in the treatment of a transvestite-exhibitionist. *Journal of Consulting and Clinical Psychology,* 1977, *45,* 908–916.

Sidman, M. *Tactics of scientific research.* New York: Basic Books, 1960.

Slovenko, R. Commentary on psychosurgery. *Hastings Center Report,* 1975, 5, 19–22.

Sotile, W. M., & Kilman, P. R. Treatment of psychogenic female sexual dysfunctions. *Psychological Bulletin,* 1977, 84, 619–633.

Stolz, S. *Ethical issues in research on behavior therapy.* Paper presented at the First Drake Conference on Professional Issues in Behavior Analysis. DesMoines, Iowa, March 1974.

Strupp, H., & Bergin, A. Some empirical and conceptual bases for co-ordinated research in psychotherapy: A critical review of issues, trends, and evidence. *International Journal of Psychiatry,* 1969, 7, 18–90.

Task force on the role of psychology in the criminal justice system. Washington, D.C.: Board of Social and Ethical Responsibility for Psychology, American Psychological Association, 1978.

Truax, C. B., & Carkhuff, R. R. *Toward effective counseling and psychotherapy: Training and practice.* Chicago: Aldine, 1967.

U.S. Department of Health, Education and Welfare. *Protection of human subjects.* Washington, D.C.: U.S. Government Printing Office, 1975.

Vera, A. Probation officer treatment for exhibitionism. *Federal Probation,* 1976, 40, 54–59.

Webster, J. S., Sanders, S. H., & Alford, G. S. *The functional dependence of several sexually deviant behavior patterns, or: I've got those multiple base-line blues.* Paper presented at the Association for the Advancement of Behavior Therapy, Chicago, 1978.

Witzig, J. S. The group treatment of male exhibitionists. *American Journal of Psychiatry,* 1968, 125, 75–81.

Wolf, M. M. Social validity: The case for subjective measurement, or how applied behavior analysis is finding its heart. *Journal of Applied Behavior Analysis,* 1978, 11, 203–214.

Zechnich, R. Exhibitionism: Genesis, dynamics and treatment. *Psychiatric Quarterly,* 1971, 45, 70–75.

Zuckerman, M. Physiological measures of sexual arousal in the human. *Psychological Bulletin,* 1971, 75, 297–329.

AUTHOR INDEX

Abel, G. G., 111, *112*, 160, 164, *180*, 216, 217, 238, *247*, 300, *308*, 339–392
Abraham, K., 68, *81*
Abse, D. W., *58*
Addis, J. W., 190, 221, *251*
Adesso, V. J., 85, 87, *115*, *117*, 161, *183*
Adler, 298, 299
Agras, W. S., 157, 161, 163, *181*, *183*, 211, *247*, 302, *308*, 359, *387*
Alford, G. S., 342, *392*
Allen, D. W., 59–82, 296, 297, 298, 299, 300, 306, *308*
Almansi, J., 67, *81*
American Civil Liberties Union, *337*
Anastasi, A., 362, *387*
Annon, J. S., 160, 161, *180*, 303, *308*, 349, 375, *387*

Ansbacher, H. L., 298, *308*
Ansbacher, R. R., 298, *308*
Application of indecent exposure statute to nude sunbathing, 38
Armitage, P., 207, *247*
Armstrong, E., 86, 108, 109, 110, *117*
Ashem, B., 188, 189, *247*, 248
Association for the Advancement of Behavior Therapy, *387*
Atkinson, G., 127, 146, *149*
Austin, W., 325, *337*
Aversion therapy and the involuntary confined, 330, *337*
Azrin, N. H., 141, *148*

Baer, D. M., 86, 87, *112*
Bakan, P., 128, 144, 145, *148*
Bancroft, H., 4, *9*

AUTHOR INDEX

Bancroft, J., 85, 86, 88, 91, 92, 93, 94, 109, 112, 113, 164, 180, 348, 354, 359, 387
Bancroft, J. A., 159, 160, 180
Bancroft, J.H.J., 238, 247, 250
Bandura, A., 152, 176, 177, 180, 241, 247
Barlow, B. A., 214, 215, 229, 247
Barlow, D. A., 95, 115
Barlow, D. H., 154, 155, 156, 157, 158, 160, 161, 163, 164, 168, 170, 172, 175, 179, 180, 181, 183, 211, 247, 249, 301, 302, 308, 341, 347, 358, 359, 361, 362, 363, 366, 367, 369, 373, 379, 386, 387, 388, 389, 390
Barr, R. F., 110, 116, 156, 184
Barry, S. M., 342, 390
Bastani, J. B., 227, 237, 247
Batchelor, I.R.C., 193, 249
Becker, J. V., 339–392
Becker, R., 211, 247
Bellack, A. S., 162, 181, 183, 365, 373, 374, 387, 389
Bem, S., 349, 387
Berecz, J., 109, 113
Bergersen, S. G., 362, 363, 391
Bergin, A., 127, 340, 388, 392
Bergin, A. E., 340, 350, 387
Bergman, A., 67, 82
Bernstein, J. G., 230, 247
Bernstein, T., 87, 113
Best, J. A., 89, 111, 117
Bieber, B., 156, 159, 181
Bieber, I., 156, 159, 181
Bieber, T. D., 156, 159, 181
Bigelow, G., 112, 117
Bion, W. R., 42, 58
Birk, L., 156, 181, 304, 308
Blair, J., 35, 38
Blair, L., 328, 337
Blakeney, P., 375, 389
Blanchard, E. B., 164, 180, 308, 340, 347, 348, 358, 359, 361, 362, 363, 364, 365, 366, 379, 386, 387, 388, 390
Blitch, J. W., 161, 181
Bogan, J., 323, 337
Bond, I. K., 95, 111, 113, 155, 181
Bond, I. M., 341, 388
Brenner, C., 77, 81
Bristow, A. R., 366, 387
Britles, C. J., 93, 115
Bross, I., 207, 247
Brown, C. W., 228, 249
Brown, P. T., 94, 118, 159, 186
Brownell, K. D., 95, 115, 151–186, 214, 215, 229, 247, 249, 300, 301, 302, 306, 308, 341, 342, 388
Burdick, W. R., 215, 247
Burger, D., 86, 118
Butterfield, W. H., 87, 113

Cabanis, D., 8, 10
Callahan, E. A., 157, 171, 181
Callahan, E. J., 90, 91, 95, 97, 113, 211, 215, 216, 247
Campbell, D. T., 341, 344, 350, 388
Carkhuff, R. R., 365, 392
Carlisle, J. M., 153, 185, 229, 250, 300, 309
Carrigan, W. F., 363, 391
Castell, D., 94, 118, 159, 186
Cautela, J. R., 155, 157, 161, 171, 181, 215, 217, 248
Chang, A. F., 86, 109, 117
Christenson, C., 38, 338
Christenson, C. V., 65, 81, 378, 389
Christenson, C. Y., 10
Church, R. M., 91, 92, 93, 113
Claeson, L., 89, 113
Clancy, J., 108, 111, 112, 160, 216, 217, 238, 247, 361, 387
Clingempeel, W. G., 376, 391
Coe, W. C., 125, 149

AUTHOR INDEX

Cohen, H. D., 146, *148*
Cohler, B., 156, *181*, 304, *308*
Coleman, E., 365, *387*
Colletti, G., 177, *181*
Collins, M., 45, 50, 58, 202, 250, 304, *309*, 316, *338*, 344, 348, 377, *390*
Colson, C. E., 189, *248*
Conrad, S. R., 160, *182*
Conway, J. B., *113*
Copemann, C. D., 89, *113*
Covvey, H. D., *114*
Cox, D. J., 3–10, 253–293, 298, 300, 306, *308*
Cronbach, L. J., 351, *388*
The cruel and unusual punishment clause and the substantive criminal law, 330, *337*
Csapo, K., 101, *114*
Curran, D., 156, *182*
Curran, J. P., 161, 162, 178, *182*, 191, 215, 217, 241, 245, *248*, *249*

Dain, H. J., 156, *181*
Daitzman, R. J., 8, 9, *10*, 253–285, 289–290, *293*
D'Alessio, G. R., 303, *308*
Davidson, W. S., 86, 87, 88, 91, 92, 93, 108, 109, *113*
Davis, D. E., 86, *118*
Davis, P. W., 292, *293*
Davis, S. K., 292, *293*
Davison, G. C., 153, 156, 158, 160, 176, *182*, *183*, 186, 188, *248*, 302, *308*
Diamet, C., 188, *248*
Dince, P. R., 156, *181*
Djenderedjian, A., 362, *386*, *387*
Dondis, E. H., 339, 377, 378, *388*
Donner, L., 188, *247*
Drellich, M. G., *181*

Eacott, S. E., 289, *293*
Eber, M., 228, *248*
Edwards, N. B., 161, *182*
Eidelberg, L. A., 300, *308*
Eisler, R. M., 162, 178, *183*, 241, *249*, 363, 365, *388*, *391*
Ellis, A., 170, 174, *182*
Ellis, H., 152, *182*
Emmelkamp, P. M. G., 188, *248*
Erhardt, A. N., 163, *185*
Ersner-Hershfield, R., 177, *181*
Ethical principles in the conduct of research with human participants, *113*, *388*
Ethical standards of psychologists, *113*
Evans, D. R., 85–118, 155, *181*, 346, 354, 377, *388*
Ewalt, J. R., 202, *248*
Exner, J., *338*

Farnsworth, E. L., 202, *248*
Fay, A., 170, 174, *184*
Feather, B. W., 302, *309*
Feldman, M. P., 93, 94, 98, 102, *114*, 115, 155, 156, 157, *182*, 215, *248*, *250*, 349, *388*
Fenichel, O., 64, 65, 66, *81*, 297, 298, *308*
Fensterheim, H., 189, 215, 229, *248*, 301, *308*
Finch, B. E., 162, *182*
Fine, B. D., 62, *82*
Fisherow, W., 20, 21, *38*
Fishman, S. T., 89, 111, *115*
Fookes, B. H., 89, 90, 94, 95, 97, *114*, 159, *182*, 188, 202, 238, *248*
Foreyt, J. P., 188, 189, *248*, *249*
Forgione, A. G., 89, 91, 92, 93, *114*, 143
Foy, D. W., 365, *388*, *391*
Frankel, A. J., 89, *114*
Franks, C., 189, *248*

AUTHOR INDEX

Frederiksen, L. W., 365, *388*
Freese, A., 35, *38*
Frei, D., 89, 95, *115*, 124, *148*, 239, *249*
Freud, S., 62, 63, 64, 65, 67, 68, 76, 77, *81*
Freund, K., 163, 170, *182, 183*, 202, *248*, 349, 359, 363, *388*
Fried, R., 189, *248*
Frisbee, L. V., 339, 377, 378, *388*

Gagné, R. M., 109, 112, *114*
Gagnon, J. H., *10, 38*, 65, *81*, 153, 155, *185, 338*, 378, *389*
Galin, D., 145, *148*
Gaupp, L. A., 159, *183*
Gaylin, W., 161, *185*
Gebhard, P. H., 4, 7, 8, 9, *10*, 35, *38*, 65, 67, *81, 82*, 153, *184*, 311, 322, 329, *338*, 378, *389*
Gelder, A. M., 238, *250*
Gelder, M. G., 160, 163, *183*
George, F. S., 189, 192, 199, *250*
Gigeroff, A., 28, *38*, 311, 323, *338*
Gilbert, F. S., 161, 162, *182*
Gittleson, N. L., 4, *10*, 289, 290, 292, *293*
Gliksman, L., 101, *114*
Glover, J. H., 109, *114, 115*
Goldfried, M. R., 158, *183*
Goldsmith, J. B., 162, *183*, 241, *248*
Goldstein, L., 127, 146, *148*
Gordon, A., 369, *390*
Graham, J., 317, *338*
Graham, K. R., 145, *148*
Grand, H. G., *181*
Grassberger, R., 8, *10*
Gray, K. G., 339, 354, *398*
Green, R., 162, 163, 164, *183*
Greenacre, P., 63, *81*
Grundlach, R. H., *181*
Guild, D., 362, 379, 386
Gunn, J., *293*

Gur, R. C., 128, 144, 145, *148*
Gur, R. E., 128, 144, 145, *148*
Guttman, O., 62, *81*

Hackett, T. P., 68, 81, 202, *249*, 295, 297, 299, 302, 306, *308*, 316, 328, *338*, 339, 344, 348, 354, 364, 365, 375, 377, *389*
Hadden, S. B., 348, 364, *389*
Hagan, R. L., 188, *248*
Hallam, R. S., 92, 109, 110, *115*
Haney, J. R., 89, 90, 91, 94, 108, *116*, 216, *250*
Hanson, R. W., 85, *115*, 161, *183*
Harper, R. A., 170, 174, *182*
Harris, G. A., 359, *391*
Hayes, S. C., 95, *115*, 155, 157, 177, *181, 183*, 214, 215, 229, *247, 249*, 301, *308*, 341, *388*
Haynes, S. N., 161, *181*
Hearn, M. T., 101, *114*
Heiman, J. R., 359, *389*
Heller, 127
Henderson, D. K., 193, *249*
Hendin, H., 161, *185*
Hendrix, E., 328, 329, *338*
Henry, G., 35, *38*
Henson, D. E., 210, *249*
Herman, S. H., 161, *183*, 302, *308*
Hersen, M., 162, 170, 178, 180, *181, 183*, 341, 364, 365, 373, 374, 387, *388*
Herson, M., 241, *249*
Hershfield, S. M., *181*
Heseltine, G.F.D., 101, *114*
Hilgard, E. R., 125, 144, *148*
Hinrichsen, J. J., 108, 109, *115*
Hodgson, R. J., 301, *309*
Hollander, M. H., 228, *249*
Holmen, M. L., 363, 364, *390*
Holmes, T. F., 362, *391*
Holz, W. C., 141, *148*
Hoon, E., 179, *186*

AUTHOR INDEX

Hoon, P., 179, *186*
Horan, J. J., 190, 221, *251*
Huddleston, W., 156, *181,* 304, *308*
Huff, F., 159, *183*
Hughes, R. C., 95, *115*
Hutchinson, H. C., 95, *113,* 341, *388*

Ivey, A. E., 101, *114*

Jackson, B. A., 160, *183*
James, S., 238, *249*
Janda, L. H., 188, *249*
Jenkins, J. O., 365, *388*
Jerry, M. B., 10, 97, 104, *116,* 228, 237, *251,* 339, *390*
Jerry, M. D., 62, 64, *82*
Johnson, V. E., 375, *390*
Jones, H. C., 359, *387*
Jones, I. A., 216, *251*
Jones, I. H., 3, 10, 89, 95, *115,* 124, *149,* 239, *249*
Jones, I. V., 124, *148*

Kanfer, F. H., 161, *184*
Kantorowitz, D. A., 160, 161, *184*
Kaplan, H. S., 375, *389*
Karpman, B., 62, *81,* 354, *389*
Kaslow, F., *338*
Katahn, M., 108, 109, *115*
Kazdin, A. E., 342, 344, *389*
Keil, W. B., 216, 218, 245, *251*
Keil, W. E., 89, 95, *117,* 124, *149*
Kennedy, W. A., 189, *248, 249*
Kerlinger, F. N., 344, *389*
Kernberg, O., 62, 64, *81*
Keutzer, C. S., 188, *249*
Kiesler, D. J., 344, 346, 350, 351, *389*
Kilman, P. R., 375, *392*
Kinder, B. N., 375, *389*
Kinsey, A. C., 153, *184*
Kinsey, C., 62, 64, 65, 68, *82*
Kinsey, N., 215, *249*
Klemp, G. O., 91, *115*

Klockars, C. B., 381, 383, *389*
Klotter, J. K., 207, *250*
Kohut, H., 62, *82*
Kolarsky, A., 360, *389*
Kopel, S. A., 323, *338,* 342, 355, 364, *389, 391*
Krafft-Ebing, R. von., 68, *82,* 152, *184,* 295, *309*
Kraft, T., 159, *184*
Krasner, L. A., 152, *186*
Kremer, M. W., *181*
Kushner, M., 89, 90, 101, *115*

Lacey, J. E., 135, *148*
Lamontagne, Y., 85, *116*
Langevin, R., 168, *182–183,* 349, *388*
Larson, D., 159, *184*
Lasègue, C., 3, 61, 68, *82,* 152, *184,* 295, *308*
The Law Enforcement Assistance Administration, 384, *389*
Lawrence, C., 112, *117*
Laws, D. R., 210, 214, 215, *249,* 359, 363, 364, *389, 390*
Lazarus, A., 170, 174, *184,* 303, *308*
Leitenberg, H., 90, 91, 95, 97, 157, 171, *181,* 211, 216, *247,* 341, 359, *387, 390*
Lester, D., 317, 328, 329, *338*
Levin, S. M., 342, *390*
Levis, D. J., 111, *112,* 160, 180, 216, 217, 238, *247,* 361, *387*
Lieberman, M. A., 42, *58*
Liebert, R. M., 341, 344, 346, *391*
Liebson, I., 112, *117*
Liechtenstein, E., 188, *249*
Linehan, M. M., 354, *390*
Lipton, S. D., 60, *82*
Little, L. M., 191, 215, 217, 241, 245, *249*
Logan, D. L., 86, 87, 88, *115*
LoPiccolo, J., 159, 160, *184*

Lovaas, O. I., 164, *185*
Lovibond, S. H., 91, 92, 93, *115*
Low, B., 164, *185*
Lubetkin, B. S., 89, 111, *115*
Lutzker, J. R., 241, *249*

McConaghy, N., 110, *116*, 155, 156, 160, 184, 216, 238, *250*, 359, *390*
McCreary, C. P., 8, *10*
McCue, P. A., 109, *114*, *115*
MacCulloch, M. J., 93, 94, 98, *114*, *115*, *117*, 155, 156, 157, *182*, 215, 245, *248*, *250*
MacDonald, J., 5, 9, *10*, 152, *184*, 328, 329, *338*
MacDonough, T. S., 215, 238, *250*
McFall, R. M., 162, *183*, *185*, 241, *248*
McGuire, R., 153, *185*
McGuire, R. J., 300, 301, *309*
McGuire, R. L., 229, *250*
McHugh, G., 349, 375, *390*
McKnight, R. D., 85, *116*
Maclean, P. D., 66, *82*
MacMahon, B., 4, *10*, 289, 290, 291, 292, *293*
MacNamara, D., 11, *38*
Madlafousek, J., 360, *389*
Mahler, S., 67, 80, *82*
Maletzky, B. M., 94, 95, 101, 111, *116*, 155, *184*, 187–251, 289–293, 305, *308*, 324, *338*
Malm, U., 89, *113*
Marks, I. M., 4, 8, *10*, 89, 90, 91, 97, *117*, 155, 160, 163, *183*, *184*, 210, 211, 216, 217, 228, 238, *250*, *251*, 362, *391*
Marquis, J. N., 160, *184*, 302, *309*
Marmor, J., 297, 299, 306, *308*
Marshall, W. C., 160, *184*

Marshall, W. L., 85, *116*, 360, *390*
Marston, A., 162, *185*
Martin, C. E., 62, *82*, 153, *184*, 215, *249*
Martin, R., 88, *116*
Martinson, W. D., 161, *184*
Massey, F., 365, *391*
Masters, J. C., 85, *117*
Masters, W. H., 375, *390*
Mathis, H. I., 85, 89, 90, 95, 108, 111, *116*, *390*
Mathis, J. L., 41–58, 202, *250*, 304, 309, 316, *338*, 344, 348, 364, 375, 377, *390*
Matthews, A. M., *247*
Mavissakalian, M., 362, 363, *386*, *390*
Mees, H. L., 160, *185*
Mehta, B. M., *10*, 289, *293*
Meichenbaum, D., 86, 89, 111, *116*, *117*, 229, *250*
Mellor, V., 349, *388*
Meyer, R. G., 311–338
Miller, E., 156, *181*, 304, *308*
Miller, H. L., 89, 90, 91, 94, 108, *116*
Miller, N. E., 141, *148*, *149*
Miller, P. M., 216, 241, *249*, 364, 365, *388*
Miller, S. A., 160, *185*
Mischel, W., 350, *390*
Mohr, J. W., 3–4, 8, 9, *10*, 28, *38*, 62, 64, *82*, 97, 104, *116*, 228, 237, *251*, *338*, 354, *389*
Mohr, M. W., 339, *390*
Money, J., 162, 163, *183*, *185*
Moore, B. E., 62, *82*, 157
Moreno, J. L., 41, *58*
Morganstern, M. P., 354, *390*
Morgenstern, K., 189, *251*
Mowrer, O. H., 92, *116*, 141, *149*
Murphy, W. D., 339–392
Murray, E. J., 141, *148*

AUTHOR INDEX

Nagler, E., 163, 182, 183, 349, *388*
National Commission for the Protection of Human Subjects in Biomedical and Behavioral Research, Department of Health, Education and Welfare, *390*
Neal, H. C., 86, *118*
Neale, J. M., 341, 344, 346, *391*
Newman, L. E., 164, *183*

Obler, M., 159, *185*
O'Brien, J. S., 89, *116*
O'Leary, K. D., 152, 159, 170, 179, *185*
O'Neil, P. M., 90, *116*
Orne, M. T., 141, *149*
Orwin, A., 238, *249*
Ovesey, L., 161, *185*

Pachman, J. S., 365, 373, 374, *391*
Parr, D., 156, *182*
Patch, V. D., 89, *116*
Patel, U. A., 86, 108, 109, 110, *117*
Pauly, I., 163, *185*
Peck, M. W., 62, *82*
Pedophilia, exhibitionism and voyeurism: Legal problems in the deviant society, *338*
Pernicano, K., 145, *148*
Peters, J., *338*
Phillips, J. S., 161, *184*
Pinard, G., 85, *116*
Pinchof, J. M., 349, *388*
Pine, F., 67, *82*
Poimerory, W. R., *10*
Pomeroy, W. B., 62, 65, 81, *82*, 153, 184, 215, *249*, *338*, 378, *389*
Pomery, W., *38*
Pratt, J. H., 41, *58*
Pullman, B. P., 359, *387*

Quinsey, V. L., 359, 362, *391*
Quirk, D. A., 341, *391*

Rachman, A. J., 202, 239, *251*
Rachman, S., 86, 87, 88, 91, 92, 93, 109, 110, *115*, *116*, 301, *309*
Rader, C. M., 8, *10*, 317, 328, 329, *338*
Rado, S., *185*
Radzinowiez, L., 9, *10*
Ramsey, R. W., 159, *185*
Ratliff, R. G., 159, *183*
Raynes, A. E., 89, *116*
Rehm, L. P., 85, *116*
Reich, A., 297, 299, *309*
Reitz, W. E., 89, 95, *117*, 124, 149, 216, 218, 245, *251*
Rekers, G. A., 164, *185*
Reppucci, N. D., 376, *391*
Reynolds, B. S., 375, *391*
Reynolds, E. S., 163, *181*
Rhoads, J. M., 295–309
Rich, R. A., 365, *391*
Rickles, M. K., 202, *251*
Rickles, N. K., 62, 64, 78, *82*, 298, 299, *309*
Rickles, N. R., 364, *391*
Rimm, D. C., 85, *117*, 188, *249*
Roback, H. B., 228, *249*
Robitscher, J., 328, *338*
Rodin, J., 91, *115*
Roether, H., *338*
Rooth, F. G., 89, 90, 91, 97, *117*, 210, 216, 217, 228, *251*, 291, *293*, 354, 362, 364, 375, *391*
Rooth, G., 5, *10*, 35, *38*, 298, *309*, 378, *391*
Rooth, R. G., 4, 8, *10*
Rosen, R. C., 146, *148*, 211, 215, *251*, 323, *338*, 355, 364, *391*
Rosenthal, R. H., 86, 109, *117*
Rosenthal, T. L., 86, 109, *117*

AUTHOR INDEX

Rozensky, R. H., 85, *116*
Rubin, H., 330
Rubin, H. B., 210, 214, 215, *249*
Rubin, H. H., 363, *390*
Russell, M. A. H., 86, 108, 109, 110, *117*

Sadoff, R., 324, *338*
Sagarin, E., 11, *38*
Sambrooks, J. E., 93, *117*, 245, *251*
Sanders, S. H., 342, *392*
Sandler, J., 89, 90, *115*
Sang, W., 5, *10*
Sansweet, S. J., 241, *251*
Sarbin, T. R., 125, *149*
Schiebel, D., 4, 8, *10*, 311, 322, 328, 329, *338*
Schmidt, E., 94, *118*, 159, *186*
Schroeder, H. E., 365, *391*
Schwitzgebel, R. K., 86, 87, 88, *117*
Sechrest, 127
Segraves, R. T., 303, *309*
Serber, M., 89, 95, 124, *149*, 155, *177*, *185*, 216, 239, *251*, 299, *309*, 325
Siddall, J. W., 87, *117*
Sidman, M., 341, *392*
Simon, W., 153, 155, *185*
Slovenko, R., 381, *392*
Smith, R. C., 303, *309*
Smith S. R., 11–38, 303, 311–338
Smith, T. E., 202, *251*
Smukler, A. J., 4, 8, *10*, 311, 322, 328, 329, *338*
Socarides, C. W., 64, 80, *82*
Solyom, L., 160, *185*
Sotile, W. M., 375, *392*
Sperling, M., 62, 63, 67, 80, *82*, 296, 298, 299, *309*
Spitz, H. H. A., 64, *82*
Stanley, J. C., 341, 344, 350, *388*
Steffy, R. A., 89, 111, *117*

Steiner, B., 163, *182–183*, 349, *388*
Steinman, C. M., 362, *391*
Stekel, W., 62, *82*
Stephenson, J., 216, *251*
Stern, R. M., 159, *183*
Stevenson, J., 3, *10*, 124, *149*, 161
Stewart, R., 160, *184*
Stoller, R. J., 35, *38*, 68, 69, 79, *82*, 154, 163, 164, 179, *183*, *185*, *186*, 296, 297, 298, 299, 300, 309
Stolz, S., 383, *392*
Strickler, D., 112, *117*
Strupp, H., 127, 340, *388*, *392*
Sturup, G., *338*

Tanner, B. A., 86, 90, 94, 101, 111, *117*
Task force on the role of psychology in the criminal justice system, *392*
Teasdale, J., 86, 87, 88, 91, 92, 93, *116*, 202, 239, *251*
Tellegen, A., 127, 146, *149*
Thorpe, G. L., 216, *251*
Thorpe, J. G., 94, *118*, 159, *186*
Trinling, D. C., 109, *118*
Truax, C. B., 365, *392*
Turnage, J. R., 86, 87, 88, *115*
Turner, R. E., *10*, 28, *38*, 62, 64, *82*, 97, 104, *116*, 228, 237, *251*, *338*, 339, *390*
Turner, R. K., 238, *249*
Turner, S. M., 162, *181*, 365, 373, *387*
Twentyman, C. T., 162, *185*

Uhlemann, M. R., 101, *114*
Ullmann, L. P., 152, *186*
U. S. Department of Health, Education and Welfare, *392*
Utne, M., 325, *337*

AUTHOR INDEX

van Brero, M., 86, *118*
Van Velzen, V., 159, *185*
Vargas, J. M., 87, *117*
Vera, A., 348, 375, *392*

Waddington, J. L., 93, *117*, 245, *251*
Wallace, C. J., 162, *182*
Wallace, J., 86, 87, *118*
Walta, C., 188, *248*
Watkins, B., 160, *184*
Webster, J. S., 342, *392*
Weitzel, W. B., 190, 221, 222, *251*
Wickramasekera, I., 89, 95, *118*, 123–149, 155, 159, *186*, 216, 220, 239, *251*
Wijesinghe, B., 89, 90, 91, 94, 95, *118*
Wilbur, C. B., *181*
Williams, C., *115*
Wilson, G. T., 152, 153, 156, 159, 160, 170, 177, 180, *181*, *185*, *186*, 188, *248*
Wincze, J. P., 160, 179, *182*, *186*

Winnicott, D. W., 63, *82*
Wisocki, P. A., 161, *181–182*
Witzig, J. S., 47, *58*, 377, *392*
Wolf, M. M., 351, 373, *392*
Wolfe, J. B., 90, *118*
Wolfinsohn, L., 342, *390*
Wolpe, J., 86, 95, *117*, *118*, 161, *186*, 188, 189, 223, *251*, 325
Woodward, M., 156, *186*

Xavier, N. S., 300, *308*

Yalom, I., 42, *58*
Yates, A., 241, *251*
Young, B. G., 153, *185*, 229, *250*, 300, *309*
Young, L. D., 366, *387*

Zajac, A., 163, 349, *388*
Zechnich, R., 354, *392*
Zerface, J. P., 161, *184*
Ziskin, J., 315, *338*
Zuckerman, M., 358, *392*

SUBJECT INDEX

ABR, see Aversive behavior rehearsal
Acceptability of treatment, see Patient acceptability of treatment
ACS, see Assisted covert sensitization
Actus reus, 12–13
Age
  of exhibitionists, 44
  of victims of exhibitionism, 290–291
Aggression, 68–69, 77–78, 140, 317, 329–330; see also Anger; Hostility
  electroshock aversion and, 239
Anger, 66, 77–78, 297, 302, 305; see also Aggression; Hostility
  group therapy and, 52–54
Anxiety, 66

Arousal problems, 347; see also Sexual functioning
Arousal scenes, see also Imagery
  construction of, 264–268
  heterosexual, 269–270
  experimental design and, 359–362
  subjective units of arousal and, 265–269
  therapist anxiety and, 268
  validity of, 362
Arrest, 306, 311–312
Assertiveness, 66, 68, 297, 364–365
Assessment
  importance of multiple, 350
  standardized initial, 349
Assisted covert sensitization (ACS), 187–246
  adjunctive techniques in, 240–241

404 SUBJECT INDEX

Assisted covert sensitization (ACS) *(continued)*
  arousal scenes in, 264-269
  assessment and, 197-210
  aversive conditioning versus, 190
  aversive imagery scenes in, 263, 271-272
  aversive olfactory stimuli in, 188-190
  aversive stimulus strength in, 203
  booster sessions in, 223-227, 263-264, 277, 285
  case report of, 253-285
    follow-up at 18 months, 283
    legal aspects of, 278-279
    patient self-report at 24 months, 284
    patient self-report of rehearsal self-exposure, 279-282
    selected therapy notes from, 272-278
  clarification of previous exhibitionistic episodes in, 255-262
  in clinical practice, 190-191
  in combination with adjunctive techniques, 233-234
  comparative efficacy of, 237-240
  convenience of, 202
  cost of, 202, 220-221
  effectiveness of, 202-210, 220-221
  experimental research on, 192-237
  frequency of exhibitionist behavior and, 200-201, 204-206, 212-213, 218-219, 225, 233-234
  homework in, 263, 275-276
  homosexual pedophilia and, 190-191
  legal status of patient and, 204
  patient acceptability of, 202, 221
  patient view of, 281-282
  penile plethysmograph records and, 212-214, 220, 226
  rationale of, 241, 245-246
  self-directed treatment and, 264
  sexual functioning and, 201
  temptation test and, 199, 201
  time required for, 220-221
  transvestites and, 191
  treatment failures of, 235-237
  treatment schedule for, 198-199
  valeric acid versus placental culture in, 203-210
  voyeuristic behavior and, 191
  wife in, 263, 275-277, 283-284
Aversion relief, 159-160
Aversion therapy, *see also* Electric shock aversion therapy
  booster sessions and, 223
  cruel and unusual punishment and, 330-331
  electrical, *see* Electrical aversion therapy
  rationale of, 109, 241, 245-246
  rule-learning model of, 110-112
    definition of rule for, 112
Aversive behavior rehearsal (ABR), 123-148
  adverse effects of, 240
  case study of failure of, 143-147
  cognitive component and fantasy system in, 145-146
  cognitive shift in, 125
  contraindication for, 145
  in vivo, 126-127
    second procedure of, 132
  cost of, 220-221, 239
  explanations of, 140-142
  fantasies and, 124, 132, 133, 145-146
  flow chart of procedure for, 128-129

Aversive behavior rehearsal (ABR) (*continued*)
  frequency records for, 218, 219, 233–234
  in vivo, 124, 126–127
  indications for in vivo, 126–127
  indications for second procedure of, 132
  modification of, 143
  motivation and, 141, 142
  patient acceptability of, 221, 239–240
  penile plethysmograph recordings for, 220
  procedure for, 125–133
  procedure for in vivo, 124
  psychophysiological consequences of, 134–138
  rationale of, 124–127
  research implications of, 140–142
  results of, 133–138, 139
  shame aversion therapy and, 216
  side effects of in vivo, 138, 140
  time required for, 220–221
  triggering events in, 127, 129
  vicarious (V-ABR), 125–126
  video-physiograph assessment procedure in, 134–138
Aversive conditioning
  assisted covert sensitization versus, 190
  mirror-imaging and, 299
Aversive imagery, 191, 263, 271–273
  aversive stimuli and, 188
  covert sensitization and, 187–188
Aversive olfactory stimuli, 188–190
  duration of, 239
  nausea and, 245
  placental culture as, 189–190, 203–210
  techniques of presentation of, 221–223
  timing in, 238–239
  valeric acid as, 189, 203–210
  valeric acid versus placental culture as, 210
Aversive stimuli
  aversive images and, 188
  covert stimulus versus actual, 187
  duration of, 239
  measurement of doses of, 221–223
  olfactory, *see* Aversive olfactory stimuli
  strength of, 203
  techniques of odor presentation and, 221–223
  timing in, 238
  valeric acid versus placental culture as, 189–190, 203–210
Aversive therapy, *see* Aversion therapy

Behavioral treatment
  assisted covert sensitization, 185–246; *see also* Assisted covert sensitization
  aversive behavior rehearsal, 123–148; *see also* Aversive behavior rehearsal
  booster sessions and, 223
  combined with psychoanalytic approach, 301–306
  case study of, 304–306
  electrical aversion therapy, 85–112; *see also* Electrical aversion therapy
  methods of, 300
  multifaceted, 151–180, 302; *see also* Multifaceted behavior therapy
  psychoanalytic treatment versus, 299–301
Biofeedback, 263–264

SUBJECT INDEX

Booster sessions, 223–227, 277, 285
   assisted covert sensitization, 263–264
   behavior treatment, 223

Characterological disorders, 329
Child molestation statutes, 30–31
Childhood trauma, 69, 297
Clinical interview, *see also* Psychoanalytic approach
   case reports, 320–341
   collateral information and, 356
   items from a structured, 355
   as source of data, 353–358
Coercion and treatment, 43, 57–58, 193, 320–321
   deception as problem of, 323–325
   legal system referred treatment and, 318–326
   mandatory attendance in treatment and, 45–47
Cognitive-behavioral procedure, 123–148; *see also* Aversive behavior rehearsal
Cognitive restructuring, 174–175, 176
   consent form for, 382–383
   erection responses and, 345
   self-report measures and, 345
Common law, indecent exposure and, 13–14
Comprehensive treatment model, 85–86
Compulsion, perversion versus, 78–79
Confidentiality, 321, 331–334
Consent of patient, 331, 333, 380–383
   electrical aversion therapy and, 88
   form for, 382–383
Consent of witness, 25

Constitutional limitations, 13, 26–27, 36, 37, 330
Covert sensitization, 3–5, 157–158
   assisted, *see* Assisted covert sensitization
   aversive images and, 187–188
   case study of, 171–173
   electrical shock aversion versus, 97, 157–158, 215–216
   erection responses and, 342–344
   frequency records and, 218, 219
   patient acceptability of, 221
   penile plethysmograph recordings and, 220
   sadomasochism and, 174
   self-report measures and, 342–344
   sexual arousal and, 172
   sexual pleasure and, 187–188
   term coined, 187
   use of actual aversive stimulus versus, 187
Covert techniques, imagery and, 245
Crime of indecent exposure, 11–30, 28–29, 36–37
   common law and, 13–14
   constitutional limitations and, 26–27, 36, 37
   exhibitionists and, 11–12, 28–29, 36–37
   exposure to children and, 30–31
   interpretation of statutes of, 12, 19–25
      anatomical features included and, 20–21
      consent and, 25
      definition of public place and, 19–20
      level of intent and, 21–24
      lewdness and, 23–24
      observers and, 21
      public morals and, 25
      public nudity and, 24

SUBJECT INDEX 407

Crime of indecent exposure (*continued*)
  juveniles and, 22
  mental incompetence and, 22
  model penal code and, 18–19
  operation of laws and, 29–30
  penalties for violation of statutes of, 27–28
  variation in statutes of, 12
    by state, 14–18
CS, *see* Covert sensitization
Cultural factors, 5, 298

Dangerousness of exhibitionists, 34–35, 314, 317, 325, 327–330, 335
  prediction of, 378–379
Data collection
  clinical interview as source in, 353–358
  inventory questionnaire for frequency, 119–122
  multivariate versus univariate, 340
  process of, 349–353
    example of, 352–353
    standardized initial assessment in, 349–350
  repeated observations in, 351
  types of, 197, 199
Deception by patient, 323–325
  erection responses and, 361–364
Demography, 123, 228
  treatment results and, 236–237
Denial
  group therapy and, 44, 50–51
  mandatory attendance and, 45–47
  treatment and, 43
Deviant behavior, 89–90; *see also* Exhibitionistic behavior
Diagnosis, differential, 48

Diagnostic groups, heterosocial skills and, 366–368
Diagnostic tests, 317
  deception and, 324
Disappointment, group therapy and, 54
Displacement, 297

Educational level of exhibitionists, 193
Efficacy of treatment, 8; *see also* Frequency recordings
  by assisted covert sensitization, 237–240
  treatment failure and, 235–237
  by aversive behavior rehearsal, 143–147
  comparative, 215–221
  demography and, 236–237
  demonstrating, 341–346
  by electric shock aversion, 103–104, 238
  prediction of, 377–378
  recidivism and, *see* Recidivism
  research issues in, 379
Electric shock aversion therapy, 85–112, 156–157
  aggression and, 239
  apparatus in, 98–99
  aversion relief in, 94
  avoidance-learning model and, 93
  case study of, 104–106, 107
    assessment in, 65
    history in, 104–105
    treatment in, 105–106, 107
  classical conditioning model and, 92
  comprehensive treatment model and, 85
  cost of, 239
  covert sensitization versus, 97, 157–158, 215–216

Electric shock aversion therapy
(*continued*)
  efficacy of, 238
  electric shock parameters in, 90–91
  electroconvulsive therapy versus, 238
  escape-learning model and, 92
  ethics of, 86–88
  frequency records and, 107, 218–219
  future research, 106–112
  general results of, 103–104
  habitual component of behavior and, 86
  informed consent and, 88
  models of, 91–94, 109–112
    punishment versus response-contingent aversive stimulation, 93
    rule-learning, 110–112
  Mowrer's two-stage theory and, 92
  objectives, 86
  patient acceptability of, 221, 239
  penile plethysmograph recordings for, 220
  procedures in, 98–104
  psychological testing and, 101, 102, 119–121
  rationale of, 88–94, 109
  relaxation versus, 97
  representation of deviant behavior in, 89–90
  self-regulation versus, 97
  stimuli, 99–101
  studies of, 95–98
    table of, 96
  systematic desensitization versus, 159
  timing in, 238
  trial parameters in, 94

Electroconvulsive therapy, 238
Electromyographic (EMG) biofeedback, 263–264
Empathy skills, 365–366
Environmental control, 230
  frequency recordings for, 233–234
Erection response, *see also* Penile plethysmograph
  cognitive restructuring technique (shame aversion), 345
  covert sensitization and, 342–343
  deception and, 361–364
  stimulus material and, 359–362
  validity of, 362–364
ESA, *see* Electric shock aversion therapy
Ethical issues, 206, 379–385
  in aversive techniques, 86–88
  confidentiality as, 384
  consent as, 380–383
  mandatory treatment and, 57–58
  rights and welfare of subject as, 383
  subject recruitment and, 384–385
Evaluation of exhibitionists for legal system, 312–317
  dangerousness of defendant in, 314
  parole and probation, 316
  plea bargaining and, 314
  preindictment, 313
  presentence, 315–316
  pretrial, 314
  technical language of psychology and, 313
  trial, 314–315
Exhibitionism, *see also* Exhibitionists
  anger and, *see* Anger
  anxieties and, 66
  behavioral approaches to, *see*

SUBJECT INDEX 409

Exhibitionism (*continued*)
Behavioral treatment
castration aspects of, 65
childhood and, 62–63
as compulsion neurosis versus perversion, 78–79
culture and, 5, 298
definition of, 3–4, 328; *see also* Crime of indecent exposure, interpretation of statutes of
history and, 3–4
psychological, 328
differential diagnosis and, 48
incidence of, 4–7
indecent exposure and, 4
indecent exposure statutes and, 11–12
legal aspects of, *see* Crime of indecent exposure; Legal aspects of exhibitionism and treatment
legal records and, 4
origin of, 62–63
predisposition to, 64
psychoanalytic explanation of, 62–69, 298–299; *see also* Psychoanalytic approach
psychological testing and, 48
recidivism and, *see* Recidivism
role of fantasy in, *see* Fantasy
scopophilia versus, 67–68
sexual functioning and, *see* Sexual functioning
social learning theory and, 152–154
stress and, 253–254, 262
syndrome of, 295
victims of, 289–293; *see also* Victims of exhibitionism
Exhibitionistic behavior
covert and overt, 197
dangerousness of, *see* Dangerousness of exhibitionists
duration of, 193
frequency of, *see* Frequency records and recording
habitual component of, 86
incidence of, 4–8
day of, 6
month of, 6
place of, 5
time of, 7
indecent exposure and, 4–12
mental exhibiting and, 61
Exhibitionistic stimuli, *see* Arousal scenes
Exhibitionists, 6–9; *see also* Exhibitionism
age of, 44; *see also* Demography
aggression and, *see* Aggression
anger and, *see* Anger
characteristics of, 140, 295–298, 306, 322–323, 328–329, 348
childhood of, 62–63
crime of indecent exposure and, *see* Crime of indecent exposure
dangerousness of, *see* Dangerousness of exhibitionists
demography and, 123, 228
denial system and treatment of, 43–44
early history of, 253–254
educational level of, 193
family life of, *see* Family life
female, 228
fetishists versus, 67
first incident and first conviction of, 8
health of, 7
latent, 227

Exhibitionists (*continued*)
  law and, *see* Crime of indecent exposure; Legal aspects of exhibitionism and treatment
    apprehension by law of, 45, 306, 311–312
    sexual psychopath laws and, 34–35
  life-style of, 50
  marital status of, 193
  narcissism and, 65
  peer relationships of, 7
  personality types of, 329
  primary, 322–323
  psychoanalysis and, 59–62
    difficulty in analyzing and, 60–62
    psychosexual development and, 77
    resistance to psychoanalytic therapy and, 59–60
  psychological testing and, 8, 9
  sample selection bias and, 6
  secondary 323, 329
  serious sexual offense and, 8
  sexual functioning of, *see* Sexual functioning
  skills of, *see* Skills
  socioeconomic mobility of, 54–55
  stress and, 253–254, 262
Experimental design, 340–346
  assessment and dependent variables in, 346
  clinical case reports and, 340–341
  controlled design in, 341
  controlled group outcomes and, 344, 346
  data collection and, *see* Data collection
  measurement procedures for, 347
  quasi-experimental designs and, 344, 346
    single-case, 341–344
    multiple base-line across behaviors, 341–344
    multiple base-line across subjects, 341–342
    reversal design, 341
Exposure to children, 30–31

Family life, 7, 64, 79, 253–254, 304
  therapy and, 47
Fantasy
  autistic, 125
  aversive behavior rehearsal and, 124, 125
    frequency of, 133, 143–144
    importance of, 132, 141
    theory on role of, 145–146
  case report of, 143–144, 167, 258, 261
  change of, 229, 303
    frequency recordings for, 233–234
  childhood trauma and, 69, 77
  early sexual experience and, 300–302
  latent exhibitionists and, 227, 305
  masturbation and, 153–154, 297, 300–302
Federal Child Abuse Prevention and Treatment Act, 31
Fees, 335
Fetishists, exhibitionists versus, 67
Frequency records and recording, 193, 197
  inventory questionnaire for, 119–122
  self-report and, 107
  for various treatment procedures, 218, 219, 232–234; *see also* specific treatment procedures
  victims of exhibitionism and, 289–293

SUBJECT INDEX

Gender identity, 64, 79, 162–163, 170, 297
Group therapy, 41–58, 304
  active participation and, 56–57
  denial and, 44
  good, 42
  mandatory attendance and, 45–47
  ethical aspects of, 57–58
  phases of treatment in, 50–56
    phase of acceptance, 51–52
    phase of anger, 52–54
    phase of denial, 50–51
    phase of disappointment, 54
    phase of termination, 55–56
    phase of upward socioeconomic mobility, 54–55
  sexual functioning and, 48–49
  treatment goal and common symptom in, 44–45
  treatment mechanisms in, 48–50
  use of male and female cotherapists in, 47
  use of term, 41
  use of term supportive in supportive, 42
  wives and significant females and, 53

Health, 7
Heterosexual skills, 169–170
Heterosocial skills, 161–162, 169–170, 302, 364
  assessment of, 366–374
    problems in, 372–374
  diagnostic groups and, 366–368
  factor analysis of components of, 373
  therapist ratings of, 369–370
Homosexuality
  assisted covert sensitization and, 190–191
  covert sensitization and, 157–158
  electrical aversion therapy and, 156–157
  orgasmic reconditioning and, 160–161
  pedophilic, 190–191
  systematic desensitization and, 158–159
Hostility, 296, 298; see also Aggression; Anger

Images, see also Arousal scenes; Fantasy
  aversive, 187–188, 194, 271–272
  in covert sensitization, 187–188
  covert techniques and, 245
  rated for sexual pleasure, 195
Implosive therapy, 276
Incidence of exhibitionism, 4–8; see also Exhibitionistic behavior, incidence of; Frequency records and recording
Indecent exposure
  crime of, see Crime of indecent exposure
  emotional responses to, 291
  exhibitionism and, 4

Legal aspects of exhibitionism and treatment, 11–37; see also Crime of indecent exposure
  arrest in, 306
  basic criminal law principles in, 12–13
  constitutional limitations, 13, 26–27, 36, 37, 330–331
  exposure to children and, 30–31
  legislative process and, 326–327
  liability in, 332–334
  reporting requirements for sex offenders and, 35
  therapist and, 311–337; see also Legal system and therapist

SUBJECT INDEX

Legal records, 197
  exhibitionism and, 4
  for various treatment procedures, 219
Legal system and therapist, 311–337
  classification of exhibitionists in reports to court, 322–323
  confidentiality and, 331–332
  consent and, 331
  constitutional limitations on therapy, 330–331
  dangerousness of exhibitionists and, 327–300
  evaluations of exhibitionists, see Evaluation of exhibitionists for legal system
  legislative process and, 326–327
  liability and, 332–334
  practical considerations and, 334–335
  psychotherapist–defendant relationship and, 317
  psychotherapist testifying at trials and, 315
  referred treatment and, 318–326
    stages at which referral may occur, 318–320
  reports of progress and, 321
    technical language of psychology and, 313
  sexual psychopath laws and, 316–317, 325
  therapist–lawyer contact and, 278–279
    example of follow-up letter, 278–279
  treatment and trial and, 319
  treatment plan and, 317

Malpractice, 332–334
Marital status of exhibitionists, 193
Measurement procedures, 347

Mens rea, 12–13, 21–24
Mental injury, 31
Mirror-imaging, aversive conditioning and, 299
MMPI diagnostic tests, 8, 317
Motivation, 141–142, 175–176
Multifaceted behavior therapy, 151–180
  case study of, 165–175
    assessment, 165–170
    sexual functioning history, 165–170
    treatment program, 170–175
  clinical issues in, 175–177
    cognitive restructuring in, 174–176
    false suppression of arousal in, 177
    motivation for change in, 175–176
  cognitive restructuring in, 174–176
  comprehensive model of sexual functioning in, 154–164
  directions for research, 178–179
  Freudian hydraulic model of sexual functioning in, 155
  self-control approach in, 177

Narcissism, 65
Narcissistic resistance, 296
Neurotic impulsive, 329
Neurotic inadequate, 329

Operant conditioning, 341
Orgasmic reconditioning, 160–161

Patient acceptability of treatment
  by assisted covert sensitization, 202, 221
  by aversive behavior rehearsal, 221, 239–240
  by covert sensitization, 221

Patient acceptability of treatment
 (*continued*)
 by electric shock aversion, 221, 239
 by group therapy, 51–52
 sexual functioning and, 272–273
Patient self-report, *see* Self-report
Pedophilia, 190–191, 304–306
Peers, 7, 297
Penile measures, 358–364; *see also* Erection responses; Penile plethysmograph recordings
Penile plethysmograph recordings, 210–215, 324, 347
 assisted covert sensitization and, 212–214, 226
 clinical relevance of, 211
 nonexhibitionist versus exhibitionist, 245
 reliability of, 210
 stimulus material in, 359–362
 validity of, 210–211, 215, 362–364
 for various treatment procedures, 219–220
Perversion, 296–297, 300
 aggression and, 68–69
 compulsion neurosis versus, 78–79
 definition of, 296
 family life and, 79
 fantasy and, 77
 fetishism and, 67
 fixations or regressions and, 62–67
 pedophilia and, 190–191, 304–306
 psychosexual development and, 77
 repression and, 67, 76–77
 splitting based, 67
 transsexualism and, 162–164
 transvestism and, 191
Placental culture, 189–190

valeric acid versus, 203–210
Plea bargaining, 314
Psychoanalytic approach, 59–80, 296–307; *see also* Clinical interview
 assisted covert sensitization in, 190–191
 aversive conditioning and, 299
 behavior treatment versus, 299–301
 case study of, 69–76
 castration aspects of exhibitionism and, 65
 combined with behavioral treatment, 301–306
 case study of, 304–306
 compulsion neurosis versus perversion, view of exhibitionism in, 78–79
 difficulty in analyzing exhibitionists and, 60–62
 directions for research and, 79–80
 family life and, 64
 gender identity in, 64
 group therapy and, 42
 mirror-imaging and, 299
 narcissism and exhibitionists and, 65
 narcissistic resistance and, 296
 penile plethysmograph and, 211
 perversions based on fixations or regressions in, 62–67
 perversions based on splitting and repression in, 67
 predisposition to exhibitionism and, 64
 resistance of exhibitionists and, 59–60
Psychological effect on victims of exhibitionism, 291–292
Psychological tests, 48, 101, 102, 119–121
Psychometry, 373, 374

414 SUBJECT INDEX

Psychotherapy, individual, 42–44
Punishment, 93, 330–331
    penalties for violation of indecent exposure statutes, 27–28

Rationale
    aversion therapy, 109, 241, 245–246
    aversive behavior rehearsal, 124–127
    electrical shock aversion therapy, 88–94
Recidivism, 8, 9, 311–312, 329, 339, 376–377
Relaxation, 97
Relaxation exercises, 263–264
Reliability
    of self-report, 355–358
    of social skills scale, 374
Repression, 67
    perversion and, 76–77
Research design, 340–346; *see also* Experimental design
Research issue(s), 178–179, 339–385
    in electrical aversion therapy, 106–112
    ethical issues and, 379–385
    funding as, 381
    lack of controlled studies as, 339
    in multifaceted behavior therapy, 178–179
    prediction of dangerousness as, 378–379
    prediction of treatment outcome as, 377–378
    in psychoanalytic approach, 79–80
    recidivism as, 376–377
    research design as, 340–346; *see also* Experimental design
    sexual functioning as, 375–376
    treatment effectiveness as, 379
Reversal design, 341
Rorschach diagnostic tests, 317

Sadomasochism, 173–174
Scopophilia, exhibitionism versus, 67–68
Self-control approach, 97, 177, 229, 264
Self-esteem, 298, 305
Self-report, 197, 212–213, 342–343, 347
    from case study, 279–284
    coerced treatment and deception in, 323–325
    in cognitive restructuring technique (shame aversion), 345
    collateral information and, 356
    in evaluation of treatment outcome, 356–358
    reliability of, 355–358
Sex education test, 347
Sexual arousal, 78–79, 295–296
    appropriate, 158–161
    Card Sort ratings of, 173
    covert sensitization and, 172
    deviant, 155–158, 168
        case study of, 168
        in treatment, 301–304
    false suppression of, 177
    heterosexual arousal, 169
        in treatment, 301–304
    measurement of, 358; *see also* Penile plethysmograph recording
Sexual functioning, 8, 152–153, 193, 254, 297, 301, 302, 304
    assisted covert sensitization and, 201
    aversion relief and, 159–160
    aversive behavioral rehearsal and, 138

Sexual functioning (*continued*)
  comprehensive model of, 154–164
  covert sensitization in treatment of, 157–158, 171–173
  effect of treatment on, 272–273
  electrical aversion therapy and, 156–157
  exhibitionist fantasy and, 69
  exhibitionist mode of, 77–78
  Freudian hydraulic model of, 155
  gender role deviation in, 162–164
    case study of, 170
  group therapy and, 48–49
  heterosexual skills and, 169–170
  heterosocial skills in, 161–162
  hydraulic model of, 155
  infantile sexuality and, 63
  model of deviant sexual behavior, 347–348
  multifaceted behavior therapy of, 164
    case study of, 165–175
  orgasmic reconditioning and, 160–161
  perversions of, *see* Perversions
  problems of, 347
  psychosexual development and, 77
  research issues in, 375–376
  sexual arousal in, *see* Sexual arousal
  systematic desensitization and, 158–159
Sexual pleasure, 194
  covert sensitization and, 187–188
  images rated for, 195
Sexual psychopath laws, 28, 31–35, 316–317, 325
  examples of definition of sexual psychopaths in, 32–33
  exhibitionists and, 34–35
  indecent exposure and, 34

Shame aversion therapy, 276; *see also* Aversive behavior rehearsal (ABR)
  consent form for, 382–383
  erection responses and, 345
  self-report measures and, 345
Single-case experimental design, 341–344
  multiple base-line across behaviors, 341–344
  multiple base-line across subjects, 341–342
Skills
  heterosexual, 169–170
  heterosocial, *see* Heterosocial skills
  social, *see* Social skills
Social skills, 347, 349, 364–374
  reliability of assessment of, 374
Socioeconomic condition, 54–55
Stress, 253–254, 262
Subject reports, *see* Self-reports
Symptom substitution, 201
Systematic desensitization, 158–159

Technical language and jargon, 313, 335
Temptation test, 199, 201, 324–325
Termination of treatment, 55–56
Therapist
  anxiety of, 268
  gender of, 47
  legal system and, *see* Legal system and therapist
  legislative process and, 326–327
Therapist ratings of exhibitionists, 347, 369
  heterosocial skills and, 369–370
  validity of, 373
Thioridazine, 230
  frequency recordings for, 233–234

Thought-changing procedures, 229
  frequency recordings for, 233–234
Transsexualism, 162–164
Transvestism, 191
Trauma of childhood, 297
Treatment
  coercion and, see Coercion and treatment
  effectiveness of, see Efficacy of treatment
  importance of multiple assessments for, 350
  procedures, see Treatment procedures
  termination of, 55–56
Treatment model, comprehensive, 85–86
Treatment procedures, see also specific treatment procedures
  booster sessions in, see Booster sessions
  combinations of therapies in, 240–241
  ethical issues and, see Ethical issues
  frequency records for various, 218, 219
  paradigm for, 242–244
  patient acceptability of various, see Patient acceptability of treatment
  problems with current, 325–326
  wife in, 53, 263, 275–277, 283–284

Valeric acid, 189, 195, 275–276
  in vivo, 276
  placental culture versus, 203–210
  self-administered, 196
Validity, 341
  of clinical ratings, 373
  of exhibitionistic stimuli, 362
  of penile measures, 362–364
  of penile plethysmograph recordings, 215
Victims of exhibitionism, 289–293, 328, 330
  age of, 291–292
  children as, 30–31
  consent of witness and, 25
  difficulties in research on, 289
  emotional responses of, 293
  psychological effect on, 291–292
Video-tape ratings, 134–138, 347
Voyeurism, 190–191

Wife of exhibitionist, 53, 263, 275–277, 283–284